D0205625

Life and Story

LIFE AND STORY

Autobiographies for a Narrative Psychology

Edited by D. JOHN LEE

Westport, Connecticut
London

Library of Congress Cataloging-in-Publication Data

Life and story : autobiographies for a narrative psychology / edited
   by D. John Lee.
        p. cm.
     Includes bibliographical references and index.
     ISBN 0–275–94095–0 (alk. paper)
        1. Psychology—Biographical methods. 2. Discourse analysis,
     Narrative—Psychological aspects.   I. Lee, D. John.
     BF39.4.L54   1994
     150.19′8—dc20   93–19093

British Library Cataloguing in Publication Data is available.

Library of Congress Catalog Card Number: 93–19093
ISBN: 0–275–94095–0

First published in 1994

Praeger Publishers, 88 Post Road West, Westport, CT 06881
An imprint of Greenwood Publishing Group, Inc.

Printed in the United States of America

∞™

The paper used in this book complies with the
Permanent Paper Standard issued by the National
Information Standards Organization (Z39.48–1984).

10 9 8 7 6 5 4 3 2 1

To Frank, Gord and John,
thank you for your words
and a portion of your lives

Contents

Life and Story

Introduction

D. John Lee

C. S. Lewis once said, "When I have something really important to say, I tell a story."

The Prince and the Magician

Once upon a time there was a young prince who believed in all things but three. He did not believe in princesses, he did not believe in islands, he did not believe in God. His father, the king, told him that such things did not exist. As there were no princesses or islands in his father's domain, and no sign of God, the prince believed his father.

But then, one day, the prince ran away from his palace and came to the next land. There, to his astonishment, from every coast he saw islands, and on those islands, strange and troubling creatures whom he dared not name. As he was searching for a boat, a man in full evening dress approached him along the shore.

"Are those real islands?" asked the young prince.,

"Of course they are real islands," said the man in evening dress.

"And those strange and troubling creatures?"

"They are all genuine and authentic princesses."

"Then God must also exist!" cried the prince.

"I am God," replied the man in evening dress, with a bow.

The young prince returned home as quickly as he could.

"So, you are back," said his father, the king.

"I have seen islands, I have seen princesses, I have seen God," said the prince reproachfully.

The king was unmoved.

"Neither real islands, nor real princesses, nor a real God exist."

"I saw them!"

"Tell me how God was dressed."

"God was in full evening dress."

"Were the sleeves of his coat rolled back?"

The prince remembered that they had been. The king smiled.

"That is the uniform of a magician. You have been deceived."

At this, the prince returned to the next land and went to the same shore, where once again he came upon the man in full evening dress.

"My father, the king, has told me who you are," said the prince indignantly. "You deceived me last time, but not again. Now I know that those are not real islands and real princesses, because you are a magician."

The man on the shore smiled.

"It is you who are deceived, my boy. In your father's kingdom, there are many islands and many princesses. But you are under your father's spell, so you cannot see them."

The prince pensively returned home. When he saw his father, he looked him in the eye.

"Father, is it true that you are not a real king, but only a magician?"

The king smiled and rolled back his sleeves.

"Yes, my son, I'm only a magician."

"Then the man on the other shore was God."

"The man on the other shore was another magician."

"I must know the truth, the truth beyond magic."

"There is no truth beyond magic," said the king.

The prince was full of sadness. He said, "I will kill myself."

The king by magic caused death to appear. Death stood in the door and beckoned to the prince. The prince shuddered. He remembered the beautiful but unreal islands and unreal but beautiful princesses.

"Very well," he said, "I can bear it."

"You see, my son," said the king, "you, too, now begin to be a magician."[1]

C. S. Lewis also said, "Do you think that I am trying to weave a spell? Perhaps I am; but remember your fairy tales. Spells are used for breaking enchantments as well as to induce them."

AUTOBIOGRAPHY FOR A NARRATIVE PSYCHOLOGY

A collection of autobiographical essays has an autobiography.

Five years ago, I was preparing to defend my dissertation on "Memory for Naturally-Occurring Events." On my reading list were two edited books, one by David Rubin and the other by Theodore Sarbin.[2] The first one, *Autobiographical Memory*, presented the mechanistic or information-processing approach to exploring why and how people remember events from their own lives. Sarbin's book, *Narrative Psychology: The Storied Nature of Human Conduct*, was a collection of original essays arguing for and demonstrating the usefulness of a contextualist or narrative root metaphor for doing psychology. Rubin's and Sarbin's anthologies held a lot of significance for me since they represented what had been done and what could be done in the area of autobiographical memory. In addition to conceiving memory as information retrieval and autobiographical memories existing in a store-house with other "naturally-occurring events," the study of autobiographical memory could be exploring the purposes, processes, and effects of "telling one's story."[3]

In the fall of 1990, I invited several psychologists to write their autobiographies.[4] I had two purposes in mind. The first was to provide an opportunity for some significant people to tell their story. My invitation was made in recognition for what they had contributed to the development of my narrative perspective in psychology. However, if one adopts a contextualist approach in psychology, then "telling your story" can actually become a requirement. If understanding human experience and behavior demands reviewing the historical and cultural context in which they occur, then understanding the writings of a contextualist demands reviewing the context of that person. A narrative psychology involves hearing the narratives of its psychologists. That is, this book is not only in honor of the contributors' scholarship but a requirement for their scholarship! This book offered the contributors a forum to describe, in their words, the context from which their scholarship has emerged. I believe that the essays in this book should and will play a crucial role in interpreting the contributors' professional work.[5]

I gave three guidelines to the participants as they embarked on their autobiographies. The first was with regards to style and content. It is worth quoting from my letter of invitation here:

> You may adopt any form or style that you desire, but please do not treat this as a forum to make arguments or to propose theories. Certainly, you may find yourself arguing a position or making a recommendation, but this kind of discourse should not dominate your story . . . unless, that is *your* story.

I gave the contributors the freedom to decide how they would tell their stories. But, given who I was dealing with, I knew there would be a temptation to tell only the "academic" version of their lives. I wanted their autobiographies to be more than intellectual histories.

Due to publishing parameters, the second guideline was to limit the length of the essays to somewhere between 35–40 pages each. The third guideline was a request that participants, after completing their essays, describe how writing their autobiography had affected them. As it turned out, some authors weaved their reflections on the act of autobiography throughout their essays, while others did as I suggested and offered some thoughts about the process after they had written their stories. The second purpose behind this book was to begin exploring the effects of writing one's autobiography. I summarize the contributors' afterthoughts about writing their stories in the Afterword.

This collection of autobiographical essays is a continuation of the development of a narrative psychology that Theodore Sarbin (Chapter 1) introduced in 1986. Thus, it is fitting that this book begins with Sarbin's story of how he arrived at the metaphor that life is storied. One of Sarbin's students, Karl Scheibe (Chapter 2), follows with his tale of how "yet another preacher's kid" found psychology. Mary and Ken Gergen (Chapter 3) offer a "duography," or the story of their lives together, in a form which recognizes that it cannot be separated from its content. Leon Rappoport (Chapter 4) offers an explanation of how a Jewish kid from the "Big Apple" ended up thriving in the "Little Apple" or Manhattan, Kansas! "Rags to riches" is also echoed in Joseph Rychlak's (Chapter 8) story as he tells of a "working class boy" making good as "scholarly loner." Brian Sutton-Smith (Chapter 6) and Rachel Hare-Mustin (Chapter 7) remember, in a reflexive fashion, how they became psychologists, playing with what Jesse Hiraoka (Chapter 9) describes as the "enigma of remembrance." The Orpheus Myth is the vehicle for some of Donald Spence's (Chapter 5) memories; the four elements of ancient cosmologies organize Robert Detweiler's (Chapter 11) memoir; and one of Stephen Crites's (Chapter 10) earliest memories guides his autobiographical song. George Howard's (Chapter 12) "teleography" is not only novel and humorous but offers a form which has numerous possibilities as a psychological method. Howard's essay is placed last because it does what I hope this book will do—review the past and look forward to the future in order to assist others in grasping the present. The present moment is offered meaning by the past and the future, by memories and possibilities, by story. I hope the stories that follow will be useful and meaningful to some others beside ourselves.

NOTES

1. From *The Magus* by John Fowles, pp. 499–500, First edition Copyright (c) 1965 by John Fowles: Revised edition and foreword copyright (c) 1977 by John Fowles Ltd. By permission of John Fowles and Little Brown and Company.

2. Both books were published in the same year (Rubin, 1986; Sarbin, 1986a) and my reviews were published a couple of years later in the *Christian Scholar's Review* (Lee, 1988a; 1988b).

3. The concept of "naturally-occurring" or "real" event memory tells the history of memory research. Memory researchers have moved from using nonsense syllables to paired associates to sentences to paragraphs to short stories to "real" or "naturally-occurring" (i.e., nonlaboratory) events as their subject matter. I hope we have finally recognized that memory content (or meaning) cannot be divorced from memory process. In another collection of autobiographies, I have reviewed the uses, processes, and effects of autobiography (Lee, 1993). James Olney and Paul John Eakin have explored autobiography as a literary art form (cf. Olney, 1988).

4. Some of the people I invited were not trained as psychologists, but had influenced the development of my narrative perspective. Three of these people accepted my invitation to participate in this collection. French literature and ethnic studies are Jesse Hiraoka's areas of interest; Stephen Crites writes in the philosophy of religion; and comparative literature is Robert Detweiler's forte.

5. Bennett Berger (1990) edited a book, very similar to this one, containing the intellectual autobiographies of 20 American sociologists. Berger's purpose was to provide the "life history data" he thought was necessary to read sociological theory. Bennett wanted his students "to get a sense of the *presence* of the theorist in the text, learn to read between the lines, and hence more fully appreciate the meanings projected in them" (p. xiv).

Steps to the Narratory Principle: An Autobiographical Essay

Theodore R. *Sarbin*

INTRODUCTION

The focus of my chapter is reflected in the title.[1] It is my intention to describe the steps in my professional journey that brought me to a particular endpoint: the recognition that life is storied, that a narratory principle guides both the interpretation of human events and the performance of human actions. To set the stage I offer a brief statement of the narratory principle.

Within the last decade, a number of influential books and papers have hailed the appearance of narrative psychology, a framework that would supplement, if not replace, the positivist framework. I contributed to the building of this framework in various ways, notably by publishing a collection of essays written by practitioners of narrative, *Narrative Psychology: The Storied Nature of Human Conduct* (1986a), and writing the introductory chapter in which I identified the narratory principle. Turning to the humanities for working metaphors coincided in time with the disillusionment of many psychologists with the outcomes of traditional methods of doing psychology.

For those who are not familiar with the proposition that human action is storied, it is important to mention that narrative psychology does not pursue the same goal as traditional psychology—the formulation of general laws of behavior for the purposes of prediction and control, a goal that has not yet been reached (nor is it likely to be reached). The goal of narrative psychology is understanding. The narrative approach is more like history and biography than it is like chemistry and physics, the models for traditional psychology.

Narrative psychology takes off from the proposition that we live in a story-shaped world. A moment's reflection will provide initial validity to the proposition. Our daydreams are storied, our nightdreams are fanciful tales. The rituals of religion and daily life reflect traditional stories. We construct accounts of our everyday conduct in narrative form. Even our hopes and our fears are storied. Survival in a world of meanings depends upon the skill in constructing and interpreting stories about interweaving lives.

The value of the narrative as an organizing principle has been demonstrated in settings that illuminate the narrative quality of experience. Nearly 50 years ago, A. E. Michotte (1946) and F. Heider and E. Simmel (1944) provided powerful demonstrations of the narrative quality of experience. They presented to their subjects filmed random movements of two or three geometrical figures. The viewers interpreted the random movements as dramatic narratives, assigning human qualities to the figures, noting common sentiments and reasons for action. All of us have the talent for emplotting apparently random events according to established narrative forms.

In giving accounts of ourselves or of others, we are guided by narrative plots. Whether for formal biographies or autobiographies, for psychotherapy, for self-disclosure, or for entertainment, we do much more than catalog a series of events. Rather, we *render* the events into a story. I have identified this human propensity as the narratory principle—the interpretation of actions and events as emplotted, as organized. The notion of plot is understood even by children—they recognize that there are beginnings, middles, and endings, and that problems are created and resolved or neutralized. Literary experts have suggested various classificatory schemes. One such classification was put forth by Northrop Frye (1971). He employed broad mythic categories: tragedy, comedy, romance, and irony. G. Polti (1916) employed 36 problematic situations identified as "emotions." A psychological classification has been offered by Kenneth and Mary Gergen (1988). They make use of three basic categories: progressive, regressive, and stability narratives. Each denotes the path of the protagonist toward reaching a desired endpoint.

The narratory principle can also be applied to action. The term "action" is not to be confused with "response." The latter category is the stock in trade of mechanistic psychology and is related historically to reflexes. "Action," but not "response," carries implications of intentionality, of goal-seeking, of agency. The choice of action in problematic situations is conditioned by one's enculturation, that is, by the acquisition of sacred stories, parables, fairy tales, morality plays, fables, adventure yarns, patriotic legends, and other narrative forms, whether rendered through oral communication, print, or graphic media (Sarbin, 1990).

The paradigm case of stories providing guides to action is the protagonist in Cervantes' novel, *Don Quixote*. As a result of exclusive reading of the adventures of knights-errant of bygone centuries, the lonely Don constructed an identity and then set out to validate that identity. Literary scholarship has identified scores of novels in which the protagonist formed an identity through assimilating stories of historical or fictional characters and then engaging in actions to make good the constructed identity. This phenomenon has been aptly labeled the Quixotic Principle (Levin, 1970; Sarbin, 1982a). Some obvious illustrations come to mind. John Hinckley's attempted assassination of President Reagan was an action consistent with a plot generated from overinvolvement in a popular movie. Reading spy novels has provided a plot and a *modus operandi* for trusted government employees to engage in espionage. Some biographies recount the influence of book reading on self-narratives. Napoleon, for example, emplotted his self-narrative on stories about the legendary Charlemagne.

Although book reading is the source of imaginative involvement in the paradigm case, other sources are available, among them, personal or vicarious acquaintance with the biographies of contemporary role models, orally presented stories, films, television, and other art forms.

In these few paragraphs, I have tried to condense a set of observations and arguments to support the claim that both experience and action are narratively constructed. Pertinent here is the observation of Alasdair MacIntyre (1981) who noted that stories are lived before they are told, and the lived stories are influenced by the stock of stories that are integral to a culture.

Having provided a sketch of the narratory principle, my task now is to illuminate the path that took me from a raw behaviorist recruit to the present involvement in narrative psychology. In reporting this personal history, I note three overlapping dynamics: contingencies, critical incidents, and turning points. Contingencies are unplanned occurrences. Critical incidents are occurrences that clearly have a major effect on the self-narrative. Turning points occur under conditions of strain when new information or new interpretations of old information cannot be assimilated to one's beliefs. Turning points have a moral quality in that the strain is between subscribing to orthodox beliefs and to beliefs that do not have the warrant of custom and convention.

In recognizing these dynamics, it becomes clear that one's self-narrative is not produced in a situation of epistemological loneliness. At every juncture, whether described as a contingency, a critical incident, or a turning point, other actors enter the drama. Any self-narrative, then, is necessarily a collaborative, negotiated enterprise. The protagonist must take into account the actions of others who are playing out their self-narratives, sometimes synergically, sometimes at cross-purposes.

FAMILY BACKGROUND AND SCHOOLING

I was born in 1911, the fourth of six children of Samuel and Annie Sarbin. My parents emigrated in the 1880s, my father from the Ukraine, my mother from Poland. They were part of the tide of Eastern European Jews who left their rural villages for a better life in America. My father was 11 years old when he arrived via steerage accompanied by two older brothers. At first he worked on a family farm in western Pennsylvania. He was soon apprenticed to a cigar maker and subsequently became a journeyman. My mother was 13 years old when she emigrated and joined family and relatives living in Pittsburgh. My parents married and settled in Cleveland, Ohio, just before the turn of the century.

Neither had any formal schooling, although both were literate and could read the Jewish newspapers. Later my father taught himself to read and write English. He spent nearly all his productive years in his trade, sometimes venturing into business for himself, sometimes working for employers. Income was always marginal. With a large family and meager earnings, our story could be characterized with the poet's line "the short and simple annals of the poor."

My parents had great respect for educated people, especially teachers. My father never missed attending open house when I was in grade school. He would shave and put on a fresh shirt and a necktie and sit in the back row taking in the teacher's lesson as if he were a pupil. When time permitted, he would attend an ongoing seminar on Talmudic teachings at the local synagogue. Both parents observed the rituals of orthodox Judaism. My siblings and I absorbed the orthodoxy without pressure from my parents. As we became more and more enculturated to American norms and values, we dropped our adherence to strict orthodoxy. By the time I was in high school, I was no longer interested in participating in religious rituals and ceremonial practices.

We lived in neighborhoods where hardly anyone went to college. None of my siblings attended college except for my brother Gene (eight years my senior) who completed a two-year university program to qualify as a registered pharmacist.

I was an inveterate reader. As long as I can remember, I made use of the public library. I read novels, biographies, plays, poetry. Reading interests, however, were not sufficient to offset the tradition of not pursuing higher education. In fact, I was a high school dropout. I had attended a technical high school and if I had had better eye-hand coordination, I could have completed the curriculum in machine shop and been employed as a machinist in one of Cleveland's smokestack industries. I was an indifferent student. During one grade period I would excel; the next period I was on the probation list. I quit school in 1928 and landed a job with a manufacturing company doing routine office work. While employed, I attended an adult evening school where I was an honor student and also the editor of the school newspaper. In 1931 I earned the high school diploma.

I quit my job in 1932 for a *wanderjahr*. Economically, it was a foolish move. It was Depression times and my plan to pick up odd jobs here and there turned out to be an unrealistic fantasy. For a few months, I lived the life of a hobo, moving about the country on freight trains and not eating very much. When I returned home, I picked up a few part-time and temporary jobs, including a stint on a WPA project as a day laborer.

A contingency became a turning point in my self-narrative. It was the summer of 1934. I had become acquainted with several social workers. It seemed that they were the only people with jobs. With continuing unemployment and the growth of government relief programs, it was reasonable to suppose that a person with a degree in social work was certain to be employed as a "relief worker." But going to college required money, and I had none. By happenstance, I met an acquaintance whom I had not seen for a year or two. He was then a senior at Ohio State University. I told him of my frustrated desire to go to college. He gave me some advice on how to attend the university on practically no money. At that time, the registration fee was $20 a quarter. Government-sponsored work study programs paying $15 a month were available to deserving students. If I could get an additional job as a "hasher" in a restaurant or fraternity house, I would be assured of meals. Acting on this advice, I lost no time in getting the necessary application forms and in September 1934, at age 23, I matriculated as a freshman at the Ohio State University. My father gave me the initial registration fee of $20 which he had borrowed from a friend. He also gave me his gold pocket watch so I would not be late for classes. Upon arriving in Columbus, I looked up an old friend who was a student in the dental school. He was the steward in his fraternity house and was in a position to offer me a job waiting tables and washing dishes. Each day I worked in the kitchen three hours or more. My compensation was three hearty meals. In today's vernacular, I had it made.

UNDERGRADUATE DAYS

It was with a sense of excitement that I went through the routines of registering, finding cheap housing, buying or borrowing textbooks, locating the college buildings, and becoming acquainted with fellow students nearly all of whom were younger than I. I was impressed with the imposing structure of the library in front of which was a larger than life statue of a former president of the university, posed as if inviting students to enter the repository of knowledge. I was delighted with the acres of green lawn on the Oval, with the mix of venerable ivy-covered brick buildings and the newer modern architecture. Being a student was an exhilarating experience. I felt exceedingly lucky that I now had the opportunity to acquire knowledge from the professors and from the world of books. And I was optimistic that I was career bound.

Unlike many of my fellow freshmen, I had a clear goal. Most of the classmates were just out of high school and regarded college days as a time for fun, incidentally acquiring an education. Eager to enter the professional world, I hoped to complete the degree in less than four years. My adviser in the social work curriculum suggested I first meet the general education requirements. I signed up for introductory courses in Italian, zoology, and psychology. My instructor in Psychology 401 was Frank Stanton, an advanced graduate student, later to become president of the Columbia Broadcasting System. After the first two or three lectures, he called on me to comment about some material in the textbook. He was pleased with my response which went beyond the information in the assignment. After class, he asked me the source of my information. I told him that I had read *Seven Psychologies* by Edna Heidbreder (1933) as part of my informal reading program before entering the university. Stanton told me that *Seven Psychologies* was the assigned text in a graduate seminar. He decided that I should be in a more advanced class. He arranged for me to take the previous quarter's final exam after I studied the text over the weekend. I passed, was given credit for the course, and enrolled in Psychology 402. This critical incident in my self-narrative convinced me that psychology was my calling. Without delay, I transferred from the social work curriculum to the College of Arts and Sciences and was on my way to becoming a psychologist.

I came under the influence of behaviorist professors at Ohio State University who reflected the Zeitgeist: human beings were machine-like creatures operating according to mechanistic principles. The standard doctrine led to the conviction that all behavior would ultimately be explained through an extension of Watson's behaviorism and Pavlovian conditioning. The intellectual leader of the department went so far as to write a textbook in which human beings were described as "electron-proton aggregates." Behaviorist theories, flowing from a mechanistic ideology, were supposed to demonstrate the futility of mentalistic constructs. As an unsophisticated undergraduate seeking to become a scientific psychologist, I absorbed these teachings. I was caught up in the enthusiasm of an intellectual movement that, in retrospect, had the earmarks of an ideology. The behaviorist credo encouraged us to think of people as complex machines. In a short time, I had become a convert to this secular religion, a movement in which John B. Watson and Ivan Pavlov were its prophets. Looking back from my present perspective, I believe that behaviorist psychology served as a comforting protection against the fearful effects of living in a world full of ambiguities and uncertainties.

In the summer of 1936, toward the end of my undergraduate program, my conversion to behaviorism was modulated by the writings and lectures of J. R. Kantor, a visiting professor from Indiana University, whose books on interbehavioral psychology supported much of the behaviorist program but cautioned against accepting the notion that the mechanistic paradigm could revive "mind" and other mentalistic constructs. He pointed to the futility of regarding the mind as a source or resultant or the actions of mechanistic forces. What impressed me and most of the other students was his compelling arguments that constructs had to be related to concrete events—events that could not be divorced from historical, cultural, and biographical contexts. This was an unorthodox idea at that time when the belief was entrenched that the secrets of behavior would be discovered in the laboratory, especially the rat laboratory. Kantor's analytical, critical, and philosophical arguments had a great effect on me. Of all my teachers, he comes closest to having been my mentor. Among other things, he emphasized the role of language in human action, but more important, he was an exploder of myths. I trace my interest in exposing myths and undressing metaphors to his influence. Later, I realized that my association with Professor Kantor had been a turning point.

I loved being a student. I interacted with fellow students who had intellectual interests, some of whom later achieved recognition in science and the humanities. When I was not attending classes, "hashing" for my meals, studying in the library, or working in the laboratory on the work study program, I would engage in animated discussions with one or another of my new-found friends. If not participating in an intellectual feast, at least I could snack on philosophy, history, and, of course, psychology. Even with a full program, I found time for some social life, recreation, and even horseplay. Because I had a good academic record, the assistant dean of the College waived the rule against taking more than 20 units a quarter (the standard was 15). I received credit for a number of courses taken by examination and I attended summer session in 1935 and 1936. Two calendar years after matriculating, I was awarded the bachelor of arts degree, *cum laude*, and elected to Phi Beta Kappa.

I had been carrying on a long distance romance with Anne Kochman, one of the social workers that I had met before going to college. We would get together for a few days between quarters. We married just before I completed my work for the bachelor's degree.

GRADUATE STUDIES

The Depression had deepened. Having a B.A. in psychology in 1936 was not a ticket to employment. Rather than remain unemployed, I enrolled in a master's program at Western Reserve University in Cleveland, my home town. A work study program paid my tuition. My technical high school background was instrumental in obtaining work in the psychology department shop. I built a number of instruments that were used in teaching experimental psychology. My courses were not very inspiring. Save for becoming acquainted with the Rorschach Inkblot Test, at that time unknown to all but a few American psychologists, most of the courses repeated much of the material that I had acquired as an undergraduate.

After being awarded the master of arts degree, I returned to Ohio State in the summer of 1937. At this point, I wanted to prepare myself to teach psychology in a college or university.

My good friend and classmate, Joe Friedlander, asked me to help with his master's thesis. He was in the process of developing a scale to measure hypnotizability. He needed a second hypnotist to help establish the reliability of the scale. Although I had had no special interest in hypnosis, I honored the friendship role and agreed to participate. We were successful in constructing a scale, and we subsequently published our findings (1938).[2]

The beginning of the story of my interest in narrative psychology was incidental to my becoming involved in hypnosis research. Prevailing hypnosis theories were consistent with a reshaped behaviorism in which dispositions, that is, traits, were central constructs. In one of several studies designed to tease out traits associated with hypnotizability, the Rorschach inkblots were used. A quantitative analysis of Rorschach categories showed only weak relationships to hypnotizability. More interesting was the observation that some of the protocols contained miniature stories. This observation led me to conduct a study with one subject. I administered the Rorschach under instructions "to be another person" and provided the names of well-known models. (Much later, I realized that I had instructed the subject to enact different roles. At that time, role was not part of my professional vocabulary.) In each condition, the subject consistently portrayed a different person. The content and the structural categories were different from the content of the protocols when she was not given explicit role instructions. For example, when the subject was told that she was Madame Curie the responses centered on laboratories, chemicals, test tubes, and other responses consistent with the notion of scientist. When given the instruction to be Mae West, the responses centered on a theatrical theme—costumes, wigs, props, and so on (Sarbin, 1939).

In retrospect, this little exercise confirmed my belief that hypnosis was more than the mechanical expression of a mental disposition released through the verbal behavior of the hypnotist. Although the language of dramaturgy had not yet been incorporated into my vocabulary, I found myself interpreting the actions of the subject as somehow similar to the performances of stage actors.

During the academic year of 1937–1938, I prepared for the Ph.D. exams and enrolled in some graduate seminars. One seminar was with W. H. Cowley, a professor of higher education, who was interested in, among other things, student personnel work. He offered me a job as research assistant to do library research. We had a warm relationship; he invited me to his home to meet his wife and daughter. Our work styles coincided. He would sketch out a grand idea and I would spell out the details.

It was the spring of 1938. I had passed my Ph.D. writtens and orals and was tinkering with various dissertation topics. Cowley showed me a letter from E. G. Williamson, at that time coordinator of student personnel work at the University of Minnesota. The letter asked Cowley if he could recommend a person to become a full time "Administrative Fellow" and work directly under Williamson. Cowley was willing to recommend me. Because job offers were still scarce, I jumped at the chance. The stipend was $133 per month.

MINNESOTA

When I took my first academic job at the University of Minnesota in 1938 I put aside my interest in hypnosis. Working with Ed Williamson was rewarding. He was writing a book on student personnel work and I served as his bibliographer, research assistant, and editorial handyman. We collaborated on a few publications. Williamson gave me a bit of avuncular advice: Always include in your schedule a time for writing papers, reviews, and books because the academic world is a publish-or-perish world. I took his advice seriously, and in the three years that I was at Minnesota, I added some 18 items to my bibliography.

At the end of the year, Williamson recommended me to Jack Darley, director of the Testing Bureau, for a position as counselor. I was one of five psychologists who worked full time counseling students. The counseling was based on interviews and a profile of a battery of psychological tests. As time went on, I specialized in seeing students whose personal problems extended beyond planning educational programs. This work brought me into collaboration with the psychiatric staff at the Student Health Service.

Because I was working full time and also writing papers dealing with counseling, psychometrics, and issues in student personnel work, I gave little thought to planning a dissertation. Before I left Ohio State, I had been assured that I could do the dissertation *in absentia*. It was Williamson who suggested a dissertation topic: a study of the relative validity of actuarial versus case study approaches to the prediction of behavior. I set up a program in which the counselors would make predictions of first quarter and first year grade-point-average for each of the student clients after conducting an interview and reviewing a battery of aptitude, achievement, and interest tests. Subsequently, I compared the accuracy of these predictions with predictions constructed from a regression equation derived from past experience with only two variables: score on a college aptitude test and rank in high school graduating class. The results demonstrated that the clinical predictions were no more accurate than the actuarial predictions. This was a counterintuitive finding. Involvement in my dissertation problem directed me to ask further questions about the nature of clinical inference—a topic to which I returned some years later.

At a colloquium given by Normal Cameron, then Professor of Psychology and Psychiatry at the University of Wisconsin, I was introduced to the concept of role-taking. Cameron's presentation was a draft version of his later widely cited paper on paranoia (1943). A central category in his explanation was role-taking. Cameron's exposition of role-taking, the skill to take the role of the other, was an exciting and novel idea. The protagonists in his case studies were men and women who were inept role-takers and who constructed pseudocommunities in trying to make sense of their unpredictable worlds. Acting as if the pseudocommunities had the same ontological status as social communities, these hapless men and women ultimately became candidates for psychiatric diagnoses. My attendance at Cameron's colloquium was a critical incident. His discourse supported my doubts about the official position that abnormal conduct was the product of occult forces activated within the abstract mind. In rejecting mentalistic explanations, I found myself thinking of people engaged in intentional, purposeful actions in order to make sense of an imperfect, ambiguous, and sometimes confusing world of occurrences. For the first time, I found myself using role-taking conceptions in talking about "problem students."

In 1940 my son, Ted, Jr., was born. I now had another reason to complete my dissertation and get on with my career. I finished the writing during the Christmas holidays and submitted the dissertation in January 1941. I was called to defend the dissertation in February and was awarded the Ph.D. by the Ohio State University in March 1941.

I applied for a postdoctoral research training fellowship sponsored by the Social Science Research Council. Having worked intensively with problem students (sometimes in collaboration with psychiatrists) and carrying over the implications of Cameron's thesis, I had become interested in acquiring knowledge and skills that psychiatry might provide. My application to the council stressed the need to refresh research on abnormal behavior by working closely with psychiatric professionals who were presumably at the forefront of the discipline. I was awarded the fellowship for 12 months, and it was renewed for a second 12-month period.

CHICAGO

A few months later, I departed Minnesota. The council recommended that I make my headquarters at the University of Chicago, in part to facilitate my attending seminars at the Chicago Institute for Psychoanalysis. My sponsor at the university was the esteemed urban sociologist, Ernest Burgess. In addition to the seminars at the institute, I divided my time during the first year between the psychiatric unit at the university hospital and the sociology department. Through Professor Burgess, I met a number of sociologists who introduced me to the writings of George Herbert Mead (1934). Although Mead had died some ten years before, his ghost stalked the halls of the Social Science building. Not unlike the ghost's effect on Hamlet, the ghost of Mead had a profound effect on me. I found the dramaturgical metaphors compelling. Working with Burgess, I began to formulate some ideas about role as a possible link between social structure and personality. Conversations with Paul Wallin, William Foote White, and Rueben Hill, advanced graduate students in sociology and anthropology (later distinguished professors), emphasized the need for such a bridging concept.

Professor Burgess arranged for me to spend time in the psychiatric unit of Billings Hospital, a part of the University of Chicago Medical School. The faculty members were hospitable, and I was invited to join in seminars, grand rounds, and clinics. I was treated as visiting faculty. On the advice of the head of the unit, Dr. David Slight, I wore the knee-length lab coat that differentiated medical school faculty from residents and interns, who wore short white jackets. I put in many hours at the hospital, day and evening, sometimes sitting in on therapy sessions being conducted by a staff member; sometimes solo.

Because I had had experience with hypnosis, Dr. Slight asked me to treat a young woman in-patient diagnosed as hysterical amnesia. She had disappeared from home and was located in a neighboring city a week later. Treatment by her family doctor and by a consulting neurologist had failed to restore her memory. My hypnotherapeutic efforts over a three-day period were successful. News of the dramatic recovery spread through the hospital and I was asked to present the case at grand rounds. This was a period of intense interest in psychosomatic medicine. As a result of my presentation, referrals by the score came from other units of the hospital, and I was the designated hypnotist. I enjoyed the status of being a "doctor," of being paged on the public address system, of being consulted by eminent physicians.[3]

I made an observation at that time that anticipated my later use of narrative in the teaching of abnormal psychology. My graduate training had involved reading the experimental literature in psychology. The data in research reports were always presented quantitatively: means, variances, correlation coefficients, etc. Working with psychiatric patients involved listening to stories told by patients and/or their relatives. No means or standard deviations entered into the stories of torment, fear, unhappiness, or pain. In keeping with the rhetoric of science, "story" was not an appropriate category to include in a medical report. At best, my colleagues would speak of the "case history" or the "anamnesis."

During the final six months of my fellowship, I worked at the Elgin State Hospital, an hour's ride from Chicago. My clinical experience was augmented by working intensively with inmates of the hospital, most of whom were diagnosed as schizophrenic. I had difficulty in accepting the official doctrine that so many different life stories could be tagged with the same diagnosis. Many years later, variability in the self-narratives of so-called schizophrenics was the starting point for my critical studies of the schizophrenia hypothesis.

At the Institute for Psychoanalysis, I was exposed to Freudian thought in seminars conducted by such well-known authorities as Franz Alexander, Thomas French, and Teresa Benedek. My critical posture made me skeptical of Freudian doctrine. One observation, however, left its mark. All the theoretical work discussed in the seminars was based on Freud's published narratives of five cases.

Taking a leaf from Freud, who had successfully advanced his theory through constructing narratives, I presented several of my hypnosis case studies to a colloquium sponsored by the Department of Psychology. Rejecting explanatory categories that were part of the older mentalistic baggage, I proposed a fresh set of metaphors. With the aid of role concepts, such as performance skills, validity of role expectations, and congruence of the hypnosis role with self-conceptions, I described the conduct of the reference cases before, during, and after the hypnosis induction. I offered the hypothesis that hypnosis was a social role and whatever variables were useful in studying other social roles would be useful in studying hypnosis roles. My notes for the colloquium served as the basis for my first article on role-taking (1943).

To anticipate somewhat and to make my story line clear, it was the elaboration of role concepts over several decades that paved the way for my development of narrative psychology. My first use of role was narrow; I did not see role as actions constitutive of the construction and negotiation of self-narratives.

INDEPENDENT PRACTICE

At the conclusion of my fellowship in 1943, I had three choices. I could return to Minnesota, I could apply for a commission in the military, or I could enter independent practice. I would have preferred a teaching job, but during the war years such jobs were scarce. I applied for a position as a military psychologist but was rejected because of my poor eyesight. The prospect of counseling students at Minnesota seemed bland after such intensive work with psychiatric patients at Billings Hospital and at Elgin. Because my colleagues had regarded my clinical work as exemplary, and because working with troubled people was challenging, I made the decision to enter independent practice in Chicago. I had no difficulty filling my calendar. I maintained some contact with academic life by teaching extension classes at Northwestern University.

Like many others who suffered the cold winters, I gave serious thought to moving to southern California. After visiting Los Angeles to explore the possibilities, I decided to move. I closed my office in Chicago and relocated in Los Angeles. Shortly after the move, my marriage ended.

Like most practitioners, I had little time or inclination to engage in a writing program. I found time, however, to do an informal study of role-taking by interviewing a number of professional actors, some of whom were well known. I was able to confirm the notion that actors generally operate with "divided consciousness," that is, the actor must monitor not only his or her interactions with other actors, he or she must be attentive to audience reactions that provide cues regarding how well the action is being portrayed. I was impressed with the actors' description of their use of "imagination" as the secret of preparing for a role. Actors imaginatively create a story about the character that goes beyond the script. Because of the pressures of the practice, I did not write up my observations. I used role concepts in my clinical work, but I did not develop additional theoretical formulations.

After several years as a clinical practitioner, I experienced an acute sense of dissatisfaction. Doing therapy in independent practice was not the same as working in a university hospital where one could interact with colleagues and submit ideas to critical examination. I let it be known that I was interested in teaching. The Long Beach City College had a one-semester vacancy. Although it was a long commute, I arranged to spend four mornings a week teaching introductory psychology. When I completed that assignment, I taught a few evening courses at Los Angeles City College. In 1947, to satisfy the need for collegial relations, I arranged my schedule so that I could devote two days a week to working in the Veterans Administration Clinic. Although I was doing well in the practice, I felt unfulfilled. I longed for the academic life and the opportunity to expand my horizons. I expressed my dissatisfaction to my friend and confidante, Genevieve Allen (who was to become my wife), who encouraged me to go all out and seek an academic appointment. I was not very optimistic, having been away from university work for five years. At her prompting, I informed colleagues and friends that I was eager to get an academic appointment. One of the staff members at the clinic, Ruth Tolman, told me of a one-year appointment at the University of California, Berkeley. After an exchange of letters, I was invited in May 1948 to come to Berkeley and give a colloquium to the psychology faculty and graduate students. My talk dealt with the psychology of role-taking. I was offered the job.

BERKELEY

Before moving to Berkeley, Genevieve and I were married. We moved into a delightful house north of the campus. Genevieve's two sons, Jim, age 15, and Ron, age 11, joined us after we had set up housekeeping. A few months later, my son, Ted, age 9, came to live with us. We were a freshly melded family, about to embark on a new adventure in domestic life.

Most of my energy was devoted to teaching and supervising graduate students in clinical psychology. My first teaching responsibility was a clinical training seminar in which students who were engaged in practicum internships would present their cases. The seminars were held in the evening. We introduced an innovation: holding the seminars in our home. The ambience of a family home appeared to bring out the best in the students. Years later, some of these students wrote me that sharing our home made them feel like persons, rather than just students.

I was certainly an unwitting narrativist at that time. Most of the students had been indoctrinated with psychoanalytic theory and were looking for "the dynamics" to account for their patients' behavior. I insisted on their telling the story, to look for reasons for action rather than psychic causes. A good deal of my energy was directed to convincing the students that psychoanalysis was not the only royal road to understanding conduct.

My research program was guided by the need to make sense of the process of clinical inference, a process that I had begun to study in my doctoral dissertation. Involvement in the further clarification of role concepts was incidental to my main mission—to do the necessary research and scholarship to move to a position on the academic ladder and subsequently to achieve tenure as a member of the faculty.

In the early 1950s I published a series of experimental studies, some in collaboration with colleagues or graduate students, designed to illuminate the process of role-taking. These studies were conducted along traditional lines. Influenced by trait theory, I looked for internal characteristics that could account for individual differences in the ability to take roles. Although skill in role-taking was unlike dispositional characteristics that were central to the study of personality, such as introversion or neuroticism, the only available methods for studying such a skill were those taken from contemporary personality research. My early attempts at understanding the full meaning of role conceptions only hinted at the construction that later became central to my thinking—that role was a necessary bridge between personality and social structure. The units of social structure are positions or statuses; roles are organized patterns of conduct expected of persons occupying such positions or statuses.

The social structural element of position was not as readily apparent in the hypnosis situation as more clearly articulated social positions, such as mother, president, teacher, or shortstop. The status of the hypnosis subject had to be construed from the relations between hypnotist and subject. The actions of the subject claiming posthypnotic amnesia, for example, served to validate his or her occupancy of the structural position in the dyad.

An opportunity for a more complete development of role theory was afforded by an invitation to write a chapter for the 1954 *Handbook of Social Psychology* (Sarbin, 1954). The source of the invitation illustrates a contingency in my narrative, a contingency that led to the writing of the chapter which in turn became a critical incident. The contingency was my reading an article by the late Theodore Newcomb in 1947 in which he discussed the process of taking the role of the other. At that time, Newcomb was in mid-career, responsible for developing the interdisciplinary program in social psychology at the University of Michigan. Although we were strangers to each other, the contents of the article prompted me to write him a letter in which I pointed out certain features that were not consistent with G. H. Mead's formulations. Newcomb saw attitude as prior to role; I argued that role was prior to attitude. His gracious reply to my letter acknowledged my criticisms, and he included a sentence to the effect that this was the first time in his career that anyone had written a three-page letter discussing his work. A decade later, after I had had a number of personal contacts with him, Newcomb told me that it was he who had recommended to Gardner Lindzey, the editor of the *Handbook*, that I be invited to write the role theory chapter.

When I cite this episode as a critical incident, it is because it provided me an opportunity to publicize role theory as a viable alternative to other theories described in the *Handbook*: field theory, psychoanalysis, learning theory, cognitive theory. Especially important was the description of the central variable: role enactment. This variable was unlike the central variables in other theories, variables that were usually construed as context-free responses or as internalized dispositions. Role enactment carried the meaning that the conduct was dependent upon social structural context. Thus, human action had to be perceived as interaction. An additional, and not unimportant, outcome of this episode was the association of my name with role theory.

During this period, the end of the 1950s and early 1960s, my work moved along two divergent paths. I have already alluded to the work in role theory. The other path led to the study of cognition, specifically clinical inference. This work was quite removed from the genre of role theory. The interest was in determining how people make judgments on the basis of limited cues. Although some role theoretical ideas insinuated themselves into the arguments, the project was more consistent with statistical models.

When I first came to Berkeley, Ronald Taft, then a graduate student (now Professor Emeritus of Psychology, Monash University, Australia) paid me a visit to discuss my published prediction papers. We were like-minded in recognizing that clinical predictions followed from the use of inferential strategies. We co-authored a privately printed essay on the subject, and later, Daniel Bailey (then a graduate student) joined us in expanding the essay. The rapidly developing field of cognitive studies influenced our output. Our book was published under the title *Clinical Inference and Cognitive Theory* (Sarbin, Taft, and Bailey, 1960). Two contingencies were antecedent to this outcome: Taft's having read my prediction papers and finding them congenial with his own thinking, and Bailey's being a graduate student looking for a professor who would be responsive to his interests in statistical inference and cognition.

In 1957 I was promoted to the professorship and appointed as chairman of a newly organized research unit at Berkeley, the Center for Social Science Theory. It was a small faculty group, at first made up of two economists, a sociologist, and myself, later augmented by an anthropologist and another psychologist. The sociologist was the late Erving Goffman whose name has become a household word. Intensively sharing ideas with Goffman steered me to a turning point in my career. Although my lectures in abnormal psychology had become increasingly critical of the medical model, it was not until I associated with Goffman on a one-to-one basis that I was able to give voice to the view that so-called abnormal conduct could be accounted for with the same explanatory categories as so-called normal behavior. His dramaturgical approach to conduct influenced me to enlarge my conception of role. Roles need not be stereotypes. Persons create and modulate roles in response to changing contexts. So-called abnormal behavior was intentional: It served purposes; it served the interests of impression management. No longer perceived as the victim of occult forces, the identified crazy person could be perceived as trying to adapt, usually under great handicap, to an imperfect and sometimes hostile world.

In 1962 I was awarded a senior Fulbright Fellowship at Oxford University. I had ample time to study and to reflect on psychological theory. I had no duties other than to make myself available to faculty and students and to pursue my own research interests. In response to an invitation from Michael Argyle, Reader in Social Psychology, I delivered a series of eight lectures on abnormal psychology during the Trinity term. I recast my lectures and developed a model of intentional conduct that brought into play the role-theoretical concepts that I had developed earlier. The model directed students to look for the existential and social antecedents of strain-in-knowing, and to observe the role behavior that people (so-called abnormal or others) perform to resolve such strain. In the context of studying deviant persons, it was important to recognize that we live in a moral order and there are always persons, usually more powerful than the targeted individual, who are ready to make moral judgments on that individual's efforts to resolve his or her strain-in-knowing. These theoretical developments led to the conclusion that abnormal psychology was more properly a branch of social psychology, not a branch of medicine. Instead of sick minds, it was more productive to speak of inept role players.

The period at Oxford was a turning point. I discarded the remnants of my earlier adherence to positivism and I identified myself as a symbolic inter-actionist. To know persons, one had to move away from the relics of mentalistic psychology and incorporate sociological and anthropological conceptions, such as social status. The conversion did not come about, however, without some antecedent preparation. I have already mentioned the early influence of J. R. Kantor and the later influence of Erving Goffman, as well as writings of G. H. Mead. Equally important was my participation in the Tuesday Morning Group. This was a group of graduate students who met with me every week for a period of more than two years, beginning in 1960. Although the members of the group had different interests, they all shared the notion that current theory ought to be the object of searching criticism, that dramaturgical and social structural constructs should be imported into psychology, that glib Cartesian explanations were unacceptable. In some of the meetings, I discussed the place of metaphor in scientific constructions. The concentration on metaphor moved me in the direction of examining literary sources, a great help in the later development of narrative psychology.

The members of this informal group were indeed instrumental in my own intellectual development. I acknowledge their participation as significant figures in my story—as collaborators in my self-narrative. The group grew and coalesced around weekly meetings with my research assistant, Vernon Allen, later Professor of Psychology at the University of Wisconsin until his untimely death in 1986. He contributed to my further understanding of role theory. He challenged orthodox methods and explanations in social psychology. Rolf Kroger joined the weekly meetings and demonstrated the effects of contrived contexts on psychological test profiles. A Professor of Psychology at the University of Toronto, he has since become a leader in the ethogenic movement in social psychology—a movement congenial with symbolic interaction. I invited Karl Scheibe to join our group as a means of countering his dissatisfaction with the lack of intellectual stimulation in the department. He influenced me to study superstitions and paved the way for a more complete understanding of so-called delusions and hallucinations. He has been Professor of Psychology at Wesleyan University for many years. Milton Andersen, Professor of Psychology at San Jose State University, had a critical and philosophical bent. He joined me in doing experiments in hypnosis and helped to formulate a more complete theory. Equally important was his introducing me to the study of metaphor, a study that facilitated my de-mythologizing many psychological constructions. Eldred (Al) Rutherford, formerly Professor of Psychology at San Jose State University, brought to the group a critical understanding of life span development and a social consciousness. Kenneth Craik, who became Professor of Psychology at the University of California, Berkeley, worked with me on the perception of time. He brought to the group a rich background in the humanities. Robert Sullivan, currently coordinator of research at North Dakota State University, imparted a unique flavor to the discussions. Somewhat older than the others, he brought experience from outside the academy to enliven sometimes solemn discussions. All members of this group save one collaborated with me in writing research reports or conceptual essays. Such formal collaboration was intellectually enriching, but the informal collaboration had more lasting consequences on the construction, negotiation, and elaboration of my self-narrative. It is important to note that the relationship with my students did not close with the granting of the degree. Their influence on my self-narrative continues, even to this writing. For example, a few years ago, Al Rutherford persuaded me to prepare a paper for a conference, Ethics and Practice of

Care in Public and Private Settings. This was a new topic for me. Preparing the paper required that I move into uncharted areas. I proposed a formulation in which care is administered through contract or through covenant. I elaborated the two models with the aid of stories depicting the different psychological outcomes for persons subject to contractual care or covenantal care (Sarbin, 1986c).

Two conditions facilitated the cohesiveness and productivity of the Tuesday Morning Group. First, the meetings were held in the living room of my home. There was usually a crackling fire in the fireplace. Second, my wife Genevieve served as a mother-substitute not only for the students but also their wives. Not only did she provide refreshments for the seminars and arrange for social interaction with spouses, she also organized appropriate celebrations to accompany such rites of passage as passing prelims, completion of dissertations, having a baby, and getting a job. Even after being awarded their degrees and dispersing to various sections of the country, members of the group (augmented by my graduate students from other generations) would join us at APA meetings, sometimes participating in scheduled role theory symposia, but always arranging a party in which a contributor would receive the Role Theorist of the Year Award. At the party held during the 1978 APA meeting in Toronto, the "Associated Role Theorists" presented an award to my wife with the inscription: "To Genevieve Sarbin, Mrs. Role Theory, in gratitude for your love and encouragement."

During the rest of the 1960s, I alternated between two pathways. In retrospect, both were instrumental in my later construction of the narrative as a root metaphor. One was the study of imagination; the other was the construction of a theory of social identity. Both programs turned out to be extensions of role theory and prolegomena to the narratory principle.

The studies in imagination emerged from my attempts to understand the conduct of hypnosis subjects who report hallucinations, who behave "as if" certain nonevents have ontological status. To understand the "as if" formulation, I put together a theory of imagination, followed by a series of research and conceptual papers, some in collaboration with Joseph Juhasz, then a graduate student (now Associate Professor of Environmental Studies, University of Colorado). My work on imagination was facilitated by a Fellowship Award from the Guggenheim Foundation, 1965–1966. In our paper, "Toward a Theory of Imagination," Juhasz and I laid the groundwork for a theory that placed the imaginer in a more active role than in traditional theories (Sarbin and Juhasz, 1970). Other papers provided empirical data and theoretical elaboration. The study of hallucination was an extension of the study of imagining. In developing the theory of imagination, I began by comparing the process of imagining with the process of imitating. In imitating, a person copies another's behavior with the model present. In imagining, the model is absent. The act of copying with the model absent is best described as muted role-taking, a more apt metaphor for imagining than "pictures in the mind." I was unaware that at this point I was only one step away from recognizing that the muted role-taking followed narrative patterns.

During the same period, a theory of social identity was taking form. In the summer of 1965, two alumni of the Tuesday Morning Group, Karl Scheibe and Rolf Kroger, were visitors at Berkeley. We had earlier agreed that theories of the self had limited utility unless they could incorporate social structural variables. This conclusion was consistent with G. H. Mead's view that the self was the product of social interaction. The outcome of our discourse was a model—a three-dimensional solid—that allowed us to locate a person's social identity at any given point in time. It also allowed us to plot the promotion or degradation of identity. The first dimension was social status. One end of the dimension contained primarily ascribed or granted statuses, such as family membership, age, and gender; at the other end were primarily achieved statuses, such as plumber, violinist, and quarterback. The second dimension was degree of involvement, and the third dimensions allowed us to plot the valuations declared by others on one's role enactments. A unique feature was the recognition of two kinds of valuations: respect and esteem. Respect inheres in granted positions and can be revoked for violating cultural norms; esteem is conferred for attainments. We were able to show the differential effects of such valuations on the conduct of the individual. This model helped us account for the social ordering of persons and, most significantly, for the upward or downward transvaluation of identity (Sarbin and Scheibe, 1980).[4]

The first test of the plausibility of the model occurred when I presented it to a conference at the University of Wisconsin Institute of Psychiatry. I had been invited by my former student, Professor Norman Greenfield, to participate in a conference on evaluating mental health programs. I spoke of the transvaluation of social identity. My comments included descriptions of how persons are transvalued into mental patients and, under certain circumstances, into nonpersons as the result of legal, medical, and nursing routines (Sarbin, 1968b). I provided a social dimension to the theme of the conference. Over the next few years, the model was used to explicate a number of phenomena, among them, deviance, the culture of poverty, "schizophrenia," nationalism, the dangerous individual, and even the success of cross-age tutoring.

As in the study of imagination, the complex model of identity formation contained in it the seeds of the narratory principle. Unlike theories of the self that adopt a homunculus model, the social identity model requires that selves (or identities) are the products of social interaction. The social identity model recognizes that moral judgments of others on one's enactments enter into self-narratives. This construction is consistent with the narratory principle that all identities are necessary collaborations between the actor and other actors. Again, I was but one step from recognizing that in using the social identity model I was dealing with self-narratives. It is significant that most of the observations from which we constructed our model were narratives about particular people, e.g., the French chef who killed himself when his restaurant was downgraded from three stars to two stars.

For several years, I had been engaged in studies of delinquency. In 1965, the recently appointed dean of the School of Criminology, Joseph Lohman, invited me to join his faculty. The school's faculty came from several disciplines: law, psychiatry, sociology, forensic science, and psychology. In reorganizing the school, Lohman wanted me to lead the psychology contingent. We arranged for my devoting one-third time as professor of criminology. It was a challenging assignment. I had opportunities to advance ideas about social identity as a neglected aspect of the study of criminal behavior. One outcome of my work in the school was a collaboration with Nathan Adler, a member of the faculty. Adler had been a student in my seminars when I first came to Berkeley and later I was his dissertation sponsor. Together we prepared a paper, "Reconstitutive Processes: A Preliminary Report" (Sarbin and Adler, 1971). This was another step on the way to formulating the narratory principle. Guided imaginings was a central feature modeled after the *Exercises of Loyola*. We spelled out some notions about the parameters of significant psychological change. The paper reflected my interest in imagination and in social identity, and Adler's in the self and symbolic processes. It was singled out for an Essay Award by the editors of *Psychoanalytic Review*.

During the academic year 1968–1969, I held a Fellowship at Wesleyan University's Center for Advanced Studies (later the Center for the Humanities). This was another critical incident. I was free to pursue my own interests in a liberal arts atmosphere. I had no teaching or committee responsibilities. More importantly, I could participate in formal and informal discourse with other Fellows of the center and with Wesleyan faculty members and students. Coming from the Berkeley beehive, it was refreshing to hold leisurely conversations on a daily basis with novelists, literary experts, philosophers, and other representatives of the humanities.

I remember long stimulating discussions with Paul Horgan, Pulitzer prize-winning historian and novelist. A bond was created between myself and Philip Hallie, Professor of Philosophy and director of the center. We spent many hours discussing issues in social philosophy, especially the issues central to his then-current writing project on cruelty and freedom. The novelist Jerzy Kosinski provided an international and cosmopolitan flavor. Members of the Wesleyan faculty would join in our scheduled seminars and I learned much from historians, literary specialists, and philosophers. It was a productive year. My longtime association with Karl Scheibe blossomed into a deep and enduring friendship. We had almost daily contact elaborating the social identity model. I also completed the final draft of a book co-authored with William C. Coe: *Hypnosis: The Social Psychology of Influence Com-*

munication (Sarbin and Coe, 1972). We advanced the contextualist position and developed in a more detailed way the antecedents of role-enactment.

It was during this period that I became aware of a shift in my own identity. The intensive exposure to the wisdom of the humanities was preparatory to my identifying myself as a member of a community of humanistic scholars. It was a turning point in that I now rejected the idea that we could know others based on probabilistic data. A single case could nullify conclusions drawn from such data.

THE SANTA CRUZ ADVENTURE

In the fall of 1969, rather than return to the Berkeley campus, I accepted an invitation to join the faculty at the recently established Santa Cruz campus of the University of California. The transfer to the Santa Cruz campus was not capricious. When I first came to Berkeley, the psychology department was a community of scholars. Interactions with faculty were frequent and rewarding. Over the years, the department added more and more personnel. The frequency of interaction tapered off. Berkeley had become a large and impersonal workplace. Each of the 50 members of the department was a specialist and intellectual interaction was quite limited. Furthermore, most of the faculty members directed their energies to their own research and the teaching and supervising of graduate students. Teaching undergraduates had a low priority. Faculties tended to be isolated from each other. I was fortunate in being able to modulate the effects of this intellectual isolation. Two nonpsychologists with whom I had collegial relations at Berkeley were the late Henry Nash Smith and Marvin Rosenberg. Smith, a distinguished Professor of American literature and one-time curator of the Mark Twain papers, was a fount of information on the humanities. We discussed many topics, including the psychological analysis of novelistic figures. Even after I moved to Santa Cruz, we had occasional correspondence about his or my papers in preparation. Rosenberg was a Professor of Dramatic Arts, a Shakespeare scholar, with whom I continue to share ideas about dramaturgy and narrative. It is noteworthy that these collegial relations were initially nurtured, not at the Faculty Club, not in committees, but on the fairways of the Tilden Park Golf Course.

The Santa Cruz campus was organized on the model of Oxford, small liberal arts colleges within a larger university. The emphasis was on developing viable undergraduate programs, a far cry from the emphasis at Berkeley. Stevenson College provided the continuity for the interdisciplinary work that I had begun during my stay at Wesleyan. The academic climate encouraged interactions with scholars in the humanities as well as social scientists. It was an ideal setting for further development of my interest in incorporating humanistic ideas into social psychology. The first year at Santa Cruz was an exciting one. Not only was I part of an experiment in undergraduate education, but my wife and I served as preceptors in one of the residence halls. We adopted these new roles with enthusiasm. We had most of our meals with the students in the Dining Commons. The experience was similar to my perceptions of life in an English boarding school. In fact, some of our colleagues referred to us as Mr. and Mrs. Chips.

I renewed my acquaintance with the distinguished philosopher, Stephen Pepper, who was on campus as a visiting professor. I had known Pepper at Berkeley but had had only casual acquaintance with his book, *World Hypotheses* (1942). Another visitor was James Mancuso (Professor of Psychology, State University of New York, Albany) with whom I had had an earlier collaboration. Pepper's book described four world hypotheses, or metaphysical positions: formism, mechanism, organicism, and contextualism. After some delightful conversations with Pepper and studying his book, Mancuso and I came to the realization that we were like Molière's M. Jourdain who discovered that he had been speaking prose all his life. We had been unwitting contextualists. We had already expressed our skepticism about the value of the mechanistic world view, the underlying metaphysic for most of scientific psychology. The root metaphor of contextualism, the historical act in all its complexity, seemed to provide more appropriate guidance for the human sciences.

During the same year, Phillip Hallie, the social philosopher with whom I had worked at Wesleyan, was also a visiting professor. The experimental atmosphere at Santa Cruz supported our jointly teaching a graduate seminar entitled Temptation, Degradation, and the Devil. Our lectures and the papers presented by the students were all guided by an interest in telling a compelling story. For example, I gave a lecture on the Faustian legend, employing the social identity model as a framework. The subtext of the legend is the barter of respect (which is granted to the occupants of ascribed statuses) for esteem, a valuation that is conferred for mere achievements. Having no basis for respect, and living only with the surface rewards of achieved roles, persons who live out the Faustian drama are metaphorically described as hollow identities.

From this point, my work focused on the application of contextualist ideas to various phenomena and to the further development of the social identity model. Mancuso and I began a collaboration that year on a critique of the schizophrenia hypothesis. Ten years later our efforts were rewarded with the publication of our book *Schizophrenia: Medical Diagnosis or Moral Verdict?* (Sarbin and Mancuso, 1980). We argued that the published research on schizophrenia, carried out under the guidance of the root metaphor of mechanism, had failed to support the disease concept. We presented a full discussion of the difference between contextualist and mechanistic approaches. We showed how socially generated contexts could lead a person into a path of downward valuation and ultimately to patienthood. One implication of our analysis included the recognition that conventional research centered on diagnostic classifications rather than on personal lives.[5]

It was in the early 1970s that I began to think seriously of the narrative as a root-metaphor. In my classroom lectures, I described the conduct of deviant persons as suffering from an inadequate stock of stories or from stories the subtext of which departed from the plots that were central to local social life. My seminars served as platforms for further developing the idea that narratives are the source of our interpretations of the world. I had commingled the dramaturgical ideas with narrative ideas that came from the Quixotic principle and a variety of humanistic sources.

In the fall of 1975 I was invited to give the keynote address at the Nebraska Symposium on Motivation. The theme of the Symposium was Personal Construct Theory, a theory of personality that had been developed by George Kelly in the 1950s. The title of my paper was "Contextualism: A World View for Modern Psychology." Here, too, I contrasted the results of traditional psychological work carried out under the guidance of the mechanistic world view with work carried out from a contextualist perspective. Among other things, I made the case that the search for causes of conduct, central to the mechanistic doctrine, had not been successful. To approach the complexity of human conduct, the psychologist had to cast a wider net and make sense of persons' actions through discovering how they emplot their lives. Although I used mainly dramaturgical metaphors, my treatment of emplotment brought out the need to focus on narrative as a necessary conception in contextualist thought (Sarbin, 1977).

POSTRETIREMENT EXPLORATIONS

I took early retirement in 1976 at age 65. I continued to teach an occasional course or seminar, but now I had more time to follow my interest in developing dramaturgical and narrative ideas. I also retired from my post as Psychologist at the Community Hospital of the Monterey Peninsula where I had been working one afternoon a week since 1970. The director of the Mental Health Center, Dr. Fred Ziegler, had invited me to help with staff training and didactic seminars. I also engaged in some therapy sessions with selected clients. After I retired, I set up a small independent practice in which I conducted therapy that might be called "narrative repair." This perspective is consistent with "rebiographing," a concept developed by my former student, Mordechai Rotenberg, currently professor at the Hebrew University, Jerusalem (Rotenberg, 1987).

It was at a symposium at the 1979 APA meetings that I first expressed to a professional assembly my views on the narrative structure of experience. I served as a discussant on a panel that recognized the ecumenical movement in psychology. The panel was arranged by Karl Scheibe and included Kenneth Gergen, Rolf Kroger, Robert Hogan and Joseph Juhasz. I employed the concept of narrative to tie together the varied substantive materials discussed by the panelists. I was pleasantly surprised that my thoughts on narrative as a central feature of the psychology of personality were enthusiastically received. The rough notes that I had prepared for the discussion were useful when George McKechnie and I later collaborated on a chapter, "Prospects for a Contextualist Theory of Personality" (Sarbin and McKechnie, 1986).

During the same year, an opportunity arose for elaborating the narratory principle in connection with the theory of hypnosis. In 1979, for a special issue of the *Journal of Abnormal Psychology*, William Coe and I prepared an essay that made use of a number of concepts that were consistent with the narratory principle. To account, for example, for subjects' apparent amnesia for the events of the hypnosis session, we made use of such unorthodox concepts as secrets, deception, and, especially, self-deception. These were strategic actions employed by subjects to maintain a degree of consistency in their self-narratives.

Self-deception is a complex topic exemplified by the person who claims amnesia for events in the hypnosis session. That is to say, the person claims ignorance under conditions where remembering is expected. In the case of hypnosis, after ruling out purposeful deception to account for the counter-expectational conduct, self-deception is an apt label. We attempted an analysis of this complex human activity employing the narratory principle. Whether creating a novel, a biography, or an autobiography, the narrator takes bits and pieces of fact and fancy and renders them into an intelligible story. The narrator is necessarily selective, elaborating some items and ignoring others that would render the plot too cumbersome, absurd, or unconvincing. The author in any genre has poetic license. Extrapolating poetic license from literature to the self-narrative is not unreasonable. All of us are poets, story-tellers, and creators of meaning. Self-deception, then, is occasioned by the "spelling out" of certain features of our lives and "not spelling out" other features. It is not unlike the biographer's strategy of selecting certain facts and not others for elaboration, a strategy legitimated by the convention of poetic license. (The Society for Clinical and Experimental Hypnosis selected this paper to bestow its award for "Best Theoretical Paper Published in 1979" [Sarbin and Coe, 1979].)

At my retirement party in 1976, two members of the before-mentioned Tuesday Morning Group, Vernon Allen and Karl Scheibe, volunteered to edit and publish a selection of my writings under the title, *The Social Context of Conduct: Psychological Writings of Theodore Sarbin* (1982). It included some previously unpublished papers. The selection of papers was dictated by their construction of my theoretical framework. They screened out earlier works that were written from the positivist perspective and only selected papers reflecting my contextualist, belletrist, and humanist orientation. Because I had made some tentative inroads into the study of metaphor (Sarbin, 1964; 1968a), the editors "commissioned" me to write two systematic papers for the book (1982b; 1982a). Among the ideas developed in the papers was the "metaphor-to-myth" transformation. I had earlier done some research in collaboration with Ki-Taek Chun when he was a graduate student. We identified some of the conditions that facilitated the transformation of a metaphor, initially employed to indicate an "as if" state of affairs, into a myth as a guide to action. One of these conditions was the use of enigmatic language to express a metaphor (Chun and Sarbin, 1970). The essays that I wrote for the book made clear that neither myth nor metaphor can be fully appreciated outside the narrative framework.

My first explicit writing about the narratory principle appeared in a volume edited in collaboration with Karl Scheibe: *Studies in Social Identity* (1983). In this book, we brought together a set of studies by historians, social psychologists, a criminologist, a Shakespeare scholar, and personality and clinical psychologists. These studies illuminated the complexities of the human practice of constructing answers to the constantly recurring question "who am I?" I joined James Mancuso in preparing a chapter with the title "The Self-Narrative in the Enactment of Roles." Following G. H. Mead and William James, we examined the distinction between the grammatical constructs, *I* and *me*. We presented observations and argument to support the notion that the *I* and the *me* are essentially features of a self-narrative. The *I* is the narrator, the agent, the organizer; the *me* is the actor, the player, the performer. In the self-narrative, the *I* as narrator prepares a script for the *me* as actor to perform. Thus, in the self-narrative the protagonist is the self as actor, enacting his or her roles vis-à-vis other actors who are enacting their reciprocal roles. When people explain or articulate their ongoing self-stories, they act as if they hold the belief that the self-as-story-teller, the *I*, has authored a script to guide role-enactments as heroes, rogues, clowns, or whatever (Mancuso and Sarbin, 1983).

During the past decade, I have continued to pursue my interest in narrative psychology. An invitation to participate in a NATO conference on role transitions provided me an opportunity for further development of narrative psychology. Role transitions are the very stuff of literature. Forced or voluntary changes in the enactment of ascribed roles place strains on the coherence of participants' ongoing self-stories. One example is the case of a woman entering the occupation of coal miner, in her cultural area an exclusively male occupation. The woman's act and the reactions of the miners provided the material for a social drama. Not the same as personal dramas, social dramas deal with the outcomes of efforts to resolve conflict that have significance beyond the immediate interests of the participants. The self-narratives of the protagonist and her antagonists had to accommodate to a breach of societal norms. A more recent example of the effects of role transition is the story of Lisa Olson, the sports reporter, and the widely publicized locker room incident in which several football players insulted her by intentionally violating modesty norms.

To resolve the strain, actors engage in various kinds of adaptive actions. Principal among these are strategic actions—verbal and nonverbal. These are rhetorical acts aimed at influencing others. The identification of two qualitatively different forms of rhetorical acts help in our understanding of social dramas and enrich the interpretive possibilities for the study of narrative construction. The two forms of rhetorical acts may be called *dramaturgical* and *dramatistic*. The first flows from the assumption that "it is *as if* life is theater;" the second from the assumption that "life *is* theater." In using dramaturgical rhetoric, the protagonist engages in strategic actions of impression management through the use of symbolic mirrors, masks, lies, and secrets (see Scheibe, 1979). The protagonist is the author of such strategic interaction scripts, improvising during encounters with co-actors, and monitoring his or her performances. Exemplifying dramaturgical rhetoric are the intentional verbal and gestural acts of the football players in the Lisa Olson case mentioned above.

Rhetorical acts of the second kind, dramatistic, are performed in parallel with dramaturgical acts. They, too, are intended to influence others. They have a different authorship, however. In contrast to dramaturgical scripts where the actor is scripted by the self as author, in dramatistic scripts the identity of the author is lost in the misty past. Dramatistic scripts are patterned after half-remembered myths, legends, folktales, fables, parables, and other story forms. Not taught and learned in a systematic way, the plots of these stories are assimilated as part of one's enculturation. The content of these dramatistic roles are moral judgments, intentions, and actions that together comprise the patterns of behavior that are conventionally identified as emotions or passions (Sarbin, 1984).

The recognition of the passions as being central to role transitions steered me into developing several papers on emotion, all overlapping but with different emphases. The pivotal notion is that the patterned actions usually called passions or emotions are rhetorical acts in the service of maintaining or promoting a particular self-narrative (Sarbin, 1989). In the Lisa Olson case, her "emotional" expression of outrage exemplified dramatistic rhetoric, a set of actions consistent with moral rules acquired from ancient narrative sources.

In the spring of 1983 Brian Sutton-Smith (Professor of Folklore and Education, University of Pennsylvania) invited me (along with several others) to participate in an APA symposium on psychology and the narrative. I took the opportunity to write a paper, "The Narrative as a Root Metaphor for Psychology," in which I made the claim that the narrative and the historical act were cut from the same cloth. Recall that Pepper identified the historical act as the root metaphor for the contextualist world view. It is clear that both the historical act and the narrative are dependent upon time constructions: past, present, future; beginnings, middles, and endings.

The meaning of the historical act includes the concept of history, and we know that the word *history* refers to more than a catalog of annals and chronicles. The concept of history requires the inclusion of a historian who, with the aid of imaginative skills, renders a narrative account of what happened. Thus the historical act and the narrative are overlapping, if not identical, constructs. With this analysis I proposed that the narrative be regarded as an alternative descriptor for the root metaphor of contextualism.[6]

A few years before, I had planned to edit a book of contributed chapters by scholars interested in the narrative. After composing the root metaphor paper, I put the plan into action. Thirteen scholars accepted my invitation to participate. Most represented clinical, social, and developmental psychology, but religious studies, archeology, and psychoanalysis were also represented. The book was entitled *Narrative Psychology: The Storied Nature of Human Conduct* (1986a).

Perhaps I am too involved to make an objective judgment of the quality of the papers. Each was an exercise in creativity. The reviews were favorable. I cannot summarize the contents because of space limitations. Suffice it to say that the arguments and the data presented in each paper added to the corpus of knowledge that gives support to the claim that stories are fundamental to shaping experience and to providing guides to judgment and action.

William McKinley Runyan was present when I delivered the invited address that served as the scaffolding for this autobiography. He pointed out to me the number of times I developed a paper as the result of an invitation from an editor, a colleague arranging a symposium, etc. Such invitations generally require an effort to say something new, something different, to validate the confidence placed in me by the person tendering the invitation. Runyan's observation fits nicely into my claim that self-narratives are not solipsistic enterprises, but the resultant of social interaction. The inviters became unwitting collaborators in my self-narrative.

In the mid–1970s John Kitsuse, Professor of Sociology at Santa Cruz, and I developed first a professional relationship and later a friendship influenced by our common advocacy of the rhetoric of criticism to identify how social problems are created, negotiated, and transformed. I mentioned before that after my official retirement, I continued to teach a seminar or undergraduate class, usually one quarter each year. In 1986, and again in 1987 and 1990, Kitsuse and I jointly taught seminars dealing with social constructionism. The topics were many and varied and included, among other topics, a constructionist analysis of deviance, social identity, creativity, and emotions. One effect of this teaching enterprise was the sharpening of our ideas about social constructionism. We decided to put together an edited volume, inviting psychologists and sociologists interested in social constructionism to contribute chapters (Sarbin and Kitsuse, 1993). In reviewing the contributions, it became apparent that the underlying structure of constructionist accounts is the narrative. For example, one contributor wrote a historical narrative going back to the nineteenth-century eugenics movement to trace the origins of the notion of intelligence and its popular index, IQ.

Unexpectedly, a new world opened up for me in which I could further develop my interest in narrative. Upon retiring from the Santa Cruz campus, we moved to Carmel where we had had a vacation home for many years. Only a few miles away is the Naval Postgraduate School in Monterey. In 1979 I was asked to join a research seminar engaged in an attempt to understand military deception. I was the only psychologist in the group; the others were military officers, a historian, a former intelligence officer, a professor of political science. The narratory principle was useful in accounting for both successful and unsuccessful efforts of military strategists to deceive the enemy. The purpose of deception strategies is to influence the enemy to construct a particular narrative and act on it (Sarbin, 1982d).

In 1986, I became a member of the Personnel Security Research Center, operating out of the Naval Postgraduate School. The center was organized in 1986 following the recommendation of a commission that pointed to the need for research on the phenomenon of citizen espionage. Because it was known that I had a background in criminology and in role theory I was invited to join the center on a half-time appointment. Espionage, being a statistically infrequent event, does not lend itself to traditional hypothesis-testing methods. To know the conditions that influence a presumably trustworthy citizen to engage in treasonous conduct, one must penetrate his or her self-narrative. Some offenders have told of being influenced by novels and journalistic accounts of spies and secret agents. As in other instances of the Quixotic Principle, the literary sources provided both moral and performance guidelines. The offender's reasons for engaging in espionage and the *a priori* moral justifications become intelligible only in the context of his or her self-story (Sarbin, 1988).

Now to close. I have given an account of a journey that began more than a half-century ago. I have sketched some of the contingencies, critical incidents, and turning points that influenced a movement away from conventional psychology that was guided by the underlying metaphor that human beings are machine-like creatures. In its place I have embraced a construction more congenial with the humanities. There is still a place for conventional psychology. But for understanding persons with proper names, narrative psychology is more rewarding.

Because of the editor's reasonable restrictions, I have had to ignore important features of the self-narrative, some of which were tangential to the career aspects of my identity. I have identified some, but by no means all, of the people who were collaborators in my self-narrative. Space limitations make it impossible to identify all who participated in the construction of that narrative figure that is subsumed under the pronoun *I*. At the end of the story, I single out my wife, Genevieve, without whose multifarious contributions my self-narrative would have been impoverished, and my students, who added zest to my life.

L'ENVOI

The editor of this volume gave the contributors complete freedom to employ whatever expository style they preferred. He made one stipulation, however: The authors were to incorporate into their stories an answer to the question "What did I discover in the course of reconstructing my self-narrative?"

In reviewing my career covering more than 50 years, I became aware of a pattern. It is in the nature of a discovery, or more accurately, an awakening. In whatever subdiscipline I worked, with hardly an exception, I had adopted a theoretical posture that was contrary to conventional beliefs and to standard conceptions. Whether exploring the phenomena of hypnosis, prediction, imagination, hallucination, deviance, schizophrenia or emotions, my theoretical claims were contrary to the claims advanced in prevailing theories.

In reviewing the various counterclaims to conventional theory, I realized that I have long held allegiance to social constructionism without identifying it as such. Only in recent years have I become involved in a movement the guiding postulate of which is the claim that social objects do not exist in nature but are constructed, negotiated, and transmitted by persons. From the viewpoint of mainline thinking, constructionism as a theory of knowledge, and contextualism as a world view, are still marginal.

My advocacy of the narrative as a basic category for understanding human action is a logical extension of my commitment to contextualism and constructionism. It is contrary to the claims made by subscribers to the positivist tradition who seek confirmations of propositions that will lead to the ultimate and invariant Truth.

Such contrary claimsmaking serves two narrative purposes. The first narrative purpose is to construct a *social* drama; if the counterclaims result in changes in social policy and practice, then fairness and justice become available to larger numbers of people, especially those who have been victimized by professional or bureaucratic practices rooted in conventional theories. The second narrative purpose is to help construct a *personal* drama. Claimsmaking may enter into validating a self-narrative. It is to this personal drama that I turn.

After awakening to the observation that my career reflects the adoption of an oppositional, nonconforming posture, I speculate on its possible origins. The reasons are undeniably multiple, but two stand out.

I am reasonably sure that one of the origins was my absorption of a mythoclastic rhetoric from my mentor, J. R. Kantor. At the time when behaviorism was in full swing, Kantor promulgated "interbehaviorism," a psychological system that was contrary to the ahistorical approach of Watsonian behaviorists. He was especially effective in exploding myths about the "mind." Also, as I mentioned in the text, he was critical of psychological theories that failed to take into account the importance of language in human functioning. Not unimportant is the nature of our relationship. During the two summer sessions he served as a visiting professor from Indiana University, we had numerous conversations outside the classroom in the cafeteria and in his office. He was a kind and patient man and showed a fatherly interest in my welfare.

Another reason for my oppositional and critical behavior was suggested during the continuing dialogue I held with myself as narrator during the writing of this autobiography. From the time I entered graduate school, my academic and professional conduct was influenced by a desire to excel and to establish a reputation as a productive scholar.

My reconstruction of the development of this goal begins with my days as a graduate student at Ohio State University. From today's perspective, it is almost incredible that antisemitism in academia was a fact of life. The prejudice was of the gentlemanly variety—no baiting or bashing, only exclusionary practices.

As an undergraduate, I was unaware of the extent of the practices that supported the prejudice. But when I entered the doctoral program, I came face to face with the fact that the university was not a shelter from prejudicial practices. Like most minority group members, I experienced instances of discrimination that might be called annoyances. But two poignant events stand out in my reconstruction. The first was a conference with my thesis advisor, Professor Harold E. Burtt, the longtime chairman of the department. He called me to his office during my second quarter in the doctoral program (1937) to discuss my progress. In the course of the discussion, he asked what my ultimate goals were. I responded that I would like to teach psychology in a college or university. He wanted me to know that it would be virtually impossible to place me in an academic job because I was Jewish, even though it was the department's policy to find academic jobs for all its doctoral students. To his knowledge, only two or three members of the APA were Jewish. He went on to assure me that, personally, he was not prejudiced, but departments of psychology in universities and colleges recruited mainly gentile, white males, especially since jobs were scarce in the midst of the Great Depression. He wanted me to know the facts, and not to labor under any illusions about becoming an academic. Because he was interested in my welfare, he urged me to consider other options.

The second event that smacked of antisemitism was my not being invited to join the graduate student fraternity in psychology. The fraternity had no residence. It was more of a club that met once a month to hear a speaker, usually a faculty member, report on research in progress. Only two of the

20 or more graduate students were not invited: Both were Jewish. My classroom relations with fellow graduate students were cordial. In fact, several of us studied together to prepare for prelims. Two or three were very competent and later became well established in their respective specialties. Most were uninspired pedestrian students and made no impact on the discipline after they received their degrees. In seminars, none ever challenged a professor or even a fellow student. They conformed to the prevailing ideology.

I am offering the hypothesis that my oppositional behavior, my taking positions on the margins, was a way of demonstrating that the traditional frameworks—with which I identified those who excluded me—were unproductive and not useful for the psychology of human action. It may appear irrational to equate conventional views—the targets of my counterclaims—to the professors and graduate students who excluded me from membership in an academic society. At the time it did not occur to me to engage in political action, to mount a soap box and tell the world about the injustice produced by stereotypes. Instead, goes my hypothesis, I would deal with this insult to my identity by demonstrating that the professors and students were wrong in excluding me: I resolved to become visible as a productive scholar. The model for scholarship was my mentor, J. R. Kantor, mentioned above, one of the few Jews to hold a professorship. Kantor's erudition and mythoclastic criticism of conventional psychology had made a great impression on me. Underlying my resolve was the subtext of an ancient story exemplified by the biblical account of David and Goliath: A champion rises to do battle with what appears to be an invincible antagonist. An auxiliary narrative model is the story of Don Quixote in which the protagonist moves from adventure to adventure challenging the existing moral order.

I have located the energy for my story in events that occurred in the hazy past. Their motive effects have certainly dulled with the passage of time. Nonetheless, I continue an active writing program centering on the challenge to traditional ways of doing psychology and advocating the narrative as a root metaphor for a contextualist, constructivist psychology. This continuity requires some explanation in the light of the fact that during my career I received a number of prestigious awards, attesting to my having earned a reputation as a professor and a scholar. The concept "the functional autonomy of motives" is a first approximation to account for my continuing to chip away at the traditional footings of conventional psychology, many years after my personal drama had reached its denouement.

Many writers have found the ending to be the most difficult part of the narrative enterprise, partly because every ending is a new beginning. The writing of this self-narrative might be thought of as an ending to the story of my career. Perhaps it is. I would prefer to construe this essay as yet another step toward the narratory principle.

NOTES

1. This chapter is based in part on an invited address delivered under the title "Narrative Psychology: A Personal History" at the 71st annual convention of the Western Psychological Association, Burlingame, California, April 25, 1991. I prepared the address in response to the gentle persuasion of the program chairman, Robert Pellegrini, and the encouragement and helpful advice of Ki-Taek Chun and Karl E. Schiebe. Conversations with John Kitsuse provided an intellectual backdrop for the enterprise. I am grateful to Genevieve Sarbin and Ralph M. Carney for their valuable substantive and stylistic suggestions.

2. For a detailed narrative history of my involvement in hypnosis theory and research, see Sarbin (1990).

3. Julian Lewis, Research Professor of Pathology, invited me to collaborate on psychosomatic research. We conducted some experiments, one of which was published (Lewis and Sarbin, 1943).

4. Because of conflicting commitments, Kroger did not participate in the writing of the basic document. He contributed significantly to the original structure of the argument. In the 1968 edition of the *Handbook of Social Psychology*, Vernon Allen and I incorporated the social identity model into our chapter on role theory (Sarbin and Allen, 1968).

5. I updated my critique of schizophrenia research at an international conference held at Clark University in 1990. The critique is one of the chapters in a book recording the conference (Sarbin, 1991).

6. I expanded this proposal in a chapter prepared for a conference on contextualism (Sarbin, 1993).

2

Yet Another Preacher's Kid Finds Psychology

Karl E. Scheibe

Early in my psychological education, I learned that many famous psychologists had fathers who were ministers or at first intended to follow a religious vocation. G. Stanley Hall, Carl Jung, Carl Rogers, and James Mark Baldwin are examples of the type. William James came eventually to be installed as my unattainable ego-ideal, in part because of his lifelong preoccupation with religious issues. This provided a major chord of resonance with my own thoughts. Even William James' father, I discovered, was absorbed by religious questions and was an authority on Swedenborg, if not an actual minister.

This knowledge of the religious background of psychologists was reassuring to me. Reasoning by analogy, I thought I might actually have some of the qualifications required of a psychologist, since my own father was a minister. At the same time, this progression from religion to psychology troubled me. I wondered if psychology might be a secular religion—a moral enterprise conducted without Bible or God, protected insecurely under the aegis of Science. Noting the tribulations of my father in trying to keep the Christian faith alive in a world that seemed to need religion but not to want it, I vowed when young never to become a minister. My avoidance of a religious vocation was also part of a design to find a more comfortable way of living with sin than was evident in my family, wherein I could not help but remark the contrast between the steady piety of the pulpit and the tumult at home. Even so, I was not bold enough to eschew religion—merely the religious vocation. Now introduced to psychology, I seemed to have found the ideal substitute vocation. But psychology, my doubts said, might be nothing more than a spiritually dead affair, wherein one might putter about in a vague pursuit of Truth and attempt to do good, but without promise of a result to match salvation.

In my world, spiritual questions were alive and real—vivid and oft-repeated. These questions—of good and evil, of our nature and origins, of the meaning of a person in the cosmos—animated then and animate now my inquiries and work. Despite my doubts, I opted for psychology and for the life of a professor rather than the life of a minister. I have no regrets for this decision and am relieved not to have become ensnared in the rhetoric of salvation. But as I trace my career as a psychologist, I am reminded of the persistence of the tension between church and classroom—a tension which provides a theme for this narrative.

GERMAN ROOTS

My father, John Henry Scheibe, was born in Germany in 1901. In 1911, his mother took him, two sisters, and a baby brother to America—and to the wheat fields of Kansas. Life in Kansas soon proved to be a distinct improvement from the impoverishment and privations of village life in Germany, where the family was expected to live on "one pig a year." My father was undernourished and sickly as a young boy, but in Kansas he prospered, and after learning English in the rural schools, he became an eager and successful young scholar, working steadily on the farm and learning building trades under the tutelage of an uncle. But in his mid-teens, young Henry suffered a crisis of fear. The terror was intense but nameless, perhaps the consequence of a life too abruptly jolted from one culture to another. The crisis was resolved for him by a religious experience, which took place while he was hunting jackrabbits in a wheat field, and which resulted in a release from fear, a soothing and joyful reassurance, and a permanent, unwavering identity as a Christian. He joined a Northern Baptist congregation near Ellenwood, Kansas, and was soon followed there by other members of his family.

Progressing rapidly through the grades at school, Henry came to feel a vocational conviction to enter the ministry. To prepare to enter a seminary, he entered Tabor College in Hillsboro, Kansas, where he boarded with the Friesen family. Tabor College was and is affiliated with the Mennonite Brethren of North America. Jacob Friesen was a Mennonite and proprietor of the local lumberyard, having settled in Hillsboro after a series of peregrinations that carried him from his Alsatian birthplace to Canada, to California, to the state of Washington, and finally to Kansas—moves intended to placate his insistent wife, Hanna. Hanna had been born in Russia, on the Volga, daughter of George Burgdorff, a German tutor to the family of a Russian duke. When George Burgdorff became a Mennonite minister, his religious zeal caused him to be expelled with his family from Russia, and from thence to emigrate to Canada.

Henry, as a Baptist, found favor with the Friesen family—for he was obviously intelligent, ambitious, hardworking, and German-speaking, as were the Mennonite Friesens. Henry fell in love immediately with the youngest and most beautiful of the Friesen daughters, Esther. They were married in 1925, when he was 24 and she but 18.

THE PREACHER'S FAMILY: CONTRADICTIONS

It was from the start not a happy marriage, for Esther rightly saw Henry's driving ambition to become a minister to be a severe limitation of her young life. Even so, she attended classes with him at Tabor, worked with him at his family farm in the summers, and when he graduated went with him to Kansas City Seminary, where he duly completed the course of study and was ordained as a minister at the Oak Park Baptist Church in Kansas City. There followed a series of four children and seven churches—the children all male, and the churches all in Illinois. I was the third son, born in Belleville, for the little town of Marissa in southern Illinois had no hospital.

From Marissa we moved to Taylorville, and from Taylorville to Sterling, in northern Illinois. From Sterling we moved for a year to a farm near Freeport, where Dad had no church, but made a living farming and selling cattle feed. From Freeport we moved to tiny Esmond, where Dad assumed the ministry of two small Methodist congregations—the Methodists, being unable to find a minister of their own denomination to serve in these desolate places, were apparently willing to settle for a Baptist. As a 12-year-old in Esmond, I learned to milk cows and to do the general routines of farm work. In back of our parsonage, next to the church, a barb wire fence separated us from a cornfield. I remember staring at that fence one summer afternoon and being overcome by a feeling of certainty that I was destined for a life that would take me far from cornfields and chicken coops. It was an oddly pleasurable epiphany, something I have thought back to frequently. After Esmond, there followed a year of Delavan, Wisconsin, with Dad again not preaching but making a living as a salesman, this time of steel radiator enclosures. The final preaching assignment was at First Baptist Church of Hillsboro, Illinois, where we moved in 1951 and remained long enough for me to complete high school.

Why all this moving about? As I have said, it was not a happy marriage. The attractive young wife of the preacher was often more flirtatious than she should have been—her way of escaping the deadening boundaries of rural and small-town life. Yet divorce was out of the question, for this would put an immediate end to the preacher's career. As it was, it took my father's considerable persuasive skills to win permission to try yet another time to serve yet another congregation faithfully; these skills he exercised as well, repeatedly and forcefully, on my untamed mother, to keep the marriage together.

He was a preacher of force and conviction, extemporizing his sermons from brief notes, enriched by a fine memory for scripture. But sooner or later the congregations would discover that all was not well at home and bid us move on. Henry Scheibe's career as a minister was a downward spiral for 25 years.

Our home life embodied a mass of contradictions. We were poor but were never in want of the essentials. I am sure my father's salary as a minister never exceeded $2,500 per year, and in the depression years, it was about $15 per week. But we lived in parsonages, always had gardens, and Dad usually won permission from his congregations to supplement his income by running a repair shop from the basement or selling door-to-door. My oldest brother, Bob, was frequently truant from school, was constantly in trouble, dropped out of school at age 16 and worked at an airport, where he soon became the youngest licensed pilot in the state of Illinois. Later, in the Air Force, he had a conversion experience, and the family's bad boy was soon in training to become a missionary, now visiting home with a view to convincing the rest of the family—including his minister father—to "get right with God." The second brother, Paul, was brilliant as a student, always a ladies' man, and a good athlete. But after one year at Washington University in which he enjoyed success in all these domains, he was convinced by Bob to join him in missionary training. In 1953, both were in training by New Tribe Missionary Society to carry the gospel to Brazil.

My parents fought constantly and yet managed to maintain an atmosphere of caring and responsibility in the home. We seemed always on the brink of one disaster or another—nothing seemed permanent, everything was temporary and provisional. And yet Dad would plant fruit trees wherever we lived and, in later years in Brazil, had a passion for introducing macadamia nuts into that country. He planted much, worked at cultivation prodigiously, but harvested little. Mother was restless, mercurial, moody, interested in the fast life and somewhat addicted to betting at the race track—not an ideal taste for the preacher's wife. In 1960, after Dad had lost his last church, and after several frustrating years of trying to make a living in various ways in St. Louis, he sold out everything and joined his oldest son, Bob, as an agricultural missionary in Brazil. He went alone and, after years of trying to get Mother to join him, finally agreed to a divorce.

COLLEGE OR MISSIONARY TRAINING?

In my senior year at Hillsboro Community High School in 1955, I applied to two schools—Northwestern University, where I thought I might study chemical engineering, having had a longtime hobby of fiddling with a chemistry set, and Trinity College, where I thought I would major in psychology. Psychology had been Paul's major at Washington University before he resigned, and I had read one of his texts with fascination while visiting him there. Also, I thought Trinity too small to have much of a program in chemistry. One April day, upon returning from a track meet, I found a telegram waiting for me, announcing that I had been designated an "Illinois Scholar" at Trinity and would receive a full scholarship for my studies. This proved to be a decisive event in my life—a major choice node in my story.

I had applied to Trinity without knowing anything at all about the school or ever having been east of Illinois or ever being interviewed. My application was prompted by a brochure describing the Illinois Scholarship program which came into the hands of the high school guidance counselor, Alice Neylon. Mrs. Neylon urged me to apply, for my high school scholastic record was excellent and my SAT scores were said to be excellent, though I was not and am not privy to those numbers, for it was policy then not to reveal scores to those who took the tests. I later came to marvel at the large consequences of small occurrences and to be forever grateful to the alert Mrs. Neylon for having attended to one of the little pieces of paper that came into her mailbox and for thinking of me. I also came to be grateful for being the beneficiary of the kind of meritocracy provided by standardized tests, for I doubt I would have won my way to Trinity without my test scores.

But my decision to go to Trinity College and to major in psychology was not yet quite sealed when I graduated from high school, though I thought it was at the time. By the time of my graduation, both of my elder brothers were completing their missionary training, both were married, and both were urging me to consider a different path than the secular one I had marked out for myself. I was thrown into a profound conflict, for my fundamentalist brothers considered that my intention to go away to an eastern college and to major in psychology was to avoid a more spiritually correct calling. After some cajoling, I finally agreed to leave my summer job as a warehouse worker at the Hiram Walker distillery in Peoria in order to attend a summer missionary bible school run by the New Tribes Missionary Society in Milwaukee.

During the six-week bible school, I found myself living in a kind of urban commune with a group of about 40 people, all in training to become missionaries. We studied the Bible, had long and involved discussions, wrote papers of commentary, memorized passages of scripture, and had many worship services. I found myself handing out gospel tracts on the downtown streets of Milwaukee, and witnessing to passersby. The elders of the group counseled me to reconsider my decision to enter Trinity College in the fall— and reconsider I did. Near the end of the summer program, my parents made a visit to Milwaukee and learning of my vacillation, began some counseling of their own. Mother's counsel was expressed in an outburst of tears and desperate pleas not to give in to "these nuts." Dad was more controlled. He told me simply that if it were he, he would go to college—that going to college did not preclude me being able to lead a Christian life. On the contrary, he told me that college would open opportunities for me to live such a life to much greater effect. I accepted this counsel with gratitude, for despite my behavioral conformity with the missionary trainees, I was far from happy about the prospect of becoming a missionary. But my conscience nagged.

LIFE TAKES SHAPE AT TRINITY COLLEGE

Trinity College was from the outset a magically inspiring place for me. Its English Gothic quadrangle, set off by the majestic Episcopal chapel seemed wonderful to me—emblems of culture, cultivation, and serious learning. I was assigned to an English professor, Samuel F. Morse, as an advisor. He was the first true intellectual I had ever spoken to and I was mightily impressed. He was supportive of my intention to major in psychology—and it was he who assigned me in his Freshman English class to read Freud's *General Introduction to Psychoanalysis* (1920) and at the same time provided a sharply critical view of Freud, which I came to share. Morse was an authority on the poet Wallace Stevens, who had just died in Hartford, and to whose papers Morse was given access. Morse was himself a poet and was an exacting teacher, particularly of writing skills. He informed me that learning to write is a lifelong task, never fully achieved. This counsel has helped me survive bouts with punctilious editors.

I didn't take the time to look at the psychology department at Trinity before deciding to major in it. The department consisted of three faculty members, all freshly minted Ph.D.s and recent arrivals at Trinity. The introductory course was offered by R. D. Meade, who was to teach a half-dozen of my courses before I graduated and who became my advisor. The chairman of the department was Andrew Souerwine, and I credit him for defining my vocation in psychology—for he actually issued a call. I took social psychology from Souerwine in the second semester of my freshman year. Once, after I had responded (with sweating palms and palpitating heart) to a question about the recent Asch conformity studies, Souerwine said, for all the world to hear, "You are sounding like a psychologist!" Later, he offered me a job as departmental assistant—there being no secretary to run off ditto copies of exams, type memos, and help out with chores. One day as I was working in the department, Souerwine told me that he thought I had the makings of a psychologist and a professor, and I quickly, eagerly, incorporated this reflection into my identity. Later in my college career, when Souerwine left Trinity to work as an industrial psychologist at Travelers Insurance Company, he offered me summer and part-time academic year employment as a research assistant in the personnel department, where, textbook in hand, I learned statistics and employed them in doing turnover studies and determining the validity of selection tests.

The third member of the department was O. W. Lacy, who was to become my friend and protector and with whom I worked closely when in my senior year he became dean of the college and I was elected president of the Student Senate.

Despite misgivings about the arid behaviorism and hide-bound mechanism of the psychology of the time, I found enough of promise and challenge in psychological inquiry to provide a permanent claim on my interest. My first attempts at experimentation were crude and not exciting. I did not demonstrate then and have not developed since much imagination as an experimentalist. But I found greater interest in writing on such topics as hypnosis, imagery, the self, and the history of psychology. My senior project excited me greatly—it was an attempt to evaluate the concepts of Jungian analytic psychology in terms of the canons of experimental psychology. Alas, my final report appeared to my tutor to be more of a defense of Jung than the reduction of his concepts to the dustbin, which he considered to be their appropriate destiny. I was required to rewrite my final project in the month before graduation in order to graduate at all and in order to save my Woodrow Wilson Fellowship and my admission to the University of California at Berkeley.

The Trinity curriculum outside of psychology was a richness in science, literature, philosophy, history, religion, the arts, and linguistics. I found all of these fields vitally connected to psychology, and I was encouraged to cultivate these connections. I think in retrospect that psychology by itself would have quickly bored me, leaving me limp and gasping for air. But psychology in the nexus provided by all these other areas of inquiry—particularly history, linguistics, philosophy, and literature—seemed to me full of undeveloped promise, and I quickened to the challenge.

My years at Trinity provided the most important formative period of my life. Not only were vast intellectual and scholarly horizons opened for me there, but I also acquired experience as a leader in student organizations and discovered I had a taste and talent for such leadership. While I used my Baptist background to defeat the pretensions of Episcopalians, I also came to use the learning and sophistication of the Episcopalians to defeat the Baptist in me. In this fashion, I came free of any sort of denominational or narrow sectarian loyalty, while continuing to accept the value and authenticity of religious experience. I read William James's *Varieties of Religious Experience* (1902) under the tutelage of a philosopher in my senior year at Trinity. If James could take religious experience seriously, then clearly I could as well. And if James, though then out of favor, could be identified without embarrassment as a psychologist, then that was obviously good enough for me.

While worlds were opened to me as an undergraduate at Trinity, in one important respect the place was restrictive. I had dated freely in high school. Trinity was at the time an all-male school, and I had difficulty establishing any sort of meaningful contact with women through the rituals of mixers and weekend trips to nearby women's colleges. My social life at Trinity was a continual suffering, though this perhaps contributed to my academic successes. In the summer after my senior year, I lived with a group of fellow students in Hartford, Connecticut, while working at Travelers Insurance Company. Just before my departure for California, one of my housemates, Terry Mixter, gave me the telephone number of his sister, who had just graduated from Smith College and was installed in San Francisco with several friends from college. In this way, my years at Trinity closed with a final and most important formative bent, for I was given a ticket to meet my future wife, companion, and lifelong friend, Wendy.

GRADUATE SCHOOL AT BERKELEY: TAKING THE PLUNGE INTO PSYCHOLOGY

I went to Berkeley in 1959 with my brother Paul, who after three years as a missionary in Brazil had decided to return with his wife and adopted daughter to complete his undergraduate degree, choosing to attend the University of California, in the state of his previous residence prior to going to Brazil. He managed, with a loan from my Woodrow Wilson Fellowship stipend, to buy a house just blocks from the Berkeley campus, and there we lived.

If Trinity was immediately exhilarating to me, the psychology department at Berkeley was discouraging. Apart from the pleasure of living with my brother and his family and my developing relationship with Wendy, the rest was hard work. O. W. Lacy had warned me that graduate school would require total commitment, and my experience with my senior thesis had left me uncertain and jarred. On entering Berkeley, I had no idea what sort of psychologist I would like to become, and when I reflected this uncertainty to my advisor, Leo Postman, he summarily handed me the formidable prelim reading list and suggested that I spend my time reading in the library. That was all the advice I ever received from Postman, and while it was cold it was also useful. Read I did. I came in with a class of about 50 graduate students, and I immediately became aware that my background in psychology was not particularly strong. No one seemed to have heard of Trinity College, which I had thought to be an academic mecca.

Very little course work was required at Berkeley, apart from a first-year proseminar and a seminar on research methods, which I took with David Krech. The proseminar was organized by a team including Theodore Sarbin and provided, over the course of the year, some exposure to just about everyone in the Berkeley department. It was a rigorous, demanding, and uneven course, but it settled for me the question of what my special areas of interest would be as a psychologist, and most important, it gave me an introduction to Ted Sarbin, who was to become my mentor and lifelong friend—the humane saving grace of a department which in other respects remained rather forbidding.

Another major formative influence for me in my first year at Berkeley was provided by Julian Rotter, visiting in that year .from Ohio State. I took Rotter's graduate seminar on social learning theory. Rotter impressed me with his clarity, his convictions, his broad scope as a psychologist, as a theoretician who kept his theory honest with practice, and as a practitioner who kept his practice powered with theory and research. That seminar was filled mostly with advanced graduate students, including Danny Kahnemann. The methodological and theoretical sophistication of the discussions far surpassed anything I had encountered at Trinity, making me bear down even harder in the library, where I spent scores of hours every week.

It was in Rotter's seminar that I encountered a problem which was to become my thesis topic. Social learning theory posits the independence of expectations and values, the two major theoretical terms in its behavioral equation. This clearly was a facilitating assumption, itself without empirical foundation. I chose to write my seminar paper on this question for Rotter, and while he resisted my argument that the assumption was flatly wrong, he agreed that it made sense to address it empirically, with a view perhaps of introducing some needed qualifications to what was stated as a naked universal.

In my second year at Berkeley, I was assigned to be a teaching assistant for the advanced statistics course, taught by Rheem Jarrett. This created the odd coincidence of my older brother being my student in a section of statistics—a circumstance he always has remembered with amusement. My association with Jarrett led to my working for him as a research assistant in my third year at Berkeley. Jarrett had been working with Edward Tolman on a project having to do with cognition and language prior to Tolman's death in 1959, shortly after my arrival at Berkeley. Jarrett and I tried to pick up the pieces of this project in 1961, but what emerged was a rather straightforward verbal learning study, exploring mediated associations between words. This resulted in my first publication—a jointly authored article with Jarrett, appearing in the *Journal of Verbal Learning and Behavior* (Jarrett and Scheibe, 1962). This was a competent piece of experimentation, but it seemed to me then and seems to me now that the yield in new knowledge or new ideas from such studies is paltry in relation to the vast questions one might have about cognitive processes. Once again, I proved myself able to do experimental psychology if it were to be required, but theoretical questions interested me more than the mechanical requirements of the laboratory.

I spent the summer of 1961 working with Martin Orne, who had his hypnosis laboratory located at Harvard Medical School. This job had been arranged by Ted Sarbin, who knew of my plans to marry Wendy at the end of the summer and knew that her parents lived in the Boston area. Orne wrote me at Berkeley and asked me to familiarize myself with the literature on sensory deprivation, which I did extensively and in detail. When I first met Orne, I was suffering under the impression that we were going to do a study on sensory deprivation. He asked me if I had read the literature. When I said that I had, he immediately responded, with a wave of his hand, "It's a bunch of crap." As I recovered from my shock, he explained to me his concept of "demand characteristics" and argued that the studies on sensory deprivation were strongly contaminated by these artifacts of experimental procedures.

We then set about the development of an experiment which would demonstrate the contribution of nondeprivation factors to the production of sensory deprivation effects. This was the first experimental study I conducted that I genuinely found to be intellectually exciting, even though it was boring to watch subjects do nothing for three continuous hours. The results succeeded in demonstrating the effect of demand characteristics in producing differences between experimental and control subjects, with highly subtle manipulations of conditions.

This was certainly the most instructive summer of my graduate career, and the most productive. Not only did Wendy and I get married in September as planned, but I also established an association with one of the most powerfully ingenious psychologists of our times and produced a study which when published would become widely known and cited (Orne and Scheibe, 1964). The "panic button" study was entirely of Orne's conception and design, but the work of doing it—from finding and adapting procedures to drafting the final report—was mine. I was honored to be included as junior author on this study. In the summer of 1961, Orne also wrote his famous *American Psychologist* article, launching the concept of demand characteristics within psychology (Orne, 1962). It was exciting to be included in discussions of the development and ramifications of this concept, for it provided a critical, even revolutionary perspective from which to evaluate standard research in human psychology. My work with Sarbin had prepared me to take a social psychological view of the psychological experiment. The work with Orne, including my observations of his research on hypnosis, further encouraged me to take a dramaturgical view of the goings-on between psychologists and their subjects or clients.

Midway through my graduate career, Sarbin convened a group of his students to meet weekly at his home for informal but often highly intense discussions of their research or of other research or theoretical issues of the day. We came to call ourselves "The Tuesday Morning Group"—though we often met at other times. Rolf Kroger, Vernon Allen, Al Rutherford, Milton ("Bud") Anderson, Bob Sullivan, and I were the original members. Later, Ken Craik joined the group, and Joe Juhasz, Ki-Taek Chun, and Danny Goldstein were frequent visitors. This group functioned in a variety of positive ways. We studied together for our qualifying examinations, and when one of us passed or won some other distinction, Sarbin would throw a party, to provide what he referred to as a "rite of intensification." Beyond socializing with each other, we developed and fortified in each other a strongly critical perspective on current psychological research. I remember reporting back on my research with Orne. The group gave cordial reception to a piece of work which would cast major interpretive doubt on much of the human psychological research in the literature. Sarbin's role-theoretical perspective provided a unifying theme for the group, but often group members would differ markedly with our leader on his radical application of the concepts of role theory. Even when Sarbin was away in the 1961–1962 year on a Fulbright in England, the group continued to meet, not only to discuss our own research, but to engage in wide-ranging and often scathing appraisals of the kind of psychological research and training we saw going on around us and to speculate fruitfully on how we might do it better. Members of this group continued to collaborate on research and writing long after we all left Berkeley—to meet at APA conventions, often to organize and conduct symposia, and to enjoy the convivial presence of Ted Sarbin and his wife, our adoptive mother, Genevieve.

In retrospect, the 1959–1963 period of my graduate training seems the end of an age—in psychology as well as in our nation. Sigmund Koch published six of the projected seven volumes of *Psychology: A Study of a Science* in this period. The epilogue to Volume 3 of that series received much attention in our group—for it effectively pronounced an end to the "Age of Grand Theory" in psychology and the beginning of pluralism and a problem-centered, less unified psychology (Koch, 1959). The failure of Koch to produce his seventh and final volume of the projected series seemed testimony to a loss of heart—an inability to pronounce a forward-looking set of conclusions which would cheer on the coming generation of psychologists.

When I entered Berkeley, psychology seemed entire, so that I was not even required to state a special field of study on my application and only settled gradually into personality-social-clinical wing of the department. When I left, evidence of fragmentation was everywhere. Social psychology was approaching its protracted crisis—a crisis to which Orne's work, including my own minor efforts, contributed. Mischel (1968) was soon to issue his scathing critique of the notion of fixed personality traits, a position already well visited and defended by our little group at Berkeley. Soon the Berkeley department would abandon the idea of presenting a single, year-long proseminar to the entire entering crop of graduate students, heeding David Krech's call to "divide and conquer" and getting on to more specialized training from the outset of one's studies.

When I left Berkeley in 1963, no one I knew had tried LSD and I never saw or smelled marijuana. While there was political activism on campus, it was focused against the House Un-American Activities Committee investigations and other vestiges of McCarthyism. The Free Speech Movement was yet to be launched. It was pre-Beatles, still Camelot, pre-hippie, still beatnik. I remember seeing a "Get Out of Vietnam" poster before leaving

Berkeley, but I had no idea what it referred to. The assassination of John F. Kennedy in November 1963—in my first semester at Wesleyan—marks a watershed—for me, for psychology, for the nation, and for the world. Later, in writing about the psychology of national identity, I developed the argument that human psychology could not pretend to be ahistorical—to ignore historical context as psychologically determinative—that events occurring at the level of the modern nation-state powerfully influence our own sense of self, our own sense of meaning and possibility in life (Scheibe, 1983). Without doubt, the Kennedy assassination was the event pushing this argument onto the page.

WESLEYAN UNIVERSITY—A GOOD FIRST JOB

My doctoral dissertation grew out of the problem encountered in Rotter's seminar in my first year at Berkeley. I devised an elaborate experiment to determine the conditions under which expectancy statements would and would not be influenced by values assigned to outcomes in a psychomotor pursuit task. I also devised a parallel questionnaire study to explore the effect of the same set of variables on assertions of belief. Sarbin was my thesis tutor, but we collaborated little on the actual design and conduct of my research. Instead, our conversations centered on the broader theoretical questions of the nature of human beliefs, the situational determinants of their expression, and the philosophical underpinnings of the notions of value and utility. Sarbin encouraged me to look at this question of the relation between beliefs and values from a variety of perspectives—philosophical and literary, as well as experimental. Our first jointly authored article presented a theory of superstitions and was published in the *British Journal for the Philosophy of Science* (Scheibe and Sarbin, 1965).

As my dissertation neared completion in the spring of 1963, I found myself faced with the prospect of finding a job. Rotter had offered me a postdoc to come and work with him. I sent my vita out in late spring to a bunch of schools, and such was the job market at that time that I received a set of job offers without so much as a campus interview or visit. But the job offer I accepted was a result of happenstance. Bob Thompson was professor and chairman of the psychology department at Wesleyan, and he happened to be making a West Coast trip in early 1963. A notice was posted for interested students to line up for interviews with him for an opening at Wesleyan. I signed up for the interview, since I knew of Wesleyan from my undergraduate days at Trinity, even though the opening was in the area of experimental or physiological psychology. A fellow graduate student, Dick DeBold, was offered this position within a few weeks of Thompson's visit. But then in late May I received a call from Wesleyan, offering me a second position—for the faculty member teaching social psychology at Wesleyan had suddenly resigned. I believe my candidacy received a boost from DeBold, for I had recently provided him some help on a complex analysis of variance problem for the completion of his dissertation. So I accepted the job at Wesleyan, without ever having visited the campus, based on my 20-minute interview with Thompson and supported by whatever words DeBold might have pronounced for my benefit. Thus, it happened that two newly minted Ph.D.s from Berkeley arrived in Middletown, Connecticut, in fall of 1963 to compose one-third of the psychology department at Wesleyan.

I thought of Wesleyan as a good first job. The school was well endowed and enjoyed an enviable reputation in psychology for a small college. (David McClelland established his initial fame there and had only recently left for Harvard.) It was familiar territory for me, allowing some contact with former teachers at Trinity. Most importantly, it was near Wendy's family in Boston, and it pleased us both to be nearer to them.

It was clear from the outset that Wesleyan expected its professors to excel both in teaching and in research. Tenure anxiety was intense—and the word within the junior faculty was that few of us would survive the drastic scrutiny of our seniors. As things came into focus, tensions became evident in the department—between the experimental, physiological, and comparative wing, represented by Bob Thompson, and the humanistic and personality wing, represented by Bob Knapp. Both were excellent teachers and active scholars, and fortunately both were supportive of my initial efforts at teaching and research. Classes were small, the students were excellent, and the general faculty environment at Wesleyan stimulating, progressive, exciting—if at the same time anxiety-provoking. It was an easy place in which to get involved, not only with psychologists but with faculty members from a variety of other disciplines as well.

At first, my research at Wesleyan was a direct continuation of what I had been doing at Berkeley. I finished the piece with Sarbin on superstitions and worked my thesis experiment into shape for publication (1964). But the most immediate influence for my research was to come in a wholly unanticipated way. Jules Holzberg was at the time the director of psychology at Connecticut Valley Hospital (CVH) and an adjunct professor at Wesleyan. In the spring of my first year at Wesleyan, he offered me an opportunity to prepare a research proposal to do an evaluation study on the effectiveness of a state-run program in which a group of about 100 college students were to work for a summer in a "Service Corps" on the chronic wards of the four state mental hospitals in Connecticut. I viewed this task as something like a graduate student assignment, and I completed it within the two-week spring break. I was able to draw heavily on my course on psychological assessment with Harrison Gough and my work for him at the Institute of Personality Assessment and Research, where I had worked as a kind of computer donkey. In short order, the grant was approved, and I suddenly found myself as co-principle investigator with the commissioner of Mental Health of the State of Connecticut on a project, later to extend for five years, funded by the National Institute of Mental Health. I was able to hire a staff—Wesleyan students, a secretary, students from the University of Connecticut and Yale, buy office equipment and supplies, and to implement a comprehensive evaluation effort. I quickly sought the counsel of former teachers as consultants—Rotter, Orne, Sarbin—and was off and running on a project which was to yield a good number of publications, including a monograph, and to provide me with an extraordinary set of experiences and opportunities (Scheibe et al., 1969).

But it must be said that the substance of the research I was doing did not connect well to my fundamental concerns as a psychologist or scholar. In retrospect, this project seems more important now than it did at the time, for it was an evaluation of one of the many entering wedges in the general and massive process of deinstitutionalization that was about to sweep mental institutions throughout the country. We were able to show that college students spending ten weeks on a chronic mental ward could dramatically change the generally lethargic atmosphere of such wards and could develop meaningful interactions with patients who were thought to be beyond reach. At the time, I inwardly reproached myself for being opportunistic—for allowing my research activities to be dictated by the availability of funds. It was a demanding project, involving mountains of data, five different research sites throughout the state, and supervision of a staff of as many as 20 people. But I wondered if I was selling out, a version of a familiar struggle of conscience.

Relief from this applied research was provided in 1965, when Sarbin arranged for some of the members of the Tuesday Morning Group to spend the summer at Berkeley, supported by his own research grant. Rolf Kroger and I worked together intensely that summer, sharing an office and developing scores of ideas for research, only a few of which were practicable. While my own research team worked away in Middletown, I worked with colleagues at Berkeley on topics of a theoretical nature.

It was in that summer that Sarbin, Kroger, and I developed a theoretical model of social identity, which we called "soapy" because I carved a representation of the relation between three dimensions of the model in a bar of Ivory soap (Sarbin and Scheibe, 1980). The model employed the classic distinction between achieved and ascribed roles, together with the dimensions of involvement and evaluation to produce an integrated way of thinking about positive and negative transformations of social identity. This model was to provide something like a theoretical kernel, from which scores of applications were soon to follow. My first application was in a paper jointly authored with Phil Shaver, at that time an undergraduate research assistant on my grant project, on the transformations in the social identity of patients participating with college students in the Service Corps program (Shaver and Scheibe, 1967).

The model we developed also provided a way of thinking about religious experiences and conversions, provided an account of the power of revolutionary ideology in shaping thought and conduct, and generally linked such sociological concepts as deviance and mass movements with psychological concepts. This work was as exciting and stimulating to me as the evaluation research was onerous (Sarbin and Scheibe, 1983). Fortunately, I was able to forge ahead both on the theoretical and applied fronts of research and writing.

THE BRAZILIAN ADVENTURE

In the summer of 1966, another unanticipated event was to have substantial impact on my life and career. My oldest brother, Bob, had continued in the interior of Brazil as a missionary, even while Paul left this life in favor of getting his degree and later developing a successful career in business. In August 1966, on the day of my arrival in San Francisco to visit Paul, we received word that Bob had been killed in an airplane accident—where he as pilot was teaching a Brazilian student to fly. My father was living with Bob in Brazil, building a machine shop and developing agricultural projects as part of their mission effort. I was devastated by Bob's death and was reminded again of the agonizing choice of a worldly life over one of more transcendent meaning. I resolved to learn Portuguese and to take my young family to Brazil for the 1967–1968 year, so that I could be of support to my father, who had no profession to continue in the United States, and who was resolved to continue his work in Brazil—even after Bob's death and the departure of his wife and children for the United States.

Fortunately, several factors contrived to make this possible. First, my younger brother, Steve, had spent time in Brazil previously, had learned Portuguese, and could help us make living arrangements. Second, I was due for my first Wesleyan sabbatical and could draw some additional support from grant research funds for the year. Third, I was able to hire Jim Kulik, a new Ph.D. from Berkeley, to serve as acting director of the Service Corps research projects. Fourth, in 1966–1967 Wesleyan had two Brazilian students in residence, and one of them, Roberto Bouchardet, was a native of Belo Horizonte, where we intended to live for the year. Bouchardet proved to be a gifted and dedicated Portuguese tutor, and the first of many generously supportive Brazilian friends we have come to know.

Thus it came to pass that at the end of the summer of 1967, Wendy and I embarked for Brazil, with two young sons—David, age 3, and Daniel, age 6 months. We were met at the airport in Rio by Steve and Bouchardet, and with their help, and most particularly that of Bouchardet's family, we were able to install ourselves in an attractive and commodious house in Belo Horizonte and to begin our Brazilian adventure.

The decision to take the family off to Brazil for the year, learn a new language, adapt to a new culture, and nurture my father along in a totally strange environment was obviously driven more by passion than by reason. I marvel today that Wendy was willing to go along with what seems in retrospect a most unpromising prospect. Yet the year turned out to be immensely successful for all of us. I completed the manuscript of my first book, *Beliefs and Values* (1970), as well as the final monograph and several papers from the Service Corps research. We did learn Portuguese, and I was able to offer two short courses, delivered haltingly but in the language, at the Federal University at Brasilia in April 1968. Steve lived with us in Belo Horizonte, and Dad divided his time between living with us in the capital and working at his machine shop in the distant interior town of Montalvania. Wendy grew her hair long and wore her shirts short, in the style of the times, and was avid in absorbing Brazilian culture. To cap it all off, I received a terse and totally unanticipated note from Jules Holzberg, who had come into the department as chairman upon his retirement from CVH. I quote the note in full:

> Dear Karl:
>
> You have just been awarded tenure. More later.
>
> > Congratulations,
> > Jules

Despite the high value that I must obviously place on being awarded tenure, this was still not the greatest achievement of the year. Our year in Brazil established for us a lasting attachment to that country—its language, culture, and people. From that time on, we have had a steady stream of Brazilian visitors at our home in Middletown and have traveled to Brazil many times, including twice as a Fulbright fellow at the Catholic University of São Paulo, first in 1972–1973 and later in 1984. I have had the opportunity of teaching courses at several Brazilian universities and of collaborating with Brazilian students and colleagues on research—a collaboration which still continues.

Because of my interest in Brazil, I have been able to attract several Brazilian scholars to visiting appointments at Wesleyan. Developing fluency in a second language has been a great satisfaction for me. Developing a first-hand knowledge of another culture is even more valuable, and I am convinced this has made me a better teacher and scholar.

CONTINUING EDUCATION AMIDST ATTRACTIONS AND DISTRACTIONS

As a professor, one never ceases being a student. While my undergraduate education provided a decent foundation for graduate school, and while my graduate education provided a serviceable beginning for my teaching career, it seems to me now that the preserved result of my formal training is quite minuscule in relation to what I have learned since in teaching and in writing. I have been carried on waves of enthusiasm for certain topics, certain authors, certain projects.

One of these waves is certainly named Brazil and it seems permanent. Machado de Assis is Brazil's most famous author, and his wry perspective on life has taught me much.

Someone gave me a set of George Orwell's journalistic writing and essays, and this led to reading everything that Orwell had published and to his installation in my small pantheon of heroes. I found that Orwell had a good deal to say about the psychology of self and identity, in particular national identity, and while he hardly thought of himself as a psychologist, it was easy for me to appropriate him as such.

While I had read William James in graduate school for my history prelims, it wasn't until I taught History of Psychology at Wesleyan that I read James in any depth. His essays, "The Will to Believe," "The Moral Equivalent of War," and "On a Certain Blindness in Human Beings," have become centerpieces in my own thinking, and Jamesian pragmatism, embracing as it does the fundamental validity of all human experience, has served as my philosophical standpoint.

Sometime in the mid–1970s I discovered the Spanish philosopher Jose Ortega y Gassett and devoured his writings with great pleasure and advantage, for Ortega's conception of human history is intimately connected with the requirements of individual psychology. Armed with Ortega, it became clear to me that psychology had to be the bridge connecting universal science with secular history—that psychology had to accommodate to determinism and indeterminacy at the same time.

Other sources of insight and inspiration for me included Mark Twain, George Santayana, Carl Jung, Thomas Mann, Oscar Wilde, Abraham Lincoln, and Erving Goffman. An odd collection, it would seem, and not a psychologist in the lot—but each of these authors gave me something fundamental—crystal clear ideas expressed in words, providing me with the texts I needed to focus my thinking, my teaching, and my writing.

I have tried reading murkier writers—Hegel, Husserl, Merleau-Ponty, Foucault, Lacan. I find I have no taste or talent for these authors and have grown increasingly impatient with obscurity and what seems either intellectually ponderous or self-consciously cute. Some writers pay me well with new ideas and memorable insights; some do not. This is no universal judgment upon those for whom I have discovered no mental meeting, but I do not spend much time with bad matches.

Meanwhile, carried along on my series of private enlightenments, I found myself willy-nilly drawn into a series of institutional involvements which, viewed from the standpoint of scholarly progress, are clearly distractions, but which in honesty I must say I have enjoyed. Beginning shortly after my first visit to Brazil, I began to serve on a number of central and powerful committees at Wesleyan, including the faculty committee on promotions and tenure. I also served on the Board of Fellows and later as a trustee at my alma mater, chairing major committees there and serving on a search committee for a new president. I began to chair the psychology department at Wesleyan in 1973, just after my promotion to full professor and did this duty more often than not over a period of 15 years. In 1974, an opportunity came up to serve as the director of the review panels for the National Science Foundation's Science Faculty Professional Development program, and I performed this consulting role for seven consecutive years. I have served as a trustee and as moderator of our Congregational church and have chaired a search committee for a new minister there. Some of these leadership roles have exposed me to difficulties—with quarrelsome colleagues or warring factions of this or that organization. Even so, I have enjoyed these jobs, have not shirked them, and have learned and grown from the scrapes as well as the successes.

Perhaps the most negative effect of my efforts at administration has been that some well-meaning friends have proposed that since I seemed to take to these tasks so well, I might well aspire to become a college president or assume some other full-time administrative role. For a brief time, I admit that I waited anxiously to see whether any of these little seeded aspirations would spring into hardy reality. Alas, they did not, and I have learned to accept this limitation as a blessing, for my energies came to be absorbed in more mature writing, more venturesome teaching, and in becoming a practicing as well as a professing psychologist.

CONNECTING THE DOTS

In reviewing tenure cases, I have often heard the reproach that some candidate's research and writing is "not programmatic," which I take to mean that the research does not relentlessly bear down on some narrowly defined topic. This characterization certainly applies to my own research and writing, for after publishing my first dozen articles I looked up to discover in some astonishment that no two of them were published in the same journal and that they were rather wildly eclectic in content—ranging from standard experimental psychology to philosophical essays, to experimental social psychology, and to empirical evaluation studies. But I do not reproach myself for the variety of style, topic, and outlet and have no longing to be identified with a specific research program. This has been relatively easy for me, since my mentor, Sarbin, presented me with a model of rather zig-zagged scholarly peregrinations. Also, Wesleyan is not a place in which one is obliged to write one's name ever larger in the same portion of the scholarly firmament. Wesleyan has encouraged and rewarded my eclecticism, and I count this a blessing.

Even so, my research and writing in later years has certainly coalesced around a more limited set of topics—themes have emerged. The first and most important of these has been a preoccupation with the general problem of predictability in psychology. I consider *Mirrors, Masks, Lies and Secrets* to be my single most satisfactory statement to date (1979). It employs the dramaturgical perspective of Sarbin, notions of strategic interaction derived from Goffman, and the philosophical views of James and of Ortega about the relationship between history and thought to yield a general statement about the sorts of predictability to which psychology might and might not aspire.

This book has served as a text in a teaching experiment I have developed at Wesleyan over the past dozen years—a course called "The Dramaturgical Approach to Psychology." The course is active, participatory, and uses plays as a way of getting psychological problems and issues on stage for discussion. The course is run as a workshop, with groups of three to four students charged each week with developing exercises—improvisations, tasks, games, recitations—sometimes employing rather standard psychodrama techniques, often inventing their own devices for involving the class. Each class meeting is structured by an assigned work—usually a play—and a set of topics. For example, "Who's Afraid of Virginia Woolf?" is assigned with the following topics: "appearance and reality, secret bonds, betrayal, sex and aggression, biology and history." The task of the leaders is to devise a set of exercises which will involve the entire class in an exploration of these topics, focused about the content of the play. I meet with the leaders both before they begin their planning, to make suggestions, and just before the class, to make corrections. For the rest, I act during the class pretty much like one of the students. Over the dozen years I have taught this course, an evolution has taken place. Certain plays, techniques, and dramatic devices have become standard. But an essential feature of the course is its risky openness, its indeterminacy, the anxiety-provoking possibility of failure. The class is given to 21 students—mostly seniors, many of them theater majors as well as psychology students. The last time I gave the course was typical: Not a single cut by any student for the entire semester, a remarkably cohesive group produced from a bunch of strangers and splendidly successful didactic experience for all of us—students and teacher alike.

"The Dramaturgical Approach to Psychology" is leading to the composition of a new book, "The Drama of Everyday Life," which is about half-finished at present. A major objective is to show that the dramaturgical approach to psychology is useful both pedagogically and conceptually. The joining of psychology and theater enlivens both.

Another book is already drafted and is being prepared for publication within the year. *Self Studies* (in press) also derives in large part from a course I have taught over the years, "The Psychology of Self and Identity." The theoretical basis for this book comes from the summer of 1965, when Sarbin, Kroger, and I produced the "soapy" model at Berkeley. Since then, I have written for other books a number of chapters dealing with self and identity themes. *Self Studies* pulls this material together, with a general updating and several original chapters.

PRAXIS

In 1984, after returning from a semester teaching and writing in São Paulo, Brazil, I was presented with an opportunity to consult with clinicians at Stonington Institute, a nearby private hospital for drug and alcohol rehabilitation—primarily to introduce group techniques to their clinical staff, but also to inaugurate some outcome research. This involvement gradually increased, and I found myself growing more and more interested in the process of treatment. Soon I began to do counseling with individual patients and families as part of the clinical staff. Then in the summer of 1987, because of a sudden resignation, I was asked to be acting clinical director at the institute.

Because of my increasing activities in counseling, I sought and obtained licensure as a psychologist in Connecticut. This was not easy, for instead of regular internships and supervised residencies, I presented a hodge-podge of clinical experiences and involvements, some of them formal, some informal—and my Ph.D. had been granted 25 years before, when licensure requirements were just coming into being. But after affidavits from former teachers and colleagues and a fair amount of sweating the bureaucracy, I was finally allowed to take the state examination, and in 1986, I became a legitimate practitioner.

Way leads onto way. By the late 1980s I had been teaching at Wesleyan for over 25 years and had been strongly involved with various leadership positions within the faculty during that time. In this period, Wendy decided to resign her position as associate dean of admissions, which she had held for almost 20 years. Our boys had both graduated from college and were embarking on their careers with admirable independence. It seemed time for me to make a change, and my license and developing experience with drug and alcohol counseling provided a means of making the change.

The most experienced clinician at Stonington Institute was Duff Chambers and we became friends. He was growing restive after over 20 years of institution-bound clinical work and was, too, looking for a change. Together, we planned to launch a private practice. In July 1990, having purchased and rebuilt a house to be our offices, we launched the Saybrook Counseling Center, in Old Saybrook, Connecticut.

Over the same period of time, I developed a relationship with psychologists at the Center of Alcohol Studies at Rutgers University and began doing some collaborative research there, which involved taking some most useful training in psychodiagnostics. In this fashion, I became a Visiting Professor at the Rutgers Center of Alcohol Studies.

Over the past few years, my counseling experience has deepened and broadened. Initially, our clients were almost exclusively in recovery from substance abuse. But soon I began to see couples, then individuals suffering from depression and a more general range of disorders. I have found the practice of psychology to be immensely instructive and gratifying. It has been difficult to curb my tendency to treat counseling sessions as if they were tutorials, and to fall into teaching. But I have found that all of my years of teaching and research do have application when dealing one-on-one with someone who has a problem. Therapy and teaching have much in common.

I have found myself becoming increasingly interested in the problem of addictive conduct—the idiosyncracies of excessive appetites. Recently, I have written a chapter for a volume edited by Sarbin on the social construction of reality—the idea that our concepts and modes of thought, as well as our made objects, are products of social fabrication. My paper concerns the careers of cocaine users, with special attention to the enormous individual differences in the patterns of those careers, and is based in large part on my experience in counseling with cocaine users over the past several years (Scheibe, 1993). I find myself finally realizing the value of advice offered by Rotter when I was a first-year graduate student—that the teacher/researcher benefits from practice, and that the practitioner benefits from participating actively in developing and imparting the base of knowledge, technique, and concept that is psychology. This happy melding has not been without strain, for I have started a new career without leaving the old one. I am still Professor of Psychology at Wesleyan as well as director of the Saybrook Counseling Center. This means very long hours at work and diminished free time. But I am finding my clinical experience to be a source of distinct enrichment to my teaching and writing, and my academic work remains a source of pleasure and fulfillment.

REFLECTIONS ON THE PROCESS OF TELLING THIS STORY

I remember years ago reading a biographical account of the linguist, Benjamin Lee Whorf. Whorf, like me, was the son of a minister—in his case, an Episcopalian. He became interested—more than interested, consumed—with the question of the authenticity of the Bible, for it did not take him long to discover that it was not dictated by God in English. This led him to become interested in the problem of translation and to consider the trail of successive translations which has led from some unknown original text to our modern Bible. This led in turn to a fascination with the relation of language to thought, and eventually to research on ancient Mayan texts, and finally to the formulation of his famous hypothesis on linguistic relativity and other contributions to modern linguistics. Along the way, of course, his primordial motivation to discover the extent to which the true word of God is preserved in our modern Bible came to be neglected if not forgotten.

This story is memorable to me, for it seems to parallel my own quest. Without question, the most burning and urgent questions for me as a child were spiritual. These questions led me along the paths I have outlined here into my identity as a psychologist. But always there is the lingering doubt: Have I taken the right path? I think so. I don't know where life would be better. I certainly believe it would not be better for me or anyone else if I had chosen to become a foreign missionary, for I have known this species and aside from the occasional Albert Schweitzer, I do not admire them. But my work as a psychologist bears many traces of my early religious background. I commonly begin lectures with a text, and my style probably does get preachy on occasion. With the development of my counseling work, the parallels to the minister grow even closer. And I still sing in the choir at the local Congregational Church—an exercise which I consider to be not just therapeutic but sublime.

James argues in his chapter on the self that the stream of consciousness is continuous—that part of us is timeless (1890). This exercise of composition has reinforced the validity of this claim. Another metaphor for the development of self is that of the chambered nautilus, a creature which builds ever larger houses for its growing mass, while carrying the accumulating spiral of vacated chambers as physical testimony to the previous chapters in its life narrative. It is a pleasure for me to contemplate my own set of vacated chambers and previous chapters, but I would not wish to return to any of them—or for that matter to spend too much time viewing them, lest I be afflicted with a kind of museum fatigue.

I close with what came to me as a powerful experience just as I was preparing to compose this chapter. In reviewing my professional development, I was frankly overwhelmed by the evidence of the extent to which my mentor, Ted Sarbin, has contributed to my professional and personal life. He has provided me with many opportunities—and more than this, with a model of gentle and humane caring—one human being to another achieving the joy of communion. My father was a minister and an admirable man. My mentor is a psychologist and a mensch.

3

Let's Pretend: A Duography

Mary and Kenneth Gergen

Narrative and action exist in a state of mutual interdependence, as does the dialogue that spices and splices the disparate segments of "self-understanding" together.
—KJG and MKG, "Toward reflexive methodology," in F. Steier (Ed.), *Research and reflexivity* (London: Sage, 1991)

... "U.S. troops authorized to fight in Vietnam" ... "Race Riots Rage in Watts" ... *Zorba the Greek* ... First issue of *The Journal of Personality and Social Psychology* ... *Woman's Room* ... "The miniskirt and Twiggy: New Fashion from England" ... *The Graduate* ... *Light My Fire* ... *Sergeant Pepper's Lonely Hearts Club Band.* ...

GENESIS: WHO IS THAT MASKED MAN?

It was the fall of 1965. Michael and I had just moved from Minneapolis to Watertown, Massachusetts, where he was taking on postgraduate work in architecture. Architect friends invited us to a Halloween costume party. We hustled up some last minute "campus rebel" costumes and arrived to find the basement "rec room" crowded with bizarre figures. As we descended the stairs we were greeted by the hosts, who informed us that a contest was in progress to identify the psychological concepts that Kenneth and Eleanor portrayed in their costumes. Since I was completing an M.A. in counseling psychology perhaps I could succeed where other guests were failing. The gentleman in question—scarcely a gentleman at that—was unshaved and half naked, barefoot, hairy chested, wearing ragged shorts, with a guitar over his shoulder. (This was not going to be easy!) But his wife, in trim white leotards and turtleneck, black boots, and whip helped to suggest the solution: clearly the Id and the Super Ego. Later, Eleanor mentioned that Ken had a grant and was looking for a research assistant. Perhaps I might apply.

Like Michael and I, most of the couples were composed of grad-school husbands at MIT and Harvard and full-time wife-mothers. At first I was skeptical to hear that Ken taught at Harvard, in part because of the status of the others, and in part because it was unbelievable that at my first party in Boston, having just arrived from Minnesota, I should be conversing with a "real" Harvard professor. We sat on the basement stairs and talked at length about how people define things in a variety of ways. He made the extravagant claim (I thought) that even what we call "pain" could be called "pleasure" under the right circumstances. I was very excited about our encounter—both intellectually and sensually. Later, he encouraged me to join him in a Greek dance led by our hosts, Phyllis and George. His grace and attentive charm plus the exotic (to a midwestern prairie girl with Swedish, German, and Irish roots) nature of the dancing, whetted my desires for adventure. Perhaps Ken's invitation at evening's end to call him the following week was just that.

I thought a lot about this call: Was Monday too eager, would Thursday make it seem an afterthought:? I settled on Tuesday. When he answered, I said, "Hello, this is Mary." There was a silence on the other end, and I realized with embarrassment that he didn't have a clue as to who "Mary" was. At the time I did not realize that as head tutor of all Social Relation majors, he might have had dozens of "Mary's" in his charge, working and playing in William James Hall. I explained who I was, and the cordial and interested tone I was longing to hear thankfully returned to his voice. He asked me to come in on Friday afternoon at 1:30 to talk about the research position. I thought of little else as the week progressed.

I was prompt and explained my presence to Joy, his secretary. She, in turn, seemed unsettled: Her boss was not there. He had rushed away to his home over the lunch hour and had not returned. Time passed slowly, and after half an hour she called Ken's home. She handed me the receiver after explaining my visit, and he told me there was an emergency but he would soon return. After a tortured hour and a half we had our appointment. We entered his spacious second floor office, impressive with its Oriental carpet of blue, a sofa, wooden university chairs, bookcases, and a lovely old liquor cabinet (a gift from Henry Murray), from which he offered me a sherry late in the afternoon. After long discussion, he asked me if I knew French and gave me some Merleau-Ponty to translate. I don't think he was very impressed with my basic French ability. In fact, I doubt there was much to be impressed about, now that I was sitting opposite him in his academic setting. I don't know why he hired me. Perhaps he felt sorry for all the delays, or perhaps it was the enthusiasm I exuded—a blend of eagerness for the job or him. In any case, my life took on a new dimension—every Monday, Wednesday, and Friday.

SATURDAY NIGHT SHUFFLE—A SECOND SOUNDING

If one comes to a costume party "dressed" as the Id what is there to do but indulge the senses? And was I not eminently deserving of such indulgences? To steep themselves against the untrammeled exuberances of four young boys, my parents—a mathematician and a cultured New Englander—had enforced an array of demanding rules of household decorum. I later added to these suppressions by developing a deep idealism, expressed—to my parents' dismay—in a youthful commitment to the Southern Baptist Church. Perhaps the culminating expression of self-bondage was a premature marriage to Eleanor—a very fine woman, but whose very virtues placed tight restrictions around all forms of deviance. Only the spontaneous energies of our children—Laura and Stan—provided a sanctioned form of impulsivity. And now the sixties were upon us, and I was beginning to respond to its rhythms.

And in that crowded, smoky basement of a Greek hairdresser—with the crisp and elemental sounds of the bazuki boiling the blood, what greater sensual pleasure than to observe this high-cheek-boned olive-skinned, broad-smiled lass? And what greater pleasure to find that she indeed found me curious? The evening was on! But what I was scarcely prepared for was the slow turn from glib phrases, elusive glances, cascading laughter, to matters of substance. Stanley Schachter had recently spoken at Harvard, and I was very impressed with the implications of his work for conceptions of the self. During graduate work at Duke with Ned Jones, I had become enthralled with what seemed a protean plasticity in self-conception. Contrary to individual psychology, with its emphasis on mechanisms and structures, self-conception seemed processual—ever-immersed in a changing sea of relationships. Schachter's work on emotion seemed to confirm this. And this lovely creature before me actually seemed enthralled by it all. It was late when I emerged from this ego excursion. God, did I also offer her a job . . . this person with the simple name of Mary? Am I out of my mind? Eleanor arrived to remind me it was time to go home.

Life moves fast for a young man on his first job—eager to explore all his potentials, open all the doors, savor all the possibilities of this cultural capital. I was riding high—with enthusiastic classes, National Science Foundation money, a position as head tutor, a seat on the august Committee on Educational Policy, and a place at the cutting edge of a new and bold adventure in a self-consciously experimental social psychology. There was also the prevailing ethos of sensual liberty: the psychedelic, flower power, rock n' roll evolution of cosmic energy—up, up, and away, dancin' in the streets, doin' it in the road—all this against the backdrop of a marriage straining itself to the breaking point and two small children touching me to the core. So how can I be blamed that I was an hour late for an appointment with a name that scarcely stood out from the overcrowded calendar on my desk. There were fires aplenty to put out before I could attend to the new spark.

> . . . "Martin Luther King Shot by Sniper" . . . "France Nearly Paralyzed by Protesters" . . . "Bobby Kennedy Shot in LA" . . . "Soviet Tanks Invade Defiant Prague" . . . "Israel Smashes Arabs in Six Day War" . . . "Police Battle Mobs as Democrats Meet" . . . "Vietnam Reds Launch Tet Offensive" . . . "Joan Baez Arrested in Anti-War Protest" . . . "Make Love Not War: 10,000 Hippies Rally in New York Be-In" . . . *Soul on Ice*. . . .

EXODUS: A ROAD TO ROME

It is late summer 1968. Leaving New York on an Italian ocean liner with Ken and my two preschool children, Lisa and Michael, was a dramatic and wonderful turning point in my life. Until that moment, I was not sure that the fantasies and plans for a year in Rome would actually materialize. We had a joint bank account into which we had put extra monies we had made, and we had ordered tickets, but not until we actually saw the last rope cast away did I realize that we were truly committed to this fanciful plan. Had we listened to too many fairy tales in our childhood, listened to too much radio make-believe, or seen too many Hollywood spectacles? Was this life copying art, or as Woody Allen suggests, bad television? (Reflecting on our actions, I wonder now if our bold and ultimately wise decision did not give us the courage to travel a great many uphill grades.)

The ocean crossing was as exciting as any pulp romance. It was our first experience living together, although traveling on a ten-day cruise scarcely qualifies as "ordinary life." Our only brush with "reality" came when Ken ran into his mother's next-door neighbor, who was the first to inform his mother that he was traveling to Italy *en famille*. (She forgave us, I still think, because she also lived in novels!). The kids loved Ken, who was a doting father, and their presence helped erase the only dark cloud, which was the loss of contact with his own children.

In most respects, living together proved to be quite easy. Ken was a master of every aspect of life, I thought. He somehow managed to be aware of every contingency, able to communicate, juggle foreign currencies, find the best arrangements, the nicest views, the right train to Rome. I was his companion, his lover, his friend. Being cared for, protected, and cherished was a wonderful new role for me that took me back, in a sense, to a childhood time. The kids and I were secure in a way I had never felt before as a married woman. But there were little costs accumulating. One day we were in Amalfi visiting the cathedral. (I was carrying the heavy blue Hatchett's guide, from which I had to read to Ken the most intimate dimensions of every edifice of Italy, while he carried the large 35mm camera and took all the pictures.) He had bought some mints, and I asked for one. He was considering a photo opportunity, and said, "Not now." The comment crystallized a sense of helplessness which had been bothering me, and I began to criticize our arrangement. The gist of my mesage was that I was not a child, to be told to wait patiently, and that I wanted more control over things. His position was that he had all the responsibilities and could not always satisfy my every whim instantaneously. It was not a pleasant interchange. In a state of pique, he shoved his wallet, passport, tickets, and car keys—along with the mints—into my handbag—"for me to control." To this day I carry all the official necessities and now make almost all the travel arrangements. The colonial quality of the relationship was beginning to recede.

Yet, the suffering continued at another level. The problem—as I saw it—was that I was being sucked up by a personality greater than my own. In exchange for a totally compelling love affair, I as a distinctive individual was disappearing. I, who had taken my individuality for granted, who took a measure of pride in my competence, intelligence, independence, and good judgment, began to feel inferior and helpless. For example, sometimes in the evenings we did complicated art puzzles together. I began to notice that he could assemble the pieces faster than I could; he just seemed to know intuitively where they all went. I began to be nervous, and the more I thought about it, the less able I was to find any pieces. One morning I awoke early and tiptoed into the study where our puzzle lay, and sat for an hour working calmly and effectively. I was up to speed. At the same time, Ken didn't seem to notice or be concerned with this deficit on my part. In fact, he was never critical of me in any way; nor did he ever seem to try to give me an impression of superiority. (It was just another superior trait he had. I was the one to complain, be irritated, angry, afraid, jealous—emotionally inferior. Fortunately, my usual nature is upbeat, and so it was I who also saw the lighter side—laughed, teased, made jokes, seduced, and caught him off-guard with the obscure.)

In January 1969 we gave our relationship a bit of an extra test by taking a month long research expedition around the Mediterranean. We circled the sea from Rome via Palermo on a ferry boat to Tunis, and then in our Fiat 124 through Tunisia, Algeria (where the United States had no diplomatic relations at the time) and Morocco, then by ferry to Spain, through France, and back home to Rome. Ken had a grant to do foreign aid research and to pay me as his research assistant. During the year, we interviewed some 40 foreign aid officials. On this trip, I began to stretch my wings again in the outside world and to feel more active and contributing to a partnership with

Ken. Finding one's way through a medina to an appointment with a public official, without benefit of street signs, language, or maps daunted even Ken, and his dependence on me increased significantly.

And the playing field was becoming more level. On the trip a late night game of cards became our ritual. We had learned Scopa, a medieval game, in Rome from our language teacher and friend Franca Severati. The first night we played in the lobby of the St. George Hotel in Tunis. I recall the setting was worthy of a Humphrey Bogart movie, where spies lurk in every dark and mysterious corner. At first I lost the game each night. Now and again I was lucky, but Ken was the shrewder player. It was amusing, however, and kept us engaged after long and arduous days. However, as Ken became increasingly bored I was improving. By Monaco, after a short night at the casino, during which "lucky" Mary lost our limit of $35 in half an hour, we returned to our dingy hotel. We were exhausted, tired of the hot drive, and eager to get back to Italy. As usual, we finished the day with Scopa, but I was simultaneously watching *Gone with the Wind* on the lounge television. Ken was aware of my mixed concentration, and irritated that I wasn't paying attention to the game. Worse still, I seemed to be effortlessly winning every hand. Ken finally terminated the game in disgust. That was our last game of Scopa.

Again in Rome, our lives settled into a joyous routine. The trip seemed to have lingering effects on our lives—drawing us closer than ever. I no longer feared that I was disappearing; I could sense that I made an important difference to Ken. Somehow through me, he gained in himself, and I, through him, was growing as well. The partnership was establishing roots.

ANOTHER RO(A)MING

A moment of epiphany—early afternoon in an olive grove, flat on my back, arms akimbo, regaled with fresh bread, cheeses, and grapes, sated with Frascati white wine and a tumble in the grass, with the spirits now drawn to the heavens by the towering pines of Hadrian's Villa. The previous months at Swarthmore—where I had taken the position as chair—were agonizing . . . for me, my family, and friends. The grief of separation had at last given way to a glimpse of heaven. But what was this "run to Rome" with Mary—cinematic fantasy, a leap into the absurd, the firm footing of a new beginning? I hadn't a clue, but was hell-bent on the exploration. It was all so clear that I had a *mate* in that Australian sense—happy to hang with me atop a flea bag hotel in Athens (where one could also behold the Acropolis in the moonlight); bear up under the thunderous tone of a Tunisian cabinet minister as he lambasted American foreign policy (and us as its carriers); sleep in the crack between the only two single beds the four of us could find on the edge of the Sahara; stay cool as the hostile border guards at a renegade outpost in Algeria questioned our legitimacy; toughed it out as our Fiat, in a small collision, was settled out by a yelling Arab crowd in Marrakesh; and swear in Italian at the landlords who cheated us out of our deposit.

So what if she didn't like to read to me from the guide books as I planned my snaps, stood solid against the most astute of reasoning, preferred that we take siestas instead of using those precious hours for work? As I was slowly learning, there were severe limitations to the responsible, goal-directed, rationally well-defended manner to which growing up in an Anglo-Germanic home had so well prepared me, and for which Yale had been the finishing school. Here was a creature of different stripe, dedicated to my well-being, who continuously suggested deviations from the direct, who chided and tempted and tugged so that I might cease to be a tin man. I often balked—even with scorn. But this moment in the olive grove was not one of those. I wrote a small book that year, *The Concept of Self* (New York: Holt, Rinehart, & Winston, 1971), and dedicated it to "Maria at Hadriana."

One of the most compelling features of this relationship was its potential for collective insanity. Either of us could place an absurd idea, image, or fantasy in motion. And, rather than examining its impracticality, its costs, or its nonsensical nature, the other would actually treat it seriously—as an entry into a possibly reasonable universe. The whimsy might be embellished, embroidered, or extended in myriad directions. These reactions, in turn, were often treated as reasonable and virtuous and precipitated still further twists and turns. Neither of us seemed willing to play the voice of the parent, the teacher, the authority. And thus, new realities were minted, and because of their palpability, we would often press them into action—sometimes scary, sometimes disastrously, but always with rapped vitality. And so we found ourselves taking nude photos on the Bernini bridge in front of the Castello St. Angelo, squirting water from our second story apartment to wash our grimy Fiat on the street below, climbing the barricades of an occupied university building to search for our mail, or visiting Venice only to fall in love with a Hundertwasser print for which we sacrificed the remainder of our vacation.

But there was common reality aplenty. Oppression, suffering, and revolutionary impulses were everywhere apparent—and absorbing. Somehow the laboratory exploration of abstract theoretical issues no longer seemed so relevant—academic exercises for an ideologically insensitive elite. It was thus that research interests were cast outward. Drawing from earlier interests in exchange theory, and a professional literature that treated altruism as an unquestioned good, the hope was explore the effects—both good and ill—of foreign assistance. Too often, it seemed, such assistance led not to the forming of positive bonds, but to resentment and resistance. Interviews with aid officials—from the United States and a dozen another nations—along with visits to sites where food was dispensed, orphans protected, and mountains reforested, were to furnish insights. Fortunately the project had appealed to the Guggenheim Foundation. However, the silence was deafening when the results were later presented at the State Department.

And in the background there was the constant sense of sadness and self-censure. My children . . . their laughter and tears haunted me. We were torn from each other, and was I not responsible? The dozens of letters and carefully wrapped gifts could not assuage the despair.

> Over twenty-five nations are now engaged in bilateral international assistance programs . . . .This aid is basically aimed at increasing the power or welfare of the donor State, and as such, the donor's motives are always suspect. . . . The bilateral aid relationship also poses the greatest potential threat to the self-esteem of the recipient. The very act of giving in this way implies the inferiority of the recipient. . . . In effect, bilateral aid may never be a fully effective mode of transferring resources or knowledge from the 'haves' to the "have nots." KJG & MMG, "International assistance from a psychological perspective," *Yearbook of World Affairs*, Vol. 25.

> . . . "Mankind Makes Its Greatest Leap: To the Moon" . . . "Thousands Overwhelm Woodstock Festival" . . . "250,000 War Protesters March in Capital" . . . "567 Massacred at My Lai" . . . *Hair* . . . *Easy Rider* . . . *Midnight Cowboy* . . . *Zen and the Art of Motorcycle Maintenance* . . . "Steinem, Millett, Friedan, & Abzug Speak at Women's Movement Conference in New York City" . . . "Millions March at First Earth Day" . . . "Kent State Shootings Shock Nation" . . . "Jimi Hendrix & Janis Joplin—Drug Fatalities". . . .

HOMESTEADING IN HEAVEN, 1969

Coming home, to a place I'd never been. I recall the first moments of crossing the Walt Whitman bridge into Philadelphia. First the smell of the oil refinery, then the sight of rusted, damaged cars piled up in a gigantic nightmare of trash, then the flames of the gas tanks, the bleak dirty landscape of South Philadelphia, the constant aroma of filth. Then we passed the airport and the swamp (which today is a national treasure, one of the last remaining inland marshes) and then Chester—a town left behind by industrial sprawl. I secretly regretted every snide comment I had ever made about growing up on the Minnesota prairie. The bleak highway finally gave way to the oasis of Swarthmore "ville." The college, itself, was small, quaint, peaceful, and almost lonely with its sparse buildings settled along grassy meadows and walled in by forest land. Our destination was nearby in Rose Valley. We were too alimony-poor to rent a furnished house in Swarthmore, so our friends from the college, Molly and David Rosenhan, found us a steal: for $238 a month we could buy one-third of an eighteenth-century country inn, where a stone wall and picket fence separated us from Possum Hollow Road. It was a crumbling affair with a Byzantine interior, but we adored it from the first moment we saw it. We were married here on October 4, 1969, with our children and few friends, Greek music accompanied, and a sociology professor/Unitarian minister presided. It was a beautiful and joyous day, as we exchanged our golden rings we had designed in Rome. The night of our wedding, we slept in our two-person sleeping bag, which was to be our bed for the next three months. Our living room had no furniture for a year, but these were times when cushions on the floor were frequently preferred to chairs and couches. We had already had our honeymoon.

Outside our house, the world was in turmoil. It had a monstrous impact on the college: Faculty and students were torn in many parts. (The president who hired Ken, Courtney Smith, died of a heart attack during a sit-in in his office.) A Quaker school in origin, the campus was at the forefront of war resistance. Yet, many faculty believed that civil disobedience and suspended classes were not the proper response to the crisis. Meetings, strikes, antiwar demonstrations and protests combined with a feeling of revolutionary high that had strong sensual overtones. Our major involvement was to develop a nationwide network of students and faculty to carry out a survey of college students, 10,000 strong, attempting to document the negative impact of the war on American university life. We tried to show that the protest movement was spurred on by the best and brightest of the generation, not by marginal, fringe, "hippy" types who were trying to evade their civic responsibilities. I worked in the trenches on this one, and together with Ken, the findings were taken to the public. We went to Washington to see the special advisor to the colleges, issued a press release that was picked up by *Time*, and in the summer of 1970, while living in Minneapolis (where I had taken my new husband home to meet my folks), we tried to write a book about it. In the end, we abandoned the project. Time was rapidly passing, and world concerns moving on.

> Thus the war gives rise to a tragic crossfire. On one side the students see the university as a tool of the immoral and militant Establishment. On the other, the Establishment punishes the university for acting as an incubator for anarchists. Meanwhile the faculty is losing its capacity to educate its students and to extend the bound of knowledge through research. University administrators are becoming powerless, and many are fleeing a sinking ship. (MMG & KJG, "How the War Affects the Campuses," *Change Magazine*, 1971)

BEGINNING AGAIN

The challenges were enormous—a new marriage, a "new" but empty house, the challenge of chairing a department in transition, new classes to organize, and a politically explosive ambience. But perhaps the most difficult challenge of all was attempting to blend children from the two families. Laura and Stan lived close by with their mother, and many hours were set aside each week for "family time." But in spite of our attempts to organize games, sports, museum trips, ice cream breaks, field trips, movies, and art projects, often we dealt with situations in which rivalries surfaced, tears flowed, or sullen silences crept in. Who loved whom, how much, for how long, how was this possible, why did it seem otherwise—the relational dynamics were so intense that "quality time" left me utterly exhausted.

Campus life had taken on a surreal dimension. The student-faculty distinction was giving way—all were politically engaged, wore denim and love beads, used phrases from black culture, from Marx, and the psychedelic movement. Marijuana was as common as cigarettes; a faculty-student party welcoming a philosopher featured a rock and roll band. (Campus police who were being co-opted by the FBI came by to check us out.) I developed a course in group dynamics—a free-wheeling, experiential, self-reflective potboiler rendition of a course I had taught with Freid Bales at Harvard; it became so popular that Mary was hired to teach an additional section. A national guide to campuses described the course as one of the major educational events at Swarthmore. Now as I think back on some of the exercises we engaged in I shiver with amazement and some trepidation. On one moonlight evening I recall, the class met in the arms of the blooming apple tree outside the psychology building, with each of us, shrouded in pink blossoms, occupying separate limbs. Psychology became one of the most popular majors at the school.

Our work in the field, and now on the antiwar movement, on drugs, and political activism also meant further changes in my views of psychological science. The field that had once excited me because of its promise of precise, empirically grounded principles of broad generality and enormous utility for society was becoming more suspect. Psychology's claims to political neutrality seemed dangerously naïve, experimental methods seemed increasingly manipulative and intrusive, laboratory findings seemed increasingly artificial and irrelevant to common life, and the theoretical claims increasingly limited to particular historical and cultural circumstances. I presented some of my views at the meetings of the Society for Experimental Social Psychology. John Lanzetta, the editor of the central periodical of the field, *The Journal of Personality and Social Psychology*, was worried about the creeping conventionality of the field and asked if he could publish the piece. Although he had difficulties locating anyone to review the manuscript, he reluctantly published "Social Psychology as History" as the last paper in a 1973 issue (Vol. 26, 309–320). I was totally unprepared for the shock waves that were to follow. Some were enthralled with the fresh air of reflective critique, but more were outraged—their professional lives now thrown into question. There were few who weren't moved to opine on the subject. Lanzetta was also having second thoughts on the monster he had helped to create and decided that the journal would not be a forum for any further debate—save for a single retaliation by Barry Schlenker in a lead article the following year. What came to be known as "the crisis in social psychology" was on!

Joint Actions: "Correlates of marijuana use among college students." *Journal of Applied Social Psychology*, 1972, 3, 1–16 (with S. J. Morse). "Individual orientations to pro-social behavior." *Journal of Social Issues*, 1972, 28, 105–130 (with K. Meter). "Deviance in the dark," *Psychology Today*, October 1973, 7, 129–130 (with W. Barton). Reprinted in *Psychologie Heute*, and in *Readings in social psychology: Contemporary perspectives* (D. Krebs, Ed.) New York: Harper & Row, 1976.

. . . "One-third of U.S. Students Tried Pot" . . . "5 Burglars Caught in Watergate Offices" . . . "Nixon Quits, First President To Do So" . . . "Carter Elected President" . . . *The Norman Conquests . . . Saturday Night Fever . . .* "Elvis Presley Is Dead" . . . *Last Tango in Paris . . . The Structure of Scientific Revolution.*
. . .

TALES OF GENJI

In 1972, we left for another sabbatical, this time to Japan. We chose Kyoto in order to be more attached to the indigenous culture, and Ken established a working relationship with Professor Takao Umemoto. Ken received an NSF award to do cross-cultural work on reactions to help, and I served as a part-time research assistant. En route, we stopped at the APA meetings in Hawaii—Ken's home while a naval officer. Because Ken was terrified of flying—a holdover from a navy experience in which his ship searched for the bodies of a downed plane on which he had been traveling weeks before— we waited in Hawaii for six weeks for a ship to take us to Japan. Lisa and Michael went to school each day, and during the afternoons, we often went down to the beach to learn surfboarding—a tranquil interlude before the more vigorous challenge of living in Japan. The entry to Japan was the most traumatic experience. Approaching Yokohama, we sailed through the eye of a typhoon, a hair-raising experience which also introduced us to cultural differences. The Japanese passengers headed for the first-class lounge where they huddled together on the expanse of beige carpet; after the bar closed (due to dangerous flying glass), Westerners sought solace in their private cabins.

Upon arriving in Yokohama, we made the wrong choice of trains, boarding a commuter sardine can with nine suitcases and two small children. The Japanese were very gracious and quiet as we shoved on. But the train was so crowded that our assemblage of bodies and objects was suspended in midair, with only Ken's feet actually touching the floor for the bulk of the trip. The people were very still, although the quiet was sometimes briefly suspended when a baby would see Ken's beard and burst into tears. Others marveled at Lisa's long blond hair. Throughout the year, the family stuck rather closely together; we engaged the culture as a co-operative team. With help from various people, including our maid, Hatanaka-san, who "came with" the apartment, and a former Swarthmore student, Jean Kristeller, who worked for Ken, we began cultural entry in earnest. We began to feel we had made it when we contracted for bit parts in a Japanese gangster film. By the time we left Japan in the summer of 1973, we felt an intense sense of separation from the joys of the culture we had only begun to perceive behind the rice paper walls. Later when we moved to a larger home, our first project was to construct a Japanese tea room, where we could "live" Japanese style from time to time, wearing Japanese robes, sleeping on tatami, drinking green tea, and even playing a koto we had brought back with us.

In the summer of 1974, Ken was invited to Ottawa for a meeting on the future of social psychology arranged by Lloyd Strickland. Faculty and graduate students from Canada, the United States and Europe were invited. Among the Europeans were Henri Tajfel, Hilda Himmelweit, Erika Apfelbaum, Jos Jaspers, and Ragnar Rommetveit. The meeting broke down rather quickly with Ken rapidly propelled into a position of leadership among the "radicals"—which also included most of the graduate students. I was somewhat embarrassed by the turn of events because it seemed to me that Ken was becoming aligned with the marginal people and in conflict with the others who were more senior. At the same time, he seemed very self-righteous about his deviance. I recall distancing myself from him in certain situations, trying to keep some sense of connection to everyone. I sensed the danger to Ken's reputation in the field and tried to prevent him from going over the edge. It has taken me years to become a relaxed deviant.

Over time, I also began to feel that I couldn't keep pace with the action in my role as "wife-research assistant." I had access to the top of the social psychology pyramid as Ken's wife, but I could feel the sense of being second class. The worst times were during psychological conventions, and once I went on a crying binge in the car somewhere in Canada before an APA because I didn't have a Ph.D., and I feared that no one would talk to me. Ken was very comforting, but it was also clear that there were increasing numbers of women with Ph.D.s, and a limited future for the old model of dedicated wife, who makes her husband's career success her only measure of achievement. I did fear by entering graduate school I would upset the delicate balance of intimacy that we had come to share. Perhaps if I were not available I would lose something more precious than a silly epigram behind my name. In August, on a beach in Sardinia, I decided the die must be cast. I sent letters to two doctoral programs in Philadelphia: Penn and Temple. As fate would have it, my letter to Temple arrived the day a new doctoral student withdrew from the program. As the faculty there knew me in my quasi-professional role at Swarthmore, they agreed to accept me provisionally. By the following year I began to teach courses as a part-time instructor. I had found a new niche.

As for the feared alienation, this was not the major outcome. I did grow more independent and less available, and we could not spend as much time together. At the same time, I began to be a "source" for our intellectual life. Instead of the perpetual "assistant," I became a walking compendium of the latest issues in the field. We spent dinners speaking of Pepper's metaphors, Nelson's models, and Wittgenstein's metamorphosis. Joseph Margolis's ideas on the philosophy of the behavioral sciences, and the growing impact of feminism on psychology also inspired my enthusiasms. A happy relationship developed between my graduate work and my home seminars with Ken and the many friends and colleagues who visited. At the same time, these clandestine discussions were at great variance with most of the mainstream positivism featured in my courses. Trouble loomed in contemplating a thesis. The topic of attributions was definitely mainstream in those days, but researchers (including, not irrelevantly, E. E. Jones, Ken's mentor) tended to treat attributions as true or false. We developed the idea that people's attributions were stock from the cultural trade and were neither true nor false. I worked out a means of applying this view to lifespan development and particularly to the aging population. It seemed to me that people got taken in by their attributional styles, and that their well-being (and perhaps their longevity) depended on the explanatory dispositions they adopted. With Ken's strong hand behind me, I pushed through a thesis that combined the theoretical position with some fancy statistical footwork that supported my case. In 1980, with the additional support of Ken's mother (who had sacrificed her career to the achievements of her husband and four sons), and a close friend (who rewarded me with his doctor's greens as a graduation gift), I received my Ph.D.

TALES OF GENGHIS

Swarthmore had a generous leave policy: three years teaching and the fourth free with half salary. These occasions were excitations to our collective madness. Where in the world would we wish to be; how are we to make a living there; how can this be integrated into the remainder of our lives? The first choice in this case was Kyoto, Japan—in a tiny apartment with a two-matted bedroom overlooking a rice field. Even if sometimes arduous, it was a superb choice in terms of growth—both personal and collective. We spent innumerable hours immersing ourselves in "otherness"—the dislocating patterns of eating, talking, working, and socializing, and an equal number in making it all intelligible. After all, how was it sensible that I was required to make an official apology—with appropriate bows—to the rector of the university for leaving a library book in a taxi-cab, that a sweet potato could cost $3.50, or that we would be swarmed by hundreds of Japanese autograph seekers as we made our way to a temple garden.

We learned to appreciate the glorious and often strange cultural treasures of Japan—the wild northland of Hokaido, sunny resorts of the inland sea, somber caste of Hiroshima, neighborhood temples, sushi bars, Kabuki, Sumo, Ikebana, the ceremonies of Nara and Isea, prints of the Ukeyoye, shrines and ryokan "inns," practices of Zen Buddhism, Shinto, the language, and the literature. Within this novel frame, we began to form a bonded unit. We were at once experiencing things alone as a couple, cut away from our friends, families, and supporting institutions. And the challenges were also generating an internal dialogue—an extension and elaboration of our "ontological space." As a result, we generated strategies that sometimes required the interdependence of trapeze performers. The singular unit of "us" was becoming effective in itself. This same sense of being parts of a single mechanism also carried over into Mary's later graduate school days. As we brought the fruits of differing associations into our common conversations, the resulting concoctions were mutually fortifying. A true catalytic motion was begun. And if the context failed to provide excuses for such mutuality, we would often seek out possibilities. For example, I had long been a tennis player and Mary had not. Over time, she acquired real strength as a player, and we now take our racquets with us on most of our travels. Similarly, I picked up cooking skills from Mary and began to enjoy preparing dishes for us and for company.

The major challenge to this interknitting was generated by our embeddedness in networks of other relationships. To create an autonomous unit of two is no more possible than the quest for truly individual autonomy. We exist in a sea of relationships—family, colleagues, friends—without which our existence as a couple would be impossible. But if one of us were to sign a book contract with a publisher, initiate a project with a colleague, spend special time with one of the children, or feel the energies of an outside attraction, there was a potential cost to the relationship. As we found, there are no overarching rules for dealing with such challenges; each day is a new day. However, we also learned ways of reducing jealousies and friction, and sometimes for turning tensions into treasures. Occasionally, we could turn the outside relationship into a joint venture—for example, writing a text jointly instead of privately, finding a way of expanding the project to include the other, or bringing a special friend into our relationship. We developed ways of sharing an experience by taking an empathic perspective—the other is oneself—that is, feels the drama, sees the significance, hopes for a good outcome—in effect, creating the other as a joint party to the effort. At other times, the partner became an "object," and in a different sense, the outside connections might make a strong contribution to our well-being. For the other to make a sacrifice for a good cause, succeed at an important task, be sought after, or present an interesting line of thought, for example, could generate positive feelings—feelings of admiration, gratitude, or attraction.

These same issues haunted the work in which I was engaged. By training, I was an empiricist psychologist; I had developed a substantial reputation in this field, was committed to many friends, students, and colleagues in this domain; and could see how, for certain purposes, its assumptions were reasonable. However, as I had questioned the tradition; had been roundly scolded for my queries; and for purposes of defense had dug more deeply into emerging developments in philosophy, sociology, history, and anthropology, it became clear that my earlier misgivings were profoundly understated. How, then, were these various investments to be reconciled? Were joint ventures possible? On what grounds? Could there be some form of mutual enrichment? By what standards? And what if there were no rapprochement possible? What course would professional life then take on? And what would the future be for new Ph.D.s, like Mary, who were no longer willing to jump through the old positivist hoops? Intellectually, these were exciting times, but we moved toward an uncertain future.

Joint Actions: "The women's liberation movement: Attitudes and action." *Journal of Personality,* 1974, 42, 601–617 (with J. Goldschmidt and K. Quigley). "Perceiving others." In K. Gergen, D. Rosenhan, R. Nisbett, and G. Clapp (Eds.) *Social Psychology,* CRM Books, 1974 (with L. Bogyo). "What other nations hear when the eagle screams," *Psychology Today,* June 1974. "Attribution in Kontext socialer Erklarung." In D. Gorlitz, W. U. Meyer, and B. Weiner (Eds.) *Bielefelder Symposium uber Attribution,* Klett-Cotta, 1978.

> ... "Khomeini in Iran, Greeted by Millions" ... "3-Mile Island Atomic Leak" ... "1980: "Reagan Is 40th President" ... "John Lennon Shot by Fanatic" ... "Egyptian Soldiers Murder Sadat" ... *Mille Neuf Cent* ... *Philosophical Investigations* ... *Against Method.* ...

TALES OF TWO CITIES

Mary: Living in Paris in 1976–1977 was the realization of youthful dreams for us—dreams born, we feared, of too much Hollywood. We occupied a small apartment between the fashionable Place de Vosges and the rugged Bastille. With a sense of unfolding adventure, we adjusted to the noise, the cramped quarters and the difficulties of communicating with our local shopkeepers. We created little games out of life's privations, for example, trying to distract the other so that he or she would be the one to step into the liberal dollops of dog shit that lined our narrow sidewalk; lying that we had bought the day's meat in the horse market, not the beef market; pretending to understand more French at the Alliance Française than the other. Ken had won a Fulbright research fellowship and spent his days shuffling between the *Laboratoire de Psychologie Sociale* at the Sorbonne and our apartment. The "shuffles" were as much fun as the intellectual exploration—long walks through historic quarters with interludes at well-situated cafes. Because the Fulbright is more generous in honor than money, we also found ourselves woefully short of funds. I thus arranged to teach English four days a week to foreign students, many who had come that year from war-torn Lebanon, in exchange for Lisa's tuition at the American School. Our apartment was above a bakery, and Michael—now struggling through a French bilingual school in Sevres, an hour's metro ride away—became an expert at sniffing the moment the fresh baguettes and pain chocolat were placed in the bakery case.

Ken: Yes, these were very special times, and we could go on musing for pages about moments both glorious (at concerts, gardens, galleries, and restaurants) and inglorious (such as trying to turn the Isle St. Louis into an outdoor track, late night trash picking, and Lisa's shadowy attacker). But I think we should say something about the central place that the process of dialogue came to occupy that year. So much of our life in Paris seemed to revolve around verbal interchange—animated conversation with colleagues and friends—in cafes, restaurants, on long walks. We were especially struck with the discussions of conceptual substance—not simply professional politics, methods, or polite exchanges of information that seemed so common in American professional life. Nor was so much emphasis placed on "being published," again a seemingly American fetish that placed a premium on social isolation. Most important here was *carrying the argument forward*— whatever the topic—passionately, vigorously, and with whatever rhetorical tools could be brought to bear. What we took away from this—in addition to the challenging ideas of Erika Apfelbaum, Ian Lubeck, Serge Moscovici, Vreni Aebischer, Peter Burch, Denise Jodolet, Robert Pages, and many others—was the significance of dialogic process. It was not in the individual, sequestered mind that creative conceptual work took place but within a relational form.

Mary: Yes, these discussions were supercharged. At the same time, I think they gave us a greater consciousness of ourselves as a couple—"the Americans"—which I should add, was not always a pleasant realization. The French view of Americans and of our political involvements in other countries, especially their accusations of the clandestine CIA activities in countries such as Chile, had a reverberating impact on our sensibilities. Erika's accusations and assaults against the United States in general, and me, in particular, often had to be smoothed out by Ian. These were painful moments, and I don't think either of us could ever experience our culture again as confidently as before. At the same time, they reinforced some of the ideas we were developing about our relationship, and within it, our relationship to others. For we could now see that on the intellectual level, our discussions with each other were interdependent with our conversations with others. It seemed all the more useful, then, to look at our relationship—in all its dimensions—as interdependent with our connections outside.

During the spring, Ken was invited by Wolfgang Stroebe to teach courses in Marburg, Germany—a blessing, not only financially, but in terms of Marburg's distinct beauty and the gracious charms of Maggie and Wolfgang. From the United States, Marburg had looked quite convenient to Paris, and only when Ken began the overnight nine-hour commute did its isolation become painfully apparent. In Marburg, our "European tutorial" on relational process was extended through our relations with Maggie and Wolfgang. During one of our weekend walks in the countryside together, we passed through an old graveyard. As we read from the stones, we began to locate a pattern in the death dates for husbands and wives: If one died, it seemed, the likelihood of the other's death was greatly enhanced. Over an evening dinner, we became increasingly excited by the implications of this pattern. The next morning, in a driving downpour, we examined and recorded dates from the stones. This work became the basis for establishing "the loss effect," and a collaboration continuing until the present.

Ken: It was also that semester that I gave a colloquium at Heidelberg. The house was packed, and I was all the more thrilled when two young assistants, Horst Gundlach and Alexandre Metraux, decided—as a result of the talk—to visit me in Marburg. We stayed up almost the entire night, wrapped in discussion over paradigm shifts in psychology. Two years later, when Mary was "on the road" consulting with AT&T, I went to Oxford to prepare an address on the state of social psychology to be delivered at the centennial meetings of the APA. After the address, Carl Graumann from Heidelberg invited us to spend a year in residence there. We were thrilled by the opportunity.

Mary: Our year in Heidelberg began in the fall of 1980, with Ken giving a seminar at the Alpach conference in Austria. It was there I began to appreciate the powerful implications of the constructionist ideas we had been working on, but simultaneously, the depth of the resistance that they evoked. In Heidelberg, we settled into the university guesthouse overlooking the Neckar and shared a spacious office at the history-rich *Institut* on the Hauptstrasse. We felt very much part of the department; we had daily coffee and kucken at the cafes near the institute, enjoyed intense discussions with colleagues, and helped entertain the enormous flux of colleagues and friends visiting the department—especially at the Wolfsbrunnen, a seventeenth-century inn tucked away in the Heidelberg hills. The attractions of intense and liberated life styles drew us into dangerous games of exploration. Yet, the risks seemed only to sharpen our appreciations for each other, and our awareness of what we shared.

Ken: It was there along the Neckar that two significant pieces of work were beginning to take shape. I was finally completing the project begun in Paris three years earlier, namely an attempt to specify more clearly the problems of an empiricist psychology and to struggle toward an alternative conceptualization—now emerging more clearly as social constructionism. The result was the volume *Toward Transformation in Social Knowledge*, published in 1982 by Springer-Verlag. The second was a joint project—to bring into focus the possibility of a specifically historical form of social psychology. As we later wrote in the preface of our volume *Historical Social Psychology* (Erlbaum, 1984),

> "Social psychology as history" provoked broad controversy in the field. . . . As this dialogue ensued, however, it also became apparent that there was developing in various research domains an increased sensitivity to cross-time transformations in social pattern. Theory and research were beginning to move beyond the static vision to explore new horizons of change. It was an awareness of this emerging pattern that struck the two of us during the winter of 1981 as we drove through a perilous route in the Austrian Alps. Issues of permanence and change were much on our minds. As we began to discuss various names and works that focused on the problem of change, it became apparent that there was indeed a corpus of significant work at hand.

This investment also sparked our interest in narrative theory, an intellectual investment that later carried Mary into her first tenure track position—at Penn State University's campus in Delaware County.

Joint Actions: "The psychological evaluation of international aid." In R. Eells (Ed.) *Perspectives on international aid*. Columbia University Press, 1979. "Behavior exchange in cross-cultural perspective. In H. Triandis and R. W. Brislin (Eds.) *Handbook of cross-cultural psychology*. Allyn Bacon, 1980 (with S. J. Morse). "Der Kummer Effect: Psychologische Aspekte der Sterblichkeit von Verwitwetlen," *Psychologische Beitrage*, 1980 (with W. Stroebe and M. Stroebe). "Causal attribution in the context of social explanation. In M. Baltes and D. Gorlitz (Eds.) *Perspectives on attribution research and theory*. Ballinger, 1980. *Social Psychology*, Harcourt, Brace, Jovanovich, 1981. Second edition, Springer-Verlag, 1986. Translated into Italian as *Psicologia Sociale*, and into French as *Psychologie Sociale* (Second edition, 1992, with S. Jutras). "The effects of bereavement on mortality: A social psychological analysis." In R. Eiser (Ed.) *Social psychology and behavioral medicine*. Wiley, 1982 (with W. Stroebe, and M. Stroebe). "Form and function in the explanation of human conduct." In P. Secord (Ed.) *Explaining social behavior*. Sage, 1982. "Narratives on the self." In K. Scheibe and T. Sarbin (Eds.) *Studies in social identity*. Praeger, 1983. "The social construction of helping relationships." In J. Fisher, A. Nadler, and B. DePaulo (Eds.) *New directions in helping*. V. 1, Academic Press, 1983. "Interpretive dimensions of international aid." In J. Fisher, A. Nadler, and B. DePaulo (Eds.) *Applied research in help-seeking and reactions to aid*. Academic Press, 1984.

. . . "Gorbachev Chosen to Lead" . . . "World Rock Festival Held for Famine Relief" . . . "Rock Hudson Dies of AIDS" . . . "Challenger Explodes as Horrified Nation Watches"... "Chernobyl Accident Releases Deadly Atom Radiation"... *The Unbearable Lightness of Being... After Virtue... Philosophy and the Mirror of Nature....*

DOG DAYS

We had moved to a new house, a sprawling, three-story stone structure nestled in the woods near the campus. While it had "wonderful potential," it exacted an enormous price in time and resources to peel back the layers of decrepitude and to locate the once elegant landscaping under choking vines. Soon after acquiring the house, we also acquired a foster daughter, Erika, whose parents had been tragically taken from her. We now had from zero to five children between us—depending on the vantage point.

As the house was finished, and the children began to leave home, we seemed to be gaining on our challenges. In 1984, Mary began her tenure track job at a local campus of Penn State, an ideal job for combining her various interests. Difficulties began, however, when after a wonderful ski holiday in Wengen, Switzerland, Ken remained to give lectures at the Graduate School of Business in St. Gallen. Perhaps we should have seen the handwriting on the wall. It was the coldest winter in both Switzerland and Philadelphia in 100 years. Life was miserable apart. Ken was put up with an 85-year-old landlady, Frau Fherlien, who proved to be the single oasis of warmth and comfort. In April 1986, Mary, who had taken on the challenge of developing funds and speakers for a large conference at Penn State, produced the faculty colloquium on feminist thought and the structure of knowledge. It was a gratifying event, gathering together a wide variety of speakers, who led off the conference with personal expressions of their development as feminists. At the conclusion of the conference, however, she felt drained, empty, and depressed, and she cried over nothing but the relief of nine months of stress. At home, Ken and John Shotter lifted her spirits with champagne.

Three months later, the shattering news is made known: Mary is suffering from cancer and requires immediate surgery. Moments from the "cancer ward": The terror is shared. It is happening to us. Who is suffering more? It is not clear. Do we have a chance; do we have a future? Again the grim ambiguity. We are together in hospital rooms; we join in a fog of anesthetic; we sit together watching Wimbledon on the hospital bed; we eat wonderful patés and white wine smuggled in to celebrate a completed operation. Our friends, especially Bobbie and Gudmund Iversen, Maggie Skitarelic, and the Stroebes are enormously supportive; many others join in to prevent the bastard from grinding us down. The operations are effective, and six weeks later, Ken arranges for us a week's holiday in London. But the possibility of microscopic cells lingering is present, and she cannot evade chemotherapy. On the Wednesdays of her sessions, he arrives at the door of the purgatory room with a rose. On each session a new rose, and counting. Her hairless, scar torn body is now battered with the curing poisons. It tears at his insides to hear the wretching. At midnight, it ends, and she curls around him, making a connection so that her head and arm enclose him, and her leg touches his, making a circuit of healing energy that floods her body. On Fridays she returns to a day of teaching. The following summer—with a clean bill of health—we celebrate with a summer of revenge in Europe.

Professional life also continued, but the terrain became ever more treacherous. Intellectual adventures were easier in the smaller enclaves of discontent; here one experienced keen appreciation for the various lurchings toward social constructionism, feminist standpoints, historical understanding, and reflexive critique. However, as this work began to surface—as its implications drew notice in the more established wings of the professions— the savagery began. Especially Ken was pilloried. In the *Handbook of Social Psychology* (Random House, 1985) his mentor, E. E. Jones, likened him to a dog barking in the night; as Ken addressed an Oxford conference, his undergraduate professor at Yale, Bob Abelson, took out his newspaper and began spitefully to read; at an Alpach seminar, Karl Popper publicly addressed him as "the enemy"; and at a conference in Gerona, Spain, John Searle spontaneously leaped to the stage after Ken's address and loudly lashed out for a quarter of an hour. But then again, perhaps the donkey kicks hardest when the thorns are most piercing. Fortunately, we were also blessed by the close and supportive friendship of colleagues: John Shotter, Jill Morawski, Anne Marie and John Rijsman, and many others.

> In the case of the romantic saga, the participants are created as by-products of an extended context of events. They are creating memorable high-points, troughs, and dramas of change. As a result they are positioned to establish a new and more palpable definition of relatedness. This definition, which can be termed *deep communion*, will be of a specific kind: At its core it will define relatedness as a movement through highs and lows. . . . It will be the result of goods and bads, thicks and thins, sickness and health, wins and losses. However, this emerging definition of deep communion should engender a greater sense of reality than that resulting from the initial unification myth (pp. 284, 285). KJG and MKG, "Narratives of relationship." In R. Burnett, P. McGhee, and D. Clarke (Eds.) *Accounting for relationships.*

Joint Actions: "The discourse of control and the maintenance of well-being." In M. Baltes and P. Baltes (Eds.) *Aging and control.* Erlbaum, 1986. "Narrative form and the construction of psychological science." In T. R. Sarbin (Ed.) *Narrative psychology: The Storied nature of human conduct.* Praeger, 1986. "The self in temporal perspective." In R. Abeles (Ed.) *Life-span perspectives and social psychology.* Erlbaum, 1987.

RECENTLY FOUND OBJECTS

- Mary's edited volume: *Feminist Thought and the Structure of Knowledge* (New York University Press, 1988). From the preface: "I have imagined the impact on various institutions, especially academic ones, if the voices of feminism might be raised in unison. . . . The chapters seem effervescent with enthusiasm for new ways of doing scholarly work, ways that rely less on power, domination, and right, and more on open dialogue, imbued with expressions of values and feelings, and with self-reflexivity. . . . I wish to thank Kenneth Gergen for his involvement and support. His intellectual perspective has been a vital force in the development of our feminist views."
- An honorary degree from the University of Tilburg, The Netherlands, is awarded to Ken. The laudatio praises Mary's contribution to his efforts.
- Erika's wedding in Santa Barbara to Joe Littera, a joyous step for our Antioch graduate.
- Air tickets for a round-the-world trip to press postmodernism and feminist theory at the International Congress in Australia and then to work and play for a year at the Netherlands Institute for Advanced Study. This year is very important to Mary's sense of professional identity. She enters the institute full of trepidation over her ability to fit in and leaves with confidence in her capacities and potentials. Ken is spending much time in Heidelberg, as he was awarded the prestigious Humboldt award. Although the only social scientist among 49 natural scientists, he is asked to give one of the plenary lectures at the ceremonial gathering of the prize-winners. We each drink deeply to the development of the other.
- A fiftieth birthday celebration for Mary at the Wolfsbrunnen in Heidelberg. Thirty guests from Europe attend. Ken reads a lengthy poem that brings tears to Mary's eyes. We dance until we are asked to leave at 3 A.M.
- A postmodern feminist performance at the Aarhus conference is presented by Mary in boa and beads. From "Mod Mascul-linity to Post-mod Macho: A Feminist Re-play": "My text is thus a lament couched in ironic teasing and an angry chastisement . . . against all those who assume ontological freedom, transitivity, solipsistic solitude; who proclaim the immediacy and oneselfness to separation and dissolution, and who revel in the phallic superfluidity that denies connection, relationships, and the possibility of love."
- A marriage—Stan Gergen to Stephanie Goddard—and our twentieth wedding anniversary.
- A $10,000 plumbing bill for a new system of water pipes in our old house.
- A positive tenure decision for Mary, in spite of her free-wheeling record of "weird" publications and a scarcity of empirical research. She is then elected to the University Senate and forms a women's caucus. One of her favorite publications: "Life Stories: Pieces of a Dream." In G. Rosenwald

and R. Ochberg (Eds.), *Telling Lives*, New Haven, Conn.: Yale University Press, 1992.

• *The Saturated Self*, Ken's first attempt to write for a general audience, is published by Basic Books (1991). A front-page glowing review in *The Washington Post* but condemned in *The New York Times*. The book sells out in six months and goes into paperback.

• A wanna-be Black Lab named Jacques, a new entry in our relationship network—helping to anchor us in a rising storm of technology.

• A room with a view at the Rockefeller Study Center in Bellagio, Italy, for a month's repose in splendor and tranquility—highlights include an evening dialogue with Sissela Bok, Don McClosky, and John Searle for the assembled crew.

• A joint colloquium at Rutgers University—on the topic of psychological discourse—complete with interactive vignettes and audience participation. We are engaged in creating a new relational form of presentation.

• And other handful of collaborations: "Narrative and the self as relationship." In L. Berkowitz (Ed.) *Advances in experimental social psychology Vol. 21*. Academic Press, 1988. "Toward reflexive methodologies." In F. Steier (Ed.) *Method and reflexivity: Knowing as systemic social construction*. Sage, 1991. "Broken hearts or broken bonds: Love and death in historical perspective." *American Psychologist*, 47(10), 1205–1212 (with M. Stroebe and W. Stroebe). "The word: Revenge and revitalization" (in press). *Proceedings of the Oldenberg Lecture Series*. Tilburg University Press. In press, 1992. "Narratives of the gendered body in the popular autobiography." *The Narrative study of lives* (1993). "Autobiography and the shaping of gendered lives" (in press). In J. Coupland and E. Nussbaum (Eds.) *Discourse and development across the lifespan*. Sage, in press, 1992. "Attributions, accounts, and close relationships." In J. Harvey, T. Orbuch, and A. Weber (Eds.) *Interpersonal accounts*. Blackwell, 1990:

> The constructionist investigator faces the challenge of envisioning and making intelligible new forms of accounting, alternative means of relating. . . . The investigator takes an active part in the construction of cultural life.

An almost perfect day: September 20, 1991, diary entry written at
its close

The weather is "San Francisco"—sunny, cool, and promising optimistic events. It is a godsend Saturday—no compelling deadlines, guests, appointments, dire needs or evening plans. We are at leisure. But this does not mean sleeping in. Ken never learned the pleasures. He is thus up at a reasonable 8:15 and makes his way with our companion, Jacques, to the kitchen. Later, they return to the bed to rouse Mary with tray and newspapers. Because of Ken's Friday trip to the farmer's market, we are treated to fresh orange juice, green zucchini bread, and a rosy pear. Ken adjourns to his study after breakfast to work on a book manuscript due in several weeks. After a more thorough look at the papers, Mary clears the dishes and makes a soup. As she finally reaches her study, she is distracted by the sounds of Nana Mouskouri—romantic, Greek/French music coming from Ken's study. The music is turned up for his morning shave. Mary can't resist the scene and joins him for a hug and a snoutful of morning air flowing through his open window.

Dressing, we prepare to go out to buy pine trees at Frank's Nursery's half-price sale. At the corner, we spot some antiques sitting on a lawn and, after looking them over, negotiate for an 80-year-old rocking chair—just the right addition for our late night drink in Ken's study. Onward through the countryside to Frank's. The evergreens are to cover the area returned to us from the state, as the mudfields outside our grounds slowly take shape as an interstate highway. We brace against the new rape by technology.

It's growing late, and we return home for a quickly made picnic. We locate a spot in the dappled shade, orienting ourselves toward the outlandish marigolds and impatients, which never learned about fall's arrival. We joke about our menu of memories: an Appenzeller cheese—recalling Ken's stay in St. Gallen—a Cheddar-Stilton mix—introduced to us by Maggie Stroebe—and some Black Forest ham, which Ken "smuggles" in on every trip home from Germany. Suddenly lawn mowers in the distance break our tranquility. But there is joy in our hearts to know that we are relieved of that unceasing burden. We joke that we may be cut to bits in minutes, as the outrageous lad with earphones whirls through our turf at 20 miles per hour.

After lunch, we make a date for later afternoon and return to the Macintoshes and the Metropolitan Opera—a dynamic duo. Two hours pass and we slip away from our cerebral companions for an assignation. Jacques waits patiently, then he leaps onto the bed to share whatever tenderness he can. He can spot an orgasm at ten feet.

But the day still retains its beauty, so we locate another excuse to be outdoors—this time it's tennis. At the high school courts we drill, play tricks on each other, and indulge in point-free games—enjoying the movement without stress. (A totally different tennis from our miserable mixed doubles on Sundays.) Then Mary goes to purchase groceries for the family dinner of the next day, and Ken takes Jacques for a bike ride. We have decided to go to the college for a concert, and we are running late. Quickly we shower, cook, dress, and feed Jacques and Lynx, our old tomcat. Finding ourselves left with only eight minutes to eat, we tell ourselves, "Calm down, for eight minutes we can be completely relaxed." The bean soup is tasty with weisswursts and a half bottle of left-over red wine. But Ken complains that his stomach has been rebelling at the eating practices of the past three nights: We must stop this rushing at meals.

With the complaint duly acknowledged, we race out the door to the Swarthmore campus five minutes away. Our destination is the Lang Performance Hall where excerpts from a new opera about the life of Malcolm X are being presented—a contribution to the multicultural emphasis that Al Bloom has brought with him to the college presidency. Embarrassingly informal in our dress, we exchange greetings with Al and Peggi and others collected there in their formal dress. The performance is very special—a postmodern pastiche of themes and rhythms from myriad cultural climes. Afterwards, we return to our studies for a short time while the jacuzzi heats up. The night air is crisply cool and adorned by a full moon. We cannot be indifferent—either to this or the fortunes of the day we have experienced. We remain with the sadness of the January death of Mary's sister, the last remaining member of her nuclear family to succumb to cancer. At least one important legacy is a vastly enriched appreciation of our remaining moments in nature.

It is time for bed, but like the irresponsible children we have always been, we dawdle. Let's stop in to graze late Saturday night television. Some of it is disappointing—teaming commercials, grade C movies, Saturday Night Live with Eddie Murphy standing around in an open black leather jacket, trading tired jokes with a hapless foil. But we are rescued by a wonderful Swedish company performing a barefoot modern dance; women in nightshirts react to the lovers who invade their dreams . . . mostly by ignoring them despite their romantic and sexual charms. After this, we are content to wrap ourselves up in our little French bed with purple flowered sheets, with Jacques lying on his blanket—pretending to guard the house as we drift into slumber.

Me: It's really difficult to imagine who would appreciate reading all this stuff, especially this last bit. That is surely the most superficial account in the whole chapter—a description of no substance at all.

You: But when you raise this question you seem to presume a stern and critical reader (perhaps a father?). Why do you think your reader isn't interested in who we are—in those trivial details that make us persons instead of personae. And what is this about superficiality? Doesn't this presume that something profound lies behind, inside, somewhere out of sight and that properly formed words will reveal what is truly there? What kind of presumption is that for a constructionist?

Me: Now you are forcing me into a binary; if I use the word *superficial*, you want to charge me with the presumption that I am committed to some form of oppositional term like *depth*. As a feminist, I can scarcely accept this move. Let's look at it in a poststructural way. I figure many of the readers will be viewing these texts will their scholarly hats on. This being so, they will only find the piece filling if it puts challenging concepts or arguments on the plate. Mere chit-chat about life's ups and downs will just be a crashing bore.

You: I can appreciate what you are saying in a relational sense. There isn't just one story, a fundamental reality that we could capture with a careful account. We could tell a lot of different stories, true enough, and in the present telling, it would be collectively solipsistic to disregard the dispositions of those to whom we are relating, namely the reader (or is it our fantasy of a reader, or a fantasy of ourselves reading our own lives?). In any case, we don't want to put people to sleep, or God forbid, cause them to dislike us. But don't you think there is intellectual content in all this, not so fully in the content as in the form?

Me: Well, you know I have to agree. We had already talked about this privately. So I guess this question is a hortatory maneuver to get me to talk publicly about the significance of the form. So, stand by for my little lecture on the four underlying principles of form. . . .

You: That little sarcasm isn't like you, it's more like me. So who are you trying to be in that display? You or me, or someone else? But I agree, some of it is pretty obvious, like moving from strong "I" positions at the beginning to a blending of identities as the tales unfold. And there is a slightly subtler narrative embedded here on the undoing of the empiricist commitment, the slow replacement with constructionism, and the place of a dramaturgic constructionism in the very formation of our relationship—a kind of "living constructionism" that proceeded the professional articulation some 20 years later. But I don't think everyone would be so alert to see the themes that were worked out in the KJG extravaganza, *The Saturated Self*, for example.

Me: I guess you are right here. That book tried to show how concepts of the person have changed from the romantic to the modernist era, and how they are now being eclipsed by the shift to postmodernism. Our treatment here reflects a similar shift—from a romantic conception of our relationship (two souls discovering each other), to a modernist view (the well-formed machine), to a postmodernist view in which we both disappear into an ever shifting relational matrix, where the difference between the actual and the virtual is erased, and the very idea of a narrative trajectory—a life story— is subverted.

You: Whoa . . . hold on there. I'm still very much here.

Me: But then again, just who are you?

You: You nut, I'm just *me*.

Me: But wait, that's who *I* am . . . I think we've got a problem. Maybe we should go somewhere to talk this over in private. But then again, if all we can do in our tête à tête is exchange language from the public coffers, how could we ever be "private"?

EXEUNT

With an Additional Cast of Supportive Characters

Raymond Bauer . . . Judy and Larry Anastasi . . . Kurt Back . . . Claus Bahnson . . . Ted Baker . . . Ellen Barry and Mike Florio . . . Michael Basseches . . . Uschi and Peter Becker . . . Didi Beebe . . . Jeffrey Bell . . . Ellen Berscheid . . . Jerry Bruner . . . Kate and Tom Cottle . . . Pru Churchill and Larry Plummer . . . Win Churchill . . . Tom Cottle . . . Esther and Robert Cohen . . . Deborah Curtiss . . . John Darley . . . Jane and David Denman . . . Patty and Bob Dreher . . . Helen Drutt . . . Lothar Duda . . . Shel and Eve Feldman . . . Anne and David Gergen . . . John and Jackie Gergen . . . Steve and Lorraine Gergen . . . Carol and Jim Gilligan . . . Gabi and Rudi Gloger-Tippelt . . . Jeffrey Goldstein . . . Harry Goolishian . . . Chad Gordon . . . Don and Donna Gorton . . . Ginnie Greer . . . Judy Greisman . . . Janie and Al Grove . . . Justine Gudenas . . . Linda Harris . . . T. George Harris . . . Elmer Johnson . . . Sara Kiesler . . . Gunter Kroger . . . Hannah and Arie Kruglanski . . . Lenelis Kruse . . . Lance Liebman . . . Cindy Lisle . . . Sally and Steve Lisle . . . Sam and Lilian Maitin . . . David Marlowe . . . Gunter and Brigitta Mayer . . . "Riki" Mayer . . . Sheila McNamee and Jack Lannamann . . . Harvey S. Shipley Miller . . . Jill Morawski . . . Stan Morse . . . Nancy Nichols . . . Wojciech Sadurski . . . Gigi Santow and Michael Bracher . . .

Walter Paynter . . . Jamie Pennebaker . . . Jerry Platt . . . Adele Saul . . . Arthur and Mary Schneider . . . Anne Shephardson . . . Paul Stanley . . . Sally and Norman Smith . . . Sandy Strine . . . Sybe Terwee and Joan Meyer . . . Judith Tipton . . . Robert Vartdal . . . Regine and Emile Walter-Busch . . . Dagmar Westrick . . . Ladd Wheeler . . . Diana Whitney . . . Rhoda and Peter Woytuk . . . Katherine Young . . . Bob Z . . . Jan and Meilan Zielonka.

And Assorted Producers

The National Science Foundation, The Fulbright-Hayes Foundation, The Guggenheim Foundation, The Alexander von Humboldt Foundation, The Barra Foundation, The Deutsche Forchungsgemeinschaft, The Netherlands Institute for Advanced Study, the Lang Faculty Fellowship, our parents, . . . and Cream of Wheat.

4

Playing in the Rough

Leon Rappoport

I have come to love the dog days of August in Kansas—the hot winds, white light sun-glare, and all-pervading dryness. If you don't fight it, life slows to a near inorganic level, and awareness of one's unity with nature is inescapable.

When I came to Kansas State University as a 32-year-old assistant professor in August 1964, the weather seemed awful, a perfect match with the inert countryside. We had driven through from New York, my wife and two-year-old son, in a Rambler station wagon with no air conditioner, and had not the slightest clue we would remain here for the next 27 years or that she would earn a Ph.D. and both our sons would graduate from the University of Kansas in Lawrence, or that I would find at Kansas State everything I needed for a satisfying career, or, least of all, that I would learn to love it here in August. But, of course, that's life.

Mine began in New York City, in 1932, with immigrant Jewish parents from *Fiddler on the Roof* country. They ran a Mom and Pop grocery-delicatessen on the upper West Side. The family atmosphere was generally warm and secure, but not without conflict. There was my sister, five years older and, therefore, in command of everything, including me. We shared some good moments, like regular Saturday afternoons at the local movie theater and sodas afterwards. But for the most part, until I got big enough by age 12 to forcefully assert independence, we ranged from uneasy coexistence to open warfare, with the little guy usually the loser.

Also, and far more formidable when aroused, there was my mother, an archetype for almost every Jewish mother story in existence. My father, who spent nearly 14 hours a day, six days a week in his store, was a more remote

figure, vaguely benign, whose standard response to any matter of consequence raised by us children was "ask your mother."

Several years ago I wrote the following short essay on some aspects of my
childhood in order to dramatize the concept of reification.

Reification: The Word Made Flesh

New York City, the 1940s; lower-middle and working-class Jews of the first generation: in this life space of my childhood, no one, not the parents, not the teachers,
and certainly not the kids, ever questioned the use of IQ scores, achievement tests,
or grades, as measures of personal worth. These were the currencies by which
children were valued, just as then the almighty dollar was the value criterion for
adults.

Not only did kids and their parents both blindly accept the indices of worth applied
to children by the school system, they tended to believe that the measures were
equivalent to the substance measured. Thus, holistically speaking, and regardless of
all their other personal qualities, kids were seen essentially as the embodiment of
their scores and grades. In this context, words were made flesh to such an extent
that for all practical purposes signs became their significates.

A child might get in trouble with the police, for example, for stealing milk bottles,
or pennies off a newsstand, but if he had good grades he was given latitude. "A little
spanking and he'll outgrow it." "What do the dumb Irisher cops know anyway about
such a smart boytchik!"

Yet if *he* (the sexist "he," of course, because in that time and place it was only the
boys who had to be smart; the girls just had to know enough to get a good husband
when they grew up)—if he had been tested and measured—God forbid—as a dummy,
then no amount of decency, warmth, or sensitivity could forestall or ameliorate the
inevitable stigmas: *Dummkopt, goyeschekopf*, or just plain *schlemiel*. Kids in both
the smart and dumb categories learned their roles in this scenario early and, like
their parents, accepted their fates. The former, naturally would become doctors and
lawyers, dentists and professors. The latter would be butchers and grocers or go to
work in the garment center.

The serious heartbreakers of petite bourgeoise Jewish mothers, however, were
those few of their sons who fell in between the standard categories. The ones with
good intelligence scores but low grades, or with clever hands and high achievement
performances but also frequent bloody noses and torn knees from getting it on with
Irish kids across the avenue. Such sons were of the category which would be named
in the future—after another decade of progress in educational research—as "under-
achievers." In my day they were just called "bummers" or "good-for-nothings" who
seemed bent on deliberate humiliation of their parents in addition to their own self-
destruction.

Based on intimate personal knowledge of this particular "case," I can testify that
despite its retrospective humor, it was no laughing matter when, on seeing a report
card containing anything less than a fifty-fifty mix of A's and B's, my mother would
either (a) grab up her largest carving knife (we were always in the kitchen so it was
handy) and thrust at me with the handle, urging me to take it and stab her to death
immediately rather than torturing her slowly. Then, at least *one* of us could be happy
while the other rested (not in peace mind you) with the worms, who couldn't eat

her up inside with aggravation any more than her own son. Or (b) run frantically to the hall closet, muttering curses in Yiddish, there to pull out a wire coat hanger and begin pursuing me through the apartment, whipping my ass with it.

Whether she did (a) or (b) depended on her mood. Like Shakespeare's Hamlet, during moments of depression, my mother went to soliloquies over the knife, and during more manic phases to hot pursuit of the culprit. The latter was always preferable, because I could move pretty good and a number of relatively safe stalemate positions were available: locked in the bathroom was best; crawling under the center of the large double bed she slept in with my father was next; and circling back to the hall closet was a poor third, since she usually could pull the door open against my effort to hold it shut, and then I'd be trapped behind the overcoats . . . which at least impeded her swing.

The point is that much later in life, as a professor who had finally written enough books and fathered enough children (two is par in both fields) to make his mother *moderately* happy (she could never accept the big Honda and the downhill skiing), I discovered the concept and process of reification: "treating a concept or symbol as if it were real." It was love at first sight! At last it was clear what it was that me and my mother and all the other Jews of my old neighborhood had suffered from! Reification, indeed, and the New York City Public School System that in those days was its most righteously powerful agent, but which now, thanks to the new breed of militant minorities and dissident academics, seems to have lost all its former high standards.

Later childhood, from about age 9 to 14, was dominated by World War II. In common with all the other boys of this cohort, I was a super-patriot who ate, drank, and played war constantly. With a few cans of baked beans and an old canteen of water, we would survive for hours in Fort Tryon park, armed to the teeth with cap pistols, tommy guns fashioned from the ends of orange crates, and our heaviest weapon: a discarded automobile muffler resembling a water cooled machine gun.

The war was omnipresent. At school we followed it on maps, bought 10- and 25-cent defense stamps, planted "victory" gardens; at home we built models of planes and tanks and fantasized about the heroics we saw in war movies like *Bataan*, *Sahara*, and *The Flying Tigers*. I loved every bit of it, probably because the closest I ever came to the reality was during a summer vacation on Long Island where debris from torpedoed ships occasionally washed ashore.

My closest friend or "chum" during these days was Johnny Clark. He was one of the barbarian Irish who lived a few blocks away across the Great Divide of ethnic prejudice. Our friendship cut right across the grain of prevailing family and peer-group ideologies and was the direct consequence of our grade school bureaucracy.

In those days, each grade level included classes enumerated from 1 to 3 or 4. The "1" class was for the brightest, and the "2," "3," and "4" classes were for the slow, slower, and slowest (the preferred term among scientific educators was slow, not dumb, but this fooled no one). There was also a smaller so-called opportunity or rapid-advance class for exceptionally bright children who were selected, by virtue of their IQ scores and scholarly diligence—the latter apparently defined by the fact that most of them carried briefcases or schoolbags, whereas the rest of us would have died of embarrassment to be caught with such a thing—to skip the fourth grade. They did, but by the time they were in fifth grade, the class was too small to meet required standards and had nearly twice as many girls as boys. The authorities decided to correct the problem by assigning to this class two boys from the "1" class who were thought bright enough to warrant the honor. So Johnny and I found ourselves sitting side-by-side at the back of a room full of certifiable "smarties" and feeling like apprehensive young wolves surrounded by a flock of sheep. It took no time at all before we became virtual blood brothers; any differences in background being pale by comparison with the awful fate we were forced to share.

For the next few years, through grade school and junior high, we were Tom Sawyer and Huckleberry Finn, covering each other in schoolyard scuffles, sneaking into the subway without paying, and sharing all the adventure books we could find in the public library.

I dwell on this at such length, partly because the friendship was the prototype for "male bonding" experiences later on, and partly because of its extraordinary conclusion. Johnny and I drifted somewhat apart in high school, for all the inevitable reasons. After high school he went to an out-of-town college, I stayed in New York, and then we were both in the army, and just never saw or heard of each other again . . . until 1989.

I was scheduled to present a paper to a discussion group of historians, psychiatrists, and psychologists at the Menninger Foundation. One of the participants was a historian from the University of Kansas in Lawrence. A colleague of his noticed an advance copy of my paper on his desk and remarked that he had a close childhood friend with the same unusual name as the paper's author. One thing led to another very quickly, we spoke on the phone, and that's how I discovered that Johnny was a history professor and had been teaching at Lawrence, 80 miles away from me, for more than 20 years. We have visited a few times since then and both been struck by how similar we still seem to be in our values and temperaments.

Turning back to the chronology, all that remains in memory of my high school years is dull routine with a few bright spots in history and English classes. I spent much of the time reading escapist fiction, mainly Zane Gray and Max Brand westerns and anything to do with war. Two close friends were also insatiable readers. Abner devoured detective novels: Ellery Queen, Perry Mason, and so on; Ray's thing was historical fiction: Kenneth Roberts and C. S. Forrester, and we often traded books. (Ab became a lawyer; Ray a high school history teacher and ultimately school system superintendent.) For the rest, I had the usual after school and Saturday jobs available to teenagers: delivery boy for a local dry cleaner, stacking groceries in my father's store, and, best of all, at 16 and 17, messenger for the Mercury Messenger Service, working from a small office in the Hotel Maryland on 49th Street. With this job came some exposure to the whole range of Damon Runyon characters who could still be seen, in the late forties and early fifties, standing around the sidewalk outside Lindy's.

From 1949 to 1953 I attended the Washington Square College of New York University. By this time, I was reading stronger stuff: Hemingway, Faulkner, and the big postwar novels by Irwin Shaw and Norman Mailer. At college, I began by majoring in biology; I had vague notions of becoming a physician. Apart from pleasing my parents, this was largely based on a deep sense of achievement experienced after removing an infected splinter from Ray's foot while we had worked together at a summer camp the previous year. My "true" ambition, however, was more straightforward: I just wanted to become Ernest Hemingway.

Toward these ends, I took literature courses along with the standard package of premed classes. Both went reasonably well until my sophomore year, when premed came to a halt because of organic chemistry. My grades in the class were so low that by midsemester I quit going to it, and I recall one fellow in the class who was making a C, but was thinking seriously of suicide because without a minimal B he would probably not get into med school.

My preoccupation with literature faded more gradually. In one class, after developing an intense enthusiasm for the work of Walt Whitman, I wrote a term paper arguing against the unthinkable charge that he could be a "homo." (Me and my friends all knew that homos were degenerates; "fruits" who dressed up—ugh!—as women. It would be quite a while yet before I discovered Vidal, Mishima, E. M. Forster, and would become faculty adviser to the first gay organization on the Kansas State campus.)

In another class, I fell hook, line, and sinker for the mystique of Ambrose Bierce and wrote a long term paper portraying him as a precursor of Hemingway. The paper came back with a C, and the instructor's comment that much of it read so well that he was sure it had been plagiarized. So that was that; no Hemingway man would waste any more time on those fools in the English department!

None of these things actually bothered me very much. I was 20, college was a drag, and there was a war in Korea that I really thought I should experience first hand. No such luck: When my mother heard I was going to volunteer she immediately threatened suicide. Since I didn't quite have what it took to put her to the test, and since my new brother-in-law who still had some shrapnel in his leg from World War II added more manly arguments, I stayed in college. Twenty-odd years later I had a small thrill of recognition when reading F. Scott Fitzgerald's remark, somewhere in *The Crackup*, that one of his great disappointments in life was not seeing combat in World War I.

In my junior year, while the Korean War went on without me, I changed my major to psychology. Having had a relatively easy time of it making an A in the introductory class, and finding some of the material on personality and social behavior particularly interesting, psychology seemed attractive. It was also a relatively new field, wide open, challenging, and uncertain. One might become a God-like shrink, or better yet, one of those ingenious investigators working to reveal further secrets of the mind. But I was also enjoying and doing well in history courses, so for a while it was a toss-up between psych and history.

The decisive move to psych came from having a class in social psychology. I still recall the instructor, Professor Vetter, who gave wonderfully dramatic lectures on the topics of prejudice, conformity, conflict, and aggression. About this time too, Otto Klineberg came to give a guest lecture. He was some sort of big wheel at UNESCO, and his talk left me with a firm impression that social psychology research probably offered the best hope for world peace and social justice in general. Compared to this, history was small beer! Besides, one could always read history as a hobby.

The further I went in psychology, the better I liked it. Readings in the Newcomb and Hartley (1947) anthology seemed to confirm impressions gained from Vetter and Klineberg, and in experimental psychology, Gestalt demonstrations showing how people could easily misperceive the world around them added further excitement. I was also struggling to understand *The Authoritarian Personality* (Adorno et al., 1950) and reading some Freud on my own. It was all heady stuff; I began smoking a pipe.

The pipe was not entirely an affectation. I had a part-time sales job for several months in a Wally Frank Ltd. tobacco shop near Wall Street, and the pipe was mandatory. This was one of the several part-time school-year and full-time summer jobs that helped pay college tuition and in retrospect seems to have helped my "identity formation" immensely.

One summer I was groundsman at an expensive boys camp in Maine, cutting grass, rolling tennis courts, and cleaning 36 toilets every morning while the kids were at breakfast. The job paid more than what the counselors were getting, and it's a little embarrassing to admit how much I enjoyed the blue collar image that went with it. I lived in a cabin with the cooks, dishwasher (an unemployed merchant seaman), and a local teenager who looked after the riding horses. Against the rules, early one morning, he let me try riding in the training ring. My cowboy fantasies lasted about three minutes. As the horse broke into a trot, I fell off the left side. The horse stopped. When I reached up to get my left shoe out of the stirrup where it was stuck, he spooked and headed full tilt toward the gate facing the stable, swinging me in toward his left hind hoof pounding down inches from my head. By reflex, my left arm went out dragging on the ground and pulling me away. The horse galloped to the gate, saw it was shut, and made a sudden swerve that jerked my foot free. Except for losing considerable skin from my left arm and side, I was okay, but me and the horse handler were afraid we would lose our jobs if anyone found out, so he painted my wounds with the gentian violet solution he used on the horses and we both pretended nothing had happened.

Another summer I worked on a 40-foot Chris Craft cabin cruiser docked at Pelham Bay in the Bronx. The owner and his wife usually took it out on weekends when I would handle the lines and anchor (he had back trouble and a hernia), rig the fishing rods, and carry the baggage and groceries aboard. There was a close call here, too, when I slipped on the deck on a rainy day and one leg went down between the transom and the dock, nearly getting crunched in between.

I also spent one school year working afternoons as a shipping clerk for Irving S., a resident fur coat buyer in the garment center. Irving himself had started as a shipping clerk and personally taught me to properly box and tie up the minks, persians, and whatnot that I would then carry down to the trucking company that moved the goods to his out-of-town customers. The box-tying skill has served me well all these years.

Later on I worked afternoons and evenings for Nationwide Packing, a garment district truck outfit. From 3:00 to 6:00 P.M., we would take in boxed goods at a long line of windows, fling them on a scale, write the weight on a receipt, and throw the box on a conveyer belt leading to the loading dock. After closing down at the windows, we would go out to the dock and use hand trucks to load stuff into the truck trailers that were backed up to it. This could also be hazardous sometimes.

I didn't know it then, of course, but the varied social experiences and occasional risks associated with these jobs were, developmentally speaking, invaluable. They provided a still-enduring sense of respect for blue-collar workers and confidence that I could hold my own among them with as much easy camaraderie as I had with my college peers.

And I must say too, even though space does not permit much elaboration, that I had a wonderful group of college friends. There were several of us, male and female, each in our own way something of a character, either majoring in or wavering between history, psychology, biology, or English, who regularly hung out together at "our" table in the college cafeteria. And we had some grand, high times there. It wasn't exactly the old Heywood Broun–Dorothy Parker round table at the Algonquin but it had that quality.

As college graduation approached, I applied to the graduate psych program at New York University (NYU) and was rejected . . . poor grades. Not too surprised, I soon picked up a job as an assistant floor supervisor at Youth House, a city-run detention center for juveniles being held for trial, and began taking graduate courses at NYU as a nondegree student. I also spent as many weekends as I could that winter on a pair of $15 downhill skis at Bear Mountain where they had a killer rope tow and runs that were more ice than snow.

The courses were wonderful (social psychology with Marie Jahoda, a seminar on prejudice with Gerhardt Saenger, and a class on thinking with T. C. Schneirla); the job was wonderful (learning to like the 3 to 11 P.M. shift with 30–40 screwed up 15 and 16 year olds, not to mention a relationship with an attractive young woman on the nursing staff); and the skiing was wonderful (I never got hurt).

Meanwhile, the Korean War ended but the draft continued. No longer entitled to a student deferment, I was expecting to go at any time, yet as the year passed nothing happened, and I got tired of seeing kids locked up every day, tired of being a student, even in classes with remarkable instructors, so in the fall of 1954, without informing my mother, of course, I volunteered for the draft.

The army: I could easily do 50 pages on the two years, but a brief take must suffice. Eight weeks of basic at Fort Dix (November and December, wet and cold); 13 weeks of radio school learning morse code ("here comes the bride" is dah-dah-di-dah, Q for Queen), and in April 1955 away to Germany on a slow troop ship (ten days, wet and cold), then through the replacement pipeline to *Worms Am Rhein* (wet and cold), where my home for the next 18 months was the 12th Armored Infantry battalion better known throughout the 2nd Armored Division as the "fucked up twelfth."

I had met a Hunter College girl during my first weekend pass from basic. We dated on all the subsequent passes until orders for Germany arrived and then agreed she would come to Europe after her college graduation and we would get married. She did, we were, and to the surprise of all concerned, including us, still are. We lived off-post in a small cold-water flat, toured through much of Europe on my 30-day leave, and when I wasn't out with the battalion (wet and cold) practicing to fight the Russians, it was the next best thing to sliced bread.

Early in the fall of 1956, with my discharge date approaching, I applied to the graduate social psych program at the University of Michigan. This time I received a personal rejection letter from Dan Katz explaining that I didn't have enough graduate credits to enter the Ph.D. program, but I had too many to enter the master's program. Grades weren't mentioned, possibly because I had A's from Jahoda and Saenger.

By November we were back in New York. My wife began working as a substitute teacher, and I found a job in the statistical department of the Elmo Roper opinion research firm on the 46th floor of the NBC building. We moved into a trendy studio apartment in Riverdale, bought a hi-fi set, and I rode the bus and subway every day in my new uniform: charcoal grey flannel suit, button down shirt, dark knitted tie, cordovan oxfords... the whole shmear. The job mainly involved setting up analysis tables designed to answer questions posed by the upper echelon project directors, for example, what percentage of women over 30 or men over 50 smoked Phillip Morris, drove Fords, voted Republican, and/or blah-blah-blah.

By prevailing standards of the time it was a very good job. Elmo and his son, Burns (Bud) Roper, were enlightened, liberal employers. Everyone was on a first-name basis. We all used the same washrooms. Bud often presided graciously at birthday lunches for employees at the nearby Taft grill. But after about six months, it began to feel like a soft prison. I had mastered the work and it was getting monotonous; the suit and tie became increasingly irritating; the bus and subway stultifying, and I was more and more missing the straightforward roughneck atmosphere of the 12th AIB. I began to day-dream about re-enlisting; one lunch hour I went to a Broadway shooting gallery just to fire a weapon again only to find that the little .22s felt like toys.

There was one outstanding bright spot, however. Paul Lazarsfeld, who was then director of the Columbia University Institute for Social Research and one of the most prominent social scientists in the country, was a consultant to the Roper firm. He gave a lengthy seminar for the entire staff once or twice a month on such issues as representative sampling, interviewer bias effects, and the "opinion leader" research technique. It must have been quite obvious to him that I enjoyed his discussions a great deal. I usually hung around afterwards asking questions, and after several months, I think we developed a sort of instinctive rapport, probably because we were the only ones in the place who really didn't give a damn about the commercial applications of the theoretical concepts. I should have known from this, as well as my other symptoms, that I was not likely to ever succeed in business, but it took about a year for me to begin thinking seriously about graduate school again.

By this time my wife Karen was also fed up with life in the city and work in the public schools, so we sat down with an atlas, picked out some places we thought we'd like—Colorado, New Mexico, and California in that order—and I sent for graduate school applications. Lazarsfeld readily agreed to write letters of recommendation, but said that if I wanted to study sociology he could phone some of his former students teaching at Berkeley and get me right in! (It was 1957; nobody questioned old-boy networks.) I cautiously demurred, holding out for Colorado, not mentioning that the reason was the skiing. A few years later while sitting on a chair lift with Mike Wertheimer, he told me that he had taken a teaching job at Boulder for similar reasons.

On the strength of Lazarsfeld's letter, I suppose, Colorado gave me a provisional acceptance stipulating that I would have to take one or two undergraduate psych courses and do well in other first-year graduate classes. I was delighted. I recall thinking that it was like receiving a pardon from serving life in penal servitude. In the spring of 1958, we gave up our apartment and got jobs at a summer camp in upstate New York, me as counselor for the teenage boys and Karen for the teenage girls. It was outdoor fun, free room and board, and a thousand dollars for the forthcoming move to Colorado.

We drove west with all our belongings in a 1953 Dodge donated by my mother, who still put education *über alles*. You can first see Boulder nestled against the Rockies at a point where the turnpike from Denver begins dropping into the Boulder Valley. For us it was something like a religious vision; the start of another new, free-er life after Germany and New York. It now seems to me that almost everything in my life from this time onwards was relatively smooth sailing, because there in Boulder at almost age 27, I had, as they say, found my niche.

The graduate psychology program was rigorous. There were comprehensive "area" exams and reading exams in two languages, as well as the ultimate prelims to contend with, but as time went on I found myself handling the coursework and other demands pretty well and liking the town, the university, the psych department chaired by Vic Raimy (who as legend had it, occasionally rode a big Harley at breakneck speeds), and most of the faculty and grad students. There was a nice informality and idealism in the air too. Most of the faculty were only about a dozen years away from their service in World War II, and they projected a strong sense that psychology research could really make a difference in the world. Indeed, that any time now breakthrough work might be accomplished that would open a path toward the elimination of prejudice, conformity, authoritarianism, and almost any social problem you'd care to name. I ate it up.

Soon after I arrived, Howie Gruber, who was reading Piaget in French and lecturing about this seemingly bizarre new qualitative theory of cognitive development, hired me as a half-time assistant to work on a study evaluating the effects of a cultural enrichment program for undergraduates. The study was run out of the Behavior Research Laboratory: a few rooms on the top floor of the university library that also housed a medical school evaluation project directed by Ken Hammond.

It was a causal gesture by Ken that profoundly shaped my early research career. He stopped at my desk one Friday afternoon as he was leaving, said something like "Here's a book a man like you might like to read," and handed me a thin paperback he had just received. It was *Multiple Probability Learning* (1955), a dissertation recently completed at Oslo University by Jan Smedslund. I started reading and could hardly put it down.

Based on Egon Brunswik's theory of probabilistic functionalism, which emphasizes that organisms adapt to uncertain environments by learning the probabilities or conditional associations linking surface cues to remote or covert objects or events, Smedslund had constructed a multiple cue learning task. It involved variations in the size, position, and other qualities of circles drawn on a deck of cards with numbers on their backs. The task was to examine the circle on the face of each card and guess the number on the back before turning the card over to see the current number. As a person continued through the cards this way, his or her guesses would become more accurate and better than chance, thus demonstrating the type of adaptive, probabilistic learning required to master what Smedslund called his "artificial miniature environment." He also observed that people who took a more relaxed, intuitive approach to the task did better at it than those who tried to figure it out logically.

I was enthralled; the theory seemed to fit perfectly with my own experiences in uncertain situations, and the task seemed to provide an elegant little laboratory model for the study of such experiences. I'm sure I shared my enthusiasm with Ken, but he was busy with other things, and I didn't see too much of him. While taking a class with O. J. Harvey, however, I had been exposed to his ideas about individual differences in cognitive and emotional rigidity. I got along very well with O. J. He could hold forth wonderfully at parties, often proclaiming at appropriate moments, "I'm not in psychology to be a psychologist, I'm in psychology to be O. J. Harvey!" Aside from that, he had just developed a questionnaire to measure personal rigidity-flexibility, and I thought we might use it to predict how people would perform on Smedslund's probability learning task. He agreed to sponsor this as my master's thesis under the title "Multiple Probability Learning and Personality." It took about a year, but although the task itself worked beautifully, the results showed no significant relationships between personal rigidity and task performance. Very disappointing, but lots of other interesting things were happening by then.

Ken had obtained a grant to study person perception and I became his research assistant, working with Fred Todd, who was his full-time research associate. Fred and I quickly became good friends. We spent about two years applying various cognitive structure models to the problem of describing how people organized their impressions of others. The project eventually was published in the *Journal of Abnormal and Social Psychology* (Todd and Rappoport, 1964).

It was around this time, too (circa 1960–1961), that the first generation of computers became available to us, and I worked up computer analysis procedures for our impression-formation data. The "computer revolution" as we saw it would open exciting new possibilities for studying all sorts of judgment and decision-making processes from the perspective of probabilistic functionalism. Research on judgment was emerging elsewhere as well. At the University of Oregon, Paul Hoffman was doing interesting work on clinical inference (the judgment processes of psychotherapists) and at Michigan, Ward Edwards was doing studies to demonstrate that Bayesian probability statistics could describe other forms of uncertain decision making. Hoffman and Edwards both visited to discuss their work with us and a handful of other graduate students—Cam Peterson, Lee Beach, Karen Signell, Joe Uhlela, Dave Summers—who had begun working with Ken. Ken also arranged for Jan Smedslund to spend a year with us as a visiting scholar, only to discover that Jan was now more interested in Piaget than in Brunswik. Jan and I had many interests in common, however, and I gained a great deal from talks with him, which turned out to be the basis of a lifelong friendship.

In sum, by the early sixties I was happily part of an enthusiastic research group created by Ken Hammond. We had a rather elitist attitude; felt that we were at the leading edge of a new field—judgment/decision-making—and a new paradigm—The Brunswikian Lens Model—for research in this field. And along with Ken, I believed that Brunswikian theory could provide the basis for understanding and ultimately resolving serious social problems caused by erroneous or inappropriate judgment processes. Furthermore, thanks to my assistantship, G-I bill money, and my wife's job teaching in the local schools, we had been able to buy a small house in Boulder Canyon and a new Hillman Minx convertible; I was getting pretty good on skis, we had many friends, and we loved living in the mountains. After passing the prelim examinations, I even had a good idea for a dissertation.

Based on my master's thesis, I thought that if two people learned to rely on different cues in a multiple cue learning task, and then had to work together on the same task, not knowing that "their" cues were no longer valid, they would probably fall into serious disagreement, each arguing for their own point of view. And this might prevent them from catching on that some other cue would now allow them to make more accurate judgments. Such a study could serve as a good laboratory analogue for the sorts of conflicts that can occur between husbands and wives, bridge partners, or allied nation states—any conflict, that is, between persons or groups who have the same goal, but whose prior experience leads them to think differently about how to attain that goal. If it worked, it would also allow the testing of various conflict resolution techniques.

Most of my colleagues thought it would fail because the manipulation was too obvious; people would realize that they had learned different cues and not take their disagreements seriously. When I tried it out, however, it worked very nicely, and Ken and I were both enthused because it seemed to offer a way to study social conflict as a cognitive phenomenon, rather than just a matter of competition or antithetical emotions.

While conducting this study in 1962, two other things happened. My first son was born that summer, and as a result of conversations with Smedslund about the role of intuitive feelings in social perception situations, I applied for a postdoctoral fellowship to spend the following year working with him in Oslo. This came through in the spring of 1963 as the dissertation was getting wrapped up, but Ken, thank goodness, convinced me to stay in Boulder for another few months to write it up for publication (1965). Then, delighted with the opportunity to see Europe again, we sold our house and took a Norwegian-American Line ship to Oslo.

Smedlsund, meanwhile, had arranged an apartment for us and also taken an offer to work with Jerome Bruner at Harvard for the year. His friend (and soon to be my friend) Ragnar Rommetveit took over as my sponsor in

Oslo. I had read some of Rommetveit's work and liked it, and he, like Smedslund, was thoughtful, creative, and interested in the things that interested me, so we hit it off immediately. But Rommetveit was busy with a book about the social psychology of language, and after finding me some office space at the psychology institute, it was agreed that I would work more or less on my own for the year, just checking in with him occasionally.

How lucky can you get? My family was comfortably situated in a modern apartment close to a state forest (Nordmarkke) full of hiking/ski trails; I could go and come as I pleased to the psychology institute, and had a fair range of colleagues available for discussion. These included not only the faculty and students at the institute who invited me to their daily tea/conversation hours, but some other American scholars who were on Fulbrights at the Institute for Social Research. With the assassination of President Kennedy, we soon had a lot to talk about. The Norwegians all concluded immediately that the killing was a right-wing conspiracy, whereas most of the Americans, including me, thought it quite likely that Oswald had done it on his own. I had almost argued some of the Norwegians around to this view when Jack Ruby ruined my position.

In pursuit of my social perception project, I went carefully through Heinze Werner's *Comparative Psychology of Mental Development* (1961) and Fritz Heider's *The Psychology of Interpersonal Relations* (1958). Both provided solid, reasonably compatible grounds for research on the intuitive feeling-tone aspects of impression formation. (I had no idea then that Werner and Heider had known each other in Hamburg.) I worked away at outlining and testing an experimental scheme centered on the use of soft vs. hard, smooth vs. pointy, and bright vs. dull-colored free-form figures as person object cues. (In case anyone cares: hard, pointy, bright colored figures are seen as aggressive, intelligent, cold, fast, unfriendly, etc.) This was all done in Norwegian. I was learning some from a grammar book and from watching "The Flintstones" on television with my 18-month-old son; it had Norwegian subtitles.

Another noteworthy event was the beginning of an enduring friendship with Steinar Kvale, who was then a graduate student in Oslo and is now Professor at Aarhus in Denmark. Steinar and his close friend Karl-Erik Grenness went about characterizing themselves as existential-phenomenological experimental psychologists and loved to provoke arguments over their claim that B. F. Skinner was the supreme American existentialist. We had some fine, good-humored discussions; Steinar and I skied together, and later on a vacation trip to Bergen, my wife and I had a pleasant visit with his parents, who had spent considerable time in the States.

Oslo is a charming city, and we liked most of the people we met there, but by December, between the dark winter days and the friends, family, and conveniences we missed—not least of which were pizzas, cheeseburgers, and Chinese food—we decided not to apply for a second year. (Norwegian cuisine and the lines at the post office were two inevitable topics of conversation among visiting Americans.) This meant finding a job in the States from Oslo, but I wasn't too concerned because at that time, 1963–1964, the universities were still expanding, and if you were any good, your former professors would usually find a position for you through their old-boy connections. And it *was* virtually an all-boy system; if this sounds unabashedly sexist and elitist, take it as a sign of how much things have changed, at least on the surface.

I soon had leads to social-personality positions at Michigan State, UCLA, and Kansas State. When the opening at UCLA was cancelled, and a solid offer arrived from Merrill Noble, the department head at K-State, emphasizing a two-course teaching load and research-friendly atmosphere, I took it, partly because it was much closer to Boulder than Michigan and partly because I liked (can you dig it?) the "feeling-tone" of Merrill's letters! Moreover, like several other faculty lifers at K-State we would later have as close friends, Karen and I thought that we would stay for only a year or two before moving on to a more attractive cultural/geographic location.

Since this is not the place for an extended essay on the subtle pleasures of life available in Manhattan, Kansas, suffice it to say that (a) Merrill did indeed turn out to be a great guy and fine "boss"; (b) my new senior colleagues in the personality-social area were Jerry Phares and Franz Samelson, both fine scholar-researchers, warm and reliable friends to this day; (c) Franz shared my love of skiing and critical theoretical-philosophical discourse, and our families would spend many skiing vacations together; (d) I got along well with the other psychology faculty, including Harry Helson, our distinguished "elder," and especially Bob Haygood, another new assistant professor with an adjoining office who had spent several years before graduate school as a piano player in cafes and nightclubs; and, finally, (e) Manhattan was and still is a near-ideal community for raising children. This last point was not lost on us; our second son was born about a year later in 1965.

The next several years, from about 1966 to 1973, were crowded with so many simultaneous personal, professional, and academic events played out in the intense atmosphere created by the Vietnam War, the civil rights struggle, and the counterculture movement that I can only note them briefly, as they show up in a blurry kaleidoscope of memory.

My family thrived. We had a comfortable house on a quiet street that was a 20-minute walk from the university and close to a good grade school. Karen completed a master's degree in education and began teaching remedial reading once our children were in school, and of course we had the cat, the German Shepherd and the station wagon . . . the whole middle-class cliché, and it was great! (When Mort Bard from CUNY visited to give a talk, he remarked that it all reminded him of old Andy Hardy movies.)

I continued the social perception research begun in Oslo but was also in regular contact with Ken Hammond and spent a summer in Boulder as his

research associate. With the help of an excellent team of associates and grad
students (Dave Stewart, Berndt Brehmer, Dave Summers, and others), he
elaborated a quantitatively rigorous, computer-based approach to decision
making and began applying it to real problems, such as weather forecasting
and medical diagnosis. At the same time, I developed a realistic multi-cue
task requiring pairs of people to estimate the levels of racial strife present
in hypothetical communities. Much of this work was done with the excellent
help of George Cvetkovich, the first student to earn a Ph.D. with me, now
professor at Western Washington University.

Late in 1966 there was an army major from nearby Fort Riley in my social
psychology class. During a discussion of attitudes to the war, he said that
he commanded a casual company of men recently returned from combat in
Vietnam and most of them were very bitter about their experiences. This
was confirmed by their responses to an attitude questionnaire he distributed
for me. In order to investigate why they felt this way I began interviewing
these and other combat veterans. The interviews often turned into dramatic,
cathartic affairs, especially with the college-age youngsters, and I began
getting pretty bitter about the war myself.

Then Jack Gore, an economist friend at Colorado University who had
become a central figure in the regional antiwar movement, more or less
plugged me into it. I solicited faculty signatures for antiwar ads in the *New
York Times* and joined with a few others at K-State to form the "faculty
action committee" against the war and for civil rights. I was also connected
with the formation of a Black Student Association through Lodis Rhodes, a
black former football player who was doing his master's thesis with me. He
became locally famous for, among other things, marching out alone one day
onto the football field armed only with his black turtleneck and dark glasses,
to demand that the university band quit playing "Dixie." And they finally
did. (Lodis is now professor of sociology at the University of Texas.)

Most of the action of the faculty action committee consisted of little more
than organizing meetings, arranging public debates, and submitting statements to the campus newspaper, but when a campus building was burned
down, it was widely believed to be the work of black activists. The Faculty
Senate passed a resolution condemning the action committee for encouraging
violence. Some of our group then wanted to resign from the university in
protest, while others were afraid we would all be fired; we compromised by
circulating a petition condemning the Faculty Senate! It all blew over after
LBJ threw in his hand in 1968 and public opinion shifted definitively against
the war.

At the 1968 APA convention in San Francisco, I gave a paper on my
interviews with veterans which received practically a standing ovation. It
was also written up with my picture in the *San Francisco Chronicle* (the
reporter said he wanted the picture because I had very short hair!). It was
at this convention, too, that Howie Gruber challenged psychologists to work

against the war and organized Psychologists for Social Action, which I immediately joined.

Back at K-State, one of the early antiwar people was George Kren, a history professor several years my senior. He was interested in the application of Freudian psychology to history; I was interested in the application of history to psychology, and we were both keenly interested in the Spanish Civil War, the psychosocial/historical dynamics of the international brigade, Orwell, Malraux, Hemingway, Koestler, and all that. George had an impressive beard, used a long cigarette holder, and rode a Honda, wearing his self-proclaimed Polish cavalry boots. We became good friends almost immediately, then started teaching a seminar together focused on the psychosocial implications of various historical crises. One of the crises covered was the Holocaust. We became absorbed in this and so frustrated by the lack of satisfactory psychosocial-historical interpretation that we decided to write a book on the subject.

I was at this point working on a lifespan personality development textbook that grew out of one of the classes I taught and had also finally completed an article on my social perception project. Since that project ended up drawing heavily on Fritz Heider's work, I sent him a copy. He responded with some very kind remarks and an invitation to visit him in Lawrence (he had just retired from the University of Kansas). I went, and together with his wife Grace, we had a delightful afternoon of tea and conversation. It was the beginning of a marvelous friendship that lasted until his death and still continues with Grace. I would visit them a few times a year, sometimes with a few graduate students; they came to K-State for him to give a talk, and Karen and Grace also became good friends. When Karen was later working toward a Ph.D. in Lawrence, she would often stay at their home.

During this same period, 1967 to 1969, Ken Hammond began holding annual research conferences on judgment and decision making in Boulder. At one time or another, almost everyone who was doing anything interesting in this field came to discuss their work, and early on, Ken suggested that the world needed a book of readings describing the various approaches and problem areas under investigation. Most of those involved agreed to the idea of writing original papers for such a book, but all of them claimed to be too busy to act as editors, so this mission fell to me and Dave Summers, who had just begun teaching at the University of Kansas.

It turned out to be a very sticky job because, with the notable exception of Paul Slovic and Sarah Lichtenstein (God bless 'em), hardly anyone would work on a paper until we had a publisher, and hardly any publisher would consider the project until they saw the papers. Ultimately, but not without some hilarious moments of near despair when Dave and I discussed running away to Mexico rather than admitting failure to our mentor Ken, we obtained a contract from Holt, Rinehart and Winston, and the book started going forward.

That about does it for those first several years in Kansas. In retrospect, considering everything I've mentioned, let alone other things precluded by space limitations and discretion, it's hard to believe that I ever had that much energy.

By 1972, when I turned 40, my family was still thriving, several research articles and reviews had been published, the personality textbook was in print, the decision-making anthology was in galleys, I was heavily engaged with Kren on the Holocaust manuscript, and at his inspiration, I bought my first motorcycle. We did a lot of backroad riding over the next several years. We thought of this as therapy for our immersion in the Holocaust horrors.

Franz Samelson and I had, meanwhile, become (a) expert downhill skiers from going alone every January (we took our families in the spring) to Vail, Aspen, Jackson, and so forth, and (b) highly critical of mainstream social psychology. In the latter, of course, we were not alone. Many important critical articles were appearing, not the least of which, in 1973, was Ken Gergen's *Social Psychology as History* (1973). We had intense discussions of critical theory and other Marxian critiques of "normal" social science. Franz was beginning to do meticulous critically oriented research on the history of social psychology, while I became more and more caught up in the Holocaust material, which seemed to me to reveal the flawed ontological and epistemological assumptions underlying much of social science. (About ten years later, I wrote a long, rather opaque article on this theme for an anthology edited by Ken and Mary Gergen [1984].)

I spent most of 1973 at Manhattanville College in Purchase, New York, as a visiting professor. This was a pleasant year; the college provided a house for us on the campus, and my sons were able to attend a good grade school nearby. Steinar Kvale visited from Duquesne University where he was teaching for the year. He had been involved in the European student movement and was ahead of me in the Marxian literature, but it was mutually gratifying to find that we were thinking along similar lines. There were other interesting contacts too: with Miriam Lewin (Kurt's daughter) who was teaching at Manhattanville, Howie Gruber, who was at the Rutgers-Newark campus, and Mort Bard at CUNY. But we began to miss Kansas, where traffic or parking was never a problem, trips to the bank or supermarket didn't take hours, and our kids never came home from school asking how much money their father made.

It was probably sometime in 1974 that Klaus Riegel stopped to give a talk at K-State on his way to present a paper at the Nebraska Symposium in Lincoln, Nebraska. He had just then worked out a theoretical critique of developmental psychology based on Hegelian dialectics. Franz and I found both him and his ideas very stimulating; we got into an enthusiastic discussion which ended with us driving him the three hours to Lincoln. Along the way, he suggested that efforts should be made to apply dialectical concepts to social psychology. We agreed, and several months later with the help of

Philip Shaver (then at NYU), who arranged facilities, there was a conference on dialectical social psychology in New York. About 25 to 30 people attended, including Klaus, Franz and I, Ken Gergen, and a handful of Marxian graduate students and faculty from SUNY Stonybrook.

This meeting, like those concerning social and developmental psychology that followed over the next few years, now seems to me to have been more about personal and scholarly consciousness raising than anything else. But there were a few substantial things accomplished. I, and then Howard Gadlin, edited a dialectical psychology newsletter; several symposia were put on at APA conventions, including one I organized on dialectical social psychology, and Klaus brought out a textbook and a theory book on dialectical psychology.

I think it was in 1978 that Klaus died. The dialectics movement did not last long after him. He had been the center, holding together a varied group of Hegelians, hard and soft Marxians, feminists and (as I thought of myself) epistemological anarchists. The core people stayed together for a while but soon moved off in different directions, at least partially because in reacting to the pressures of radical scholars, feminists, and minorities, mainstream psychology became more and more open to concepts like contextualism, historicity, and the interpenetration of opposites.

During the mid–1970s, I worked on some practical decision-making projects, such as how nuclear power plant inspectors could tell whether or not nuclear material "unaccounted for" was being stolen or diverted to weapons use, but I was losing interest in the field. It had become dominated by relatively a-theoretical, nonpsychological approaches: computer-based linear information processing/integration models which were generally seen as superior to mere humans, whereas I was more concerned with how mere humans could come up with Auschwitz. George Kren and I finally had this figured out to our satisfaction in 1978. Our book, *The Holocaust and the Crisis of Human Behavior*, was published in 1980 and put us firmly on the map of Holocaust scholarship. We have continued working together on the subject (an expanded new edition should be out in 1993), but less intensively than before, as my interests shifted toward the study of foodways.

Why foodways of all things? There were several reasons. First, when seeking ways to dramatize dialectical philosophy in concrete terms, food consumption provided an ideal illustration: the transformation of animal flesh into gourmet dishes into . . . shit. Second, while studying behavior in Nazi death camps, it struck me that all it takes to strip people down to a demoralized state of primitive survival is systematic starvation; that food, indeed, is the bedrock of all culture (cf. Claude Levi-Strauss), and so much taken for granted in modern societies that its psychosocial implications have been largely ignored. Third, I had become involved in Zen Buddhist philosophy and practice, which places a special metaphysical importance on food and the cook or "tenzo" in charge of its preparation. And fourth, I began running into all sorts of fascinating material on the subject, such as the Norbert Elias history of table manners, and the fact that American POWs returned from North Vietnam were found to have healthier cardiovascular systems than their peers, presumably because of their enforced fish heads and rice diet. I also thought that foodways offered a very practical domain of research as well as broad scope for all my philosophical, historical, and psychosocial theory pretentions.

The interest in Zen meditation practice, and then yoga, began in the early 1970s when one of my students gave me a copy of Herrigel's *Zen and the Art of Archery*. This account of a lived experience with the embodied philosophy of Zen seemed as if it had been written specifically for me. I soon found other Zen books, the most impressive being works by the American master Phillip Kapleau and the Japanese masters Daisetz and Shunryu Suzuki, which confirmed my impression that Buddhist thought and practice, including its humor and aesthetic style, was a near-perfect manifest expression of my own latent world view.

Based on the readings, I started taking a little time each day to try the recommended beginners meditation exercise of counting breaths, from one to ten. And I was amazed, as most beginners are, to find that I couldn't do it; couldn't get even to six or seven, without losing count because of interference from the stream of ordinary ego consciousness that Zen masters often call the "monkey mind." This experience only made the practice more intriguing to me. I mentioned it to a colleague in the math department who was interested in Eastern philosophy and was also exploring meditation. He had heard that Zen master Taizan Maezumi Roshi would be giving a public talk in Boulder, and we decided to go and see for ourselves whether anyone could really represent, in their person, the values and style we found so attractive in books.

Sitting on cushions in a hall filled with about 200 people, including the poet Alan Ginsberg, we just more or less had our minds blown by Maezumi and his two American disciples. Their personification of Zen exceeded our expectations. Later that year we attended an arduous weeklong meditation retreat (sesshin), started our own little meditation group in Manhattan, and began taking regular instruction from Dainin Katagiri Roshi, abbot of the Minneapolis Zen Center.

I was also fortunate to meet in Manhattan a retired professor and former foreign service officer who had mastered yoga while stationed in India. Because of the intense pain I had trying to meditate in traditional cross-legged or half-lotus postures, I needed all the yoga I could get. It took a few years of steady practice, but eventually I could do pretty well in both the half- and full-lotus, and even manage a passable headstand.

Although it isn't possible to fully explain the meaning of regular meditation practice, I can say that at a minimum, it has for me, in one sense, been like mental weight lifting because it strengthens the mind and, in another sense, like a powerful detergent bath that dissolves cognitive-affective *dreck*. As one of my favorite Zen aphorisms has it, the point is to learn how to "exist in muddy water with purity like a lotus."

Meanwhile, apart from Zen, some other interesting things were happening. In 1982, I spent part of a sabbatical in Paris working on the problematics of foodways with Erika Apfelbaum, a French social psychologist I knew from one of the dialectics meetings. She came to Kansas to interview Fritz Heider in 1980 or 1981, then stayed a few days with us in Manhattan and immediately flashed on the foodways topic when I discussed it with her. She was full of good ideas about the subject—"Americans eat with their eyes; the French eat with their noses"—and I still have almost a hundred pages of notes from the time we worked together in Paris, but although she later did an excellent paper on the psychodynamics of anorexia, time and distance prevented further collaboration.

I am still chewing away at foodways, have accumulated a filing cabinet full of partially digested sources, and one of the chapters I have cooked up for a projected book on the subject concerns usages of the language of food and cuisine, as illustrated in this sentence. The book keeps getting postponed, however, because the sources running through anthropology, sociology, dietetics, and psychology are so diverse, and because I have been working with a few local colleagues on empirical studies of food cognition, that is, how people conceptualize food in everyday life. This relates closely to the field of health psychology, so I began teaching a course in that subject a few years ago.

True to my by-now obvious pluralistic form, moreover, I have also been trying to bring my personal experiences with Zen meditation and yoga to bear on some issues in the area of transpersonal psychology. The foodways, health, and transpersonal content areas have a great deal of theoretical overlap, and I think they may ultimately converge to provide the basis for important advances toward a more holistic psychology.

It remains only to add that by guess or by God, my family marches on. Karen has become the leading authority on reading in the local schools, and our sons survived adolescence and college with a few close calls but no permanent mind-body damage. The oldest has a master's in political science; he now works at unspeakable things in Washington, D.C. The younger has a graduate degree in film/TV production; he currently pursues the muse editing television commercials in New York. Both get along well with dogs, cats, and children; are expert skiers; and I'm pretty sure you wouldn't mind being stuck on a chairlift with either one.

SOME REFLECTIONS ON TELLING THE STORY

I thought this would be quick and easy; it turned out to be slow and difficult. Just the mechanics of the writing alone are noteworthy because contrary to familiar expository theoretical/empirical writing, this first-person narrative form required considerable effort to avoid repetitive, egocentric sentences and paragraphs, and it isn't clear to me yet if the effort succeeded.

Another more surprising problem concerned the extent to which I found myself getting immersed in the various life contexts under discussion. There you are trying to describe the fabric of a particular incident or event, and the threads start leading off in unanticipated directions, and after the inevitable, sometimes prolonged ruminations about dead friends, long unthought-of girlfriends, good buddies, or supporting players whose names you can't even recall anymore, you have to pull out and impose manageable boundaries lest you never get out of college or the army.

Furthermore, while busy excavating the past, you can't help keeping an eye on the present and future. How many good friends may be disappointed to find they were left on the cutting room floor? I've only mentioned, mea culpa, one of the dozen-odd students who completed their doctoral theses with me and were all, for a while, surrogate sons or daughters. And who else might read this? My 88-year-old mother, after all, is still capable of going for the coat hanger or the knife!

This is all quite apart from the insights. Some seemed almost too trivial to mention, such as the realization that my romance with Hemingway ended when my first son was about a year old. I was as pleased then with my recent achievements at diaper changing and bottle feeding as I was a few years before at being seventh highest man with the carbine in my battalion. So it was a real disillusionment to see in a biography of Hemingway that the poor bastard apparently never changed a diaper in his life. The heroes of our youth never last.

A more significant insight following from the rule that what is *unsaid* can be as important, if not more so, than what is, was the whammo realization last night that there is not a word about personal health or the joys of teaching/ research anywhere in this essay! The former is easy enough to understand: I've been so fortunate in my health—never spent a day in a hospital; haven't consulted a physician more than a few times for the past 40 years—that I take it too much for granted. And I have also probably taken it too much for granted that any reader will see between the lines, so to speak, that for me the joys of teaching/research have far outweighed any sorrows. Just for the record, however, let me say that while these experiences have sometimes been downers, the euphoric highs associated with good new theory-research ideas, having the text of a paper flow just right, or spontaneously blowing students' minds in a class discussion, are in the same category with the float down through deep powder on a sunny day in Jackson, Wyoming.

There is one last, perhaps banal point. Before working on this essay, I never seriously thought about how much my life seems to have actually been several lives, each with its own thematic scenario, cast of characters, sets and props. I have sympathized with the recent critiques of Erikson's ages and stages approach to life span development for being "Eurocentric" and an implicit reflection of American liberal ideology, yet in my own life I see a whole series of distinctive age/stage life histories. Of course, these are wheels within the wheel, and not entirely independent of one another. The bookish, nonconforming, somewhat risk-seeking qualities of the child and youth show up all through adulthood, but if they have persisted through radically different circumstances, is it because they were so unaccountably strong to start with, or because I just consistently lucked out with relationships and events along the way?

In this autobiography, Fritz Heider handles this sort of issue by concluding that he must have had a mischievous angel watching over him. I have neither the achievements nor the character required to support such a conclusion, but I am prepared to acknowledge more than a bit of mystery.

5

The Orpheus Legend and Its Surprising Transformations

Donald P. Spence

From as far back as I can remember, the Greek myth of Orpheus and Eurydice has always carried a special meaning for me, and I find it coming to mind in any number of situations. The story, as everyone knows, tells how Orpheus traveled to the underworld to bring back his former wife; how his wish was granted on the one condition that he not look back until they had reached the upper world (or, in some versions, had crossed the River Styx); how, when he saw sunlight approaching, he realized that they were almost safe; and how, forgetting that she was still several steps behind him (and therefore not quite out of danger), he turned too soon. He saw her slowly slip out of sight, lost forever.

Why this myth and why its fascination? Could it be (and Freud has made the same point) that my fascination with the myth and my attempts to construe each new version are attempts to repeat and also change some long-ago happening? What form did it take—this long-ago encounter—and when did it take place? To write a memoir like this is an attempt to discover some of these answers.

Each time the myth has surfaced in my life, it has taken on a somewhat different version. When I was in the seventh grade, we had just moved to a new apartment on 120th Street and Amsterdam Avenue (in Manhattan), much closer to Teachers College where my father was a professor. Moves always upset my mother and this move, combined perhaps with the pressure of endless decisions that surround any change, proved one of the worst. All during the fall, we had the sense that she was somehow slipping away from us—smiling less, talking less, going off on long walks by herself, going to church alone—in all these ways, much unlike her usual self. The days were also getting darker, and she loved sunlight, plants, and flowers; the change to Standard Time was the final blow. She took to her bed and not long after, she was taken off to the hospital with what was called a "nervous breakdown." My clearest memory of this time goes back to a cold, overcast afternoon in early winter when my father asked me to take my sister Carol (four years younger) out for a walk so that she would be out of the way when our mother was being taken away. I felt honored by the assignment but also frightened by what my sister wasn't supposed to see; what were they afraid would happen? We walked down Amsterdam toward 125th Street and I have a clear memory of wondering how far to go, what was happening back in the apartment, and when we would see her again. When we came back, she was gone.

As I begin to reconstruct that winter, all memories from that time seem overcast, like the day I took Carol for a walk. Most frightening of all was a moment, close to the time my mother left, when my father and I were in my bedroom and we heard a sudden noise, like a venetian blind being rapidly pulled up. My father rushed out of the room (thinking that something awful was happening); I could make nothing of the noise but felt frightened by his sudden rush to the bedroom. I realize now that it was usually the response of other adults during this period that made me concerned; thus, I remember riding to a friend's house, sitting in the back seat, and telling in a conversational way about how my mother had gone off to the hospital. I suddenly was aware that everyone else had stopped talking and were listening in a kind of hushed silence. It seems clear that grownups, all during childhood, become our eyes and ears; much more than our five senses, they become the means we have of discovering the world, and when they seem alarmed or disturbed or more than usually intent, it's a sign that something important has happened. We are now beginning to realize how serious are the consequences when this link is cut (as in the case of autistic children), and how much of the time, learning what really counts is mediated by someone else.

This early rerun of the Orpheus myth—my mother slowly slipping away from us—had a happy ending because even though she had disappeared, she also returned, some time in the spring, and seemed the same as ever. We had done what Orpheus—with all his marvelous charms and talents—could not do. In hindsight, with the advantage of all that is known today about the effects of seasonal change on depression, it now seems clear that my mother was reacting as much to the encroaching darkness (intensified by the fact that the back bedroom, where she spent much of her time, was in a courtyard and cut off from all sunshine) as to the move, and that the use of modern light therapy could well have prevented a trip to the hospital. I am presently treating a patient in just this way, and every fall, when the days grow shorter, I marvel at the effects of ordinary fluorescent light— better than any drug.

A second time the myth surfaced came during the middle of basic training in the army. It was the fall of 1944, not long after the Normandy invasion, and I had been assigned to the 71st Division at Fort Benning, Georgia, learning how to be a radio operator. One day our commanding officer got a call from the Signal Corps of the 14th Armored Division; they needed a small number of replacements and I was chosen to go. Not bothering to wonder why the rush, we traveled all night, daydreaming about life in the Signal Corps and its vast store of high-tech, highly mobile AM and FM receivers and transmitters—and all safely out of harm's way. We arrived at the base in Kentucky to find that the division was busily packing up and on the verge of pulling out and going overseas! Our group was sent down to Signal Corps HQ and lined up, army fashion, in alphabetical order. The noncom began calling off names and making assignments and once again, I saw Eurydice—this time in the guise of a highly touted position in the Signal Corps—gradually fade from sight. By the time the sargeant got around to calling the S's, all Signal Corps positions were gone. Those of us remaining were assigned to a troop of mechanized calvary (armored cars) with the assignment of forming the point—lead vehicle—of an armored column once we got into battle. In less than five minutes, I had gone from the hopes of a rear-echelon position in Signal Corps HQ to the reality (and the worries) of becoming a radio operator at the head of an armored column.

The most recent time the myth has surfaced took place in the course of setting up an electronic mail link between Rutgers and Yale. The task was complicated by the fact that Rutgers is part of one network, Yale part of another, and only certain kinds of messages can cross the network boundary. We thought we were in contact and able to speak back and forth; then we discovered that while one of us could both send and receive, the other could only send brief notes; the bulk of the message would disappear. Once again, I had the sense that Eurydice was fading from sight.

I am slowly learning that when that happens—when a connection is lost or an open channel is closed—I react with more than the normal amount of concern and dismay. Several years ago, when my mother was expecting eye surgery and seemed to be moving into another depressive state, I made arrangements to have her seen by a recent graduate of our residency program (in psychiatry) at the medical school. He agreed, saw her once, and made arrangements for further meetings, but in the meantime, she became quite distressed and I needed to reach him quickly. Long after I left a message on his answering machine—more than 12 hours, as I remember—he called back, and I remember being angry that he had waited so long, and then not believing that, if he had waited so long, he really cared. We switched to another doctor, and he must have wondered why I became so upset.

The Orpheus myth not only weaves a thread all through my childhood and adult life, but it can also be read as a lesson in how things are not always what they seem to be. So long as Orpheus does not look back (and therefore sees nothing), Eurydice is safe and all is well; once he looks back (and sees her), she is gone. Not only are appearances deceiving but what is called

psychic reality (the play of the mind) may sometimes be a better guide to
the world than the standard five senses. The trick is to know when to believe
in one and when in the other.

How are appearances deceiving? Rear-echelon Signal Corps positions
could turn, overnight, into front-line assignments; E-mail connections could
suddenly break down and prove disappointing. Surfaces which look one way
from one angle could mean something quite different from another. One of
my favorite examples comes from E. M. Forster's *A Passage to India*. Aziz,
the Indian physician who wants to be everyone's friend, is visiting a Mr.
Fielding and chatting with him as he gets dressed. When Fielding accidentally spoils his last collar stud, Aziz immediately offers him one of his own,
pretending that he has some to spare. What he does, in fact, is to take off
the one he is wearing, hoping that his collar will stay in place during tea.
Teatime rolls around, his collar starts misbehaving, and all of the well-bred
guests are quick to notice. "Aziz was exquisitely dressed," said one, "from
tie-pin to spats, but he had forgotten his back-collar stud and there you have
the Indian all over: inattention to detail; the fundamental slackness that
reveals the race." What the guests never realize—and what Forster so wonderfully reveals—is that this "inattention to detail" was caused by a spontaneous act of kindness.

Not only are many things seldom what they seem, as the song from Gilbert
and Sullivan would have it, but appearances, I discovered, could often be
transformed into something else, something much closer to what we want
to believe. Starting in fourth grade, I began to collect card tricks and carefully
study the magicians we would see at Christmas parties. One of my father's
friends had made a second career of playing practical jokes on any vulnerable
professional; thus he would gleefully tell of dressing up in overalls, going
up to a dentist's office, and officiously marking up the floor in preparation
for a soon-coming "remodeling." The dentist, of course, had been told nothing of this new plan and his frantic questions were met by an understanding
nod and something mumbled like "I only do what they tell me." I was
fascinated by these stories and the power of suggestion; how quickly could
a sizeable piece of mischief be set in motion. Many years later, while in
France and moving up to the 7th Army front at night, sitting in the back of
a jeep, I would amuse myself by pretending that we were really traveling
backwards. (The fact that backwards also meant going away from the front
gave the game a special kind of satisfaction.) I would close my eyes, force
myself to believe that we were driving backwards, and then open them; I
would always be greeted by a kind of sudden shock when the "backward"
world started going forward. The shock was both startling and amusing and
took my mind off my gradually numbing hands and feet—and wondering
about what was in store for us when we arrived.

Thinking along these lines reminds me of another misunderstanding which
could be a metaphor for the general theme. One of my frequent jobs as

radio operator was to tune the receiver to a standard frequency and in the course of this tuning, we would start with a high pitch and then slowly turn the dial until the whistle had reached its lowest point. When this was done several times, starting at a high whine and then rapidly descending, it sounded almost exactly as if we were under attack from incoming artillery fire. More than once, men in our unit—particularly those who had seen a lot of combat—would drop to the ground when we started tuning our receivers, and even though we would try to warn them in advance that the sound meant nothing that was life threatening, they would still be unable to remain standing. Much more than appearances were involved here; they were also suffering from a kind of conditioning that they had no control over and could do nothing to disregard.

EARLY YEARS

In going back over favorite stories that I remember and used to read, I am always impressed by the special magic I find in illustrations. Looking at old editions of *Treasure Island* or *Winnie-the-Pooh* brings back some special feeling that doesn't belong to the words alone. I have always assumed that this power comes from the fact that pictures spoke to me long before words did; that since I could recognize objects long before I learned to read, the pictures of a story became the windows to what it was about. I also must have looked at the pictures while I was being read to and associated them with many of the feelings aroused by the story.

What pictures? What comes to mind first are illustrations from the *Arabian Nights* by Maxfield Parrish, and those from *Treasure Island* and *Kidnapped* by N. C. Wyeth. Long after I finished the book or heard the story read aloud, I would go back to the pictures and search for what else was there that hadn't been mentioned. Each illustration was, for me, a kind of looking glass into another world which could, if studied long enough, show the way to whatever was hidden beneath appearances; each face, if looked at long enough, would tell something of what the person was thinking and feeling. Some pictures even remind me now of where I was and where we were living when I first saw them, just as Walker Percy, in his book *The Moviegoer*, has his main character remember in what part of New Orleans he saw this or that movie.

One particular moment keeps coming to mind—a wonderful discovery. My father was reading to me from, I think, *Winnie-the-Pooh* and I was looking at the drawings. We paused on one, for some reason, and my father began to draw in a balloon over Robin's head. By putting words inside the balloon, he showed me how we could read his mind and tell what he was thinking. Other balloons could be used to show conversation, and in this way, you could be transported into some other world, past or present. I was astonished, not only because of the possibilities of time travel, but because up to that point, I had thought that pictures were real and unchanging as pieces of the world. When he showed how you could make pictures become something else, I felt as if we had walked through another looking glass. (Many years later, when I began to write stories, I had the same feeling about words.)

Trying to get behind the looking glass of the illustration can also be seen as a metaphor for writing this memoir. Different scenes occur to me as I think back, but each is somewhat fixed and frozen, disembodied from the stream of happenings that must have surrounded it at the time it happened. To get into the picture again is probably one mark of a successful autobiography that discovers even as it describes. Several years ago, I experimented with remembering a key incident—an accidental, wheels-up, airplane landing in the Colorado Rockies—under different surrounding or enabling conditions and was not surprised to discover how the surroundings would affect the nature of the memory, the way it was recalled, and some of its more important details. This experience led me to believe that certain memories will always remain opaque, nothing more than pictures, unless they happen to resonate in some way with the conditions that prevail as they are being remembered. When that happens—which is largely a matter of luck—the pictures or memories become more plastic, transparent, and accessible; the world behind the mirror opens up and a new voyage begins. Modern computers, in an ironic way, hold out the same promise—and frustration. When first learning your way around a new program, everything will seem chaotic and unyielding until a lucky key stroke opens a new window which displays a new list of possibilities—a new menu—and the game is afoot.

Now we come closer to one of the ways in which the act of remembering changes what is being remembered. I don't simply call up memories as I would retrieve a file from a floppy disk; I first find a space to house them and if the space is right, the memory comes alive and may change in the process. When I was remembering the wheels-up landing in Colorado, the details being included would depend on the overall context. When the fit was good, I remembered more than I thought was "there" and surprised myself by recalling things that seemed to appear for the first time. It may be, in view of this line of argument, that attempts to remember the past or write an autobiography in chronological order, while logically appealing, may only get in the way because clock or calendar time may be the least important thread holding the past together. I see that in myself; I am (at this moment) rapidly losing interest in presenting a time line of my life because themes like the Orpheus myth or the importance of appearances seem much more compelling.

But to stay with the early years for a little longer—one of the important "presences" of our apartment on Morningside Drive, when I was in grammar school, was the danger of Morningside Park. To get to school we would walk the length of the drive to 122nd Street, then go down the stairs and across a corner of the park. Safe enough under most conditions, but never at night and sometimes not even during the day. The first year we lived in the city, when I was in fourth grade, I had been roller-skating by myself on a Saturday afternoon when I was knocked down and robbed; three or four boys had come up from the park below, grabbed my skates, and disappeared over the railing. It all happened in front of the window of a barber shop, and I remember seeing the barber looking out—and doing nothing. In a state of helpless rage, I walked the five blocks down to my father's office, found his secretary (who told me he was busy somewhere else) and then stood tongue-tied when she asked me if there was a message. I couldn't think of a dignified way to tell him (and her) that I had just lost my skates, so I shook my head and turned and walked back home. (I don't think I ever told him that part of the story.)

The park and its dangers were in our minds all the time, and even in daylight, some kind of strategy was essential. On the way to school in the morning, I would plan my route along the drive in such a way that I would meet other classmates at 119th and 120th streets so that we had a big enough crowd before we started down the stairs. But at night, it was a different story, especially after I started seventh grade. Because the school had no playing fields to speak of, the soccer and football teams had to be bussed up to Van Cortlandt Park (around 242nd Street in Riverdale) for practice and to play other teams, and by the time we got back, it was completely dark. To go home, we would avoid the park entirely and walk up Amsterdam.

But the danger was also a challenge. One Saturday morning, around fifth or sixth grade, a friend and I decided to skate around the periphery of the park but kept it a secret until we got home. Nothing much happened but we were left with a wonderful sense of having accomplished something important, as if we now no longer needed to be afraid of that thing lying below our window. But its presence would never quite go away. On summer nights when our windows were open (they looked east, over the park and toward the East River), we often heard police or ambulance sirens from somewhere in Harlem. And the quickest trip to certain parts of the city was the A train which stopped just a few blocks from school. Here again this was a safe route by day but, because it crossed a corner of Harlem, doubtful by night.

Something else is happening as I write. As I discover things about my past and how parts are connected in ways I hadn't realized before, I want to celebrate this discovery (i.e., come back to the present) and not stay with a dutiful recounting of everything that happened. Is that because the park and its dangers is making me uneasy all over again? I realize that jumping around in this way makes for a disjointed narrative but also (for me) a much more exciting one, and if I don't come back to the present now and then, I am afraid that certain insights will disappear forever. As I continue this account, I am getting a clearer feeling for when I am here, in the present, and when I can go back in time and lose myself in a memory. It's a new sensation for me, this shifting of time frames, and reminds me a little of changing focus from near to distant vision. And I'm beginning to recognize different layers of sensations that belong "back there." Some of the time, I feel very close to the early experience and feel as if I can trust my recollection and let it carry me back into the scene. At other times, I feel the memory is more opaque, less easily entered, and I am more doubtful of telling the truth about it, or of adding anything new to the recollection. The opaque memories, it occurs to me, may be largely screen memories—one of Freud's earliest discoveries (the fool's gold of the past) because they are scenes which never happened in the first place.

SAVING LIVES

The Orpheus myth shows up in yet another way—in my fascination with saving lives. On my second summer back from the army, I was working as a swimming counselor in a children's camp in the Adirondacks, and we organized a supper party at the edge of the Au Sable River at a place called Ralph's Chasm. It was long after dark when we finished eating, put out the fire, and started back to our cars along a trail that climbed steeply along the edge of the gorge. You could hear the river in the dark, far below us. The man leading the way must have been using his flashlight to follow the line of branches overhanging the trail instead of looking down on the ground, because about half-way back to the parking lot, he stepped over the edge in the blackness and fell some 100 feet down to the river.

All of us were stunned. We had to find him—somehow—but the darkness and the suddenness made it seem unreal. Before I quite knew what was happening, I was sliding down the bank, checking my fall from time to time by catching roots and branches, until I finally reached the water. There— miraculously—was Dave, mostly unhurt. Somehow—but I have no clear memory of how—we climbed back to the top, where I saw that he had two enormous black eyes (they must have been caused by hitting the water full on the face). Striking water instead of rocks might have helped to save his life.

Going down into a black gorge with a flashlight and the hope that he was still alive—could anything have been more like a re-enactment of the Orpheus myth? And yet even though the parallels seem almost mawkishly obvious, it wasn't until this present moment of trying to put that memory into words that I was aware of the link. I knew, of course, in a general way, that saving lives could be seen as a kind of undoing of the myth, but the specific details of that particular time are uncanny in their correspondence to the original story. And I'm not even sure that at the time, I was aware of the Orpheus myth and the central place it was playing in my life. The skeptic could accuse me of revising my memory to suit my story, but there is no ambiguity about the fact that Dave fell into a gorge, that it was night, and that I went after him in the dark, mostly by feel. Parallels to the underworld seem quite natural. And once again, I did the myth one better.

And there have been other times as well. We were tying up our sailboat one Sunday on the Hudson when an old friend came by in his power boat and invited us to come along for a swim. He anchored a little farther up river and some of those on board went over the side on rubber floats. They hadn't realized that the tide was coming in, and the current soon swept them upstream from the boat at a speed faster than they could swim against it. My friend, Howard, started to swim back to the boat, but soon began to tire and started to shout. I was still on board. I didn't know how to start or navigate his boat so I looked around for some other way to help. Finding the longest rope I could see on deck, I tied one end to the rail and swam the other end up river, with the current. When the rope pulled taut, I dropped it and swam on alone. I quickly caught up with Howard and started pulling him back with a cross-chest carry (I had taken a course in life saving when I was working at the camp). But it was hard work because he was taller than I and much heavier, not at all the kind of quiet "victim" we practiced on during life saving class. About the time I was starting to lose my breath, we reached the end of the rope floating in the water. I grabbed the end; those still on board started to pull; and very slowly they hauled us back to the boat. Howard started the motor, raised the anchor, and we quickly picked up the others still in the water.

After the first rescue and even more with the second, I began to realize what makes people want to join first-aid and ambulance squads and volunteer fire departments. To be able to save a life or prevent a small accident from becoming worse—this comes very close to working a miracle. But the victim, I soon learned, is not always grateful; some are ashamed that it happened in the first place and don't want to be reminded; others remember the rescue but don't want others to know. The Hollywood-style parade for homecoming heroes is more true of the movies than the way things actually happen. I've heard the same story from others.

But these adventures pale alongside a story I heard several years ago from a Harvard classmate. He was an enlisted sailor and happened to be far below decks on the U.S.S. *Oklahoma* on Pearl Harbor morning—he may have been sleeping. When the Japanese attacked, the ship sank, rolled over, and my friend and about 18 others were trapped in a compartment as the water was leaking in and slowly rising. They tapped against the outside skin of the ship (which, by this time, was out of water) and, miraculously, someone heard them. Not only were they rescued, but they have had a regular reunion every year since 1941. Not surprisingly, I find that I make a special point of collecting (and telling) stories of this kind. Once again, it seems like a way to remake the Orpheus myth.

RALPH

I had a dream about my father last night—one of the very few times I have dreamt of him since his death in the fall of 1990. In the dream, he was reading through the *American Dictionary of Biography* (if there is such a thing), and he seemed lonely and somewhat sad. I told him that we all loved him and thought about him often and he seemed cheered to hear this. Reading about biography seems an obvious link to writing autobiography, and the dream reminded me of how his death—now some 12 months ago— is still casting a shadow over what I'm thinking and feeling and is certainly affecting the shape of this memoir. I've recovered from the first sadness and shock, but I'm still discovering delayed effects—like a forgotten conversation that suddenly comes to light.

I think I've called him Ralph all my life, and that's something that deserves a little space in its own right. My sister and I grew up calling our parents by their first names and it wasn't until we were well into high school that we began to realize that there was something unusual about this practice. For us, it was simply what children did. Grandparents were different—first names would be out of the question—but even aunts and uncles went by their given names. What was more, my father was born on April Fool's Day, which made his birthday the perfect time for joke and surprise—not respect. Thinking about respect, I remember walking with him across campus to his office and being impressed by how much notice he received from other students and faculty. One day he walked me down to my fourth grade class, and my teacher (who must have known him from Teachers College) was almost speechless in her attempt to greet us. This made a big impression on me (another time when I found myself watching and learning from grown- ups). Of course, when something like that happened, I would shudder at the thought that back home, we called him by his first name—that seemed almost indecent, a kind of enormous secret that nobody must know. Once I began to realize that first-naming your parents was not the usual thing to do, I began to be more careful about when and where I did it, and when someone did overhear it, I would brace myself for the reaction. Carol and I quickly learned that it was not something you would do around grandpar- ents, and a surprising number of our friends heard it as a kind of brattish insolence, the sign of a spoiled child. (A good lesson in how things are seldom what they seem.)

But to return to Ralph's death and its effect on this memoir. Several years before it happened, he was getting more and more impatient with his growing lameness and his retreat from cane to walker, from walker to wheelchair, and from wheelchair to bed. An early follower of the Hemlock Society, he began to collect all the information he could find on ways of doing yourself in—with plastic bags, by drowning in a drug-induced stupor, or by taking pills. We would find ourselves back in the apartment after Sunday dinner, having an unreal conversation about ways to "do it," and even though he wanted my mother to join him, she always held back and let him do all the talking. Each conversation was just like the last until finally, one day, they stopped—for some reason he had lost interest. Perhaps he lost interest in trying to convince us, or perhaps his world, filled more and more with discomfort and often pain, had begun to retreat to the point where nothing outside the pain could be thought about.

Against this backdrop, his death, when it came, was both a shock and a relief. I've often found myself wondering what would have happened *had* we helped him carry it out and how such an act would have left us not only with his loss but with the burden of having brought it about—a terrible thought that might never go away. But despite all this, his death was, of course, a wrench with a jolting effect on my mother; thus it was with a kind of wonderment that I first dreamed about him last March, and then again last week (November).

I have noted how the dream was probably influenced by this memoir, but another way to read it—more primitive, perhaps, but with its own charm—is to believe that since he is reading the *Dictionary of Biography*, he must have "known" what I was up to and was trying to "help" with the "research" (and that would have been in keeping with his life's work). Who is to say whether this reading is wrong? The standard wisdom is that the dreamer dreams his dream, but since there is always a lot that can never be explained, it is sometimes hard to rule out help from other sources. And that line of thought—taking dreams as messages—has a much longer history than any other (but little in the way of systematic research).

Another effect of his death comes out in the way I think about him across the years. When I imagine being back in fourth grade and walking alongside him across the Columbia campus, being hailed by faculty and saluted by students, always looking *up* at his face to read his expression, hurrying to keep up with his pace—the Ralph in this memory is just simply not the same Ralph who I last saw in a wheelchair or laboriously moving from bed to walker, burdened by arthritis. The same name applies to both figures, but names are deceiving, and in all other respects, the two figures are clearly different people—different shape, different voice, even different cells. And the Ralph of my dream—which one is that? Does he come entirely from my imagination or is he just as real as the Ralph of my memory? If we say yes, then we can be persuaded to listen to what he says. While it's becoming fashionable these days to look for multiple personalities only among disturbed patients, a case could be made for seeing all lives as multiple and always in flux, held together by only a common name and social security number.

Which would seem to suggest another way of looking at mourning and grief. What we are doing, after a death, is not so much attempting to recover the missing person and repair the loss as to replace our most recent image—usually of someone sick, crippled, and in pain—with an earlier image from some happier time. Mourning can also be seen as an attempt to move back in time and put life back into a faded memory or forgotten conversation. It is probably no coincidence that this reading of the grieving process has an almost uncanny resemblance to the Orpheus myth; once again, I am trying to recover something that was lost and part of the past and bring it back into the light of day. And the trick lies in not turning around too quickly—not looking the memory full in the face too soon, because then it will disappear. One of Bergmann's movies (*Fannie and Alexander*) captured this well: The recent dead in the family were always seen out of the corner of the boy's eye and would disappear whenever he turned his head.

The same rule applies to this memoir. I'm beginning to realize that to look a scene full in the face tends to make it disappear and that the more evocative happenings tend to bubble up around the edges and make themselves known quietly. Perhaps this is another reason why following a time line only seems to get in the way and also explains why writing this memoir has taken much more time than I would have expected. I have the feeling that the past only comes alive when your back is turned and scurries out of the way when you go looking for it. Thus a passive stance is the first requirement; once you've achieved that, you best sit and wait for things to happen.

Some time has passed since I wrote the last sentence, and real life has once again shown its unexpected face. Since Ralph died, my mother, Rita, has gradually come back into her true self, and we keep being surprised at how well she survived his death, how tidily she accomplished her own mourning, and how spirited a woman she is now for someone approaching her ninety-sixth birthday. None of this could have been predicted while he was still alive and she was still under his shadow. Part of this rebirth has been a new set of stories about the way things were when I was young and the only child. One Sunday at lunch, we were talking about the summer when I was two and had gone with her to the tuberculosis sanatorium at Saranac Lake (in the Adirondacks) to visit my father. He had been there since early spring when he had been diagnosed with pleurisy and suddenly moved—in great haste—from Manhattan to the North Woods. The only treatment at the time was lots of rest and fresh air, and he spent most of his time flat on his back in a sleeping porch. When we arrived at Saranac, we found rooms in a boarding house with families of other patients (and some recovered patients as well!). Soon my grandmother (Ralph's mother) had news of what was happening and when she heard how we were living, she must have wondered whether it was a good place for a small child. She decided it was not, and my mother may have been relieved to have more time for Ralph. My grandmother came east some time that summer to bring me back home with her to Wisconsin.

I have no memory of the boarding house in Saranac, of any discussion over where I should go, of the trip back to the Midwest or the summer in La Crosse (my aunt Margo, then a teenager, seems to have done most of the baby sitting). But after the Sunday conversation with my mother, I found myself wondering if that moment of leaving on the train had some connection with the Orpheus myth. Something in the way Rita described that moment made me guess that when it came time to say good-by, I might have been looking out the train window, waving to her on the station platform. As we began slowly to move out of the station, she would appear to be getting smaller and smaller until she disappeared—just like the myth. And another similarity—I was powerless to bring her back. Hearing the story this time around—and she brought in more details than I had heard at other times—made me gradually understand its resemblance to the Orpheus legend. Could this early experience have been the source of my fascination with that particular Greek fable? Of my unwitting attempts to relive the myth? The pattern match with Orpheus seems too close to be coincidental, and if this early experience had really taken place, it would explain something that up until only recently had always been a mystery. I was, after all, still puzzled when I began this memoir.

By the time I returned from Wisconsin, Ralph was already back at work and pleurisy never disturbed him again. But he must have been sobered by the experience. He also acquired a lifelong wait-and-see attitude about doctors. The atmosphere at Saranac preached a philosophy of watchful waiting, along with the idea that healing is really out of your hands—all the doctors can do is make you feel better (some of the time). But he was warned, and every working day during the 1930s and 1940s, he would come home for lunch and a nap. The standard watch word in our family was always "Don't get too tired."

His deeper concern—that the pleurisy might some day reappear—was never discussed but was covered over by one of his favorite sayings. "The way to live a long life," he would announce on any number of occasions, "is to have a chronic illness and nurse it faithfully." In that way, you learned to care for yourself and take nothing for granted. He was almost 90 when he died.

What has always puzzled me, given this experience at Saranac, is how casual my parents were about the dangers of tuberculosis when I was growing up. One of my best friends in high school died from it in his twenties; his mother had died earlier; and his father was a recovered patient whom Ralph had first met at Saranac. I would go over to visit on weekends or see them in Vermont on summer vacations (where I lived in a tent with David) and my family helped make the arrangements. It seems now that polio was thought to be more of a menace; one of my friends needed a wheelchair all through high school and the news reels were full of pictures of iron lungs and crippled children. But tuberculosis was just as infectious and just as deadly, and there was no good medicine for either until after the war.

It was almost as if we had paid our dues and were safe; Ralph had spent time at Saranac, and in some magical way, that stay had immunized the family, and now we could come and go as we liked. But to polio we were as vulnerable as the next family and as a result, much more concerned.

Another thought. Tuberculosis has always been a much more romantic disease and that reputation—mostly false, of course—may have added to our complacency. From *La Bohème* to *The Magic Mountain*, tuberculosis had acquired a fanciful reputation and was, in some peculiar way, seen as more of a happy accident than a curse. Polio never had that kind of association; it crippled young, and if it didn't lead to an iron lung for life, it left the victim disabled and often disfigured. It was the single greatest terror of my childhood.

My first look at it took place shortly after we had moved back to the city, at the beginning of the fourth grade. One Saturday, I was invited to lunch with a boy of my age (his parents and my parents were friends from somewhere), and when I was brought into his bedroom, he was sitting erect, braced upright in some sort of white jacket, and could only eat by using one hand to help the other. His mother brought us lunch; I wasn't very hungry. After that we played chess, and I marveled at how small, soft, and white his hands seemed—and how one was almost completely useless. I kept turning to look at the bedclothes to make out the shape of his legs and wondering, what did they look like? Were they as shrunken as his hands and as childlike?

What I remember most about the visit was the great feeling of relief once I left the apartment. Once out on the street, I raced back home some seven or eight blocks, never stopping for breath and hardly pausing for street lights, as if I had just escaped from prison. I behaved as if paralysis was catching and the longer I sat next to him in his bedroom, the sooner I would be sick myself. To run all the way home was to prove that I could still use my arms and legs and hadn't been affected. I never went back. And I never forgot the look of their apartment house; even years later, when I went by on the bus, I would always be reminded of that lunch.

If polio was the great danger, school work was the biggest island of safety—especially reading and arithmetic. One of Ralph's best friends was a statistician and after visiting England one summer, she brought back a book titled *Mathematical Recreations and Essays* by an English mathematician with the wonderful name of W. W. Rouse Ball. It included pieces on the tower of Hanoi, the magic rings puzzle, string figures, and my favorite chapter, a piece on magic squares and how to construct them. It turns out that there is a perfectly standard formula for constructing odd-sided magic squares (3 × 3, 5 × 5, etc.) and by following a few simple sequence rules, everything falls into place. You begin with a 1 in the middle cell of the top row; then drop to the bottom row and keep working in a northeast direction, up and to the right. If everything goes well, the median number of the set will fall on the middle cell of the middle row. I thought this was deeply magical, partly because it was so simple, and I got good enough to make squares as large as 25 × 25. I don't think I got much beyond that.

For reading, we had the faculty book club. Every morning on the way to school, riding down in the elevator, I would see a set of books in brown wrappers piled on the bench on the back of the elevator cab. Fixed on the front of each book was a list of names and when our name came up, the books would turn up at our doorstep—two or three every other week. All through high school I felt as if I were on the shore of a river of reading that slowly and steadily moved forward, tempting me to put my hand out and catch whatever was going by. The pick was mostly nonfiction and strangely varied—but a good introduction to what was out there, and every so often, I found something that was hard to give up and pass on to the next family. One of the books that I still remember was called *Out of the Night*—a first-person account of life in a Soviet prison.

Along with this branch of letters, I was addicted to the *Saturday Evening Post* and especially to its serials. Each week began for me with the day the new issue came out—I think it was Wednesday—and there, with luck, would be one long continued piece by J. P. Marquand and perhaps another by Nordoff and Hall. Each serial would continue for six to ten issues, and if I didn't wake up early on Wednesdays and go down to the dock (as people did in the nineteenth century when Dickens was writing in installments), I would certainly pounce on the new issue as soon as I came home from school. There was a certain way you curled the front part of the magazine around behind the rest of the pages to make reading easier, and the hefty feeling of many pages (copies were always fatter around Christmas and other holidays) added to the excitement. Here again the illustrations were part of the magic, and there was always an electric moment when, in reading the text, I would come across the incident that inspired the picture. I would turn back to the front of the magazine, compare my picture of the moment to what the artist had drawn, and have something of the same experience I would have in the army, riding in the back of the jeep. If my image didn't quite match (which was usually the case), I would have a brief sense of puzzlement and surprise before everything fell into place.

Time to stop. Perhaps the biggest lesson I've learned from all this is a renewed sense of the plastic essence of memory and how easily it can be fitted into a particular narrative frame. There are so many ways of moving from happenings to words that once a particular theme has surfaced—such as the Orpheus myth—then almost everything seems to connect. If the theme is powerful enough, it may be impossible not to find an association. And because the memory is itself influenced by language, it becomes tempting to "remember" other pieces of what happened that seem to fit the larger picture, all the while being aware that context may be controlling recall.

All of which is to say that as the result of writing this memoir, I have begun to see the past in a different way, more connected than I had realized. The most exciting moment came when I had lunch with my mother and suddenly became aware of what might have been the cause of my fascination with the Orpheus myth—looking out the train window and watching my mother slowly fade into the distance. This discovery would not have happened unless I had been in the midst of writing the memoir at the time when we had lunch. Once again, context is controlling. And I had no idea, on the point of beginning the memoir, that I would be making this kind of discovery. I wonder what other discoveries lie ahead?

6

A Memory of Games and Some Games of Memory

Brian Sutton-Smith

THE SCHOLARLY RECORD

There are multiple ways in which to discuss one's scholarship as well as multiple ways in which to tell stories about it. There is no one scholarship and no one story. I begin this account believing that I am telling you the truth about my scholarship, and that what follows is not just a fiction. However, you must know, as well as I do, on psychodynamic or mnemonic grounds, that I cannot possibly be telling you the truth nor possibly know what that truth is. What I will hope to show is that truth in any scientific sense is not really what this is all about anyway.

But, again, for my comfort and yours I will begin this story by trying to state what the public record shows my scholarship to have been about and I will do that by a brief content analysis of the titles of my articles. At least then we will know what it is that must be explained or storied. Of approximately 300 items, including articles, books, chapters, and reviews, over half have been on the topics of children's play and games. If the topics of children's toys, drama, folklore, film making or stories are added to play and games, the count is about 80 percent for all of these items of children's expressive culture. Most of the 20 percent left has been on the topics of sibling relationships, gender differences, or developmental psychology.

This count is easily verifiable from one's curriculum vita. A 1991 survey by Christie of the way in which this work appears in the *Social Sciences Citation Index* for the years 1976 to 1989 shows that those who have consulted this work have quoted the material on child expressiveness (80 percent) only twice as much as the much lesser body of work on sibling relationships and gender concerns (20 percent) (Christie, 1991). From which we gather that the imbalance between play (expressive culture) and orthodox seriousness (siblings and gender) in this scholarly count is not appreciated as much by the reading social science public as it is by the author. This serves, I believe, to make the point that what must be explained about this scholarship is its overwhelming focus on play, and so on, despite the relatively greater social science approval of the author's other work and despite also the relatively low attention and status that this subject matter (play) has had in the history of child psychology.

THE SCHOLARLY FOCUS

Unfortunately, it is not sufficient simply to announce that one has been persistently interested in play and to find out why. The topic is sufficiently ambiguous and multilayered that we need to know also what kind of approaches have been taken by the author to this subject matter. It seems generally agreed that my own work has been eclectic. Thus, Schwartzman says, "Sutton-Smith has shown an almost unique flexibility in his studies exhibiting his adoption of a variety of research orientations (folklore, anthropology, sociology, and psychology). Sutton-Smith is also significant for his attempts to study changes in games over time or variations in games from society to society, rather than emphasizing the universality and similarity of games in all historical periods and cultures (1978, p. 82). And Spariosu: "Although some critics have charged him with a certain theoretical eclecticism or even inconsistency, for Sutton-Smith this eclecticism seems to be a conscious strategy in dealing with a complex and slippery phenomenon that cannot lend itself to any single methodology (1989, p. 202).

Obviously these characterizations need some explanation and that I will reserve for later. In addition I think a good case can be made that my own work throughout has been preoccupied with games, play, and play theory as forms of power. As Spariosu also indicates: He "is highly skeptical of a purely rationalistic interpretation of ludic phenomena. One can discern in his recent work an increasing awareness of the relationships between play and power, and in this he stands apart from a great number of his colleagues in developmental psychology who have a tendency to idealize play" (p. 202).

In my early academic decades (1950–1970), I focused more specifically on the structural development in childhood games of power roles. This was a tracing of the rise and fall of the central person role from high to low power in the folkgames played by children of 5 to 15 years of age in New Zealand. The subsequent Fulbright period in the U.S.A. with the "It" game studies with Fritz Redl and Paul Gump at Wayne State in 1955 were an attempt to interpret games as therapeutic ego control systems.[1] Here, it was the game's power over the player that was the issue. But most importantly, my cross-cultural studies with anthropologist John M. Roberts during the 1960s were meant to result in a book entitled *Games: Models of Power* (1989). Here, the games of physical skill, chance, and strategy were said to model the triad of power forms instrumental to human societies in social decision making. But even in my nonplay studies of these years, I focused upon the power relationships between siblings. My coauthor, Ben Rosenberg, and I were concerned to rectify a tradition in which only first borns were ever studied. Our book concentrated for the first time on the relative power and character of the non-first born. In our book *The Sibling*, we even jokingly included the dedication: "to our older siblings who will undoubtedly regard this as just another form of harassment" (Sutton-Smith and Rosenberg, 1970). Later at Columbia Teachers College, I worked with my student Marylou Savasta on gender differences in power, summing the work by suggesting that the sexes, male and female, tended to specialize respectively on public or private power tactics (Sutton-Smith and Savasta, 1972).

During the 1970s (as indeed Spariosu notes), I became concerned with the rational turn being given to modern cognitive play theory, including a down playing of the kinds of irrationalities that were so familiar in the earlier days of psychodynamic play theory, as well as evident in the historical record. By the 1980s, I began to believe that these rationalistic theories were not just mistakes in emphasis but served as well various rhetorical purposes in the modern domestication of childhood, contributing their own influence, witting or otherwise, to efforts to abandon recess, prohibit playfighting, prohibit war toys, as well as prohibit gender differences in play. Regardless of the intent of any of these movements, I felt that to contend that play was primarily an intrinsically motivational, funful form of personal mastery certainly helped a modern generation of theorists and practitioners to rule outside the play category for children all the older forms of nonsense, festival and rowdiness, as well as many games and sports. By that definition, they domesticated the notion of play and justified their management of play by excluding much of that which had been traditionally associated with play. In tribal life, by contrast, most play is obligatory, not optional as we define it today. The book I am currently writing is a summing up of play theory in the twentieth century from this rhetorical viewpoint (Sutton-Smith, in press). Its general position is that play theory is itself a form of rhetoric or advocacy in social science as much as an empirical undertaking. Which is to say that play theory is a form of power assertion no less than play itself. One might even argue that the phenomenon of play is a kind of labile communication medium, which gives itself to the mediation of power conflicts.

MY PERSONAL BIOGRAPHY OF POWER

From this point in the discussion, I wish to move to the way in which I remember the story of my concern with power in my own personal games rather than with the way my scholarship seems to have catalogued its em-

pirical existence. Despite the salience of my approach to play in terms of
various power discourses, I do not believe that in the beginning I was very
conscious that my emphasis was distinctive in this respect. Role theory was
a commonplace in the 1950s, and an interest in power roles was in no way
unique. Also sport sociology, with which I was associated for many years,
runs a continuing internal debate on who exploits whom in modern sports,
with respect to economics, race, and gender. In more recent festival theory
in folklore and anthropology, as well as in cultural history, there is also the
continuing debate over whether play culture is an opiate or instigation to
cultural revolution. Thinking of children's games in terms of the development
of power roles, therefore, though novel, was not surprising. None of my
colleagues found it so. Furthermore, in the 1960s, I was linked with John
Roberts who had spent a great deal of his mental life absorbed in pondering
the power strategies of human adaptation whether in war or in ordinary life.
It was a most influential colleagueship.

If we move now more tendentiously and psychodynamically to the possible
origins of this interest in games as power, then there are a number of stories
that I have told myself over the years about this interest:

1. The story I began telling myself sometime during those first two adult decades
of research (1950–1970) was that my interest in games and power began in childhood.
The memories that I relied upon at that time had the precedent of the three children's
novels that I had written 20 years earlier toward the end of the 1940s about my
childhood and my play in the streets with three other boys (Sutton-Smith, 1950;
1961; 1976). We played endlessly at the games of rugby, hockey, boxing, and cricket.
I was the youngest, and my brother was the oldest by four years. He was number
one in skill, and he played with number three. I was number four and played with
number two. Statistically, numbers one and three will typically beat numbers two
and four. And indeed, we (two and four) almost always lost, and we were all frequently
injured from falling on the gravel, from the skin off our shins and knuckles because
of the curtain rods and iron bars we used as hockey sticks, or even from the jagged
edges of the flying cigarette tins we used for the hockey ball. These were rough
social play days (1930s), and though I never wanted to be left out of the games, they
were not always at first (particularly boxing) intrinsically motivating for me. I was
there because it was not possible to envisage oneself as one who would be a coward
enough not to participate. The motive for the game was to be one of the gang and
not to lack in courage. It is not surprising that having spent much of my childhood
in such extrinsically motivated play that I do not find much credit in a definition of
play that makes intrinsic motivation the universal requirement for it.

The "functionally autonomous" sequel to this competitive arduousness of social
games was that I went on to be a captain of my elementary school rugby team, and
a member of my high school (Palmerston North Boys High) first rugby 15, as well
as the welterweight boxing champion of my year, 1941, and also placed in the mile
and in the high jump. At the age of 19 years, however, I retired from senior rugby
after my third concussion and switched to soccer, with which I subsequently obtained
a University of New Zealand blue in 1943. I also represented my own Victoria

University of Wellington in basketball and the Wellington Teachers College in softball. I was at that time, not surprisingly, offered the possibility of an educational
career in physical education. This was a highly selective system much sought after
by my peers. All of this indicates the successful side of my addiction to strenuous
physical games.

My attraction to the teachers college and the university in the first place was
motivated by my high school French teacher (Alan Thom) saying that I would particularly enjoy the teachers college because one whole afternoon a week was given
over to games play. I remember being ecstatic over such a possibility in my impending
work life. I should point out that it was war time and much of one's vacation time
away from college was spent helping farmers in their boring routines of weeding
mangols, picking potatoes, digging ditches, harvesting wheat, strawberry picking the
dags from the wool during shearing, picking the wool off dead sheep, etc. In short,
the most parsimonious explanation for my subsequent addiction to games research
is that it continued my earlier addiction to playing games.

2. Although, in the light of the first story just told, the following does seem
somewhat superficial, I have to acknowledge that early in my university student
career I got an unusual 100 percent from Professor Gould of Victoria University of
Wellington for my first essay on play theory, and although I hesitate to think that
that single reinforcement could have carried me so far subsequently, it does show
that I was already evincing an interest in the theoretical side of all this game playing.
It at least suggests that we should begin to look here for multiple rather than single
sources of motivation.

3. Thirty years later in the 1970s, while at Teachers College, Columbia University,
I combined with recreationist Eliot Avedon on the writing of a 1971 book called *The
Study of Games*. As it happened, Avedon was a collector of actual games, ancient
games, board games, etc., which he subsequently formed into a game museum and
with which he traveled around Canada when a professor at the University of Waterloo.
It was a shock for me to realize that I felt toward his enterprise as most other people
felt toward my own game research. I thought it was a kind of trivial absurdity. I had
written earlier about the "triviality barrier" that interferes with most Western people's appreciation for children's play (1970). It was a surprise and a paradox to me
to come upon this very attitude within myself. Much later in the 1980s, when my
grown-up children and some of our own older social friends liked to play social games
(*Trivial Pursuit*, *Charades*, etc.) on party occasions, I realized that I disliked them
and that participating in them had about the same emotionally enforced quality as
my play at games with my brother and streetmates. Now this was a quandary for
me because I had hitherto, unthinkingly, considered my interest in play and games
to be a general one, whereas I was now discovering it was for me very much limited
to theoretical materials about games and play.

4. Again one day in the late 1980s in my graduate folklore course at the University
of Pennsylvania on "Play, Games, Toys, and Sports," an insightful female student
from England, Jane Ashdown, pointed out to me that by and large I seemed to
glorify in accounts of rough male play but almost completely neglected the play of
females. At first, I countered to myself with thoughts of my 1971 book with Rosenberg, *Sex and Identity*, and my 1979 article on "The play of girls," in a feminist
volume. But finally, it occurred to me that she was indeed correct and that through
all of these years I may have been acting somewhat counterphobically with my macho

play accounts. I became aware that while I might enjoy such stories of rough play on an academic level, I certainly had limited taste whatsoever for that kind of behavior in everyday life. Despite my college participation in boxing, I had often congratulated myself for never having had a fight out of the ring since about the age of 11 years and not in the ring either since about 22 years. In sum, my talk might be tough, but my behavior was not. And looking back again at all my childhood and adolescent competitive social gaming, I realized suddenly that for the greater part it had been accompanied by considerable anxiety for days before each impending context. I used to tell myself as an adult that the great value of going into boxing matches when a child was that it was such a terrifying experience, that any such central or public roles in later life were mild by comparison. But perhaps a more appropriate thought for the present paper might be that this whole section, which is devoted to my concern with power in games, may itself be a story I continue to tell myself about toughness. So much of the sociology of sport is devoted to such "tough" and "real" interpretations about the dominance of power in play phenomena that it is hard to resist the view that whatever else they may be, such interpretations are themselves in part expressions of a gender ideology of masculinity.

5. So the synthesizing story here might be that the constant stress and physical pain associated with many years of game play during childhood and adolescence may have had a very different outcome than I had first believed. The critical turning point may have been in 1945 when I turned down the certainty of a fellowship in physical education and took my lower probability chances on winning an educational scholarship and proceeding on to advanced degrees. That is, at the critical point, I took the theoretical, not the practical, alternative in the study of play. The explanation for this choice might have lain not just in my avoidance of the practical and social and dangerous, but also in my more positive childhood experience of intrinsically motivated solitary play, which was the microsphere into which I retreated in Eriksonian fashion from fairly rough social seas described above. In that sphere, I played out endless fantasy games with soldiers, blocks, and plasticene of defending my city against King Kong, who was usually put to death by the soldierly spears (pins) stuck into his plasticene body. My older brother and father spring to mind as potential prototypes for such fierce invasions. It now seems to me that the theoretical study of games in the university may have come to serve a similar purpose as did my imagination in this solitary play. Both allowed an engaging retirement into my own imagination.

6. Another story to be considered is that my predisposition toward game theory rather than praxis was modeled by my father's lifelong contention that he would have preferred to have been a university professor rather than the bureaucrat postmaster of the capital city of Wellington, which he was. Considering that I ultimately realized his ambition, this alternative explanation cannot be put lightly aside.

7. Still, of these various alternative sports (vigorous child games, success in sports, anxiety about competition, withdrawal to solitary play, success in academic play theory, interest in play theory not praxis, father's values), I find it more interesting to hypothesize dialectically that my involvement in games as a *theoretical and academic* problem perhaps became for me a reconciliation of my very considerable conflict over games, which were both the success of my youth and the pain of my childhood. I have come to realize that I was never really very strongly interested in actual games other than the ones I played myself (a fairly normal recreational dis-

position), but I did find myself fascinated by the theoretical problem of the games as such. How were they invented? How could they be invented? What did they mean? In this interpretation, the lifelong conflict between the positive and negative poles of my game experience is resolved by a displacement into an abstract and fairly safe place. Instead of using a formistic metaphor, as in Pepper's formulations (1942), which is to say that games in childhood foster game interest in adulthood, we may instead adopt a dialectical metaphor. The theoretical approach to games then becomes for me the harbor for resolving the conflict between games loved and games hated. Unfortunately, neat as this formulation might be in apparently resolving some of the contraries in the above data, it is beyond the reach of my intuition. It sounds reasonable, but I can offer no personal conviction. And there is the danger that because of my long years with John M. Roberts, with our similar conflict enculturation theory of games (that conflicts induced by child rearing motivate game socialization to develop certain culturally useful behaviors), and my fascination for dialectical explanation, as in my 1978 book of the name *Die Dialektik des Spiel*, I may be just leaning here on a preferred metaphor.

Still, some things seem reasonable. Namely, that my early intensive and later successful game play provided a disposition to be interested in games. My position as a younger brother always on a subordinate level of power with my stronger older brother seems likely to have given me my special interest in games as power. Finally, it is indeed possible that I resolved my conflict over the pleasure/pain that I associated with games, as well as my father's ambitions, by pursuing them rather as objects of scholarship than of everyday reality. And to add a final twist prompted by this present essay, who is to know whether this focus on power in this paper is not itself prompted by the very same macho foci on game power throughout the described game life.

POWER IN SOLITARY PLAY

Games and play are often distinguished in the English language but not in most others. With us, games are often seen as more organized, rule bound, competitive, and extrinsically motivated. Play is seen as more free floating, imaginative, and intrinsically motivated. The distinction may well have had to do originally with the peculiar role given to the relationship between extrinsic game play and morality as it developed in the public schools of nineteenth-century England. Because of it, there is in some quarters an attempt to suggest that games are not really play forms. In a larger historical and anthropological perspective, however, there seems to be little empirical worth in such a firm distinction. Regardless of these scholarly matters, however, as we shall see, the distinction between games and play is strongly emphasized in my own biography and that is the major reason for continuing the distinction here.

During the 20 or so years that I studied games in an empirical way, I assumed that I would one day study play directly. I always felt that play was, in effect, waiting there for me to come and study it. This was, it seems to me now, a rather strangely confident assumption. The reasons seem to have been that much as I respected the strongly psychodynamic versions of play (Freud, Erikson, etc.), they were so often based on abnormality that they seemed to miss much of the material that I had witnessed in my two years of studying New Zealand playgrounds, in particular, the one at Island Bay in Wellington, where I had grown up and gone to school and where for those two doctoral years, I witnessed almost every recess period. I came to the conclusion that while oedipal and other depth psychological materials were quite apparent in such play, they seemed to me to provide the players with a common denominator of fantasy, which was used in the very hard primary work of social construction that the games required. What actually took place in social play were such things as strenuous approach-avoidance social dramas requiring complex metacommunicative skills, as well as tactics both for inclusion and success. The psychodynamic material appeared to be a supplementary fantasy recursion on behalf of social construction. It was perhaps not unlike adults using their national anthem for the purpose of emphasizing community prior to engaging in divisive sports.

Additionally, the cognitive studies of children's play that were emerging in the 1960s seemed to be even more remote from the phenomenon itself. As I saw it, the dominant scholar Piaget made play only an ancillary to thought, whereas for me, play was a cultural dynamic which had its own systems, its own rationalities and irrationalities. One of my first academic papers of 1951 had contrasted New Zealand Maori and European games. Experience with anthropological approaches always makes it difficult to be satisfied with solely psychological explanations for cultural phenomena and that was indeed the character of Piaget's work. Throughout history, play has been dominantly a collective event, not solely a psychological process. In 1963, I spent a year as a visiting professor at Clark University and received great support from Bernard Kaplan and Joseph Glick in formulating my Piagetian critique, which was published subsequently in the *Psychological Review* in 1966 and reassessed again in 1983.[2] The Wernerian psychology at Clark was a system that could apply to multiple areas of human life, not only cognitive but also perceptual, aesthetic, playful. From thence forward, I spent a number of years in pursuit of play as a powerfully autonomous system linked, one supposed, with the very basis of human creativity. It was an exciting time with psychologists such as M. A. Wallach and N. Kogan, Jerome Singer, Nina Lieberman, and Jerome Bruner making important contributions to this connection between play and creative thought; in addition, there was supportive work in comparative psychology and even in anthropology where Reynolds coined the notion of a flexibility complex (1986). I carried out studies on toy novelty, which had an impact on the play and divergent cognition literature, and my wife and I wrote a parental handbook on *How to Play with Children*, which reflected the confidence that many of us felt at that time about the relationship between play and creativity.[3]

Subsequent research has not dealt very kindly with the play creativity connection, which was from the beginning limited by the stilted character of the measures used to capture either the play or the creativity. I have continued in the 1980s with my students pursuing more ethnographic and performance-oriented approaches, convinced as always that there are some more fundamental truths yet to be discovered.[4] My preference currently is for seeking linkages between dreams, daydreams, play, games, sports, the arts, and mythology and the respective roles that they play in the ludic construction of reality. This, it seems, is the proper context for the understanding of play's proto creativity. My approach to play continues to emphasize the eclecticism that was mentioned earlier as a feature of my work. In my own mind, this orientation still seems necessary in order to understand the varied phenomena of play and games. Single disciplines seem to be mostly too insular for their pronouncements to be satisfactory. The origins in my own life of this orientation is not clear to me, except that I have always been this way. I was always attracted to history, to philosophy, to psychology, to education, to literature, to anthropology, and to folklore, and still am. Perhaps New Zealand was a place too far from the center of scholarship to become a world of convincing scholarly hegemonies. A colonial heritage for me was perhaps one of skepticism toward the derivative appearances of British glory. Or perhaps the source was in the split between the hegemonies of my brother and father or the split within my father's own bureaucratic life and his academic ambitions.

What is important here to explain narratively, however, is again the persistence of the importance I now gave to play (from 1970–1990) which I had hitherto given to games (1950–1960). One might say that for me the terms *play* and *games* were almost metaphoric icons in their ontological effects on my life. Perhaps that is the way in which Pepper's formistic metaphor works most successfully, as when scholars and others attribute a kind of concreteness and motivation to their own central ideas. This could be so even when those ideas have the scientific virtues of, say, structuralism and become icons for the movements they sustain.

I suspect that my own making of such a clear distinction between play and games has to do also with the way in which, in my own life, the two spheres of play and games are mapped onto my private and my public lives. Games were in the arduous public sphere. Play was my private sphere and was the one to be defended against intrusion by others. And from what I can remember, this kind of private play was supported by my mother during the preschool period, all of which was spent playing alone inside the house or in the backyard in the five years prior to public school, always waiting for my older brother to come home after school in the hopes of some adventures with him. In particular, I remember being allowed to play with my toys in the off-limits front bedroom and front parlor as long as I did not mess them up. They were the only carpeted rooms in the house. It was a solitary time with few peers ever available. And I continued to cherish that solitary time even in the childhood years in between the spells of vigorous outdoor play with others. One outcome of that activity was prizes for the clay modeling that I did in such private time. In my book *Toys as Culture* (1986), I make a great deal of the rise of solitary play in the twentieth century and the use of toys to sustain that solitariness. Obviously, whatever other rationalizations I present in that book, my own experiences were not irrelevant.

In adult years, I have mapped the same private public distinction onto my scholarship on the one hand and my faculty activities on the other. I am a scholar who prefers to work in his home near his wife of 40 years rather than at the university. I associate the university with social arousal and the infestation of debate, intrigue, and combat. Although not much of an activist, I was an AAUP executive member in one university fight (Bowling Green State University) where we forced the resignation of the president, and for ten years, in another (University of Pennsylvania), I was the chair for the faculty meetings, the chair for the faculty tenure committee, and was required to defend the school against faculty grievances. Faculty life is not as much like a rugby game as solitary scholarly life is like playing with your toys, but the analogues deserve some attention in this narrative. In addition, this public-private dichotomy seems reflected within my own personality as a duality between seriousness and sociability. I tend to reserve the seriousness now for the temperance of my quieter solitary activities and the playfulness where possible for my more conventional academic social activities. There has been something of an inversion in values from childhood to adulthood, with me now being more serious about the private sphere and more mocking in the public sphere. I strongly suspect that my use of humor in the public sphere is a direct derivative of my earlier combative use of words as a younger brother in the power plays of siblinghood. That the public-private distinction might be more than a personal idiosyncrasy, however, is suggested by the writings of philosopher Richard Rorty (1989).

My own interpretations of these phenomena of play and games seems to fit the way my work has been publicly interpreted by Professor Garry Chick of the University of Illinois, who says in his recent Festschrift statement: "In his own work Brian has consistently called for the need and the rights of children to play, but he has also credited children with the ability to recognize the nature of their own play. He acknowledges them for not being simply little tablets of clay onto which the environment impresses itself but actors with their own understanding and interpretation of play and the world, an understanding and interpretation that may differ from that of adults. If anything has characterized Brian's career, it has been an enduring commitment to the pursuit of truth about play, refusing to be deflected by those who would seek to encompass it within their particular political or intellectual agendas . . . an individual who has our respect and gratitude for a lifetime of devotion to a topic that perhaps he above all others has shown to be of such moment and worth (Chick, 1991).

In short, it is possible to say that if my focus on games was upon structural power dialectics, my focus in play has been on the empowerment of the solitary player or, perhaps more antecedently, on his or her defense against disempowerment. But it has been also a focus reflecting my unwillingness to give way to the various encroachments upon play flexibility, encroachments that are often to be found in the educational uses of play, as well as in doctrinaire theoretical persuasions about it. I am of the view that most of what passes for empiricism in both childhood and play research has much to do with the historically derived and underlying rhetorics of the investigators. Thus, both childhood and play tend to be seen through religious eyes, historicist eyes, romantic eyes, determinist eyes, or commercial eyes, and there turns out to be little empowerment for children in any of these. The history of childhood and of play is largely the history of intruding upon them with adult-centered paradigms.

This means that, although treating play quite differently from games, I have begun to give the theme of power centrality in these play studies also. I seem now to be fighting from a more embattled position (as younger brother perhaps), whereas in my studies of the role of power in games and culture, the power stance was more active and less defensive (as in the successful athlete perhaps). So the games and play collapse into the public and private, the serious and in the playful, and into power both offensive and defensive.

STORIES

In 1973 I received a National Institute of Education two-year grant to study the four- to seven-year-old age period as an initiation from private to public life. I was perhaps investigating my private to public distinction again as a developmental transition, although I was not aware of its personal significance at that time. When invited to apply, I saw myself as particularly interested in the social transition that took place in children's play and game life in that age span. My students and I at Columbia University set up shop in Public School 3 in Greenwich Village in downtown Manhattan. We made an arrangement with Principal John Melser (a New Zealand friend of mine), whereby we would engage in special forms of art education (photography, film making, architecture) in return for using the school as a research locus. The school was noted for its attempt to use the arts in education. I should, perhaps, say that I was in these years developing a critique of Project Zero's excessively cognitive view of the arts, a point of view expressed in my presidential address to Division 10, "Psychology and the Arts," in 1984.

In the project, however, what happened was that the larger initiation notion took second place to our collecting stories from children, and our obsession with these narratives preoccupied us until the grant money was done, and we could proceed no longer. The results were published in *The Folkstories of Children* (1981).

In pondering the emergence of this obsession with children's stories, which still persists in my mind and in my research, I told myself that it must have to do with several key events in my own life. First, the children's narratives were perhaps a subset of their play. Catherine Garvey, famed play researcher, once informed me that she could see the themes in these stories being played out in children's play a year or two earlier (Garvey, 1977). Perhaps, then, my study of stories was the study of play under another guise. Second, I began writing stories for children when I was a teacher in 1948 at age 24 years. I recollected that my father had often been a story teller to my brother and me when young. He would sit on the bed and tell us hilarious stories about a naughty dog that created havoc in the grocery store. I was told by my father that his father had been the village story teller in Scottish Waikouaiti, New Zealand, in the 1890s, where he was the local saddlesmith. He would tell his stories to a group of village children on Sundays. Remembering all of this in the 1970s, I began to assume that I was continuing in a family tradition, having likewise made up stories for my own five children when they were young. The constancy here was presumably a contextual one, going from grandparent to parent to child.

But there seems to be more to this story. Since publication of the stories, I have lectured extensively on them, contending that one of the things that cuts children's writing off at the faucet is that parents and teachers will not allow children to tell the stories they wish to tell. Instead, they impose respectability upon them and so deprive the children of much of the motivation they might otherwise have. My collections and former ones clearly demonstrate that when given their opportunity, children like to tell stories of disaster and disorder and that if permitted to do this, as they were in our PS 3 project, they often rise to great heights of narration (see Pitcher and Prelinger, 1963). I have become very fond of some of the best of these stories we collected and have taken some delight in performing them. My high point was a recitation to the first International Conference on Sexology in Montreal in 1976, when the laughter of the English listeners would be quickly overtaken by the appreciative roar of the French listeners getting their translation a few moments later. For example here is one by a four year old, which I particularly treasure:

> Once there was a dragon
> Who went poo poo on a house
> And the house broke
> Then when the house broke the people died
> And when the people died

Their bones came out and broke
And got together and turned into a skeleton
And then the skeletons came along
And scared the people out of the town
And then when all of the people
Got scared out of the town
Then the skeleton babies were born
And then everyone called it Skeleton town
And when they called it Skeleton town
The people came back
And then they got scared away again
And then when they all got
scared away again
The skeletons died
No one came to the town
So there was no people in that town
Ever again.

And here is the beginning of a story from a seven year old:

Once there was two babies
And they hung from the ceiling naked
And their weenies was so long
Their mother need 300 and 20 rooms
To fit half of it in.
But they had to chop half of it off.
And the baby had to go to the bathroom
So since they didn't have no bathroom
Big enough for his wiener to fit
He put his wiener out the window
And Nixon happened to be walking along
And he said:
"Flying hotdogs, I never heard of it. . . ."

In advocating that children be allowed to tell their own stories and performing them myself in lectures so that parents or teachers could know what it was they were doing, I was, of course, running against pedagogic tradition, which prefers to use such narrative phenomena for the purpose of more mundanely conceived and respectable socialization. While I was always politely received in putting forth this viewpoint, I never had the feeling that very many were going to make a positive response. And I told myself also that the deep puritanism in our attitude toward children was more than I could circumvent. It was a surprise to me, however, when, in Europe recently, a respected colleague told me that she thought it inappropriate for one of my status to be expressing himself in this fashion. And although I quickly put this response down to that pompous conservatism that I associate with traditional academia, I have now given it second thoughts and believe that once again, as in the case of the games, there might well be another personal narrative that is of importance here.

My children's stories, which first appeared in the central education department's journals, providing reading material for grade two New Zealand children, caused a great uproar in the 1949 newspapers, arousing discussion in parliament.[5] They were said to be full of slang and immoral happenings. As I saw it, the stories were the pursuit of the timeless in my childhood (after Wordsworth) interspersed with the impropitious (after Mark Twain). They involved such mild misdemeanors as sneaking into movies through the exit, hitting cricket balls over fences and breaking windows, playing rugby and inadvertently breaking the bones of sissy players, accidentally smashing up the furniture at a birthday party, having an underground fort's construction foiled by its placement in a dog cemetary, climbing through private yards by night, throwing eggs on shop fronts and running away from home. The contents were discussed in parliament in 1948 prior to an impending election, and the chapters were soon withdrawn from further publication in the school journal, although, as a result of the uproar, they were soon published separately as books. At the time, my mother reminded me that although the stories were full of typical boyish escapades, our own boyhoods had really been quite respectable—going to school, Sunday School, earning prizes, and so on.

Again public, the critique of these stories in 1949 now reminds me of how my later work on my Ph.D. thesis involved interviewing children about their games, in the course of which I was often told their stories and jokes. When I wrote the thesis, I included a chapter attempting to deal developmentally with their humor, some of which was obscene. My approach (1949–1951) was not unlike that taken in 1954 by Wolfenstein, giving much of it a psychoanalytic interpretation. Subsequently, I was required to eliminate this portion of the thesis by my professorial advisor because of the offense it might bring to the elected education boards who, he said, "happening upon this study in the library might in consequence prevent further research in schools." Another professional advisor, also involved in my work at that time, suggested that my "originality" (sic) would probably make it inadvisable to seek a future appointment at that university. And yet another colleague of that day has said more recently that in conservative New Zealand I was probably regarded as too much of a "risk" for such major appointments.

So, all in all, it is worth my taking seriously the possibility that I am given sometimes to unconventional self-expression, and therefore, it is worthwhile for the purposes of this account for me to dig deeper to get another autobiographical account for this chapter. My father, who told stories of naughty animals to us at bedtime and who was himself a most appropriate civil servant, was also an amateur thespian, and we would see him occasionally performing onstage as a buffoon along with the school headmaster and school secretary at the annual elementary school concert. After he had told us his bedtime story, my brother would retell the story usually with added scatology. He was a most rebellious brother, and in effect, I had two fathers growing up, the appropriate one (with much theater and humor as well as propriety) and the older brother with constant rebellious humor. My brother's rebelliousness I take to have occurred because of my father's pressure on him to do well at school and proceed into professional life. My brother, on the contrary, wished to become a farmer and revolted against most school-related requirements. He subsequently became a farmer.

With both brother and father, I learned to make wisecracks as a relatively powerless response to their orthodoxies of this or that kind. On rare occasions, my father would chastise me for my "impudence." And my brother would punch me excessively for the same thing. I nearly always had a bruised left shoulder from his punches. Amidst the speeches in a recent retirement "banquet," one of my colleagues, although otherwise adulatory, referred to me humorously as a "cheeky bastard." Another suggested I should be "roasted" not admired. And I was in fact so "honored" by The Association for the Study of Play in a roast at the Baton Rouge meeting in 1983. I was the only one so honored in the history of that society. Undoubtedly, their Festschrift to me in Charleston in 1990 was a kindly condolence. Likewise during adolescence in high school, I arrogated to myself the role of class wit and would often make wisecracks as the lessons proceeded. Mostly these led to laughter by both teacher and classmates. But on several occasions, I received a bamboo caning or a leather strapping for my impudence. It was a relatively risky pursuit.

My parents were respectable people. They gave us liveliness and affection and were most conscientious in their religion. My mother was secretary of Mother's Union and my father the vicar's warden of our local Anglican church and ultimately treasurer of the Church of England Men's Society for New Zealand. In these oppositions between respectability and impropriety, there is support for the type of interpretation made by Fisher and Fisher in their book *Pretend the World Is Funny and Forever: A Psychological Analysis of Comedians, Clowns, and Actors* (1981). They contend that such characters are often reared in highly respectable homes where their inappropriate humor would not be acceptable, but who subsequently get that respect for their disrespectful follies from the audiences that support them. I certainly have long been aware that it is my practice to make a conforming self-presentation in most public situations, while at the same time, I reserve private thoughts for fantasied bathos and amongst friends frequently use humor in a way that is less than sublime. Such an interpretation is like the one given for games in suggesting a displacement of affect. First, there is the conflict over being respected but having a mind also for the disrespectful, which is then displaced into humorous disrespect. Again a dialectical metaphor.

After consideration of the above criticism of my impropriety and after attempts to explain this biographically in the terms given above, I have, in the course of writing this account (during 1991), come to believe that this material on stories, like that on play and games, is also most appropriately subsumed into the notion of disempowerment already suggested in the earlier sections. The interest in power in games and play was also an interest in securing children against disempowerment, which results from the intrusions of parents of educators and psychologists. My claims for the worth of children's own stories, regardless of their contents, would seem to be similarly motivated. From a historical point of view, I am most clearly a romanticist about children's expressive productions but, unlike most romanticists, prefer not to see those productions stilted or bowdlerized. I like to think of children's play or story as mediators of the irrational elements in their lives without requiring that these irrational contents be further suppressed. In fact, I espouse such sublimatory expression, envisaging a world where people can appear to be quite playfully awful when they feel like it, but must not be awful in actuality. And that I like to think is what the First Amendment is really about. It is my hope that rather than corrupt us all, such mediated expressions of irrationality allow humor and play to be the vehicles of greater human kindness. Most surely, this biography, whatever its intrinsic worth as scholarship and as story, adds up to the view that behind everything I have said is a younger player's, or should we say, a younger brother's cry for power and for justice.

REFLEXIVE EPILOGUE

While I have maintained that there is a potential multiplicity of ways of relating my personal scholarship and autobiography, the account presented here has developed, surprisingly to me and perhaps to others, along increasingly coherent lines.[6] I had at first thought I could throw more randomness into the picture with details of my variegated war time work experience and the "accident" of ending up at the university, or of my academic shifts from Ohio to New York to Pennsylvania, but soon I found myself interpreting each step of the latter as increasing my freedom to follow my own focus on expressive childhood topics. And when I thought of throwing in some of the unfortunate events of personal and professional life, once again I found myself saying that the effect of these was to increase my disillusionment with the narrowness of psychology as a discipline and to permit me to increase my eclectic interdisciplinary wanderings.

So, I am impressed that although the current undertaking was meant to be an epistemological enterprise on the power of narrative, that is, to increase one's knowledge of what in one's biography caused the developments in one's scholarship, it turned out to be instead an ontological enterprise. That is, it became an exercise in making one's own life more meaningful. Thus, by making everything more coherent, I have unwittingly (until this moment) participated in an ontological act of self-validation.

And this in turn leads to several further paradoxes. The very enterprise that all of the chapters in this book tackle, which on the surface is to give us more knowledge of the interaction between the subjective narrative life experience and the objective scholarly record, between the personal and the scientific, itself rises historically out of what has been called the "aesthetic turn" in romantic philosophizing. In twentieth-century terms, this aesthetic turn becomes the willingness to believe that a central value in human life is to be found in subjective experience. Other central values of a more obvious kind in our culture are to be found in science and religion. Which is to say that the present inquiry has as much to do with this romantic or aesthetic belief as with science. A book by a group of psychologists usually takes on the aura of science, but the present one presupposes contrarily there is something of value to be found in the irrational world of their personal motivation. So our enterprise begins with a phenomenological presupposition that personal experience counts in science but what has been revealed here is that the personal experience may well count more for the individual's own sense of authenticity than it can be taken as counting in some empirical sense for science. After all, this is at best badly remembered correlational data under the duress of a powerful experimenter effect to make some sense out of it.

A further paradox is that postulating power as causally central came as something of a shock to myself. In so doing, I reduced my own ontological self-description to one of the most orthodoxly popular epistemologies of Western society—that power is the prime mover, whether discussed in Marxist, Nietzschean, imperialist, or feminist terms. Which means that my apparent pursuit of authenticity has actually been just one more manifestation of a vogue epistemology. What we have here is an epistemological hunt, which turns out to be an ontological self-validation, which turns out to be an epistemology of contemporary vogue.

Paradoxically, the biographical moves put me in step with games as power theorizing, whether from Von Neumann, Michael Maccoby, Eric Berne or Spariosu, but out of step with post-Freudian play theorizing, whether from Huizinga, Csikszentmihalyi, or the intrinsic motivation school of modern psychology. Game and play theories have tended to pull in opposite philosophical directions as this century has progressed. The ontological purpose of this book with its implied enhancement of the worth of subjectivity might have received concurring help from a typical modern play theorist but did not do so from the present game theorist.

But the worst paradox for me is that having completed the story as honestly as I know how, I am not satisfied that it is adequate. I think that while I would acknowledge that I still find intense involvement in the sound and the fury of my chosen competitive games, I am loath to believe that that is all there has been to them. In part, the lacuna in the epistemological case I have presented arises, I think, from the lack of adequate theorizing about the culturally collective and often irrational arousal values in performances of skilled action. Our tendency always to see these things in individualistic and rationalistic terms (a further expression of the twentieth-century focus on subjectivity) ignores the role of the historical and social context in human events. Which is to say, I feel, that in my account of my own scholarly preoccupations, I might well have rightly emphasized the importance of power but have, as well, contrarily completely missed the collective poetry of the human festival, which in reflection I believe, counted a great deal with me.

NOTES

1. The work with Redl and Gump is described in Avedon & Sutton-Smith (1971).

2. The controversy is reviewed in Sutton-Smith, 1983.

3. These efforts are reviewed in Sutton-Smith, 1993.

4. My thanks also to the following students whose own dissertations contributed powerfully to my understanding of play, games, and stories. I apologize for omitting the multiple other students whose dissertations contributed equally well to other subject matters: Gil Botvin, 1976, and David Abrams, 1977, of Columbia University Teachers College; from the University of Pennsylvania both in the Graduate School of Education and the Department of Folklore in the Faculty of Arts and Sciences, Diana Kelly-Byrne, 1982; Linda Hughes, 1983; Kathleen Connor, 1991; John Gerstmyer, 1991; Alice Mechley, 1992; Ann Richmond Beresin, 1992; Felicia McMahon, 1993; Justine McGovern, 1993; and Rosylyn Blyn, 1993.

5. Dominion, Christchurch Press, Dunedin Star, newspapers, New Zealand, August 18, 1949.

6. I wish to thank the following individuals for discussing with me an earlier draft of this chapter: Berit Bae (Norway), Garry Chick (Illinois), Jim Christie (Arizona), Bernard DeKoven (California), Robert Horan (Wisconsin), Diana Kelly-Byrne (Australia), D. John Lee (Michigan), Fay McMahon (Pennsylvania), Danielle Savasta (Canada), Helen Schwartzman (Illinois), and Pat Wilson (England).

7

Uncovering Clues,
Discovering Change

Rachel T. Hare-Mustin

As academic activities go, meeting with a colleague for lunch at the Harvard Faculty Club has a good deal to recommend it. It is convenient to the Yard, it allows for encounters with others at the university, and it avoids the time and effort of a foray into Harvard Square. My recollection of my first visit to the Faculty Club is of a spring day when as a young researcher I am to meet a faculty member on the research project for lunch. Arriving early, I wander into the club's library to read the paper, carefully selecting a seat where I can be seen from the entrance hall.

Sometimes one does not consider much what one is doing in day-to-day activities. One goes here, one goes there; one's mind is on other things. I was glancing through the *New York Times*, only dimly aware of the library, a vast, empty space with possibly two or three other readers in distant corners. Consequently, I was startled when a man spoke to me to discover him standing before me. He introduced himself as the club manager. One of the men in the library asked him to intervene. He regretted to inform me that ladies were not permitted in the library of the Harvard Faculty Club. He would escort me to the ladies' waiting room. My colleague would be informed where I was. I moved along beside him, across a hall, down a passageway, into a tiny room decorated with flowered ruffled chairs and lamps. I was confused and embarrassed.

I recall such feelings on another occasion. I was living in Nigeria, teaching psychology at the University of Ife and doing research on a grant from the Rockefeller Foundation on attitudes toward authority among different tribal groups. I was walking through the open marketplace and suddenly noticed that I was the only white person in the market. I was acutely self-conscious; I was painfully aware of being inside my skin. I felt strange, my scalp prickled, my movements were stiff and awkward as if I did not know how to walk. The sun glared down. The light was too bright. I felt exposed. I kept moving. This is what it means to be "out of place."

The meaning of these events arises from the context—to be in a place that renders one "out of place." Being out of place is a dis-comfort that intrudes into our waking and sleeping; it is the stuff of dreams and night-mares. In such ways, the meaning of things "is shaped by our patterns of bodily movement, our spatial and temporal orientation to the world, and our interaction with objects in the world. Human cognition is never merely a matter of abstract conceptualizations and propositional judgments" (Hermans, Kempen, and Van Loon, 1992, p. 25). In the first incident I experienced being out of place because of gender barriers, in the second because of racial differences.

THEME AND NARRATIVE

Many experiences go into being a scholar, a teacher, a researcher, a psychologist. My experience at the Harvard Faculty Club was one of a number of enactments intended to set women apart from men. Recalling what happened there, I could say that life is full of novelty and unpredictability. Or I could say that I should have been more vigilant. Or I could say that the dominant discourses provide the meanings and define the experiences in the society. In that situation, I was not "simply me," but a participant in a discourse that constituted me.

I returned some years later to Harvard as a faculty member and wandered into the library of the Faculty Club one day. It was 1980. Women were now allowed. The problem of exclusion was being played out elsewhere, perhaps in the tenured faculty—less than 5 percent were women—perhaps in the experiences of women students.

To consider the incident prototypical would not be far off. Like "high politics," intellectual life is gendered: The exclusion of women legitimizes its standing. That experience was not the first nor would it be the last I had of bias against women in the academy. Other incidents had a more critical impact on my academic career. Some were overt and customary, others indirect and denied. Did this one serve as a warning of an uncertain, risky future for a woman in academia? But if it were a warning, it was not the first, for there had been an earlier one that I had managed to forget. At Swarthmore College, my prestigious academic scholarship was withdrawn because I got married at the end of my sophomore year. Again I had been startled, unprepared. I did not know that a married woman was not expected to make a scholarly contribution. How is one to deal with such unexpected incidents? They are central to my experience; they are peripheral to my experience; they are overwhelming; they are trivial; they are boring; they sap my energy; they beg to be put aside; they are experiences one is never quite prepared for. As this story unfolds, I realize that I have launched a tale with a narrative plot familiar to Western stories: Once upon a time there was a hero (heroine) who encountered many obstacles in pursuit of a goal and overcame (some of) them.

I imagine it is not customary for a man to ask himself, "In what way does my being a man distort or influence what I am saying?" A man is not typically asked to represent men. But I am aware of representing women in this collection. I have noticed when women are positioned as opposite to or different from men, the diversity among women is overlooked. Yet, in study after study, psychologists have found that the variability among women is greater than that among men. I believe this is because the sanctions on men to conform to norms of masculinity are more severe than those on women. Traditionally, a man's greatest fear is to be thought to be like a woman. Men are regarded as true representatives of the society. Women are not.

The gender category, woman, shadowed my career and caught me unawares even after I accepted it and focused on it in my scholarly activities. "Intend the thing you fear" is Viktor Frankl's (1960) paradoxical injunction, and paradox became a way I understood the world. Looking back, I realize another way I could have protected myself would have been to identify with the male hierarchy in academia and find a man as my mentor, a familiar pattern for women in psychology. Perhaps I did not do so out of a sense of independence and individuality, for my family had given me a profound commitment to equality that in some ways ill-prepared me for the world. Only gradually, as feminist theory and postmodernism came together, did I comprehend that man is the hidden referent in our language and culture. As Dale Spender has pointed out, "Women can only aspire to be as good as a man, there is no point in trying to be as good as a woman" (1984, p. 201).

As I moved through the academic world, I often felt out of place with the local setting. My identifications, scholarly exchanges, and shared activities typically seemed to be with colleagues elsewhere. I was like Dorothy in *The Wizard of Oz*. From a distance, the Emerald City of Oz glistens and gleams and beckons, but upon arrival, Dorothy discovers the image is created by an old man behind a tattered curtain pulling levers. One sets out to find utopia, forgetting that utopia means nowhere. As Neville Wakefield (1990) has pointed out, in a postmodern age there are no homes. When you get there, there is no there there.

THE DETECTIVE STORY

A life can be described, but can it be explained? Description is not explanation. Like a sculptor, one asks how much to include and how much to carve away. Shall I be honest? Shall I be charming? Shall I speak truth to power, as the Quakers say, realizing that speaking truth to the powerful entails risks? When I use the term *patriarchal* to describe the hierarchical arrangements in society that ensure that men are predominant, I realize it is risky. Such a term makes many people defensive, but I would feel dishonest to avoid it. Similarly, with the term *feminist*, which many women now disavow in response to the conservative backlash. Of course I realize that gender is not the only issue in one's experience, but the denial of the importance of gender is what is remarkable. Gender saturates our daily lives, soaks into and permeates our being. It is so much a part of us that it often does not intrude on our awareness. When it does, gender has the power to startle, to catch one unawares.

In creating a narrative of my life, I am not unconstrained. Life narratives, as Jerome Bruner has observed, reflect the prevailing conventions about the "possible lives" that are part of one's culture (1987). Thus I select certain memories and cast aside those events that would belie the theme of this narrative, that of being "out of place." An alternative narrative might build on a theme of notable achievements, of recognition and leadership, but I avoid that. I have decided for this essay to heed Thoreau's admonition concerning notable events: Beware of enterprises that require new clothes.

The form this narrative seems to be taking is that of the detective story. Corrine Squire (1990) describes the detective story as an increasingly self-critical and self-conscious form of fiction narrative that expresses a kind of social psychological concern with subjectivity. The detective narrative sets up a problem and then resolves it step by step, fulfilling narrative's potential for completeness and closure. But there are always inconsistencies and missing clues. The text often repeats itself, the order of things is irregular, the introduction foreshadows the conclusion. Above all, the continuing moral debate within the detective story is like a morality play where uncertainties arise about both the investigator and the dubious justice system that the narrative explores and exposes. This is the form of my narrative. The underlying question I ask of myself and of every character is that of motive and opportunity.

The detective story as a narrative genre has a particular approach. It is not neutral; the method of inquiry determines what can be found. To have a method, as Gadamer (1970) says, is to have an interpretation. In focusing on different subjectivities, on my experiences as a social being, I may be neglecting the mystique of my inner being. Notions of freedom and choice, of critic and observer, are closely related to modernist notions of an autonomous true self radically separated from society. This dichotomy conveniently conceals the messy terrain of everyday behavior. I believe that the modernist view of a self-sufficient self is undermined by the interdependency of human life. One's individuality is acquired through association with others and exercised through such association.[1] It was Freud who made it acceptable to be in love with one's own unknowable self. In contrast, Michel Foucault (1980, 1988) has regarded the very concept of the self as a fiction that serves to sustain established hierarchies of power.

It is hard to give up the obsession with the uniqueness of self. I have a rich inner life, but I do not believe there is a need to be preoccupied with the self, a true self, or a false self. Louis Sass has suggested that "many who claim to disbelieve in the self seem to take an inordinate delight in dancing round its burning image" (1988, p. 552). I conclude I am warmed by other fires.

BECOMING A PSYCHOLOGIST

I grew up in a liberal family on the margins of a conservative and affluent community. I have noticed that other scholars from places like Scarsdale, Larchmont, or Bronxville distance themselves from suburban stereotypes by claiming to come from New York City or the Bronx. I claimed to be from upstate New York, because when I was growing up it seemed like upstate. Working summers at places like the *New York Daily News*, I commuted from one world to another. I learned early how to be an outsider and a skeptic.

Psychology began for me at Swarthmore College. The way gestalt psychology explained the world for me foretold the way systems theory and constructivism and discourse theory would each do so in turn. The common thread that I followed as it unwound before me was the way each added to my view of meaning as context-dependent. The future was waiting for the past.

I was late when I entered the crowded lecture hall for my first psychology class, squeezing past those already seated under the scowl of Professor David Krech. He was irascible; he was intimidating; he was inspiring. When I discovered he was leaving for Berkeley the next year, I determined to get into his upper-level social psychology course. Through those long wonderful days, psychology at Swarthmore seemed to offer one challenging experience after another. The seminar on gestalt psychology with Wolfgang Kohler was marked by his clarity, his brilliance, and his graciousness. I worked as a research assistant for Benbow Ritchie and for Hans Wallach. I discovered as a subject in Solomon Asch's research that I was countersuggestive. I coauthored two published articles as an undergraduate, one in social psychology mapping family friendship patterns, the other in experimental comparative psychology on sign-gestalt learning. Recalling the experimental design of the latter, I am still struck by its elegance and simplicity that demonstrated that the solution depended on a cognitive map rather than a reinforced response pattern.

Elegance and simplicity is the way I would characterize the perceptual principles of gestalt psychology as they described the dynamics and fluidity of a system. They had immediate appeal because they described the way I operated in the world. Closure was important to me. How was it that others did not have such a strong Zeigarnik (1927) effect? Reversal of figure and ground described the affinity for wit and humor in my family, my use of paradox, my observation that foreground shifts to background with familiarity, my attempts to understand opposition. I saw space responses on the Rorschach as readily as whole responses (and doubted the conventional interpretation). The immediacy of contrast, similarity, "pregnance," and a good gestalt fit the way I saw the world. I thought in spatial terms, I had a cognitive map. Later, in applying systems theory to psychotherapy, I echoed Korzybski's credo that Gregory Bateson put forth: "A map is not the territory" (Korzybski, 1958, p. 58). Today, as my way of viewing the world has shifted in a postmodern era, I favor Heinz Von Forster's view of the world as the map (Von Glaserfeld, 1984).

CHANGE

My childhood and early family life reflected continuity and stability. The ideals of individual responsibility and community service were omnipresent, remnants of a staunch New England tradition. To put one's principles into action seemed natural. But the basis for continuity in my adult life has been frequent change. I have adapted by first welcoming change, than later learning to be wary of change.

Movements of social activism that had small beginnings in the 1950s caught fire and blazed up in the 1960s only to later burn out. The problem of change consumed both my early scholarly and political life. As a Quaker, I was impressed by opportunities for service around the world. As a scholar, I looked to the work of psychologists who had struggled to understand the threats and appeals of totalitarianism and authoritarianism in the Nazi era. The questions they addressed were those of social change, nuclear bomb testing, disarmament, and civil rights. How could attitudes be changed? How could behavior be changed? What about fascism, racism, yea-saying, nay-saying, conformity, defiance, courage, response set? What could explain them?

As momentum built in the political arena, I responded to the exciting sense of possibilities for change. I was in the midst of actions for civil rights and ending the Vietnam War. In the inner city, the clinic where I worked often seemed under siege. On the campus, hope and disorder and danger vied with one another. The sense of personal freedom meant beards and sandals were everywhere (the prescribed uniform?). I was often in Washington at demonstrations.

Having walked the walk in protest movements, I find it hard to smoothly talk the talk about those events. Seeing people being gassed and clubbed, striving for nonviolence in response to violence, stirs up fear as well as despair. There is hope for change, but reaction could set in again: One has merely to look at the hate in the faces of those blocking women's clinics who claim to be pro-life.

The sense of community and hopefulness spawned cameraderie. But, as it became clear what women's position was in these social movements, I gradually pulled away. The emerging women's movement observed that women were always the foot soldiers in someone else's revolution.

Sometimes I watched events in America from afar. During the 1960s, I moved around the world a great deal, living here and there in what were called developing countries, first with the Peace Corps, then with grants from the Office of Naval Research and the Ford and Rockefeller Foundations. Immersing myself in different cultures with a family of four children, traveling through Asia and Africa as well as Europe, I sought to understand how change could come about. I looked at differences in the use of guilt and shame in child-rearing in non-Western societies. I studied the relation of authoritarianism, autonomy, and education in tribal groups in different parts of Africa. I researched the way Filipino children learned to balance the expectations for autonomy in the schoolroom against the dominant themes of a dependency-oriented society.

When I looked at psychology from afar, I was disenchanted with what I saw. What did academic psychology have to offer this changing world? Its research seemed irrelevant, its acceptance of psychodynamic theory faddish, its behaviorism sterile, its teaching dated and dogmatic. Other than that, though, it was terrific! Would there ever be enough evidence to charge psychologists with having made a difference?

I now recognize that I was probably suffering from culture shock on re-encountering academic life in America after sharing arduous living conditions in villages and poorly equipped universities in other parts of the world. One morning as I drifted through the Museum of Archaeology and Anthropology at the University of Pennsylvania, I decided to make a change. I presented myself to the director and was immediately hired. Still fresh from overseas, I plunged into work on African displays and Native-American collections. I still find it amazing that someone would be paid to catalogue and arrange such diverse and beautiful objects from around the world. However, by the end of a year, I had come to realize that I would have to get a Ph.D. in anthropology or archaeology if I wanted to seriously pursue those interests. Or should I return to graduate study in psychology? The director of one program told me, "As a woman, you need every degree you can get."

The last direct use I made of my international experiences (until I returned to Asia in 1981 to do research on motherhood in China) was in a little test I devised using unusual foreign languages I knew such as Bikol, Swahili, and Tagalog. Because the test involved a domain of knowledge few knew, it was essentially a guessing test that would randomly distribute experimental subjects into success and failure conditions without regard to intelligence. The test was part of my research on autonomy and creativity. It epitomized my interest in language, reframing, puzzles, and play—the simple and the artful. I liked the way other languages initiate us into mysteries even before we fully understand our own language. For example, from analyzing the phrase, "Iisipin ko ang dapat gawin," would we recognize its meaning—"I am thinking of what to do"?

I returned to psychology, receiving a Ph.D. in clinical psychology in 1969. Having been told by a senior colleague at Harvard that the work I did prior to my Ph.D. did not "count," I have remained somewhat puzzled by what should be accountable. A detective narrative asks what constitutes evidence in solving the mystery. I am reminded that any deviation from the standard career track is open to question.

THIS SIDE OF PARADOX

I grew up in a family of four children. Perhaps someone could make much of our family configuration. Joyce Carol Oates once wrote that the family is the deepest mystery, deeper than love or death. I doubted my older sister's suggestion that I must have been adopted because I did not have red hair like the other children and my mother. I was a second child—we try harder.

Systems theory was what drew me to the field of family therapy and the debates on language, cybernetics, second-order change, and paradoxical interventions. Family therapy was founded in challenge and controversy. Systems therapy, and especially family therapy, evolved from dissatisfaction with psychoanalytic and Rogerian models of therapy. The feedback processes of systems seemed to provide a better way of understanding family interaction than traditional models of psychotherapy. I was also becoming aware of how both psychoanalytic theory and practice supported woman's place in man's world.

When I once pointed out to a therapist friend that there was no compelling evidence to support psychoanalysis, I was disdainfully dismissed as an empiricist. *Moi?* But then, who has ever abandoned a theory because of disconfirming evidence?

Perhaps I am a pragmatist. I am aware of the work of Jerome Kagan and others demonstrating that early childhood experiences are not immutable. Who we are is not just produced in childhood but recursively reproduced in adult social relations. What family systems therapy focused on was the persistence of a problem rather than its origin. We cannot know the past except in the present moment. Through memories and anticipations, the present includes the past and the future. Delving into the past can be fascinating, as it was sometimes in my lengthy psychoanalysis, but it may not have much to do with change. I discovered that I did not believe that insight was necessary to produce change. Sometimes change would occur and insight might follow. Or insight might never occur. As W. Ross Ashby (1956) has noted, transformation is concerned with *what* happens, not *why* it happens. Reinterpreting the past is just one of many ways to try to influence behavior.

As I moved away from questions of social change in other cultures, I was drawn to theories of change emerging in systems approaches to psychotherapy. I could again visualize change in gestalt terms as the sudden reorganization of the field. Gestalt theory has suggested that what is hidden lies in plain view, hidden by familiarity; habitualization devours objects, clothing, furniture, cruelty, fear of war, dominance, and subordination. The little volume *Change: Principles of Problem Formation and Problem Resolution* brought these ideas together (Watzlawick, Weakland, and Fisch, 1974). The book examines how sense and "logical" behavior often fail to produce the desired change, whereas seemingly "illogical" and "unreasonable" actions succeed.

Wittgenstein is often credited with first seeing the behavioral implications of paradox. As the theory of paradoxical change was developed, second-order change through paradox—in the clinical sense, symptom prescription—was identified as a powerful and elegant form of problem resolution. The paradox is created by the patient being told that change will occur by the patient's not striving to change. This creates the contradiction that is associated with classical paradox. The use of counterintuitive tasks dramatically reorganizes perception and behavior. Moreover, understanding paradox in systems terms reminds us that to see both sides of a question is the surest way to prevent its solution because there are always more than two sides.

Just as Alice discovered she had been speaking prose, I discovered that for much of my life I had been using paradox. The sudden shift in perception appealed to me, the absurdity and astonishment, the change in meaning, the detachment, the humor, the enormous possibilities arising out of deftness and simplicity.

I was intrigued by the related ideas of John Platt on the sudden transformations and discontinuous changes in natural systems and of Rene Thom on the predictable nature of catastrophes.[2] Just as deconstructive readings disrupt a text, therapists' observations disrupt the way patients see the world, opening the way for other possibilities to emerge. My early paper, "This Side of Paradox," was followed by other articles on paradoxical change.

It has been said that paradox is more congruent with Eastern thought than with Western Aristotelian concepts of behavior seen as flowing from an object's "essential" nature. When I lived in Asia, I studied Chinese philosophy and poetry. I discovered a different view of reality as a student of Chinese brush painting. I was surprised to find I had an aptitude for Chinese brush painting as it seemed at odds with my liking for modern art and my previous art work. I found brush painting an absorbing discipline—to touch brush to paper with the requisite pressure, lightly bearing down and turning the brush, to create only that bamboo leaf which belonged in that place at that moment.

The cybernetic metaphor in family therapy began to shift to a constructivist one that viewed the family not as an interacting behavioral system but as a system of beliefs and assumptions held by the family. Family therapy was moving away from communications theory and Gregory Bateson's ideas of circular causality as well as from structural-functional theory. For me, systems theory segued smoothly into constructivism with its focus on the meanings of events for the family. For other therapists, constructivism meant a new interest in stories, narrative, and metaphor rather than behavior. Constructivism once again reminded therapists that therapy centers on meaning, and language is its medium. Constructivism does not provide a technique but a philosophical context within which therapy is done.

Family therapy was also being challenged by the feminist critique, often described as the most important development in family therapy in the decade of the eighties. My involvement in feminist theory started with others in clinical psychology in the preceding decade. From a feminist perspective, I questioned the mechanistic aspect of systems theory that disregarded gender and the associated power differences. I also questioned the hierarchical model of structural family therapy that drew on Talcott Parsons's functionalism and sex role prescriptions. Parsons viewed the survival of the family as dependent on clearly separate sex roles; his theory of separate spheres for men and women continues to influence the social sciences and public policy (Parsons and Bales, 1955). Some feminists seemed less willing to question psychodynamic conceptions of feminine and masculine natures, seeing them as a welcome contrast to the ignoring of gender in systems theory. The feminist critique challenged family therapists to examine authoritarian, patriarchal structures in the family and the larger social system. I was invited to present my ideas in the first plenary on gender of the American Association for Marriage and Family Therapy in 1985.[3] On that occasion, I pointed out that therapy that does not consider the condition of women may not be worth doing, and therapy that is not worth doing is not worth doing well.

GETTING PUBLISHED

My persistence comes to me as a surprise sometimes, particularly in regard to publication. I recall my sixth grade teacher's comment on my project on the American colonies: "Good ideas but lacks persistence." I had conceived doing the history of the 13 colonies by an exchange of letters between a settler in each colony and someone left behind in the Old World. What an endless project! I tried to escape from the tedious correspondence I had initiated by coming down with first whooping cough and then measles in my sixth grade year. Thus can scholarly pursuits ruin one's childhood.

Like other "disciplines," psychology is subject to the features of discipline in the Foucauldian sense of the word (Yeatman, 1990). It has a set of intellectual practices and rigorous gatekeeping procedures that block openness to challenges of those outside the mainstream. It is no secret that research that "discovers" gender differences that reflect the prevailing ideology gets published, while studies that find no differences do not. Another gatekeeping device is research funding. I have found that funding for problems affecting women is niggardly compared with research funding for hypertension, heart attacks, smoking, alcoholism, and other problems that primarily affect congressmen.

The editorial review process for publication can be a painful one. It can be avoided by not submitting one's work to journals, and I have colleagues who prefer to write books because they typically will receive "balanced" (read: uncritical) professional book reviews. I have found journal reviews sometimes arbitrary and often funny. Of course they are biased. And for someone like myself who longs for closure, the slow process is excruciating.

As my scholarly work began to address the treatment of women in therapy, I encountered problems getting my work published. "This manuscript treats the subject too lightly," was the editor's feedback on my first ethics article, "Ethical Considerations in the Use of Sexual Contact in Psychotherapy," submitted to the *American Psychologist*. Since there was only one review, I wrote the editor asking that the manuscript be sent out for another review. "This manuscript treats the subject with too much dignity," was the feedback on the second review. The editor again rejected the manuscript. He was apparently not troubled by that hobgoblin of little minds: inconsistency. The article was subsequently published elsewhere (1974).

Twenty years later, my most recent ethics article, "Cries and Whispers: The Psychotherapy of Anne Sexton" (1992), deals with the same question. Now I use a postmodern perspective to show how the response to Sexton's treatment reflects the dominant discourses of psychoanalysis and psychotherapy. I observe that the debate by leaders in the field on issues of confidentiality in the case has provided a smoke screen, obscuring the ethical violation involved in the sexual abuse of Sexton by the therapist who had an affair with her.

I found a paradoxical approach successful in publishing my first article on feminist theory in *Family Process* (1978). "You may not want to publish this article because it takes a feminist approach, which is not what your readers are used to," I suggested to the editor in my letter of submission. He published it. From the reviewers' comments, I discovered that men's observations about women were called science, but women's observations about men were called polemics. The article has achieved a life of its own, hailed as the first article on feminist theory in family therapy, appearing in many edited books and in translation in foreign journals and receiving publication awards—to the surprise of its author.

However, I again ran into difficulties with the *American Psychologist* when I submitted "An Appraisal of the Relationship between Women and Psychotherapy: 80 Years after the Case of Dora" (1983). Since the *American Psychologist* had not previously published anything on women and psychotherapy, the editor seemed very cautious. I had the impression he kept trying to find another reviewer who might have another criticism. The process took so long that three years passed before the article came out. By that time it should have been retitled "*83 Years* after the Case of Dora."

All scholarly activity is aimed at writing "The Book," so it is perhaps remarkable that I have yet to write "The Book." But then, as Julian Barnes observes, "It's easy, after all, not to be a writer. Most people aren't writers and very little harm comes to them" (Barnes, 1985, p. 121). Yet threats of harm hang over anyone in academia who does not write "The Book."

Why have I not written "The Book"? Let me count the reasons. First, I wanted to move into the future, unencumbered by a dissertation snapping at my heels to become "The Book." I discovered that if you work too long to improve something, you end up throwing it out. Second, I achieved tenure and promotion by publishing articles without "The Book," so I continued to do "more of the same" with my ideas. Third, I lived for many years with an academic who was always writing "The Book." Even after "The Book" was published, he started on "The Next Book." Fourth, I knew a widely disliked famous psychologist who wrote and published the same book almost every year. Was the world crazy? Yes. I had once written in my column in a psychology magazine that a person had only one great idea in a lifetime. Someone wrote in to say that Albert Ellis had two great ideas (the psychologist above was not Ellis). Fifth, I knew of someone who wrote a book that did more harm than good, and I wanted to do good, or at least do well. Sixth, the book I wanted to write, *Change*, had already been written by someone else (Watzlawick, Weakland, and Fisch, 1974). Ditto, *Authority* by Richard Sennett (1980). Ditto, *Great Housewives of Art* by Sally Swain (1988). Seventh, there are too many books. Alas.

Any investigator knows that when seven reasons are given for doing something, the real reason is none of the seven. Surely, to put forward one's ideas in a book and make an impact is a fine thing. Maybe I should think about that. No—I don't think I want to. I will just approach "The Book" asymptotically, as I describe below.

MAKING A DIFFERENCE

Psychology has largely remained on the sidelines during the debates on gender theory occurring in the humanities and other social sciences in the last decade. In those debates, I found myself puzzled by the enthusiasm with which feminists, particularly feminists who espoused psychodynamic ideas, embraced the idea of gender as difference. Privileging the essential nature of masculinity and femininity reinforces the very stereotypes that disadvantage women. Essentialist views encourage women to feel differently about themselves but leave the structural conditions in society unchanged. On the other hand, the minimizing of differences in neutered theories denies the unfortunate material conditions of many women's lives. I began to see these problems as related and as analogous to the two kinds of error in hypothesis testing in the traditional psychological research paradigm. In hypothesis testing, alpha or Type 1 error involves reporting a significant difference when one does not exist. Beta, or Type 2 error involves overlooking a significant difference when one does exist. I decided to identify the tendency to exaggerate differences as alpha bias and the tendency to minimize or ignore differences as beta bias. I first applied the alpha-beta schema to gender in an invited address in New York in 1985 and soon published it in an article. Shortly afterward I began to collaborate on ideas about gender with Jeanne Marecek.

Collaboration is a special kind of creative relationship with its own peaks of stimulation and stress, of pleasure and despair. Jeanne Marecek, a professor of psychology at Swarthmore College, and I had been discussing a joint project on ethical models in clinical practice since our collaboration on rights of clients and responsibilities of therapists in the late seventies. We began to collaborate in earnest on ideas about gender theory and published a joint article (1986) on autonomy and gender in which we explored and highlighted the relational nature of autonomy.

The collaboration worked because we sparked each other's ideas; we each drew on a different body of knowledge; we both enjoyed epigrams; we shared an interest in writing style; we wanted to explore postmodernism and feminist theory. It was to be a close collaboration, every word and phrase and concept poured over by us together for any final draft. Her strong preference for linear organization was balanced by my being more goal oriented. For me, our major difference emerged in our time perspectives, for I liked to move more rapidly. I feared the *zeitgeist* was escaping over the next hill.

When it came to publication credits, what we discovered about collaboration is that the whole is greater than the sum of its parts. Other collaborators have confirmed our observation that no collaborator ever receives proportional credit. It is always assumed that "the other one" made the major contribution.

As we explored various theories and grappled with one idea after another, the solution became the problem. We found ourselves so absorbed in the discussion of ideas and images that we became impatient about having to stop to write about them. We had notes; we had outlines; we had epigrams; we had titles; we had theories; we had gossip; we had doubts. We were entranced with ideas; we were caught in a spell. Recognizing that language is recursive, we felt it using us. Meanwhile, I worried that the *zeitgeist* was slipping away.

Our way of trying to break out of the frame we had created around our dialogues was to organize presentations at professional meetings with the intention of exposing our ideas to others. In 1987, we organized a symposium for the American Orthopsychiatric Association meetings. A symposium we organized the next year for the American Psychological Association meetings led to our article on the meaning of difference in the *American Psychologist* (1988). This was followed by our book (1990), which includes three chapters we jointly authored and a chapter each by the three other scholars we had invited to participate in the symposium.

What constitutes differentness is a vexing question for psychologists who study sex and gender.[4] The politics of gender is the politics of difference. We observed from a constructivist viewpoint that theories persist as long as they are useful. However, we were skeptical about the utility for feminists of viewing gender as difference. Whether one accepts the prevailing view that women are essentially different from men or finds that women differ little from men, the answer is spoiled by the flawed question of what constitutes differentness between women and men. We suggested that constructing gender is a process, not an answer. As John Dewey observed, intellectual progress usually occurs through the sheer abandonment of questions together with the alternatives they assume. We do not solve them; we get over them. Thus, we stated:

> Male-female difference is a problematic and paradoxical way to construe gender. What we see is that alpha and beta bias have similar assumptive frameworks despite their diverse emphases. Both take the male as the standard of comparison. Both construct gender as attributes of individuals, not as the ongoing relations of men and women. Neither effectively challenges the gender hierarchy, and ultimately neither transcends the status quo. They [lie] within the larger system of assumptions, but they leave the system itself unchanged. ... In accepting male-female difference as the meaning of gender, feminists have acceded to the construction of reality of the dominant group, a gentle slide into the prevailing hegemony (Hare-Mustin and Marecek, 1990, pp. 54–55).

Several ideas that I had been puzzling over for a long time came together in working on the meaning of difference, notably questions of authority, paradox, and meaning. Like other feminist theorists, I was examining the work of Michel Foucault (1980) and postmodern thinkers who had drawn attention to the connection between meaning and power. From a postmodern perspective, the construction of "knowledge and truth" is an expression of the power of the privileged that silences and marginalizes other perspectives. However, from a feminist perspective, Foucault's work on power is flawed because it makes it difficult to locate domination.

The problem of change appears to me as the problem of changing a system of which one is a part. This is also the predominant problem in psychotherapy—the observations of the therapist help determine the therapeutic system that is the target of change. Similarly, an alternative discourse, in trying to define what the dominant discourse leaves out, is defined by the dominant discourse. The difficulty is also evident in feminist theory where

I find myself furthering the ideas I intend to subvert. For example, to engage in research or theory development intended to dispute conventional ideas about female nature necessarily gives prominence to those ideas. As this paradox is described by Richard Sennett (1980), even when one's response to authority is defiance, that stance serves to confirm authority just as compliance does. Thus, the feminist critique simultaneously protests and protects the status quo. We drew attention in *Making a Difference* to the observation that woman is not really the enemy of the system but the loyal opposition.

DOMINANT DISCOURSES

As theories go, postmodernism can be appealing to someone like myself who has qualms about asserting the rightness of truth, positivistic models, and experimental paradigms. Feminist critiques in the 1960s and 1970s were among the first to bring to general awareness the contradictions and inconsistencies in knowledge claims and master narratives. One such grand narrative is the theory of the sexual division of labor or sex roles, which can be shown to reflect historically specific cultural constructions. Another is the privileged vision of the male subject universalized to represent every point of view. Like other feminists, I challenged the way this universalized male view continually iterates itself in language through the use of the generic masculine form.

I have found myself contesting the dominant discourses in both theoretical debates and the struggles in the "real world." In "Sex, Lies, and Headaches: The Problem Is Power," I show how the dominant discourses construct the male-female relationship to meet men's sexual desires (1991). In a current paper, "Discourses in the Mirrored Room," I challenge the idea that there is no predetermined content in the conversation of therapy. The therapeutic conversation takes form and meaning from the cultural assumptions regarding roles and relationships, thereby typically barring alternative discourses from the therapy room.

The postmodern moment has been called politics at its most intense. Competing discourses challenge established meanings and structures of knowledge. I am among those feminists who see postmodernism as a way to open up space for alternative views to the "correct" representations shaped by specific historical and political practices. Some other feminists see postmodernism as a denial of women's experience and women's essential relational nature. I can understand because I, too, have found it hard to move away from foundational beliefs. I have shared in the nostalgia for feminine essentialist qualities—caring, understanding, quilting, baking bread—and the presumed moral authority these qualities accord femaleness. I also have been reluctant to give up the Enlightenment ideal of the freedom of the (ungendered) individual. My work on autonomy attests to that. But, clinging to the ideal of the freedom of the individual creates a threshold of deafness to the question of power inequities in the social system.

Theories that valorize what are considered women's essential female characteristics, like motherhood and peaceableness, are acceptable because they do not threaten the status quo. They demand neither individual nor social change. However, they are treated by philosophers as limited and peripheral to the major ongoing theoretical debates. Feminist postmodern theories that do provide a direct challenge to postmodernism are ignored. Men who are postmodern thinkers have shown themselves unwilling to debate issues placed on the critical agenda by women. In general, what women do is not regarded as important. It is a difference that does not make a difference. Once again I am reminded that the system maintains itself, in this case by having feminist theorists debate each other, ignored by those whose interests are served by the dominant discourses.

LIFE IS ONE THING AFTER ANOTHER

My interest in process and interaction has sometimes extended beyond therapy or the family in society. In the 1960s, some critics identified organizational rules with domination by the male establishment; therefore, doing away with such rules appeared to be doing away with white male domination. But Joann Freeman (1973) cautioned that that was a mistaken notion. Just as chaos theory has made us aware that chaos is order disguised as disorder, there are orderly patterns hidden in structurelessness. What appears to be a lack of structure often means operating under informal rules that few are privy to. It gives the illusion of openness and equal participation without the possibility being realized or the means contested. Freeman has called this condition the tyranny of structurelessness. Hidden rules are like family secrets, not accessible to direct challenge and change.

The issue of rules was brought sharply to my attention one Saturday afternoon as I was drowsing through a business meeting at an annual convention of the American Psychological Association. A question arose about whether there was a quorum, the minimum number of members required to conduct business, but no one "called" a quorum. It seemed to me a good idea so I called a quorum, thus requiring a count to be made. The result was astounding. The meeting came to a dramatic halt because there was no quorum. In the ensuing uproar, the chair had a temper tantrum, and I was publicly berated for my "inconvenient" action. Shaken though I was, I concluded that knowing the rules had interesting possibilities.

Thus began a pastime that led to my exploring old tomes and tracking down information on parliamentary rules and preferential voting systems. I still liked detective work. It linked such apparently unrelated places as Cincinnati and New York City around questions of civic reform. I soon discovered that few who used parliamentary rules had gone beyond the knowledge of Robert's Rules learned at school. The ideal of equality in the democratic process gave way before an *aficionado* of Robert's Rules who could run circles around the average participant at a meeting and often did so. Realizing that parliamentary rules existed primarily to protect the minority was appealing to me as was learning of other parliamentary systems than Robert's. My becoming Parliamentarian for the American Psychological Association and other groups was one small step toward furthering democratic procedures and making them more comprehensible. I have found that being a parliamentarian is a pastime in which the form is typically more interesting than the content.

A pastime, however, takes time, and I am very aware of the passage of time. I recall how disorienting it was for me to live in the tropics where the passage of time was not so sharply marked by the changing seasons as in North America. Time seemed endless, hardly moving. Months, days, hours were but the "rags of time." I lost the sense of time. Time goes, we say. Perhaps not. It may be that time stays, we go. Time is represented for me in spatial terms as a diagram in my head, a kind of cognitive map with the year or century represented by irregular dips and gradients. Images like these are hard to explain because words are so inadequate. It reminds me that to know what one means does not mean one can say what one means. Trying to describe some images is like throwing a ball that can never be caught.

Change is elusive—hard to see, hard to measure. We observe events at different time points and label what happens in the interval as change. What have I observed over time? Some things do change. Recently I came upon a cartoon that depicts an elderly man tottering up the steps of a Southern mansion to be greeted by an old lady leaning on a cane who says, "I'm sorry Rhett, but now I don't give a damn."

As Wittgenstein observed, explanation has to come to an end somewhere. Returning to the idea of the detective narrative, I recognize that I may not have presented the "facts"—the "what" or the "why"—but scattered a few clues to suggest motive and opportunity. But then, narrative is a selective art, not a comprehensive one. Our actions are events that begin to vanish as soon as they emerge. I have pointed to some of the complexities and ambiguities in my scholarly life and have deflected attention from other aspects. I have said little of my clinical practice or my academic life. Narratives are said to be solutions to problems in living, but surely that is a modernist ideal of linear progress. What I have reflected is the dislocating experience of a postmodern era. I am the author of my life, but the only meanings available to me are those provided by this time and place.

It has been said that books are where things are explained to you, life is where things are not. Books make sense of life. The only problem is that the lives they make sense of are other people's lives, never your own (Barnes, 1985, p. 121). There is a reflexive aspect to writing one's life that makes one question many things. What kind of a witness can one be to one's own history? Is there enough evidence to show that one has made a difference? I conclude one's own life may never be solved, one's own questions never answered.

NOTES

1. For a discussion of meaning and subjectivity see Hollway, 1989.
2. See Platt, 1976; and Thom, 1975.
3. Published as Hare-Mustin, 1987.
4. For a survey of the research on gender see Tavris, 1992.

8

A View from the Fringe: An Autobiographical Sketch

Joseph F. Rychlak

My favorite reading for relaxation is autobiography and history. I prefer my fiction in the cinema or theater. So as I undertake the task of writing my autobiographical sketch, I am forced to ask myself: "What have you to offer the reader?" I was asked to be in this collection because of my writings as a psychologist. It follows that a reasonable, if not expected, approach for me would be to zero in on the content of my writings. However, our editor has asked us to avoid turning our chapters into theoretical arguments. Obviously, this could hide anything personal from entering the account.

At the same time, it happens to be true that my career as psychologist has been one long running argument with the psychological establishment. I have never accepted the image of humanity that the vast majority of my colleagues either accept, or are not troubled about enough theoretically to question. Since taking my doctoral degree roughly 34 years ago, I have been continuously developing my arguments and conducting my empirical research outside the mainstream in psychology. This calls for a certain type of person—an "odd duck" or maybe just someone willing to live a professionally marginal existence. So, when all is said and done, maybe marginality is "my life story." I leave it to the reader to decide. I will present my life events around nine headings, each of which contributed to my maturation as a person and a psychologist.

CHILDHOOD

I was born December 17, 1928, on Pulaski Avenue in Cudahy, Wisconsin. I was the first born of two children and for 13 years an "only child." Cudahy was a small, primarily blue-collar community lying just south of metropolitan

Milwaukee. The town was renamed from Buckhorn to Cudahy in honor of the Irish meat packing family that had established a large plant there. The other major industry in town at that time was the Ladish Drop Forge, but there were secondary industries as well. About one-quarter of Cudahy's then 5,000 or 6,000 population, living at the southern end of the town, was of Polish descent. My parents, both of whom were about age 20 at the time of my birth, were "first generation Polish-Americans" and fluent in Polish (I am not). They followed many of their peers into the workforce after grammar school (although my father did have some high school). In 1928 they were renting an upstairs flat on Pulaski Avenue, in south Cudahy, and in a few years moved north one street to a nicer upstairs flat where I lived out my childhood. My folks built their "dream home" after I had returned from military duty, while I was beginning college. I helped with some of the finishing work.

Today, we might say that I was brought up in a Polish ghetto. Polish was spoken everywhere. Polish accents abounded. Most of the names in south Cudahy were unpronounceable to Anglos—a minor annoyance that I have also had to put up with concerning my name. There was a Casimir Pulaski Park in south Cudahy. Even the public grade school was named after Thaddeus Kosciuszko. Across the street from Kosciuszko school was Holy Family grade school, where both my parents had received their primary education. The Holy Family Church (Roman Catholic) that my family attended adjoined this school. The teachers at Holy Family were all sisters of the Felician order.

My mother (née Helen Bieniek) was eventually to become an expert seamstress. She worked 40 hours a week until retiring at age 65. My father (Joseph Walter), after working at various laboring positions, went to "barber college" and opened his own barber shop in Cudahy. When World War II came along he took a position with a vinegar manufacturing plant in Cudahy and continued barbering part time. He was a vigorous man, much interested in political affairs. He became active in the union movement and held offices in his local. He also became active in Cudahy politics and was elected as an alderman of his ward for many years. For the last 15 years of his work career, my father was the city clerk of Cudahy (an elected position).

As my mother always worked I could be called a latch-key kid in modern parlance. But the sense of family and community that I experienced negated any such labeling. I never felt neglected or totally alone. Actually, I have *liked* being alone from early childhood. I get a sense of freedom and relaxation when I am alone. Within a two-block radius of our home lived three or four relatives who could be reached in an emergency—especially my grandparents on my mother's side. My father's parents had divorced and his father simply disappeared. His mother then died when he was about eight, and he along with three brothers was reared by a stepfather. My father found in my maternal grandmother a second mother. I too loved my grandmother very much. She was the focus of all our lives, the unquestioned leader.

Across the street from us lived one of my father's brothers. His son, my cousin Antone, was to become my closest friend—like a brother. Antone was two months older than me. We grew up together and parted when I left to go into the Air Force. This was the era of nicknames; he was "Sonny" and I was "Skip." At first I was "Junior" but my dad changed that. Antone and I had a great childhood, even though it was during the years of the Great Depression. We had fields to play in. There were huge dumps around the factories to forage in and make toys out of the junk that we found. Westerns were our favorite play themes. I was Tom Mix and he was Ken Maynard. This childhood fascination with the Old West has stayed with me. For relaxation, I now have a large collection of nonfiction dealing with the "good guys, bad guys, and Indians." I have even taken vacations to study the locale of Western historical events, such as the Custer battlefield and the OK Corral shootout.

Antone and I started grade school at Kosciuszko. My mother was not too pleased with this, as she was (and is) a very religious person. She wanted me to attend Holy Family. But Kosciuszko had a gymnasium, and dad, being what today we would call an "ex-jock," wanted his son to experience physical exercise. They also had a school library at Kosciuszko. Apparently my dad was kind of Peck's bad boy at Holy Family, continually getting into trouble with the sisters. Where I attended grammar school for the next eight years depended upon the tussle between my parents over what was most important for me at the time. I spent the first three grades at Kosciuszko, at which point my father "gave in" to mother's pressure and I moved across the street to Holy Family in order to take my First Holy Communion. I did so, only to return to Kosciuszko for the sixth grade because dad had some reason or other for me to do so. Mother won out in the next year for I spent seventh and eighth grade at Holy Family.

I detail this bouncing back and forth across the street to make the point that it was probably a good thing for my future career as a psychologist. There was tremendous competition, prejudice, and downright hostility between these two groups of school kids. But here I was, forced to shift sides every couple of years. I liked (and disliked) kids on both sides of the street. I could never really lend my complete allegiance to either side. This gave me a sense of marginality and objectivity. Also, it probably added to my tendency toward becoming a loner—to rely on myself a bit more and less on "the gang" I was with. I don't mean to suggest that I avoided others. I was always gregarious in groups and, in fact, something of a cut-up in the classroom.

When I was 13 years old mother gave birth to my brother, Don. This meant I had to learn how to change diapers and look after a baby in every way. I have always enjoyed children. My own children have been the joy of my life. But, of course, when you are 14 and 15 years old, problems can arise when you have plans to go the soda parlor to flirt with the girls and your mother decides you have to "watch the baby." But my mother was equal to the task, and I was a "good" son. The experience helped when my own children came along.

High school found Antone and me together again—walking to school and back, lockers side by side, trying out for football together, ogling the girls, and so on. I was always a good student, although hardly a scholar. My saving grace was that I enjoyed reading and understood what I read—a trait that probably accounts more for any success that I have had professionally than anything else. That is, I am in large measure self-taught and have always loved books. My father insisted that I do well in school, but he never pressed college on me. My mother did speak of college occasionally. In high school, I continued performing well enough in the classroom so that at graduation I was given an award for having the highest academic record of any graduating athlete. I preferred my own reading to classroom assignments. I once stumbled upon an edited version of Nietzsche and spouted his aphorisms for a time. I also recall reading Havelock Ellis in an effort to advance my sexual education beyond street-corner edification.

My life in high school was primarily "football." My father had seen to my development as an athlete. One of his brothers was a professional boxer, and so I had boxing gloves from the time I was six. I also had a broken nose early in life, but that happened in an accident on ice. Dad had taught me how to toss a football and swing a bat. He was a great pal to me. We went to football games together and took in the fights in Milwaukee. I never had very "personal" talks with him—at least, none that he initiated. My mother was always easier to talk with about personal matters. Dad saw all my football games but Mom never attended one. I played varsity in the backfield for three years and was the only sophomore to earn a football letter. This swelled my head a bit, but I was brought down in time by the fact that the best I could achieve was an "honorable mention" in the all-conference voting of my senior football year. I did get the Cudahy High School award as the outstanding graduating athlete of my class.

Suddenly, it was graduation time and what was I to do? I had never seriously planned for college, except in the sense that I hoped maybe to land a football scholarship. My folks couldn't send me. I was not academic scholarship material. It was 1946. World War II had ended the previous year, and all of the boys were coming home to swell the ranks of college football teams. There was no room here for honorable-mention quarterbacks. I had landed a job at the Ladish Drop Forge, working in the shipping room. Was this to be my future? I decided the thing to do would be to go into the military service and earn the GI Bill, so that I might one day have the money to go to college. Quite honestly, this was a vague goal at the time. I primarily just wanted to get out of the small town and "see the world." Antone liked the idea, but his folks would not sign for him. We were only 17 years old and needed their signatures to enlist. So, I had to go alone. That was pretty much the end of our close relationship, for we went separate ways in life (and he died much too soon).

UNITED STATES AIR FORCE

I enlisted in what was then called the Army Air Corps on August 27, 1946, and was honorably discharged with the rank of sergeant on June 29, 1949. Enlistees were sent to Lackland Air Force Base, San Antonio, Texas, for basic training. This was the first time that I had been further from Wisconsin than Chicago, where we had relatives to visit. It was exciting. San Antonio was a beautiful city, and I had some riotous Saturday evenings there with my buddies. I had visions of flying all over the world following basic training—preferably as a tail gunner on a flying fortress. Instead, I was lumped in with about 40 other guys who scored reasonably well on the Army General Classification Test and, following basic training, was sent to Barksdale Air Force Base, Shreveport, Louisiana, where I spent the rest of my hitch coding morning reports in the Statistical Control Section of the Air Training Command. We tracked the movements of all the military personnel in various training programs—machinists, pilots, cooks, and so on. It was an unromantic, dull desk job.

The day I stepped into that basement office was one of the low points of my life. I felt as though I had been sent to prison. After a few days, my supervising captain could see my desperate mood and took me aside for a long, private, fatherly chat. He made a deal with me. If I would just stick it out, he would see to it that when he rotated his assignment in a year I would be transferred overseas. I agreed to straighten-up and play the "good soldier" for a year.

But by the time that year rolled around, I had changed quite a bit. What happened at Barksdale had already begun during basic training at Lackland. For the first time in my life, I became painfully aware of class—or is it "caste?"—differences. I found myself saluting other guys, many of whom were just a few years older than me but who were supposedly "officers and gentlemen" by right of metal bars pinned to their shoulders. I was a "dog face." What differentiated them from me? In most cases, nothing except two or more years of college. It didn't take a genius to figure out that if I wanted to "go someplace" in life I would have to really and truly get through college. It was no longer to be vague talk about someday going to college—I really *wanted* to go!

So, I set about getting the best background I could for college. This amounted to a lot of reading. I got a copy of the Harvard list of Great Books and began reading those I could lay my hands on. I stumbled upon a collection of books called the Delphian Course in a used bookstore. This was a kind of adult-education series of ten volumes (for which I paid ten dollars) covering ancient history, Greek mythology, literature, and philosophy. I studied words. I spent a lot of time at the Barksdale library, which was a good one and even landed a part-time job there. This lasted only a few months but it was long enough for me to get to know the place like the back of my hand. I took extensive notes in my studies and made use of these in later years. I read a lot of philosophy and some, but not much, psychology.

Of course, I had the usual recreational pleasures of a young man in the service. I played semi-pro softball during one summer, got to play in a tennis tournament at Scott Field outside of St. Louis, Missouri, during another. Saint Louis looked like a nice city. I would be back. I caught "hitchhiking hops" on planes to Los Angeles, Philadelphia, and New York City on weekends. I went to a Mardis Gras in New Orleans on a three-day pass. But the job of coding morning reports at Barksdale was one long bore. An unexpected benefit here was the fact that in our statistical studies we made use of key punches, sorters, collaters, and printers—all of the stuff that was to go into computer processing. I got a good sense of just how all this machinery "worked" to extract and compile information.

My captain was true to his word. After about a year, he was given orders to ship out and looked into an overseas assignment for me. None was available, but he did find me a possibility in Alaska. There was no overseas pay differential for assignments in Alaska. I thought it over for a day and decided that I would ride out my enlistment at Barksdale. My work was lousy, but my living conditions in what is called "permanent army" duty were excellent. We stood almost no inspections. We did not have to march. We could wear civilian clothes after work hours. And, I was advancing intellectually. So, I declined the captain's offer. So much for the Air Force. Well, one last thing: While at Barksdale, I met a fellow who had taken some psychology in college. I decided this would be a good career, working maybe as an industrial psychologist—back at Ladish Drop Forge but this time wearing a tie instead of overalls.

UNIVERSITY OF WISCONSIN

I spent my first two years at the Milwaukee Extension Division of the University of Wisconsin, and then finished up at the parent campus in Madison. I lived at home while attending school in Milwaukee. The only serious academic problem I faced was during my first semester in an algebra class. I had neglected to study mathematics at Barksdale, doubtless because it was never my favorite subject. The instructor went so fast that she lost me after a week, and after six weeks, I was given an F in the course. I wondered for a day or two whether I really was cut out for college. But, since my other courses were going well I decided to fall back on my self-study tactic. I bought a College Outline book on introductory algebra and learned how to solve all of the problems in the class in ways other than what the professor was instructing us. She took this well, actually, and was kind enough to give me a grade of B at the end of the semester. This was one of the four B grades I took at Wisconsin. The rest of my courses were at the A level. I was honored to make Phi Beta Kappa and later helped found chapters of this society at St. Louis University and Purdue University. So, my "college prep" efforts at Barksdale did pay off. I had learned how to study.

I took a double major at Wisconsin—psychology and philosophy. Initially, I thought I would earn a master's degree in psychology and then find a job as an industrial psychologist. But I soon learned it required a Ph.D. to do interesting work in the field. I then set my sights on a career in the mushrooming field of clinical psychology. I have made a reputation in psychology as a "philosophical type." I do love philosophy, at least ancient philosophy. Modern philosophy, with its arcane arguments about language usage, tends to lose me. Also, my athletic identity has stayed with me enough so that, even though I enjoy arguing, I feel there must be some point at which the talking stops and some kind of final test is made to decide "who wins." I find philosophers willing to press on with additional talk when what seems called for is to "put up or shut up" through some kind of disinterested testing procedure. What I was after, of course, was a scientific test.

With the help of my advisor, Emmett Baughmann, I made application to a half-dozen graduate programs. I was admitted to Illinois and Stanford, but decided on Ohio State University. In the fall of 1953, I drove my 1941 Chevrolet down to Columbus, Ohio, found a room, and entered yet another new world.

THE OHIO STATE UNIVERSITY

I was very lucky to do my graduate work in clinical psychology at Ohio State. It has often been singled out as the very best such program of the 1940–1950 era. Jules Rotter and George Kelly both published their fundamental works during my tenure there. Rotter was a neo-Hullian, tempered by a strong attraction to Adlerian theory, which gave his social learning theory a fundamentally teleological cast. Surely this was true of his clinical style. Kelly, on the other hand, theorized more in the phenomenological tradition. His personal construct theory was clearly teleological, and it encompassed dialectical reasoning in the human being.

A major reason for my being considered a philosophical type stems from the prominence I have given in my writings to the role of dialectical reasoning in human cognition. Machine models are exclusively demonstrative in "reasoning" style (the distinction being drawn here is Aristotelian). Some of my interpreters have traced my arguments to Kelly's influence. Actually, Nietzsche had given me a foreshadowing of dialectical reasoning. I also had read about Hegelian dialectic at Barksdale and had seen parallels of this cognitive style in Freud. I was totally cognizant of the Aristotelian distinction throughout my studies in psychology at Wisconsin—which was a veritable "pit" of demonstrative theorizing. We were force fed the resultant mechanism at Wisconsin. At Ohio State, I saw the similarities of my views to those of Kelly's and later (after taking the Ph.D.) tried to get him to admit that he was a dialectical theorist. But he did not like this label, identifying it with Hegelian-Marxian formulations that he did not want to get confused with. Years later, I saw the wisdom of his decision.

Given the similarities in our views, one might expect that I would have taken the Ph.D. with Kelly. But I did not. I took the Ph.D. with Rotter (my master's degree was with Paul H. Mussen). As I always have given Rotter's social learning theory a teleological reading—his basic concept is that of an "expectancy"—it did not bother me that he tried to follow Hull in writing formulae for predicting behavior in quasi-mechanical fashion. I liked the clarity of Rotter's approach and the direct tie it has to laboratory experimentation. Kelly's approach is also experimental, but because he employed a kind of assessment scale (i.e., the *Role Construct Repertory Test*) there has been a different style of empirical investigation taken by his followers. I find the same thing has happened in the rapidly diminishing field of personality study, which has focused primarily on testing, the study of traits (or concepts of the same ilk). Kelly was idiographic in theoretical outlook. Too many of his followers today are nomothetic "testers" to suit me.

The interesting thing about this selection of professors is that, in the long run, I have been closer to and received more personal help from Kelly than Rotter. Rotter was closer to what my father was as a person—more direct, someone who could "level" and be "one of the guys." Kelly, as I viewed him, was more proper and restrained although extremely clever interpersonally. Initially, I took his manner to be a little too manipulative. But then, when I was going through a difficult period in my graduate training, he actually became my therapist. I had gotten into trouble for "questioning the value of clinical instruments" in my first assignment as a Veterans Administration intern. The clinical psychologists in the field were not going to promote me to the next intern level. I guess I was asking some tough questions about the rationale for instruments like the Rorschach. My questions implied that I was a hostile "wise guy" who had no respect for clinical instruments.

I was extremely hurt by this decision to hold me back in my VA internship. So, I asked Lauren Wispe if he would take me on as a graduate student in his program—that is, social psychology. This was my minor area of study. He said "yes," and I informed Rotter—then clinical director—of my intentions. I spelled out exactly what the field people were criticizing me for, and how unfair I thought it was. Rotter told me straight out that I was *not* going to shift programs and that I *would* be promoted. He arranged for a shift in my clinical placement, where I worked under the magnificent tutelage of Margaret Shuttleworth. She helped me to become an effective colleague by rounding out a lot of rough edges.

Even so, following this I had a period of self-doubt about my clinical abilities. This doubt was exacerbated by some difficulty I was having in accepting one of my patients on what might be termed moral grounds (he was a child molester). Both Rotter and Kelly supervised me in my new setting, and at one point I unburdened myself to Kelly. Strange, that I would select him! Kelly, in a most sensitive and insightful manner, quickly grasped the depth of my depression. I spent several sessions with him, and he helped me immensely. One of the most important things that he explained clinically was that aggression is not ipso facto hostility, and having a judgmental stance is not ipso facto rigidity. I think that my desire to earn accreditation from the American Board of Examiners in Professional Psychology at the earliest possible date stemmed from this period of professional self-doubt. I was also pleased by the fact that I got the "ABEPP" on the first try, which was hard to do in 1962. To me, it was like making the varsity.

On a happier note, one of the major events of my life took place at Ohio State. I got married. Lenora (née Smith) was an undergraduate student whose parents lived in Columbus. To keep us as out of debt as possible, she continued her education under her maiden name (using her parent's address) even after we were married. If she had used my name we would have had to pay additional, out-of-state fees. We were married on June 16, 1956, and by December of that year Lenora was pregnant. Ohio State was on the quarter system, so by her third quarter in the spring of 1958 "Miss Smith" was attending college in maternity clothes. This means nothing today, but in those days she faced ostracism from certain of her teachers and was given an F for missing required gym classes. We took most of this in good humor. Lenora and I have had a traditional marriage. Our family "came first" in our lives. But I always went where the best job opportunities for growth could be found and Lenora backed me up without complaint. This meant we had to forego the help of a close relationship with our respective families. In time, Lenora would take a formal role in my work.

I completed my graduate studies, plus my VA training, in four years, graduating in the spring of 1957. That summer, before taking up my first teaching position, I began what would become a 25-year alliance with Douglas W. Bray in the Management Progress Study that he was conducting in the American Telephone and Telegraph (AT&T) System. This longitudinal study followed young men (later, young women as well) through their careers to see who were successful, what the ingredients of a successful career amounted to, and so on. Data were collected during the summer months at assessment centers, set up at certain hotels around the country. I was fortunate to get a job working as a personal interviewer in this study. Later I devised a "life themes" scoring system that allowed us to put the contents of the personal interviews into numerical analyses. I even published a book on some of these data. But a major benefit to me and then my family was the travel opportunities that this consultantship made possible. We spent summers working in Washington, D.C., New York City, Detroit, Philadelphia, Minneapolis, and Denver. Also, I benefitted personally from my friendship with Doug Bray in that he was an excellent model of the sophisticated professional. Copying aspects of his style helped build my self-confidence in professional and social contacts. I also learned about wines. But I still prefer beer with my meals.

FLORIDA STATE UNIVERSITY

I was awarded my Ph.D. in the spring of 1957, and worked for Doug that summer in Washington, D.C. My friend, John Neff, helped me to land a position at Florida State University. He had moved down there from Ohio State the year before. As Lenora's obstetrician was located in Columbus, I had to drop her off at her folks' place on my way from D.C. to Tallahassee, to begin teaching my classes. On September 23, 1957, Lenora gave birth to our son, Ronald Joseph, as I "sweated it out" with John's support. One month later, Lenora and Ronald joined me.

There would be little to say about the one year spent at Florida State except for an incident that literally set the tone for my entire career. I was teaching a practicum in family/child therapy and had three male graduate students in the course. It was a Thursday morning in November 1957. I had scheduled a case review session in which other clinical staff and a consulting psychiatrist were present. I was infuriated to see my three students sitting through this two-hour review of cases without saying one word! No comments, no hypothesized interpretations, no therapy suggestions. Just three stumps, sitting there in total disregard of my embarrassing efforts to bring them out.

After the psychiatrist and other staff had left I read the riot act to them. What could have possessed them? Weren't they interested in clinical work? What was going on here? Their reply shocked and then challenged me. I have to mention here that Joel Greenspoon was teaching at Florida State at this time. He had conducted a widely cited experiment in which he claimed to have manipulated people's verbal reports without their awareness. Subsequent experiments have proven Greenspoon wrong on this point, but at the time his Skinnerian claims were receiving wide acceptance.

Well, what my students told me, in effect, was that Dr. Greenspoon had convinced them that it was pointless to do such clinical investigation as was manifested in our session, theorizing about this or that aspect of the client's case history or future prospects in therapy. "We have not yet learned how to control and predict the complete behavior of a laboratory rat. So, how in the world can we hope to control the behavior of children or their parents?" I was so taken aback by this line of argument—one that I had never heard at Ohio State, where we were always theorizing, critically evaluating, proposing, and so on—that I did a very poor job of countering it. It seemed as though my students' morale concerning clinical work was low, and now mine was beginning to plunge as well—but for different reasons. This burned me up all the more. I dismissed the class, went home for lunch, and poor Lenora had to listen to my ranting and raving for about an hour. Then, I went directly to the school library and took down the first volume of our basic professional journal, the *American Psychologist*. That afternoon I initiated a series of readings that progressed into a career emphasis. I began reading all of the papers relating to the profession of clinical psychology in historical sequence—taking my usual notes (which I still possess and use). I found that this called for study in the philosophy of science as well. Over the years, I extended my historical review of psychology to the *Psychological Review*. This journal used to be an excellent outlet for theoretical exchanges, but in my opinion, it has been ruined since the 1950s by a misguided editorship demanding that empirical data be included in most if not all of the articles. In any case, near the close of 1957, I had begun fighting for my professional life, wondering what the devil I had gotten myself into.

WASHINGTON STATE UNIVERSITY

We spent the summer of 1958 in New York City, where I was working on the Management Progress Study. Florida State University had not granted any raises and had not asked me to sign a contract. So when Jim Elder called me about a job at Washington State University (Pullman) that raised my income by almost 50 percent, I took the job "sight unseen." Jim, who was chairperson of psychology at WSU, was taking the recommendation of Paul Mussen (my M.A. thesis professor). I was looking for a raise, but there was also the lure of my beloved "Wild West." So, in late summer I moved my family from the East to the West Coast by way of Florida. Luckily, Ronnie was a good traveler.

The job at Washington State involved running a small community clinic (Human Relations Center) and teaching one course each semester. I was worried about too much time committed to clinical administration, but things worked out beautifully. I had my own facility, away from the department. I had my own secretary. Lenora and I found a nice little house a few blocks from my clinic. And I had the time to study as well as to do a number of experiments on the group Rorschach, dreams, free association, and various personality dimensions. I gave my first advanced degrees there. Gradually, I worked out a more experimental approach to the study of the person, one that permitted me to be rigorously experimental yet teleological in theoretical accounts. I also began submitting exclusively theoretical pieces to journals—encouraged initially by my friend and colleague Jerry Brams. I think Jerry felt that others should have to suffer through what I was making him suffer through during our bull sessions.

Our life in Pullman was pleasant enough, but we were far removed from family ties in the Midwest with no real financial capacity to fly back and forth. And it was too far to drive more than once a year. The summer jobs with the Management Progress Study were a godsend, for they covered our expenses as we motored to Philadelphia in 1959 and Minneapolis in 1960. Lenora became pregnant late in 1960. In April 1961, I was contacted by Saint Louis University concerning a position. I believe that Rotter had recommended me. As I had a good opinion of St. Louis (MO), I decided to look the job over. I was to fly out in mid-May, and Lenora's obstetrician said that she could accompany me. The baby was due in late June. Fortunately she decided not to make the trip, as no sooner had I checked into my hotel in St. Louis than I learned that Lenora had gone into labor. My mother flew to Pullman that very day to help out, and I continued my job interview. I landed the job and almost made it back to Pullman for the birth. But a few hours before arriving on May 16, 1961, my daughter Stephanie Dianne was born—six weeks early! I have since kidded Stephanie about this because the name "Rychlak" can be anglicized as "Early."

SAINT LOUIS UNIVERSITY

Saint Louis University is a Jesuit institution. I suspect that Rotter, knowing of my Roman Catholic identity, recommended me with this in mind. I do not consider myself "religious" in a doctrinaire manner. But I do carry with me a sense of the human need for some such loving order in existence. It seems to me that our "modern" world is losing the sentimentality that religion often engenders. I am loyal to my Catholic roots, and as a matter of fact, I am not overly happy with the changes that have occurred in its liturgical practices. I believe that religion makes a difference in one's life. But one must work at it, and I am sometimes lazy.

I have had to pay a price for my religious identity as a psychologist, for it has tended to undermine my teleological theoretical position concerning the description of human behavior. People dismiss my views more readily when they think, "This guy believes in God. Naturally he will claim that people have free will." I have often said that, from my graduate school days on, my religion has been as much the "cross" as the "crutch" that most people think it is. The truth is, of course, that teleologists are not always religious, and religious people are not always teleological in their understanding of human behavior. I was reading Nietzsche in high school with greater concentration than anything I read in my prayer books, and he claimed that "God is dead." Nevertheless, Nietzsche characterized human beings as purposive agents in their everyday activities. So, whether I keep my religion or claim there is no God is quite irrelevant to the question of *human* agency. Deity teleology need have nothing to do with human teleology. Try telling this to some of my critics!

The eight years spent at Saint Louis University were highly productive. I decided to write a book based on my studies to that point. It was not easy getting this manuscript published, but luckily Bob Rooney of Houghton Mifflin saw something in it. One of the problems my approach to psychology suffers from is that it cannot be easily categorized. I tend to "fall between the cracks." Bob helped me focus the manuscript and to work out the title, which became A *Philosophy of Science for Personality Theory* (1968). But the greatest honor he did me was to take an interest in my next project, which was to apply the theoretical framework from this initial effort to an introductory personality text. I had begun teaching personality at Saint Louis University, and it irritated me that everyone looked down their noses at this "Mickey Mouse" course. I wanted to write a substantial personality textbook, one that would be accurate, in depth, and thoroughly documented—to rival textbooks in experimental and statistics. In addition, I wanted the student to gain some knowledge of theory construction. So, Bob "signed me up" one afternoon, over lunch, with nothing more than my handshake promise that I would get him a book in five years. No prospectus had to be written, no handful of reviewers making their pet suggestions had to be put up with.

I spent one year studying Freud's works, the next studying Jung's works, six months on Adler, and so on, with the usual detailed note taking, until in four years I had a manuscript. By this time, Bob had left Houghton Mifflin. I think he was not quite the "bottom line" type they were interested in, although I am not sure. But he was the prototype editor in my estimation. It seems that we no longer have such editors in psychology. He was interested in developing talent and raising levels. I have found that even university presses today are more interested in maximizing the return on books than they used to be. In any case, my introductory text appeared when I reached Purdue under the title *Introduction to Personality and Psychotherapy: A Theory-Construction Approach* (1973). It has been a successful text, but to my disappointment the theory-construction is not what sells the book. It is the in-depth coverage of the theories that sell it, and, ironically, this is considered "too difficult" for undergraduate education in any case. So, it is used predominantly in graduate study.

Lenora and I bought our first house in St. Louis. It was a huge, three-story Georgian colonial—ten-foot ceilings, red brick, slate roof, copper rain gutters, on a beautiful but declining boulevarded street. It was also badly in need of repairs, a new furnace, paint, and so forth. The price was extremely good for the market was depressed. For eight years, we painted, refinished floors, shopped at garage and estate sales for carpets and furniture, and turned that place into what was for me a real palace. I loved that house. In fact, I used to dream about it regularly once we had left it. The kids had a great time in it too. But when we sold it we lost several thousand dollars. Well-spent losses, I'd say.

I have great memories of St. Louis, where my family and my career really began to grow. The kids went to Saint Margaret of Scotland grade school, and Ronnie began playing Little League baseball. Stephanie assumed the position of "teacher's little helper" from kindergarten on and has always stood at the top of her class. Lenora held a state PTA office and received an award for her work with the Democratic party in the city. We had a nice, traditional family life. There was the sorrow of losing Lenora's father in 1969. The Department of Psychology was young and dynamic, under the excellent leadership of Don Kausler. I attracted several graduate students, some of whom began gathering data on topics in learning and memory rather than strictly clinical topics.

I gradually but steadily was moving from a full-fledged clinical psychologist to more of a personality theorist. I worked out a method of studying learning based upon people's affective preferences, and I was becoming increasingly aware of the fact that to accomplish what I wanted to do, I would have to spend less time in the clinic and more in the laboratory. To be honest, I was finding clinical work repetitious. I had passed my ABEPP exam early in 1962. But I had this "empty" feeling that we could go on as clinicians, spinning our theories of a teleological nature, yet the "lab guys" in their white jackets would just ignore us and say, "Basic science proves that human beings are machines."

Well, I didn't believe that basic science proves that people are machines. My studies of the philosophy of science were convincing me that it was the theories of the mechanists that provide this "proof" by way of interpretation and not the evidence per se. I was sure that my telic interpretation could be equally substantiated in a rigorous experimental context. When a job opportunity came up in 1969, enabling me to shift into personality at Purdue University, I was only too ready. Mark Stephens, a friend from Ohio State who had been working at Purdue for some years, helped me land this job. So, we sold the house, packed up the furniture in a huge rented truck, and made our way to Lafayette, Indiana.

PURDUE UNIVERSITY

We had trouble finding a suitable house in West Lafayette, Indiana, where Purdue is located. There were very few places for sale in 1969. So, we ended up buying a four bedroom, garrison colonial home about five miles south of Lafayette, on an acre of land. This was to be Lenora's "dream home." It was in a new subdivision, out enough in the country that we could actually hear cows mooing from a farm across the way. There were only a handful of families in the subdivision, and they became the nucleus of a group of great friends. We had both a cat and a dog. There were good schools for the kids. I had to drive about 25 minutes to get to work. We bought a second automobile, a Volkswagen camper that became my personal treasure. Lenora got the Mercedes. Gasoline was a major item in our budget as the kids moved through grade and high school.

Joining a Big Ten psychology department as a full professor was a distinction that I did not take lightly. I worked all the harder. I was very impressed by the efficiency of the Department of Psychological Sciences, as it was to be known. Jim Naylor was the Head (actual title), and I found him to be an excellent administrator, with high standards and a sense of fair play. The plan was for Donn Byrne—who joined the faculty the same year I did—and me to form the nucleus of a new personality division in the department. And so we did. But, in time, I was asked to sit on the faculty of clinical psychology as well—which I agreed to do. Despite our theoretical differences, Donn and I got along very well, with mutual respect and support. I began gathering a number of graduate students around me and continued my experimental research on what I was now calling my logical learning theory. I was not successful in getting research grants. I recall a stretch of ten years in which I submitted extensive research applications without success. The only support I enjoyed in my entire teaching career was two small grants, given over summer months. I often felt "shot down" by colleagues who seemed to be protecting an outdated interpretation of what science involves. They equated mechanism and engineering with rigor, and I was advancing a rigorous form of humanism. Thanks to the help of many undergraduate and graduate students, I conducted experiments on college students, mental patients, kids in the school systems of West Lafayette, Lafayette, and Indianapolis. In time, I published all of this empirical work as well as a preliminary statement of my theory in a book entitled *The Psychology of Rigorous Humanism* (1977).

By this time the Management Progress Study data collection had run its course. I continued to score the interview data and, in time, published a book on the life themes entitled *Personality and Life-Style of Young Male Managers: A Logical-Learning Theory Analysis* (1982). This could not have been done without Doug's help, of course. I was getting more invitations to speak around the country and to attend conventions. Whenever possible, I tried to take my family with me to psychological conventions. We traveled to Europe a couple of times while I was at Purdue. Lenora and I took a memorable "speaking tour" around the Los Angeles area during a sabbatical leave in 1977, and I spoke at four or five departments of psychology. I also wrote the manuscript of a book entitled *Discovering Free Will and Personal Responsibility* (1979) during this semester's hiatus.

Both of our children were good students. Stephanie graduated from high school as the valedictorian. She was also a school leader, homecoming queen, cheerleader, actress, and so on. Ronald was both a school leader and an exceptional athlete, earning not only all-conference recognitions in baseball, football, and wrestling, but ranking at the state level in all these sports as well. This naturally pleased—and even amazed—the "ex-jock" in me. He was offered college scholarships in football, but did not have to take that route as he earned a full academic/leadership scholarship to Wabash College, where he was student body president. Stephanie was awarded merit scholarship assistance at DePauw University. In time, Ronald would earn a degree in law at Vanderbilt and, after working in corporation law for a time, take a position as a law professor at Ole Miss. Stephanie, after working in business for a few years, returned to earn the Ph.D. in developmental psychology at Loyola University of Chicago. Both Ronald (to Claire Lindsey) and Stephanie (to Todd Stilson) have married and have turned Lenora and me into proud grandparents.

Aside from the theoretical elaboration and growing evidence that I was accruing for my view of human behavior, I suppose the major professional development that I experienced at Purdue was my 18 months as interim Head of the Department of Psychological Sciences (June 1979 to December 1980). Actually, I was selected, quite unwillingly, by default. I had never aspired to an administrative position. My somewhat narrow view had been that administrators were the professor's natural "enemy" because they seemed always to be finding committee assignments to fill and initiating "programs" that detracted from the time one could be spending on scholarship. So, it was as a bolt from the blue when one afternoon my dean called me into his office and put the question to me: Would I take the job of an interim Head?

Jim Naylor had stepped down from the position and a replacement could not be agreed upon The department had to do another search and someone had to occupy the Head's chair. I guess hot air rushes to the vacuum, and I was the vacuum. Well, very reluctantly, I accepted. But I tried to do my best. Fortunately, my dean, Bob Ringel, was a great help to me. What made the job tough was the fact that we were moving into a new building at the time, and the various factions in the department were maneuvering for space. I found it an education, sitting in that chair. I could see how that kind of work could be interesting as well as challenging. But I didn't come into teaching to do it. One of the eye-opening things I learned is that not all problems are solvable because the people concerned really do *not* want to solve them! There is always a political aspect to any problem's solution. And political power is not conceded easily.

I was frankly amazed to see how political academics are. Politics is essential in life, of course, although I had had enough of politics just witnessing my father's involvements. Power is important, but it strikes me that academics should be concerned with intellectual power, with ideas. An "ivory tower" person like myself is interested in and willing to confront *any* form of idea in open exchange. This is what the ivory tower means—that ideas are not to be judged in the political arena, as power plays. They have power ramifications, of course, but the academic advancing them should not be using them as a tool in such manipulation. Nor should he or she be punished for expressing these ideas. There is a difference between ideas having power implications and literally seeking to use ideas in a power manipulation. I am therefore unimpressed by those who talk of "politically correct" ideas in the academic context. Academia should be as little tainted by political considerations as possible.

The early years of the 1980s decade were traumatic ones, as a number of loved ones passed away during a two-year period—including my father, my brother Don, and Antone. At about the same time, an old friend from Saint Louis University, Father Dan O'Connell, contacted me. He was now on the psychology faculty of Loyola University of Chicago, and they were having a chair funded in humanistic psychology that he felt I might occupy. I resisted at first. Stephanie had one more year to go at DePauw, and we wanted to be close to her. But Jeanne Foley, chairperson of psychology at Loyola, was very understanding of my circumstances, and things were worked out so that I could assume the chair in the fall of 1983 instead of 1982. Moving amidst the funerals detracted from the pleasure of a new career challenge for me. And I know that Lenora found it very difficult giving up her home in the country. But, the kids were now on their own, and a shift to the Chicago area would not only put us closer to my now widowed mother but also provide some excitement to our lives. So, once again, for what we both know is the last time, we packed up and moved on.

LOYOLA UNIVERSITY OF CHICAGO

I assumed the Maude C. Clarke Chair in Humanistic Psychology at Loyola in the fall of 1983. Maude C. Clarke was living when we arrived. She attended my inaugural address and Lenora subsequently had a dinner party in her honor. She was a marvelous human being, a down-to-earth, sincere kind of person. She was an ex-nurse who held the rank of Lieutenant Colonel during World War II in the Army Nurse Corps. I believe that her husband, John Clarke, had accrued the wealth which they both used philanthropically. It is said that when the Clarkes were asked about funding a chair in the Department of Psychology, Maude admonished: "I don't want it to be for one of those rat psychologists." The counter here was "Well, how about a humanistic psychologist?" Maude liked the sound of that. So, this is how I came to be the holder of what I think is the first chair in humanistic psychology in this country. My appointment was actually dual, in that I was also made a professor of philosophy. I was delighted with this dual appointment, of course, even though it does tend to perpetuate some confusion over my approach (falling through the cracks again!).

I am not a humanistic psychologist in the sense that many of my colleagues use this term—as someone interested in studying only "the higher" experience of human beings, refusing to "objectify" people in experimentation, and so on. The term *teleological psychologist* would suit me better. I am bothered by the tendency today in psychology for humanistic theorists to demean the traditional forms of experimental validation in favor of a more discursive proof, based on analytical argumentation or "dialogue" relying exclusively on what I call procedural evidence (common-sense plausibilities, etc.). Colleagues with a "politically correct" mind-set seem especially drawn to this sort of proof. I sometimes feel a little guilty about this state of affairs in psychology because my writings have helped to spell out the limitations on certainty that the logic of scientific proof entails. Too many colleagues have taken these limitations to mean that science either "proves nothing" or "proves anything it wants to." It seems to me that we are approaching nihilism in certain circles of psychology today. The tendency to confuse "theorizing" with "proving" is rampant. I have tried to keep these two sides of the scientific enterprise clear and distinct in my work.

In the lengthy negotiations for the Loyola position, Lenora and I had talked it over and decided to "count her in." We felt it would be great if she could assist me by managing the budget of my chair, as well as become more active in data gathering than she had in the past. Actually, Lenora has always given me editorial assistance in my writings. I do my own typing, even on final copy, but she is the chief editor of the work. But now it seemed a good idea in the new environment for her to actually attend the job with me as an executive assistant. We were not seeking additional salary, of course, but I wanted her to have an office at the school. Jeanne Foley and Father Lawrence Biondi, Dean of Arts and Sciences, both understood and were very helpful here. They found adjoining offices for us, set outside the Department of Psychology proper, but in good proximity to the clinical faculty. Actually, my chair is not limited to clinical, although this is my primary contact and I attend this subfaculty's meetings. But I have had graduate students taking degrees in all four of the areas offered at Loyola— clinical, experimental, social, and developmental.

Lenora looks after a budget including two graduate assistants, makes all travel arrangements, handles supplies and equipment purchases, carries out editorial and library duties, assists the graduate students working with me, and generally keeps the mayhem under control. As she is more gregarious than I am, she also presents a nice image for the Clarke Chair. She seems to know everyone. What I especially like is that she accompanies me on most of my travels these days (circa 1992). I make five or six trips each year to deliver papers, both in America and overseas. Lenora has also now become a published author. Our decision to include her in the job was a good one for both of us.

We moved into a large, older apartment/condominium near Lake Michigan in suburban Evanston. This is located just three miles north of the Loyola Lake Shore Campus and occasionally for exercise we walk to work. Lenora and I are enjoying the many cultural outlets that Chicago has to offer—from the Lyric Opera to the Chicago Cubs. We have a "restauranting" hobby these days. We are also less than two hours from Cudahy and therefore see my mother regularly.

I failed to mention that since my Saint Louis University days I have been a dedicated jogger. Nowadays, in a slow trot, or a trot-and-walk, I cover four or five miles every chance I get (at least four days per week, winter or summer). I used to run ten-minute miles, but that was years ago. I like to run alone. It gives me time to think or simply to let the mind go blank. I always feel better after a jog. I have kept it up for over 30 years, and I feel certain this has added to my level of physical and mental health. The "trick" for me to maintain motivation (I hated to run track in high school!) is to avoid making my jogs into contests. I have never run in a race. I jog for pleasure, and when it is too much of an effort on any one day, I simply walk it out.

Professionally speaking, at present I am working on what I jokingly call my *magnum opus*, which will give a detailed presentation of logical learning theory. I started this book a few years ago but found that the things I wanted to say in a preliminary way demanded a book of their own. So, I published *Artificial Intelligence and Human Reason: A Teleological Critique* (1991). This book brought out my conviction that human beings employ predication when they reason, whereas computer models and traditional learning explanations rely on a matching process through mediational mechanisms. I also began speaking of "oppositionality" rather than "dialectic" in this book because I discovered—as George Kelly seems to have realized—that the latter concept has a lot of historical baggage lugged along with it. People want to put you into an Hegelian or a Marxian camp when you use this term. And there are all kinds of dialectical theories being tossed about today in psychology. I can recall when there were virtually none but mine. The concept just "got away" from me. I could no longer convey specifically and clearly what I wanted to say in using it. I still refer to dialectical reasoning, of course, but I am doing empirical research on the role of both predication and opposition in human cognition. Actually, I show how opposition is an aspect of predication.

Now that the artificial intelligence book is completed, I can turn my attention to a volume on logical learning theory. I am hesitant to call this theory a truly Kuhnian revolution, because of course I do not really expect it, or anything quite like it, to be adopted in my lifetime. Revolutions have to take place. But I do have the confidence—or is it hubris?—to suggest that something like logical learning theory will be accepted in the future. We are learning that our Newtonian/Lockean style of theoretical description in psychology simply does not capture what people "do" mentally. We require formal/final-cause terminology and are gradually being moved in this more Kantian direction. I have lived through a fantastic change in how behavior is described by my colleagues. Mechanistic explanation has steadily eroded these past 30 years. My teleological accounts have not changed one iota. The "other side" is sounding more and more like me. At least, this is what I like to believe. Only the future will tell if teleological description will win out in the characterization of human behavior.

CLOSING OBSERVATIONS

Well, this is about all I have to say—or, is it reveal?—about my life. I can see in reviewing what I have written that the reader has been given a theme—something like: "Working class boy makes good as scholarly loner, but does not reject his roots altogether." I guess this is what I probably wanted to convey, although I did not have any such scenario in mind when I began. Intellectual achievement seems to have predominated in my adult life. I have been stubbornly focused on what interested me, and it looks now like I just might get it all recorded between the covers of a book. My family has always taken precedence in my affections over my work, but the truth is that I have a wife who encouraged and materially helped me to fulfill my professional interests. I did the best job I could, given my natural limitations. I hope some kindred spirit or two down the road of time will build on my efforts.

Winding up an autobiography like this has the dreadful implication that the life concerned is over. Like the cartoon character says at the end of an episode: "That's all folks!" I hope this isn't true, of course. I have some writing projects in mind after the *magnum opus* is finished, such as a theory-based history text. But, for the sake of narrative completion, assuming this is about "it" for my primary career, what would I like to have people think of me? As is sometimes asked, what would I like to have written on my tombstone? There is a statement, paraphrased from a song in the musical *Oklahoma*, that I would not mind having engraved on my tombstone:

"He went about as 'fur' as he could go."

9

Conditions and Will: The Enigma of Remembrance

Jesse Hiraoka

Preceding any chronology and any organized series of events are two occurrences that seem to arise from nowhere and to dominate all other events
in my life whenever I think about the totality of my existence, and it is the
same at this moment: the arrival of a McCormick Deering tractor in a year
that I cannot be precise about, and the removal of our family from the farm
in Fowler, California, in late July or early August 1942, a consequence of
the war between Japan and the United States. Both events recur without
exact dates and precise acts. Both occurrences seem to image all of the other
events and acts, be they large or small. Obviously the two occurrences gained
significance at some point in my life when the years of experience sifted
them out, at least some 15 years after they had occurred. Let them take
their place more naturally as I try to retrace events in the more usual act
of growing up and growing old.

I was born on the second day of January in 1927. I was the last of nine
children, two of whom did not survive the first few days after being born.
My father and mother were *Issei*, the first generation of immigrants from
Japan, and they had settled on 40 acres planted in grapevines and peach
trees. My early recollections are of mules and a memorable brown and white
horse named Barney, who was gentle and patient enough to be ridden by
children. There were chickens, and I spent many a spring killing flies with
a large rubber band so that the newly hatched chicks would be attracted to
the hand offering the remains of house flies. One dog replaced another over
a period of time so that there comes to mind a Jimmy or Jimmie (I never
knew because no one bothered to put it on paper) and a dog named Bull.
The names seemed to derive from whoever seemed to have the final say.
In the early years that would have been my father. As such matters of naming

became less interesting to him, I am sure that the older children decided what names were to be selected to identify the creatures that had some semblance of importance.

After all, my father had had to name all of the children, and the fact that he did not select a Japanese name for the last three children offers some proof that the matter was becoming less interesting to him. And the fact that he gave me the name of Jesse, and that name alone, would surely prove that he had lost interest in names. The source was not biblical; there happened to be a person bearing that name who drove, along with my two oldest brothers, the two GMC two-and-a-half-ton six wheelers which took the boxed peaches and grapes to the Los Angeles wholesale markets. His place was taken later by his brother named Floyd, suggesting that had their names been reversed, my life would have been altered by the incredible distance that separates those two names, Jesse and Floyd. Later, when my own first child was born, it became incumbent upon me to create a bit more history, and it led to at least a middle name of David for my oldest, since Jesse was the father of David. I know that not having a middle name, not even an initial, was of some concern to me in my early years, but it never occurred to me to add a name. All of my other brothers and sisters had created new names for themselves, choosing to add an American name to their given Japanese names, or, as in the case of my sister nearest in age to me, just adding a middle name. I felt that there was enough in that first name given to me by my father to create problems. During the early years in which many of my playmates were of Mexican parentage, I was called Jesus, pronounced in the way that those who knew Spanish spoke it. The *Isseis* gave it its own peculiar sound. Later, as I began a professional career as a professor of French, I would find it spelled in different ways, with letters addressing me as Miss, Mrs., or Ms. I wondered then as to the real source of the name my father had chosen for me. Of course, my mother could not pronounce the name easily, and I thereby became Jay to all the members in the family. Jesse became increasingly for me a written name, and a name that was sounded by those who really did not know me.

The family name was source of further concern, since the "ao" combination is not readily found in English. The name was more often than not written with "oa," after the word *oak* in English. During that early period of childhood, the eight years of elementary school, I was Jay to the family, Roak or Rugga to those with whom I played softball and basketball, and Hiraki, Hiroak, or Hirako to those who attempted to use the family name. I am fairly certain that the fact of dealing with the different pronunciations and uses of my name developed in me a variety of attitudes and some patience.

Being the youngest, I was needed less on the family farm and in the family business of packing and shipping fruit to the wholesale markets in Los Angeles. There was no set routine for me, and I began to read fables and stories in *The Book of Knowledge*, which my father purchased and had kept hidden in a large citrus box in the two-room separate building where my three brothers slept. I would go into that first room, pull the box from under the first bed and lose myself for approximately two hours reading Aesop's fables, short stories, and pieces of fiction such as *The Cloister and the Hearth*. The tales of Edgar Allan Poe were of special interest. For whatever reason, the articles on science did not interest me, and that easy turn to fiction suggests that my interests were set early on.

I attended the local elementary school and was usually rated the best student in each of the classes. Since a great deal of the work required finding the correct answers within the text, I became adept at finding the paragraphs which were significant. With the mastery of this skill, I completed workbooks two or three months ahead of when they needed to be completed. I did exceptionally well in spelling bees and in math bees. The school was considered to be a grammar school, and grammar I absorbed.

Unlike the older children in the family, I was not sent to Japanese language school, except for a period of some three months. A prestigious attorney who lived in an imposing tiled-roof mansion had asked my father why I was being sent to school on a Saturday. His influence was such that I not only was freed from Saturday classes but also received each Monday the *Los Angeles Times* comics, which included Tarzan and Flash Gordon and The Katzenjammer Kids, Hans and Fritz. My playmates came primarily from Mexican-American families, and despite occasional warnings by my parents and by older brothers and sisters, I never understood why their background was of concern. Two of those playmates were brothers and lived on a neighboring farm. Saul and Refugio, the latter suffered a naming problem that I felt exceeded my own, were exceptional athletes and very good students. I walked regularly to school with them.

The 15 to 20 students in each of the classes fell usually into three groups: three or four students from families of Japanese parentage, five or six of White, and the remaining nine or ten of Mexican. Our world was small and rural, and the simple pleasures consisted of filling pockets with raisins from boxes or trays before continuing on to school. We could also find walnuts under trees. These were good for trading with the three or four classmates whose parents ran the local grocery or dry goods store. They usually had peanuts or candy in their pockets and were willing to trade for raisins. I managed to avoid getting into fights, but I suspect that this was due more to the fact that the fathers of two or three of my classmates worked for my father. It explains the fact that one girl whose father worked for mine always gave me the biggest Valentine received by anyone else in the class, more a statement of economic position than of affection, but one took what one was given.

I did not grow as rapidly as did my three older brothers, and this was a disappointment to the coaches who had benefited from the athletic prowess of my brothers. At the elementary school level, especially seventh and eighth grades, Prairie Elementary always produced the best local teams in softball, basketball, and track and field. Since there were three classes according to size, I was able to have a bit of success at the level for the small children, meaning "C" class and not even "B" or "A." There were occasionally fully grown boys who competed at the "A" level, and they offered early examples of the value of size in athletics. Since I had met no *Isseis* of any size, let alone *Niseis* (children of Japanese immigrants born in North America), it was clear that athletics would not provide a route to success.

I could not attribute my lack of size to being sickly. I had almost lost two fingers of my right hand when my next older brother had tried to cut a board that I did not want cut. Any chance at a budding career as a pianist vanished, although I must admit that I did not know then that such a career existed. My other accident was the result of foolish grandstanding. During the fifth grade, it must have been in the fall of 1937, ten of us would have bicycle races at the lunch hour on a deserted street. As luck would have it, during my particular race, a lone car turned onto that street, and the driver, with some astonishment I am sure, looked up to see two boys on bikes coming straight at him. I was, unfortunately, looking back to see what my margin of victory might be. In the next moment, I was no longer on my bike and I could not get up. My mind was still in the race, and the gum which I had been chewing furiously was still in my mouth. This would result in a costly and taxing broken femur, since there would be a long stay in the hospital, a rebreaking and a resetting before the leg would heal.

Although I grew up during the economic depression of the 1930s, I remember only that we seemed comfortable enough and that we ate well. I continued to get a new pair of shoes to start each school year, as well as new clothing. My father who got up at five in the morning did have long and late evening discussions with my older brothers, but I was usually in bed, oblivious to whatever level of economic problems had to be faced. My father could not have the 40 acres in his name, and the fruit boxes bore the name Hiraoka Brothers, although I never felt myself to be included in that label. I wasn't contributing directly to the work, even though two or three of my classmates were already members of the picking crews. There were, after all, unread stories in the many volumes of *The Book of Knowledge* which were stored under the bed.

I saw my father in two roles: as father and as an *Issei*. Therefore, I came to consider certain situations to be beyond his control and his understanding. Since I was the youngest and without designated responsibilities, he would take me into town, Selma usually, because there was a Safeway store there. I shall always remember the incident in which one of the store employees greeted him with a cavalier "Hi, Charley." My father, stopped short by the remark, asked the employee to call the manager. In the next few minutes, I heard my father tell the manager in his functional English that his name was not Charley, and that the employee was to apologize and be taught manners. Since this was in the 1930s, a long way from the civil rights years and the quest for tolerance, it was a courageous act. I don't believe that he viewed it in that fashion. He urged us, as his children, to stand up for our rights and to not accept insults and ill-behavior. His promptings led my sister who was two grades ahead of me to urge me to abandon the eighth grade play because there would be no chance of my being given the lead. And she proved to be right.

The teacher, casting a play involving a prince, princess, courtiers, and a jester, could not conceive of having a male of either Japanese or Mexican origin playing the prince, especially opposite a White leading lady as the princess. Since there were only four or five White males to choose from, there was never a guarantee that the lines would be learned and remembered. The expectations of the town and the school would, however, be fulfilled. Knowing that my sister's perceptions were accurate, I still was willing to accept a background role, but it ultimately meant being chided each day by my older sister. My sense of practicality underwent constant testing.

I should not leave this period of the 1930s without referring to the arrival of the McCormick Deering tractor. Horses and mules had been used widely in the early 1930s. There were Caterpillar tractors, but they were beyond the reach of small farmers. In the late 1930s, both John Deere and McCormick Deering had begun to sell a more affordable tractor. A few years later, in the early 1940s, the Ford Ferguson tractor with a hydraulic lift would be developed and become widely available, even to those farming small acreage. The impact of the arrival of that orange tractor (I am still reminded of that tractor in occasional Arnold Palmer ads for Pennzoil), was that the horse corral would be torn down, there would be no more cleaning of stables, no more spreading of horse manure, and probably most significant to a child, no more truckloads of hay, with its mixtures of butterflies and grasshoppers.

The arrival of the tractor signalled the end of a way of life. Without a corral, and without horses and mules, the work routine changed drastically. The odors definitely changed, and it seemed that the outhouse which had been placed near the corral for some obvious reasons also lost its place and value. The indoor toilet had arrived, and my father had it installed in the screened porch, overlooking the pumphouse and a large grey tree. Whenever I had to get up in the middle of the night to relieve my bladder (my mother had begun refusing me liquids an hour before bed), I simply flew from the kitchen to the toilet, thereby avoiding whatever monsters slept in the pumphouse and beneath the large grey tree. Members of the family suggested that the door of the kitchen and the toilet door opened and closed at the same time. That I was distrustful of the dark is evident.

I attended the same high school that had seen all of my older brothers and sisters. Since this was a time during which teachers and coaches kept their jobs as long as possible, there was no way in which one could avoid references to other brothers and sisters. In our family, this meant that the standards set by the first two children were placed before those following. Both of my older brothers had excelled in team sports and in their classwork. The football coach had expected me to appear in my freshman year as at least a candidate for a starting quarterback position on the "B" team. The fact I weighed in at 98 pounds stripped did not augur well for the football team. Fortunately, I was a good student, and all of that early reading and preparation in English grammar kept me at the top level of the classes in which I was enrolled.

I began taking speech classes as a freshman and found that I could be quite successful paraphrasing Lincoln's Gettysburg address and in citing Emma Lazarus' lines about lifting her "lamp beside the golden door." In my first year of entering speech contests, I took third in a contest for those qualifying from 19 districts. My success could be attributed to the ability to memorize five- to ten-minute speeches, usually without halting or hesitating at any point, the training in English grammar, the early period of reading that made it easy to find simple and patriotic expressions and acceptable moral positions, and a willingness to perform, which may explain, in part, why teaching eventually became a field of interest. I had moments when I thought there was some merit in becoming a successful Methodist or Congregationalist minister. My oldest brother served regularly as the assistant to the Congregationalist pastor, who had been primarily engaged to preach in Japanese to the *Isseis*. As English became increasingly the language utilized by the flock, my brother's participation increased, and he was soon delivering sermons. At about that time, the film, *One Foot in Heaven*, with Frederic March, was attracting considerable attention, and it fueled my desire to be paid to preach. I felt that there were fairly good financial arrangements for the local pastor, or at least they impressed me in my innocent state. A car was provided, there was a monthly salary, and most important, one visited the individual families, usually, as practiced by this leader of his flock, at lunch and at dinner time. I mused on the fact, and I remember my parents' commenting on this very issue, that one could select the families that set a good table and always arrive at their homes at a time when an invitation to partake of the family meal would have to be extended. This was another of the situations that offered food for thought and, in part, raised moral questions.

My secondary school education at Selma High School lasted only two years. The Executive Order 9066, signed in February 1942, made it clear that my education would be completed somewhere else. The last six months of my stay at the high school, from January to June 1942, were somewhat puzzling. In the same speech classes that I had enjoyed during my freshman year, there were now occasional short speeches and explanations as to why the Japanese in California and on the West Coast had to be evacuated. In the similar round of speech contests in which I had done well the previous year, I became aware that there was no chance of my winning. These were, after all, speech contests sponsored by the Bank of America and by the American Legion. The same brand of patriotic words no longer elicited the responses that I had evoked the previous year. It became very clear to me that I would not be evaluated in terms of the stated criteria. A debating partner of the previous year would not even speak to me after one particular speech contest. I had expected at least a fair evaluation from this fellow student and the comment that I should really have been given first prize.

The months preceding war relocation were very active, in part, because so much was happening. Plans had to be made, new people came to purchase furniture or automobiles or tools. My father had decided to allow two families to live in an area of the barn which could be made semi-private with partitions. This gesture on his part failed since there was no way to set reasonable arrangements regarding work, wages, levels of interaction, and the future. Everything had come to a standstill, and in a country in which time had replaced space as the principal dimension, those who had lost the future would have little context for action and inter-relationships.

We were placed on board a train in late July or early August. I can never recall the exact dates, although it would be simple to uncover them. The hot weather of the San Joaquin Valley summer added to the confusion of the departure. Would we ever return? Time, as well as place, had indeed been taken away. All attachments to the "homeplace" were being cut by the act of boarding the train. My father had decided to sell the 40 acres on which we had all been raised. I would no longer be able to return to the irrigation canal, with its minnows and pollywogs. This irrigation ditch that cut the farm into two portions would no longer be available for solitary games. Unlike the arrival of the McCormick Deering tractor, which marked a shift toward mechanization and modern life, the relocation to the Gila River Internment Camp suggested a different kind of intervention. I did not understand it then, but the relocation began to serve as a kind of receptacle for the odd and sundry events that had taken place over the years, including my father's objections to the Safeway store manager, my sister's objections to my accepting a secondary role in a school play, and of course, the deliberate ignoring of my skilled performances in speech contests.

The boarding of the train would also herald a new course away from the context of my childhood. I did not know that then, but it has taken on increasingly a sense of embarking upon a different way of life. It was as if the early years of growing up on the farm without specific chores or even a specific role could no longer provide a context because that way of life would all be phased out. The animals would soon be replaced, small farms would be merged into larger ones, and even the irrigation ditches would be piped and covered for greater efficiency. This phase begun by war relocation and, of course, the war, seemed to mark the end of rural America and of a way of life that related more directly to nature. Fields in which there were rabbits, pheasants, doves, mice, horned toads, and killdeer still remained in my mind because it was not yet clear to me that even if we were to return to the farm a few years later, those creatures would have been displaced just as we were. The effects of human politics and policies had penetrated the rural areas at every level.

The major act of settling into the closed space of the internment camp was the selection of the barrack in Block 21 and of the two units that were to serve as shelter to our family of nine, plus one other who was separated from his family and who accompanied us into camp. There were options in selecting the location of what would become our temporary residence. One thought was to select the units near the block latrines and the laundry room. It was evident that there would be both odor and traffic to contend with. We picked the other side away from the latrines. It was also decided not to be too near the mess hall, since the block residents would always line up to await the opening of the mess hall. Each unit of some 600 square feet was expected to serve six individuals. Since we were ten, we were fortunate to find a widow and one son to reach the required number of twelve. Blankets were strung across the second unit to give the widow and her son some privacy.

Very early in our stay, my father decided that we should have a front lawn. That this constituted a truly absurd act did not seem to bother him. In his view, the necessities of survival included one patch of grass clearly marked by four poles and string. Since the two oldest sons were given more important matters to deal with, number three brother and I set about raking, seeding, and sprinkling. That very first night, what seemed like a million kangaroo rats came out of the desert to dine on the rich table of seed that we had laid for them. From midnight to one A.M., I counted over 100 that I had tapped into oblivion with a stick and disposed of. There were, however, too many of them to warrant staying up any longer. Enough seeds were left, and a decent patch of lawn marked our unit. Fortunately, my father was not fond of fish ponds, so this type of embellishment of the area was left to the few who were interested in catching mud carp in the ditch that could be reached some distance away.

In early September, there were classes, and I started my junior year at Canal High School, a proper designation for a school in an arid region. It was my first experience in competing with others who were of a similar ancestry, and there were adjustments to be made. In those other schooling situations in which there had been at least students of White, Mexican, and Japanese ancestry, the objective of doing well had seemed obvious. Moreover, since the teachers were White, the process of Americanization seemed to be methodical. There was a weeding process at work, a system of selection in which those who were able to garner the best grades would be encouraged to go on to colleges and universities.

To be surrounded only by the faces of other *Nisei* children did not restore a unipolar space. The principal teachers were White. I had a chemistry class from a temporarily assigned teacher who had been only two years ahead of me at the high school in Selma, but those who were in authority and who talked of the future had been brought in from the outside. Clearly, the classes in science and mathematics at Canal High School were more competitive than I could ever recall. Without having any previous information on the subject, I was led to feel that these were areas in which *Nisei* were highly competent. I turned even more, therefore, to those areas in which I had always been successful and could stand out: Speech, English and Spanish, the latter since Latin and French were not offered. There, the principal competition came from two or three female students, and the teachers were usually delighted that there was a male student interested in poetry and drama. The Spanish teacher was from New York, the wife of a naval commander, as I recall, and she would on occasion encourage me to go on to a university on the east coast and to immerse myself in opera, theater, and music. I had no real context for the information and advice that she offered, but she was attractive, cultivated, and knowing. It occurred to me only much later in my life that the merging of context and information is a long and slow process, and that one is sometimes fortunate to have any usable context within which to store advice and information which will be of use at a later date.

That junior year of 1942–1943 went rapidly. I was elected junior class president and considered myself to be a person of importance, even though I knew that I was skating on thin ice, with no objectives, no sense of the future, and only the feeling that what was past could never return. Perhaps that feeling in itself provided a sense of the future, for it meant that functioning within the immediate set of circumstances was of prime importance. Matters did get resolved quickly after two of my brothers who were of military service age volunteered for the combat regiment of *Nisei* soldiers that was being formed. The loyalty of the family was ensured by this act, and arrangements were made for the family to leave to go to an apple farm in Burlington, New Jersey. This was in late May or early June, since I had to receive permission to depart before classes were over for that academic year. We packed, there were good-byes, and my first experiences in having a close relationship with three or four persons were cut short.

The trip to New Jersey was by a circuitous route, since we needed to be legally cleared in Cleveland, Ohio, before proceeding to New Jersey. I had my first glimpse of Chicago where I would later receive my graduate education and my first teaching position. The farm to which we relocated was pleasant. There were apple trees, strawberry patches, and several buildings to house the hired hands. I worked that summer for 25 cents an hour, later raised to 30 because I had been a farmer's son and could wield a shovel. When the Jamaican apple picking crews came in, I carried water to them and did odd and sundry jobs, meaning filling whenever needed. When it rained, there was the pleasant change of putting together apple crates in the huge barn; on clear days, there were strawberries to be picked for Horn and Hardart's, a coin-operated Philadelphia restaurant that was noted for its cherry and strawberry pies. I worked with members of two families from Kentucky and had my first contact with what were called "hill people." The attitudes shown toward them by the proprietor, the foreman and his regular workers, and the local high school children hired to help pack apples reflected only another form of drawing lines as to who had a future and who did not. As in California, migrant labor was going to be viewed as no more than that. I noticed that the Jamaicans were viewed somewhat differently. Since they were imported labor, they could be accepted more easily and without consideration of consequences, since they were expected to go home after the harvest. Moreover, they sang beautifully while they picked apples, and on Sunday mornings, there would be visitors at the edge of the orchards, listening to the English hymns that were rendered in West Indies English. Their singing seemed spontaneous, but they knew that there was an audience. The singing of hymns bought them space.

The question of the high school that I would attend was quickly settled when my sister, the one just above me, received word from the Friends Society of Philadelphia, the office in which she worked, that I would go to high school in Swarthmore, Pennsylvania, and that arrangements had been made for me and for my sister-in-law's brother to be lodged and given work at the Strath-Haven Inn. My sister informed me that, as she understood it, my future would be better ensured by this change. It ruled out Burlington High School in New Jersey and staying with my parents and my oldest brother and sister. The break-up of the family, which began with war relocation, had now been completed, all within the period of one year.

The money earned during the summer went toward new clothing for the year at Swarthmore. Having had no previous experience in what one should wear on the East Coast, let alone at a high-powered, mainline high school, my major investment was in a raincoat, which would not really ever serve in those walks from the inn at the corner of Harvard and Yale avenues to Swarthmore High School. I had also to learn to pronounce the name of the town and the high school and the college as knowing people did.

The living arrangements were comfortable. We were given room and board in exchange for three hours of clean-up work in the kitchen every evening except Sunday. This meant working from eight in the evening until eleven, since cleaning could not begin until the dinners had been served and traffic from the kitchen to the dining room had become minimal. The retinue included a Black chef, three Black waiters, usually from a part of Philadelphia, a White busboy, two or three White and two Black high school girls, a White night watchman who made his rounds surreptitiously, a dwarf Black dishwasher, a second Black dishwasher who had lost a leg and could not bear the pain of wearing his prosthetic, and two other women, one White and one Black who alternated at taking care of the salads and the desserts. The overseers of this large and active group were the proprietor's wife, a licensed chiropractor who worked with the elderly who lived at the inn permanently, and a tearoom hostess who took care of seating arrangements and the maintenance of the dining hall.

I had never before met with this level of diversity, but since the period of contact was limited, it was not difficult. I helped the dishwasher and finished doing pots and pans. The two main tasks assigned to myself and to Boake, my sister-in-law's brother, who had liked the name of a radio news-caster named Boake Carter and had, therefore, appropriated that name for himself, were to mop the large expanse of kitchen floor and to spray areas where uncountable numbers of cockroaches nested and bore even more uncountable numbers of new cockroaches. The contrast between the exterior and facade of the inn, its pleasant setting overlooking a creek, its long porches with books and settees, the comfortable and sedate tearoom, and the situation in the kitchen and back area reinforced my view of space and its layers.

After classes, I would return each day, change clothing and go down into the basement area where the Black waiters relaxed before the rush of serving dinners, and where Robert, the one-legged dishwasher had a cubbyhole where he slept. From four o'clock to about five-fifteen, we would play pi-nochle, the four consisting of Willie, the dwarf dishwasher, a waiter whom we addressed as old Dollar Bill, Boake, if he didn't have football practice, or a fill-in, and myself. We played no passing, straight pinochle. I became oblivious to the untidiness of the basement area; it was not meant for the public. One day, several months later, I was called in alone to the little office in which business was usually conducted. I had noticed on every occasion that I passed through that room a cartoon of an obese person, with the caption: "I can't fight and I can't run, so I must be good-natured." I looked at it steadily while the proprietor spoke to me and advised me that I should cease playing pinochle with the Black waiters and Willie the dish-washer, since, and the words seemed to imprint themselves deeply, "It is inexorable that they go one way and that you go another." The word *inex-orable* seized me, and it struck me as too strange a word, especially since the real question for me involved playing pinochle. It was an example of the pervasiveness of a kind of social morality that permeated every corner, and in this case, every card that we played in our turn. I did not give up playing and continued to spend every afternoon that a game could be ar-ranged in the basement. On one occasion, Willie took me to a movie in Medea, where we seated ourselves in the area where he was allowed to sit. There was no specific feeling that resulted; it seemed to be a part of what was, along with the use of the word *inexorable*, expected and practiced.

The shock of falling from being best student to scrambling to stay in the upper quarter of the senior class was numbing. This was a high school in which over 90 percent were reputed to be going on to colleges and universities, with several going to the most prestigious schools. It was the first mention which reached my ears of places such as Harvard, Yale, Princeton, Haverford, Swarthmore, Brown, Dartmouth, the University of Pennsylvania, Mt. Holyoke, and Smith. A partial explanation for the level of sophistication of some of these students was, of course, that they had, from their early years, benefited from the suburban train that allowed them to go in groups, or even singly, into Philadelphia to see opera, to shop, visit the museums, and walk the informative streets of a large urban area. It occurred to me that there were, after all, different sources of passive knowledge. Mine had been grapevines and peach trees and the creatures that one found in irrigation ditches coursing the farms in the San Joaquin Valley. Theirs, at least those with whom I felt I was competing, had been urban, including even information about the Gayety theaters, the restaurants such as Bookbinders, and stores such as Wanamaker and Strawbridge and Clothier. These were names that suggested a different world than did Babcock peaches, Muscat grapes, and Tilton apricots, let alone pollywogs and toe-biters. The playing field had been determined, and I needed to learn the game, the words, and strategies that kept one in the play.

Latin class was especially troubling, for this class represented the extent of the adjustments that would have to be made. The instructor had a Ph.D. in classical studies. He was a kind and soft-spoken gentleman. With his tweed coat and grey flannel slacks and repp tie, he epitomized a new and different world. The six other, or was it seven, students were all females, all with plans to complete their higher education at a time when this was still not a general expectation. I was clearly the weakest of the group and struggled to maintain a passing grade. It was a helpful world of passive knowledge in that their expectations and level of work, as well as their general views, seemed to me then to reflect a more secure and established world. Although it was probably not the case with each of them, they seemed at that time to constitute an enclave to which access would be almost impossible. It, therefore, came as a surprise to me that in the formal English grammar tests that were given prior to graduation, quite a number of them would need two, or even three, attempts to pass these tests. As with spelling, my early training had apparently prepared me for the more standard tests. In the senior yearbook, I was categorized as the most studious male student, not a particularly significant accolade in this type of setting, for it was better to show effortless achievements, and a few of them did exactly that. That I was able to stay in the top quarter of the senior class of 98 students (and I don't know why that number comes to mind) became increasingly acceptable. Moreover, since the teachers knew that I had three hours of work each night at the Strath-Haven Inn, there were indications to me that I would receive the benefit of any doubt regarding the quality of my schoolwork.

My entrance into a totally different world was also evidenced by a minor incident. I was informed that it would be appreciated by the school if I would go to the senior prom and take as my prom date the student who had had to leave her home in London as a result of the blitzkrieg. We would be symbolic. Since it was evident that I was unaware of the extended significance of the event about to take place, two students asked for a moment when they could discuss the matter with me. They suggested that I should not attend, make a flat refusal since my liberties were being violated. They felt that the gift of two tickets, plus a school administrator's request of my employer that I be freed from work that particular evening constituted excessive pressure. The two students were reasonable and presented the other side only to make certain that I was not yielding to any type of pressure, a conclusion which I could follow only to some extent since, in other instances, I had seen that life's conditions were, to a high degree, inexorable, and, after all, there was that word again. I attended the prom in the company of the English girl, and almost everyone seemed satisfied that the proper thing had been done.

In the spring of my senior year two ladies informed me that I would need to have an interview with the Dean of Swarthmore College, since the Friends Service Committee would be able to support me with a four-year scholarship. I took the college boards and wrote on an aspect of the relocation experience that offered convincing evidence that I could compete successfully with other students at the college. Since I had no idea as to the reputation of Swarthmore College, I could not fully appreciate what was being done for me. The result was that I turned down this opportunity in favor of the Army Specialized Training Program (ASTRP) that would surprisingly send me to Johns Hopkins University, another institution whose name meant very little to me at the time. It was clearly the army part of it that made sense to me, and it was only good fortune on my part that the army needed doctors and was attempting to prepare its own corps of physicians and surgeons.

In the fall of 1944 I went to Baltimore to begin the first quarter at Johns Hopkins. I was the only non-White in that entire group from Pennsylvania, and I am led to believe that no one fully expected that Jesse was the name of a Japanese American. The group of 17-year-olds had passed entrance examinations and were expected to continue university studies after basic training, which could not begin until the reservists had turned 18. I was accepted quickly, especially by the few that came from the Pennsylvania Dutch area, and the choice I had made seemed to be a wise one. Still, I was never certain that I had actually chosen, nor did I feel that I had had a choice. Whatever had prompted the refusal of the opportunity to attend Swarthmore College remained and remains forever vague. If I had not been accepted in the ASTRP and been sent to Johns Hopkins, I would have probably waited out the time until the end of 1944 when my father and mother were allowed to return to their home in Fowler, California. I have sometimes tried to imagine what that road would have led to.

I spent only a quarter at Johns Hopkins, enough time to know that my strengths were in writing and in English, and less so in calculus and chemistry. The decision was made during the quarter that the army's needs would be in engineering. As a consequence, the group of which I was a part was transferred to Virginia Polytechnic Institute (VPI) in Blacksburg, Virginia. I felt that I was floating and treading water in rapidly changing currents. I would not have agreed to join had I been told that I would become an engineer. The fact that I had two somewhat insensitive fingers in my working hand as a result of my brother's impulsive behavior had not led me to conclude that medicine was not my calling. Another quarter or two of chemistry would have convinced me later, of that I am certain. At Blacksburg, I did well in English, but failed miserably with engineering problems. Along with a then free-floating roommate (he was to re-enlist later in the regular army and retire as a lieutenant colonel), I began reading comic books in class. Designated by the sergeant as two flat wheels (*sic*), we decided to take literally the maximum demerits allowed and were planning to fall just short of the danger line. Forty-five maximum demerits meant that we could and would risk 44. We were both asked to report to the head of the program, a colonel who appreciated our talents at soccer. We were suspended, but reinstated when my roommate convinced the colonel that I was not to blame and had not seen my parents for a long time. Suspension and immediate dismissal would have shifted us to basic training in Georgia without any furlough. The reinstatement was a relief, and I finished the second quarter at VPI. Even with the resultant poor grades, I no longer doubted my ability to study at the university level. The year at Swarthmore, plus the quarter at Johns Hopkins, had clarified that. The question was now one of deciding what to pursue. The fact of making a living had not yet reared its grinning and frightening head.

I left Blacksburg, having completed more than one year of university study because of the intensive program. My grade point average had fallen to just barely under two-point, a fact whose significance I had failed to appreciate. I felt rather that I had learned a great deal as a result of not doing well, or at least I felt the relief of not having to compete against whomever or whatever. I had two weeks of furlough and reported to the basic training army camp in Macon, Georgia. I had been sent at least to another place of learning, although again, the irony of the name was lost on me. As I completed the program in basic training, the atomic bombs had been dropped on Hiroshima and Nagasaki. I was in the final week of training, and we heard the news with relief. The question of what we would be doing in the next few years would now have to be answered by someone.

Since I was the only Japanese American in the training group at Macon, I was separated out and sent to a temporary placement center. It was clear that I would not be sent to the Pacific. Besides, my language skills in Japanese were not even recognizable. With the war coming to an end, those of us who had recently completed training were given a choice of re-enlisting for one to three years in order to establish our interest in a service career; there were inducements for the three years. The other choice was to await a date of honorable discharge, which would be uncertain. I chose without any specific reasons the one-year option. I knew that a service career was not my destiny. At the end of basic training, I had also been given the opportunity, even with that GPA of slightly under a two-point, of going to Ohio State University for further education in engineering. However, to me, the VPI experience had ruled out a career as an engineer.

In November 1945, the small remaining contingent of Japanese American soldiers was sent to Puerto Rico to fill vacancies in the Signal Corps. There was a sudden shortage of cooks, radio operators, and teletype operators. My early exposure to foreign languages, Japanese at home, Italian and Spanish in the vineyards and orchards, seemed to make learning the Morse code a breeze. I was the first to finish, or rather to reach the required level, and I was quickly dispatched to a troop transport to serve as one of three radio operators on the U.S.S. *State of Virginia*. The assignment was choice. We visited ports such as Havana, St. Croix, and St. John. We went to Kingston, Jamaica, and Curacao. The problem was that I always became seasick even on calm waters. The smell of the radio tubes and the closed room, plus the rolling motion, left me yearning for solid ground. I requested transfer after two months, but it took longer than that. An officer's secretary who knew of my weight loss, down to 109 pounds, pushed papers through and I was reassigned as a teletype operator, without code clearance since I could still be a security risk.

During my brief stint as a radio operator, it became very clear that I was expected to hit the ports and go drinking with the second and third mates in the merchant marine. We were army noncommissioned officers, but our role as radio operators gave us status. On my first round of the Havana nightclubs, I fell asleep at the third port of call, and I was ruled to be unfit for carousing. That I could not drink left me in a state of unease since the other soldiers, including some from the Japanese American contingent, viewed hard drinking as a sign of manhood.

Fortunately, my success as a fast-pitch softball pitcher and my growing ability at ping-pong were sufficient in maintaining my self-esteem. The team for which I pitched reached the finals; we lost three to one in the championship game as a result of two walks, which I gave up in the sixth inning of a seven-inning game. I was selected for the all-star team and spent the last month of military service on special duty, playing games with teams from other islands in the Caribbean. My success at ping-pong was exhilarating, and it was spiced with money gained playing pinochle, the training ground for which had been the basement of the Strath-Haven Inn. It seemed only inexorable that I and my partner would always win, no matter the competition.

The year of military service passed rapidly, and I returned to what was left of the family farm. After one year at home, it was clear that there was still no place nor role there for me, and I left for Chicago where the presence of an older sister made the transition easier. I had formulated the vague plan of going into journalism. I had by now learned enough about institutions to understand that the University of Missouri at Columbia had one of the better schools of journalism. I had heard of the *St. Louis Post Dispatch*, along with the St. Louis Cardinals who were my favorite baseball team, shades of Max Lanier, Harry Brecheen, Country Slaughter, and Slats Marion. My intention, which seemed vaguely outlined in my head somewhere, was to work and save for a year, then go to Columbia, Missouri, and enroll. I had overlooked the low level to which my GPA had fallen at Blacksburg, Virginia.

Chicago was cold and immense. I did not yet have the kind of clothing appropriate for that weather. I was interested in any type of job and found one immediately as a printer's ink millhand. I poured out the liquid onto huge stainless steel rollers and watched the ink smoothed out to where it could be put in buckets and delivered to the then growing ballpoint pen factories. I did not know until later that I had been hired because the owners wanted to break the grip of the Black union workers. When I developed an allergy to the cleaning fluid used for the rollers, and also saw the possibility of getting a hand caught in the rollers, I decided that I needed a different line of work, although I was exhorted by the foreman to stay on.

I went to Columbia, Missouri, in the summer of 1948 and was informed that I needed to take two summer courses to get back to the two-point level. I returned to Chicago and enrolled that fall at Roosevelt College, a new institution that had been forged out of the old YMCA college. I enjoyed my college life in Chicago, and the future career in journalism was soon abandoned. I did well in French and in general literature courses. My grade point average climbed rapidly, and in my senior year, I was asked to join some other select students for a course on the intellectual currents of the eighteenth century. There was a book to be read each week, with a three-hour discussion once a week. This was a three-professor seminar, and it filled large gaps for me. Roosevelt College was an unusual urban institution. Located near the Art Institute, and with professors consisting of doctoral candidates at the University of Chicago and intellectual refugees from Europe, there was a grand mix. There were all the elements anticipating the 1960s, including Black professors and students who would become well known a decade or two later. The strong backing of two labor unions encouraged radicalism and social change.

Completion of the bachelor's degree left me with one year of the GI bill unused. I could continue study and receive $75 a month for an additional 11 months. I decided to go to France and begin work on a doctorate of the university, a degree offered by the individual French universities. My interest was more French literature, since journalism had given way to ambitions of becoming a writer. My fiancée urged me to go, and I left in January 1951 for Paris. I settled in Montpellier in an attempt to stay out of English-speaking enclaves. This was a difficult year of adjustment since the GI bill allocation did not provide much leeway in levels of living. I traveled to Italy, saw Naples as I had heard one should do, and also traveled in Spain. The period was one of immense input. It was also revealing that, in comparison to my early period in California, I was often asked by French residents whether I was a painter or a pianist. The assumption was that I had to be from Tokyo and was studying at the music conservatory or was tracing the path to Sainte-Victoire in imitation of Cézanne. The level of input often left my head swimming, since I was actively learning as well as drowning in an ocean of passive information.

The following January, I returned to Chicago, having exhausted the allotted government funds, and made plans to be married and to enter the graduate program in French at the University of Chicago. The rise in the GPA and the stay at Montpellier provided entry into what I now knew to be an outstanding institution. Not having access to the gossip of graduate students, I entered in the fall of 1952 and selected courses which older and more experienced graduate students avoided. The program for the master's degree took longer than expected, and I did not complete it until 1955. There were extenuating circumstances: in the fall of 1952, I was asked to teach a class or two at Roosevelt College and the part-time pay was indispensable to our survival.

I took examinations to teach in the Chicago public schools and had received my fall assignment in 1955, when a full-time position opened at Roosevelt College, and I was hired as an instructor in French. The two paths had come upon me quickly, and again the unforeseen and unanticipated had simply been there for me. I would be teaching at the university level, rather than at the secondary level. It had been my intention to complete a doctorate in American Studies at the University of Minnesota, but their quick response had discouraged me. I would have to complete six undergraduate courses in English and American literature to qualify for admission. I also made inquiries to the Committee on Social Thought, then directed by the economic historian John U. Nef for whom I typed letters in French. It became clear that being placed in a department for a teaching position would not be a simple matter with an interdisciplinary degree. It was now clear to me that I had to complete a doctorate in French, and I transferred to Northwestern University because of the deteriorating living conditions on the south side of Chicago, as well as the more clearly marked path at Northwestern to the doctoral degree. My mentor and director of thesis at the University of Chicago had indeed contributed beyond measure to my formation, but his expectations had begun to exceed the practical, and more important, our first child had, by then, arrived. We moved to Evanston, and I began the doctoral program, which I completed in 1962.

The job market for those with foreign language skills had brightened, largely as a result of Sputnik, and I found that there were repeated requests that I consider other positions. I had been quickly promoted at Roosevelt College and had been named chair of the Department of Modern Languages, a result of conflicts among three senior faculty who asked that I take the assignment. I now had both academic and administrative skills to market. I accepted a position at Portland State College, which was growing rapidly, as were the California schools. After three years, the weather proved unsettling. Besides, there were now three children to be invited to take their play outdoors. I applied for a position at the new college being built at San Bernardino, California. This was to be a return to California on what I assumed would be a permanent basis.

I asked for, and was given an appointment at the full professor level. To some extent I had not expected that I would be able to rise so rapidly, even at smaller and less reputed universities, because much of my time was committed to helping raise four children. My wife had had difficulty with the birth of the third child, and the arrival of the fourth meant that she needed help with the care of our four children. I would usually arrive home at three-thirty in the afternoon and immediately take the children to a park, for a drive, to wherever we could spend an hour to an hour-and-a-half outdoors or in a museum. This limited my time for research and writing; moreover, from the time I had begun my dissertation, I had become critical of the kind of research and the type of articles that were being published. The 20-minute presentations at professional meetings served, in my judgment, little more than an excuse to travel to a conference, plus another entry in the curriculum vitae. I felt that little could be developed in 20 minutes, and communication seemed possible only with those who were interested in the same topic. Since I had not had the pressure of having to conform to specific established standards, in part because of my arrival in the profession when there was a shortage of professors with the doctorate, I had been able to move and advance in rank on the basis of personal judgments made by colleagues and by those who had a basis for judging my competence. I could not feel that I was being deprived of valuable research time then, and it was my choice in priorities which permitted me to accept spending the afternoon with the children, thereby allowing my wife to have some period free to spend as she pleased. And since she had an interest in English and continental literature, she read voraciously and culled readings for me, noting what really seemed significant and what was not. I was certainly aware that I would have to conform to certain criteria and that my mobility in the professional system, with its network of organizations and aspiring professors, would be increasingly limited. I had, moreover, begun to view the entire academic structure as now feeding on itself, and the charges of irrelevancy leveled by some students of the 1960s and 1970s received my hearty support. Having assumed administrative duties as dean of Humanities, I became even more convinced that knowledge had fragmented beyond recovery.

In 1971, a six-month bout with cancer led to the death of my wife, and with four children to raise, the youngest was 5 and the eldest was 15, I felt an unstoppable urge to leave the smog and·the congestion. I had made a sufficient number of contacts in organizations, state work, and in task forces, such that I was recommended for three positions. One I ruled out, lost as finalist in the one that seemed most suitable, and after much vacillation accepted the one that I had openly stated was not a viable position for anyone, a position as Dean of the College of Ethnic Studies at Western Washington State College, later a university. The pressure of minority students had resulted in an entity that was supposed to function as a small and independent college. No practical thought had been really given to its viability. Two previous deans, the first Black, and the second Chicano, had left after a year each. The first dean had been especially well qualified and would later become president of a large midwestern university.

My decision to take this position had been made for personal and not career reasons, and the first two years were difficult transitional years. I had not liked the northwest during my period at Portland State College, later to have its status changed also; I did not like the cultural and intellectual climates, too much nature, too few minorities, too few Jewish intellectuals, an inbreeding since their own graduates stayed in the region and wanted positions there. Still, I had to accept whatever conditions existed, since moving again had become almost impossible. The existence of a journal, *The Journal of Ethnic Studies (JES)*, opened one door. Only one issue of the JES had been published, and the founding editor had received a grant which could not be ignored. I was asked to assume responsibility and began what was to be a publication that would end in 1992 with my anticipated retirement from the university. It had succeeded beyond my expectations, especially as issues of ethnicity became global. I could only be reminded again, by this unexpected work as editor, of the importance of prevailing conditions in the success or failure of any undertaking.

The period during which societal conditions pressured academe opened doors to new and different programs. I became director of a large grant program in human services, primarily because no department wished to deal with an internship program in which courses needed to be developed and concepts formulated. I was able to travel extensively to Atlanta, Washington, D.C., and to three countries in Africa for projects related to human services education.

My career seemed to have completed its cycle when I returned to French language and literature and was asked to become chair of the Department of Foreign Languages in 1981. I was asked to straighten out a difficult situation and to make necessary changes. Two years later, remarriage and an exchange professorship to Asia University in Japan did in fact complete the cycle. In Japan, I became aware that unanswered questions from my childhood re-emerged and were replied to by the Japanese countryside and by its spatial arrangements. My father had always left persimmons on the high branches of the trees, and I had often argued that they should have been picked, if only to clean the trees. Seeing the persimmons on the high branches from the train going to Kyoto, I understood, almost as if my father was speaking to me, that they were there for the birds to eat during the winter, and that they were examples of persistence and stamina as they held the high branches through the cold and windy winter months. Seeing the small farm plots, I understood why the family farm had been cut up into three- and five-acre sections of different fruits and grapes. Even the irrigation ditch that flowed through the family farm and seemed to increase inefficiency in its division of the farm took on meaning and made me realize that spatial arrangements depended on one's sense of purpose.

The trip to Japan had also necessitated my participation in the English-as-Second-Language Program for Asia University students on Western Washington University's campus, leading to a bold, large-scale program on five American university campuses for 700 sophomores from Asia University, an educational objective of the forward-looking president of that university.

Now, in the first year of my retirement, I sense that a path had indeed been taken, as contrasted with what at first seemed chaotic, imposed, and a result only of conditions. Why had I not accepted the scholarship to Swarthmore College? Why the entry into French language and literature and that difficult one year spent at the Université de Montpellier? Why the departure from that field for a 10-year period to teach ethnic studies and to remain as editor of a journal in that field for 19 years? Why the entry into the field of human services and English-as-second-language? Why the desire to move, rather than staying in one city or at one institution? Did I have a choice?

I now anticipate eagerly the arrival of a new phase. There is Tokyo for at least 18 months, followed by Paris and, perhaps, Bordeaux and its celebrated vineyards where both my training in French and in ethnic studies will allow me to observe and make notes on the major changes in France and in the European societies. What awaits in each of those places arouses my curiosity. One is never finished, and nothing ever stands still.

META-NARRATION

The issue of the extent to which life's events are partially willed, or are the result of conditions and timing, has been with me for some time. On every occasion that I am asked to recount a personal experience, I find myself setting the time and place so that none of the events or acts emerge as if they were the result of set decisions. I found again in writing this autobiography that I had forgotten specific dates, even when the events and actions were of significance. I became aware that I could set the approximate periods, within the year itself, but to become more precise meant fragmenting the experience so that a specific reference could be located. I find that now, even more than previously, dates are less important and I have difficulty establishing the exact timing of events.

In my first effort at writing this autobiography, I uncovered more details than I needed, and I quickly reached 10,000 words in just narrating what came to mind. I had, however, written about my past only up to the age of 15. So many other people emerged that the nature of the relationships seemed to need narrating. It was more in the interaction with those others that my own life took on any significance.

In eliminating the narration of those relationships to reach a manageable point, I had no recourse but to become more linear in the narration. This in itself made me a bit uncomfortable, for it made me feel that there had been more agency and more will than I believe can ever be asserted by any individual. The attempt to stay within the 10,000-word limit imposed a framework with which I was not totally comfortable. I found myself trying to leave a particular state of my life in order to get on. I was reminded, in writing the autobiography, that I have been reluctant to be interviewed and to discuss such personal experiences as the war relocation of the Japanese, even where the request has been for the events alone. Even in my classes, with their specific topics and time periods, I am really teaching myself and my experiences.

10

It Was My Mother Taught Me How to Sing

Stephen Crites

RUTH

> I often think of home, Dee-oo-lee-ay
>> When I am all alone and far away:
> I sing an old refrain: Dee-oo-lee-ay
>> For it recalls to me a bygone day.

So begins the text of a sentimental song called "The Old Refrain," arranged and published in 1915 by Fritz Kreisler.[1] There was a tinny recording of it by the famous Irish tenor, John McCormack, to whom Kreisler dedicated it. This recording was a staple of the wind-up Victrolas that graced middle-class living rooms in the 1920s and 1930s and that made singers sound like voices from a damp cave, thin and gray. But I also heard the piece sung in full color by my mother, accompanying herself at the piano. She was a fine musician, with a clear, warm soprano voice, unquavering and on pitch. "The Old Refrain" was one of her favorites, and she often filled our little living room with the sound of it, beginning quietly but gathering energy in the next lines:

> It takes me back again to meadows fair,
>> Where sunlight's golden rays beam ev'rywhere,
> My childhood joys again come back to me,
>> My mother's face in fancy, too I see,

—then she would relax into a slower tempo to end the verse with quiet fervor—

It was my mother taught me how to sing
  And to that memory my heart will cling,
I'm never sad and lone while on my way
  As long as I can sing: Dee-oo-lee-ay!

Listening to Mother sing this song is one of my earliest memories. Years later I noticed as she sang that it is a song about singing, really about itself. Most songs seem to be about other things, about love or God or the Chattanooga Choo Choo. But perhaps 'The Old Refrain," for all its simplicity, expresses the deeper insight that music is about music. I always think of it as Mother's Song, not only because she loved to sing it, but because singing formed the style of everything she did. The second, final verse ends in paradise, but a paradise that will ring like our humble living room with this very song, and here she was exultant:

And when at last my journey here is o'er,
  'Twill ring more joyfully than e'er before,
For up to heaven I will take my lay
  The angels too will sing: Dee-oo-lee-ay!

My parents and older brother and I lived in what we called "the little house," next door to the big Victorian frame house built by my father's parents, who still lived there. We moved in with them when I was in my teens and they had grown too old to manage by themselves. But my boyhood home remains my orienting point in the world. Standing on the steps of the little house, I looked due south across Main Street of our rural village, Elida, Ohio, across Route 30 South which swept by it, to the tracks of the old Pennsylvania Railroad main line between New York and Chicago. On my right hand, the road and the tracks led to the neighboring village of Delphos, and beyond that to Chicago. That was west. On my left they led to the small industrial city of Lima, the county seat six miles away, where my father worked in the court house. New York was that direction: east. Even now when I am confused about directions, I imagine myself back on the steps of the little house, and if I can make out which way is south, from the position of the sun, everything falls into place. All directions begin, and end, at home, where my mother sang, and fed and warmed me, and wiped cinders out of my eyes with a handkerchief.

For living so close to the railroad tracks, still in the days of the steam engine, I assumed that cinders in the eyes were simply the universal human condition. Trains showered the village with them, so whenever the first shrieks of their whistles were heard down the tracks, housewives rushed from their houses to take down the wash, and took hankies out of their apron pockets to remove cinders from their children's eyes. Yet I loved the trains, and still do. I never saw one rushing by pellmell for Chicago or New York without wishing I were on it. The only touch of glamour I ever actually saw, except in the movies, was the glimpse of people eating at gleaming tablecloths in the dining car as the train dashed by. In later years, taking the train home from the East Coast was a great wish fulfillment; I never felt so superior to common clay as when I surveyed it through the window of the dining car. One reason the trains seem so enchanting to me is that the rhythm of their wheels on steel rails, no less than the ticking of our large clock, was throughout my boyhood the pulse and measure of daily life. Tucked in bed with my big brother, the last sound I heard before it lulled me to sleep was usually that of a long freight train passing by the village in the night.

The angels too will sing: Dee-oo-lee-ay!

Since, born in 1931, I passed my childhood during the Great Depression, I also recall hobos who had hopped off those nocturnal freight trains appearing at our door for breakfast. I doubt that Mother ever turned them away hungry, so there were often strangers, down on their luck but usually polite and friendly, eating in our kitchen. They seemed to like having a child to talk to, and since my curiosity about them made me ask too many questions, they told me lots of wonderful lies. Mother was an R.N., so she sometimes tended their ailments. She also nursed children in the village, who called her Auntie Ruth, through colds and chicken pox. Grandpa Crites had a farm outside the village where he milked a few cows, and children from neighboring families used to come in the evening with their pails for free milk. That sort of thing was not unusual during the hard times. Neighborhood men helped us out cutting firewood or moving the big potbellied living room stove out in the spring or back in the fall. Houses were mostly gray in our village, unpainted. Our house, and the big house of my grandparents, were a resplendent white, which made us seem better off than the others, and the farm provided us with plenty to eat.

The whole village was down at the tracks to greet the first run of the new streamlined diesel locomotive, which replaced the shrill old whistle with the bawl of a great calf. No more cinders! That was the first dramatic sign of the twentieth century to touch our nineteenth-century village, where even the automobiles still looked like overgrown buggies. The sleek new train also seemed to signal the end of the Great Depression, and an excited cheer went up at its appearance. That was about the time I began to be aware of news about a war in Europe.

Mother made the Elida Methodist Church the social and spiritual center of our family. The Criteses were not church people, though Grandma used to listen to radio preachers. But Ruth was the daughter of a Methodist minister who served a succession of country churches, including, from 1912–1914, the Elida Methodist Church. She graduated from high school while her family was living in Elida, and she returned at the age of 26, as the bride of an Elida man, my father, after a long courtship. His somewhat reserved attitude toward religion did not deter her from an active involvement in church and in the community affairs which for her were inseparable from her Methodist Christianity. She was keenly intelligent, she was steeped in the scriptures and in Methodism, she had studied piano and organ with a Miss Eisenbach, to whom she always referred reverently, and upon her return to Elida, she began a term as director of the church choir that was to extend for more than 40 years. She was also organist for some of that time and gave piano lessons to local children. I studied some piano with her but applied myself more seriously to the trumpet and to the singing lessons I took with an excellent teacher. My voice as a child was nondescript, but after it changed, it blossomed forth, to everyone's amazement, as a pleasant lyric baritone. I had a good ear and could sing on pitch, so Mother recruited me for the choir at age 13. I have been singing in church choirs ever since.

Now this conjunction of music with the practice of religion has turned out to be a fateful knot in my life, for ever since that time, the two things have been inseparable in my experience, as they were for my mother. Whether this conjunction was a stroke of luck or of divine providence, or whether it is even a good thing, is impossible for me to say. For good or ill, it is one of the root facts of my life, like the family into which I was born, or its low church Protestant Christianity. Given my situation in the world, the conjunction of music and religion in my experience seems fortunate, since it is arguable that the deepest spiritual currents in this Protestantism have registered in its hymnody. All its diverse sects and denominations have contributed to the Protestant hymnbook, from the stately Lutheran chorale to the earthy Negro spiritual and the raucous evangelical song. Into this rich musical broth, I was initiated at an impressionable age by my mother, the choir director. Low church architecture is largely undistinguished, its liturgy is too arid to inspire drama, and after you have named Milton, it is hard to think of a second poet. Its iconography is an embarrassment, at least since the days of Albrecht Dürer, and indeed there has always been an iconoclastic strain in Protestantism. But the hymnbook is the jewel of its piety, and when the congregation rises to sing, mostly in four parts, its men and women, rich and poor, old and young, achieve a rare harmony and equality. The congregational hymn, in full cry, is the ritual idealization of low church Protestant community life, and the nearest thing to its heaven on earth. Here, at least, is the way it ought to be. Wise and foolish virgins alike greet the bridegroom, and the whole congregation, momentarily sanctified, the pure in heart and psalm-singing hypocrites alike, enjoys a heavenly harmony as richly chromatic as a rainbow and even more ephemeral. The hymn is not visible or palpable, it lasts only so long as it reverberates in the air, and yet it is as physical as it is communal, performed with the whole body, letting an inward language of the heart find its way into the outer air, filling a large public space and making every living body in it vibrate to the same frequencies. The choral anthem is also generally an elaboration of the hymn, sung not just *for* the congregation, as if it were an audience, but *to* it, absorbed into the bodies and sentiments of everyone within earshot.

For people like my mother and me, who tend to be connected to the world primarily through the ears anyway, the Spirit is indeed invisible but not inaudible. It is sonic, musical, taking possession of mortals through tapping feet and nodding heads and the inhalations and exhalations of the breath, the forming of resonances that set every thing and every living body vibrating together.

I am on most points deeply ambivalent about my lifelong low church affiliation, but its music is what has made my quarrel with it a lover's quarrel. I am not the first child of the Christian religion to fuse or confuse Mother Monica with mater ecclesia, but my mother was the choir director, creating the triangle Mother Ruth, Mother Church, and sacred song. A mama's boy, I became the church's boy, too, though I offer a thumb in the eye of anyone who suggests that my religious ambivalence is disguised hatred of my mama! When I was a young man I was ordained to the ministry and served some little Methodist churches, with a good deal of personal satisfaction, and I still occasionally preach, marry, and bury upon request. Since I began my teaching career 30-odd years ago, I have been active in the music programs of Congregational churches and have also worshipped, sung, and preached occasionally among Presbyterians, Baptists, Lutherans, and Unitarians, as well as in college chapels. My love/hate relationship with low church Protestantism is entirely nonsectarian. I always find the theology and the moral teaching and especially the politics hard to swallow without a heavy infusion of story and song, which have redeemed many an otherwise arid Sunday morning. When I was young and still thought I had choices, I actually considered converting to Catholicism, or leaving the church altogether. But I could not actually practice anything but low church Protestantism. If I tried to break away, it would be an exercise in futility. I'd just be a disaffiliated Protestant, a Catholic Protestant, a Methodistical atheist, a backslid Protestant, still Protestant to the core. I could no more change my religious practice than I could change mothers. Indeed, church has always had a feminine face for me, and still does. Since the day after Christmas, 1990, I have even been delightfully surprised to find myself the husband of a Congregational minister (UCC) named Ann, and the recent recovery, under feminist influence, of feminine images of God entirely accord with my experience.

In fact, my parents were hoping for a pretty little girl when I was born, so it seemed a fitting compensation for their disappointment that I should perform many of the household chores usually assigned the daughter of a family. One of these was doing the dishes, usually drying while Mother washed, and we always sang over the dirty plates and plans. Hymns were our staple, with a smattering of current popular songs and light classics. She

always sang in the kitchen, so it seemed natural for me to join in. Some of
the songs had a didactic hue, for a son somewhat given to dreaminess:

> Dear Lord, we are not here to play,
>   to dream, to drift;
> We have a work to do
>   and a load to lift!

God knows Ruth lifted hers. There was a side to her that was all business.
She was briskly at work on something when she was home, and when she
went out she walked at a very rapid pace, heels clicking staccato and tempo
presto, usually down Main Street to the church. She was also a tireless
shopper. When I was a small boy, she often dragged me along on shopping
trips to Lima, making me go at a trot to keep up with her. It wasn't enough
to find what she wanted to buy: She had to check in every store that might
carry it to be sure she was getting the lowest price. To this day I dislike
shopping.

Diligence wasn't the only thing that moved her down the sidewalk at such
speed. She also didn't much like being outdoors. Home was her space. She
animated it; it was my home because she was there. Same with the church.
But even when she wasn't at home or in church, she generally preferred
being indoors. The open air seemed alien to her, a medium she passed
through as quickly as possible to move from one enclosed space to another.
She had the very fair skin that went with her auburn hair, and both sun and
wind caused her discomfort, not to speak of rashes and large welts caused
by insect bites and exposure to poisonous plants. She squinted in distress
in bright sunshine. She was vigilant about protecting me from such afflictions:
"Get out of that hot sun!" "Don't lie on that damp ground!" The sun was
always hot, the ground always damp, the night air always chilly, the river
muddy, the wind freezing. The gentle rain that fell from heaven did not
water the earth, but gave you your death of cold. She was artful in devices
to keep her home cool in summer, warm in winter, and utterly free of dirt.
Though I inherited her complexion, I rebelled against this regime, but only
at the cost of sufferings all the more grievous because the world regards
them as ridiculous: blistering sunburn, agonies of poison ivy, heat rashes,
insect bites, all evoking hilarity rather than sympathy from my peers. Nor
did our Protestant piety offer any comfort, since it is the irony of this religion
of largely thin-skinned folk that its scriptures are obviously written by leath-
ery people. You will look in vain for a psalm invoking comfort for the sunburnt
or deliverance from the bite of the pestiferous mosquito. The silence of
scripture about such matters lends support to the suspicion that we Prot-
estants are very remote in sensibility from the Mediterranean peoples who
founded our heritage. What we have made of this heritage would have

appeared so comic from their point of view that it would have made even Jeremiah laugh.

The only exception to Mother's hostility toward the out of doors was a love of gardening. Well protected from the elements in a broad-brimmed hat, gloves, and long sleeves and slacks, she tended a good-sized kitchen garden and very extensive flower gardens. Grandma Crites, similarly clad, did the same. Our two houses were on four adjacent lots, and the rear third of all four lots made up one almost continuous garden. We were locally famous for it. People out for a Sunday drive would go out of their way to view the Crites gardens. The menfolk did the donkey work, spading and manuring and mowing the grassy paths among the flowers, but Mother and Grandma did all the planning, seeding, pruning, and tending. Since the installation of hose outlets was deemed extravagant, I spent a good part of my summer evenings going from plant to plant with a bucket and dipper, watering. Mother was especially fond of roses, planting many varieties and colors with the one common feature that you couldn't water them by my method without being snagged and scratched by thorns. Only many years later did I develop a friendly attitude toward flowers, and I still have my reservations about roses.

Mother died February 17, 1991, at age 95. During the last 24 years of her life, she lived alone, mostly in the big family house, and she had to watch the gardens dwindle until there was only one ill-kept rosebush left. By then she was in her nineties, frail as a dry twig but still lucid in mind and forceful in personality: still entirely Ruth. Still, she associated the loss of her flowers with the death of her entire numerous generation in her own family. To give some inkling of the magnitude of this loss will take some explaining: Her father, the Reverend Frank Hook, and her mother, born Jenny Good, had belonged to two large farming families in Van Wert County, the Hooks of English extraction, the Goods of German. Frank's two sisters married Jenny's two brothers, and all three couples proved fertile. So besides Mother's own sister and three brothers, she had a host of double cousins, genetically like siblings and almost as dear to her, with constant visiting back and forth as she was growing up. It was a very close extended family, really a tribe, and even after her marriage she was in constant touch. When I was a boy, there were Hook-Good family reunions every Fourth of July at the Van Wert County Fairgrounds. I have a panoramic photograph of the reunion of 1933, with 66 people in it, including myself at age two sitting on the lap of Grandpa Hook. At all these tribal gatherings, and at smaller ones at more irregular intervals, there were quantities of country cooking and intense piety and affection—too intense for my father, who usually stayed home. Mother's only vacations were family visits, sometimes lasting for weeks and usually with me in tow, with her parents and brothers, or with her sister Eva with whom she was especially close. Of this entire tribe,

Mother finally found herself the last survivor, like the rosebush under her window, and she missed the others.

In other respects, she was far from solitary. She turned to the living, to younger folk in church and village, to Eva's two daughters, and to my own four daughters, each of whom formed a distinctive bond with her and traveled great distances to visit. I visited several times a year, and after my long first marriage broke up, in 1985, I spent my summers with her. We made music together almost every day, and sang together at the sink, and talked by the hour. She still had great charm and wit and affection. She was the graceful matriarch of family, church, and village, and the church and the village officially proclaimed Ruth Crites Day when she was 90, celebrated with appropriate ceremonies and festivities, including greetings from the governor of Ohio and from President Reagan, this last admittedly hokey, but such things can be arranged. Still the honor was singularly appropriate, recognition of a life that was, in the moral framework in which she lived, exemplary. She represented the values of her time and place at their best, evangelical in her zeal but liberal in her commitments, generous and indefatigable.

She was also resilient. Several times in her last years she seemed at death's door. I took emergency flights to Ohio and rushed to the hospital, but within days she would be back on her feet. Friends thought her astonishing recoveries were magical effect of my visits. That I doubt, but there was a musical if not a magical consonance between us that always had a tonic effect on us both. Only once on such an emergency visit did I find her bereft of her lucidity, the result of a treatment that had depleted the electrolytes in her brain. That was a shock to me, but she was deliriously happy. She was seeing her long-departed cousins, aunts, parents, who filled her hospital room and the hall outside her door. She was greeting them all by name and calling to those in the hall, chattering excitedly with them. They were beckoning to her, urging her to come away with them. She said she couldn't go quite yet because she hadn't said goodbye to Steve. When she realized I was there, she joyfully introduced me to one after another—"and Steve, this is my cousin Winnie I've told you so much about"—adding, sotto voce, so as not to offend them, "they're all dead, you know." She was embarrassed that she was in no position to make a big dinner for them, an awful breach of tribal custom. But then she found a happy solution: I should take them all out to a restaurant. She, of course, would foot the bill!

She believed in heaven, as matter of course. One of our most rapturous duets at the kitchen sink rendered an old evangelical hymn:

> Oh Beulah Land, sweet Beulah land,
> Upon the highest rock I stand;
> I look away across the sea
> Where mansions are prepared for me,

And view the shining glory shore,
My heaven, my home forevermore.

But her Beulah Land, I suspect, was very much like Van Wert County,
white farm houses and corn growing in black soil, where there is an ever-
lasting Hook-Good reunion in progress, with plenty of lemonade and fried
chicken.

The angels too will sing: Dee-oo-lee-ay!

Two years before her death, Mother sold the old family house. After one
last Christmas there together, my daughters Steffie and Lilli and I moved
her to an apartment house for the elderly in Delphos and cleared out the
13 rooms of the home she was vacating. The change turned out to be a
happy one. She had her snug apartment to herself, but had dinner in a
common dining room, where she struck up some warm new friendships.
Before long, she was leading the group in singing after dinner, accompanying
it with great gusto on the piano. She even took up bridge again, which she
hadn't played since she'd been in nurse's training 70 years earlier. She had
been slow to give up the old house, but after she did she never looked back.
Talking about it later, she told me it was the hardest decision she ever made,
except for getting married: "and that," she added grimly, "was a mistake."

BERYL

My father was 39 years old when he married my mother, 13 years older
than she. Until then, he had lived with his parents in the big house, their
only offspring. He never quite forgave them for naming him Beryl, more
commonly a woman's name. I had few living relatives on my father's side,
by contrast with Mother's tribe, and Dad was much less gregarious. He
could be charming in company, but it cost him a lot of effort. He was 49
when I was born, so I knew him only as a middle-aged and older man. He
had practiced law in Lima earlier, but after the Crash of '29, in which he
lost a good deal of money, he opted for a more secure but smaller income
by accepting a political appointment as deputy county recorder, and later
as deputy county auditor. We were Democrats in largely Republican territory, but by the time the Republicans recovered the court house in the
early 1940s, he was ready anyway to retire from the county seat and the
daily bus ride to town. He opened an old-fashioned little law office at home
where he served local clients and had welcome leisure for reading. In those
days before duplicating machines, the complicated land descriptions on the
deeds for farms had to be copied out on the typewriter, and I used to read
the originals to him while he checked his copies. I felt important to be
helping Dad with serious business, but I also learned that law could be

pretty boring. All that record keeping in the court house can't have been very interesting either, but he was meticulous about his work. He served the village for many years as chairman of the Board of Education and as legal advisor for the town council and other official bodies. I felt proud that people looked up to him.

Dad was a moody man. When he was in form he was funny and kind, taking pleasure in his family. I liked having him read to me when I was little, and he was a good story-teller. He was not overtly affectionate, as Mother was. Sometimes he would reach out awkwardly to give me a little pat. I never doubted he loved me in his inhibited way. Still, he could also be very grouchy and withdrawn, not abusive but giving off a lot of silent anger into the air around him. If crossed or offended, he would give us the silent treatment, sometimes taking many days to be reconciled. He didn't like for Mother to go out to church meetings in the evening or to practice music when he was around. After their marriage, he insisted that she give up hospital nursing because he thought it reflected badly on him as the breadwinner to have his wife working. Yet he was very close with money and had to be begged for things she needed. The shortage of nurses during the war gave her the excuse to return to hospital nursing, claiming it was her patriotic duty. When I wanted a favor from him, I learned early on that it would take persistence. The first answer was always "no."

Still, though he was much older than the fathers of my friends, he made an effort to be a normal Dad to me. Sports, especially baseball, offered a point of contact of the customary sort. He had been an athlete when he was young and enjoyed playing catch with me in the evening. He came to the games, when my brother and I were playing. He and Grandpa were great fans of the Ohio teams, especially the Cincinnati Reds. The ballgame on the radio was one of the familiar sounds of summer, and we often listened together and talked. When I was in my early teens, he and I would sometimes take the train to Cincinnati or Cleveland or Detroit and stay for several days in a hotel, seeing as many games as possible and visiting points of historical interest, which he was able to explain so engagingly that I came to share his enthusiasm for the historical sights as well as for the games. I remember those times together fondly.

But he also gave me something very uncommon in our corner of the world. He had a fine personal library, bookcases full of histories, biographies, novels, essays, many of them classics, and even some poetry in expensive bindings. For he was a reader. He was perhaps happiest when he could sit in his big leather chair, puffing his pipe and concentrating on a book for undisturbed hours. By the time I was in junior high, I was doing the same, except for the pipe and leather chair, which came later. Even as a child, I had been a precocious reader, and when I was ready, he opened his library to me, letting me make my own choices but suggesting books he thought I might like. He regularly discussed the books with me, sitting on the porch together or out for a walk, without pressure or pedantry always shedding interesting light on what I was reading. It slowly dawned on me that my Dad was the most intelligent person I knew, and what was even more surprising was that he showed respect for my budding intelligence as well, asking me questions not as if he were testing me like a schoolmaster but because he wanted to know what I thought. Disagreements about reading were amiable.

So I became a reader too. Now that is a very strange thing for a sensuous young animal to do! Whenever I could, just like Dad, I read not only by the hour but by the day, sometimes by the week, with only occasional breaks to meet organic demands, staring at signs on steadily turning pages, to the exclusion of the more sensuously vivid objects around me. It is a kind of trance, an immobile but obsessively active state, a focussing of the entire body on the most unphysical, abstract activity of which it is capable. I discovered that this trance is an opening into an otherwise unimaginable complexity: an intricate plot, the interpretation of a life, or a history, in a configuration of events grasped simultaneously, a many-sided theory, a dense play of images and metaphors. As I spent more and more time in this region of complexity, my own psychic life underwent a subtle metamorphosis. For reading, like any other habitual activity, trains the organism into a mode of existence peculiarly adapted to that activity, into a creature, in fact, that loves the activity that has made it what it is.

I still got together with friends, and I played sports, badly. Throughout my adolescence, I was always madly in love with somebody or other, usually without much encouragement from the object of my attentions. Athletic ineptitude and unrequited affection doubtless also reinforced my withdrawal into books, though I must say that I never soured on either sports or love. I excelled without much effort in the undemanding studies at my school. And then there was music, for which I did have talent, and which I practiced more and more, another rather unworldly region of intense concentration.

My reading and my music were turning me into a peculiar sort of boy, different from any of my peers in the rural social world in which I lived. The peculiarity would have perhaps been less evident in a community more sophisticated about such pursuits. The farm and village kids with whom I hung out were good humored enough not to make me suffer much for my peculiarities, but they were aware of them. My friends figured I was just smart, however inept in other ways, a "brain" as they said, though really I doubt I was naturally more intelligent than many of them. I had simply found a path, by way of Dad's library, that was unknown to them and that would likely have aroused little interest if they had come across it. There was only Dad to talk with about the regions of complexity into which this path led me, and he was a generous companion and guide. Being serious readers didn't necessarily make either of us better human beings, or more competent in everyday pursuits. It didn't, for instance, make him a more adequate husband and father in most respects, and it hasn't made me a terribly good husband or father either, much as both of us tried to be. Being a reader did, however, for good or ill, in significant ways make me the man I became and fitted me for a professional career as a scholar and teacher in love with ideas.

Mother wasn't troubled by this bookish turn of mine, lovingly but mistakenly convinced as she was that I could do no wrong. But when we visited her family, my kinfolk found it rather alarming. There had never been anyone like me in the family, always, as Grandpa Hook observed, with my nose in a book. He did some reading in his theological library, but with moderation, not like me, lost to the world for days as I turned the pages. He said I was a bookworm and a trifler. Like my dad.

There was, however, another side to Dad, though his father-in-law might have found it just as trifling. Dad was a musician, too. His taste in music was very different than Mother's, and for him it was less a nourishment of the soul than an entertainment. His soul, after all, fed on books. But he was an exuberant trombone player who had played for years in concert bands and marching bands and dance orchestras in Lima, and at the time when Lima had a vaudeville theater, he had spent his evenings in the orchestra pit after his days in the law office. Souza marches and vaudeville tunes were still in his blood in his later years. When he was in the humor, he could rip them off on the trombone, and sometimes he even went into a comical little soft shoe routine. He also directed a village orchestra that played for special programs, beating time with his left hand and playing the trombone with his right, and he led a Sunday School orchestra at the church that accompanied the zippier hymns and camp meeting tunes deemed unsuitable for the worship service.

He bought me a trumpet when I entered the fourth grade, so that I could prepare for the school band, and it wasn't long before I was playing beside him at Sunday School, my silvery tootling harmonizing with the mellower virility of his trombone in the brass section of the little orchestra. So in this more extroverted milieu, he had already led me on a path that had given him a lot of satisfaction, and I enjoyed it as much as he did. I shared his pleasure in the livelier arts generally, the silver screen and the radio comedy that had evolved from vaudeville, and music that could set your feet marching or dancing. So I became a performer. As a teenager, I organized an eight-piece dance band, leading with the trumpet and also singing popular ballads in the baritone crooning style of the day. Dad loaned me his precious trombone and taught me to play it enough to double on it with my band. These brassy, jazzy excursions brought out an exhibitionist streak in me. I even gave little magic acts at intermission. We were booked for school dances and played every week at the Navy Club, one of the veteran's organizations that were thriving after the war. My performing career took me into spots Mother found questionable, but Dad convinced her it was all right. He hadn't been corrupted by the seedier places he'd performed in, and he trusted me not to get drawn into anything vile. I didn't, and continued performing on the trumpet through college, divinity school, and graduate school.

I played as long as I could find an empty classroom to practice in but gave it up afterward, when the brilliance of trumpet sounds proved incompatible with bourgeois living arrangements. It was like an amputation to quit. I took up quieter instruments, recorders, that I still play for private enjoyment, but they never compensated for the loss of that marvelous sound of brass. Even now I dream sometimes that I have my shining trumpet in my hands and am making brilliant sounds with it for a bedazzled audience, but my performing impulses have been sublimated into gentler disguises.

Dad couldn't live with Mother without going to church. He even taught the men's Bible class for many years and became something of a student of the Bible. But he took an historical interest in it, without the evangelical fervor Mother invested in Scripture. He told me he thought religion was good for people's morals but admitted that he was privately skeptical about its claims to truth. When I began to read the Bible as a teenager, he encouraged my interest, but bought me a fat one-volume commentary[2] that interpreted it book by book and chapter by chapter from what he regarded as a sound historical and liberal standpoint. I read it along with the King James version of the Bible and was spared any fundamentalist episode in my religious development, as Dad surely intended I should be.

Still, I had enough musical imagination to be captivated by it on another level. Its euphonious diction, to be sure, was partly a misleading sonority created by the King James translators. I must say that the high style of that translation does stick in the mind. I haven't read it for 40 years, having soon switched to more reliable translations and having learned enough Greek to read the New Testament, but whenever I quote the Bible from memory what comes rolling out are those sonorous cadences of the King James version. But that is not quite what I mean by its music. The Bible absorbed me emotionally, viscerally, it set me vibrating to the bone, as music did, especially the vividness and fatality of Hebrew and Gospel narrative and the poetic intensity of the psalms and prophetic books. The Bible became soul music for me. For once I was reading a book in which I seemed to find more than Dad did, just because my harp was strung differently.

He died in 1967, in his mid-eighties. Mother tended him at home, and he was touching in his gratitude. But as soon as he died, she took driving lessons and bought a new car. He had never permitted her to drive, but for the next 20 years she terrorized the village with her sleek black Mercury. In one of our last family visits before his death, in the excitement of a noisy arrival, our four girls released from long sitting in the car like a flock of birds, I grabbed Dad, locked him in a long bear hug, and kissed him. It was an impulsive gesture. I wasn't sure how he took it, except for being surprised. But a few minutes later, as the girls were finding their rooms, I overheard him speaking to Mother in the kitchen: "Did you see that, Ruth? Stevie kissed me."

BILL

My brother Bill was seven years older than I, a big difference when youngsters are growing up. He was already a spiffy dresser, getting interested in girls, when I was still playing in the dirt with toy trucks, so there wasn't much between us, just amiable toleration and some teasing, without much open competition. Bill was a good athlete, quick and well coordinated. He played on the high school teams, which gave you status in our school, and I basked a little in his reflected glory. He notoriously broke training, though, taking to beer and cigarettes in his early teens, but he could still come through in a game. When I was old enough to try out for sports I trained assiduously but mostly sat on the bench at game time. On the other hand, our father's library had no charms for Bill, he had nothing to do with church after he could no longer be forced to go, and he was an indifferent student. The family joke was that he'd given his school book report every year on *Tom Sawyer*—without ever having read it except in the comic book version! But he was good looking, slicked his hair down with Brilliantine, and sported a Clark Gable mustache with the help of some eyebrow pencil.

The fact that Bill's beer and cigarettes were a breach of training was the least of the problem. His habits flouted our moral code. Our rural Protestant ethos had certain moral touchstones: good folks abstained from alcohol, tobacco, gambling, and sex outside marriage. More evangelical churches prohibited dancing and movies in addition to these evils. Methodists came down especially hard against strong drink. Giving that up was most often the crux of a decision to convert, and notorious backsliders on the drinking issue would stop showing their faces in church. Dad, to be sure, did not conform to the code with respect to tobacco, though he insisted that pipes were less reprehensible than cigarettes, perhaps because women didn't smoke them. Otherwise, he was as committed to the moral code as Mother was, whatever reservations he had about Methodist belief and practice generally. She was a lifelong member of the Women's Christian Temperance Union, but he was no less unyielding than she about the use of alcohol in any form. He'd seen plenty of drinking among dipsomaniacal musicians, and it disgusted him. He often declared that he'd never touched a drop in his life. Loose sex and gambling were also beyond the pale.

Now again, in other climes and circumstances Bill's habits might have seemed peccadillos. At most he might have been thought a little wild. But it was as if Bill set out with comprehensive thoroughness to violate all the taboos of church, village, and family. By his mid-teens he chain-smoked and often came home drunk. He carried condoms in his billfold, and at the age of fourteen brought home a venereal disease, apparently the result of a visit to a whorehouse. Precocious he was! He was also an adroit poker player, who quickly graduated from penny ante games to higher stakes at illegal gambling establishments in Lima. Anything folks thought wicked, short of outright criminality, Bill did it. Home became oppressive for him, partly as a result of his behavior, but maybe also as its cause. I remember Bill's rushing out of the little house evenings without a word, and clipping down Main Street with the very same fast gait as Mother's, but not to church. At first he was setting out for the gas station where the local ne'er-do-wells hung out, most of them older than he. With these buddies, he soon acquired wheels to the fleshpots of Lima and who knew where.

Dad and Mother were devastated. Their firstborn, whom they always recalled as having been an uncommonly sweet little boy, had turned bad, just about as bad as he could be. In their moral world, he was in fact the prototypical Bad Boy, the kind that only turned up in less respectable families, and they were utterly unequipped to deal with him. There were awful scenes. Mother prayed over him and pled with him, sometimes weeping hysterically, which was very unlike her. Dad lashed out angrily at Bill for a while, then turned his back on him in cold fury, consigning him to a permanent silent treatment. Their Bad Boy was the most bitter disappointment of their lives.

I appeared to be only an uncomfortable witness to this family melodrama. Bill and I still got along. He even took me fishing with him sometimes, our two corks bobbing peacefully side by side in the muddy river near the village. But in fact his dereliction seems to have had a profound effect on me. Since my brother was a Bad Boy, I became a Good Boy. I suppose in principle that I had a choice in the matter, but I had no experience of that so far as I can recall. Being a Good Boy was a burden. It was as if I were assigned that position in some pure geometry of family life.

I had to be the son who would make his parents proud, the overachiever, the performer who won the applause of the village. I sang with Mother and read with Dad. Bill was the sinful outcast from church, while I became the church's boy, a mainstay of the choir possibly headed for the ministry. Church folks doted on me. I was almost indecently good. Even during drunken revels at the Navy Club, I entertained the crowd without ever a convivial beer. When I went off to college, I continued to observe the code. Ohio Wesleyan was a Methodist school, but not all that Methodistical in its ethos. I was rather an exception in continuing to abstain from alcohol and tobacco. I won prizes in scholarship, music, and oratory, not sleeping much. I still kept falling passionately in love, but my love affairs were virginal despite some close calls. The romantic novels and music in which I had been steeped had formed my image of love. It did not call for any coarse groping. Gambling never has tempted me; Bill seems to have monopolized any family passion for games of chance.

Ironically, my first breaches of the code occurred when I entered Yale Divinity School, where the gentlemanly ethos of that time made tippling and pipesmoking seem fitting. Besides, Methodistical austerities were hardly compatible with the Barthian theology, Niebuhrian ethics, and Bultmannian biblical studies in which I was initiated there. Still I was pretty straight. I was an assiduous student, and I sang in the YDS choir for morning chapel. I later directed the choir, swelling Mother's heart with pride when she once visited the campus.

Only much later did I begin to entertain the wry suspicion that Bill had significantly if ironically contributed to the formation of my character. The geometry of our polarization within the family seems clear, but I am still vague about its psychodynamics. Did Bill's astonishing waywardness some-how propel me onto a straight path? Did my belated appearance on the scene, worming my way into our parents' favor, after all the years he had basked in it, turn him into the Esau of the family? Did our parents unwittingly create this polarity? Is it latent in Protestant morality? Is it an example of my own pet theory of narrative emplotment in the formation of experience? All of the above/none of the above? Whatever made him the Bad Boy and me the Good, it was a bum rap, really, for both of us.

Bill, at any rate, played his part to the end. He was married just out of high school and soon divorced. By then, he was drafted into the army, where he seems to have whiled away World War II mostly playing poker and chasing women, one of whom turned up at our door, pregnant and demanding indemnification. Dad shrewdly negotiated a financial settlement on condition that she sign an affidavit renouncing all future claims. Bill, meanwhile, went AWOL when his unit was ordered into overseas combat, and did time in the brig. After the war, he returned with a lovely young French wife and actually took a legitimate job for the only time in his life. That ended when he and Ginette were in an auto accident a few months later. They spent their convalescence with us, and Ginette became the sister I'd never had. She charmed us all, but as soon as Bill could get about he was heading down the sidewalk again, and away. He abandoned Ginette and became a professional gambler, sometimes rolling in money and sometimes scrounging. In his mid-forties he fell off a fire escape, or was pushed, sustaining head injuries that incapacitated him for the rest of his life. Mother could not bear the prospect of his being institutionalized, so she encouraged him, with promises of financial support, to marry a third time. His wife looked after him lovingly. He still had a certain charm and good humor, was often very funny in conversation, so you scarcely noticed anything was wrong with him. But he had no memory, would, for instance, read the same article in the newspaper again and again. He died in 1981 of a sudden heart attack. I don't know anyone who slipped through life, and out of it, with less effort.

The remains of Ruth, Beryl, and Bill Crites lie buried under a single broad gravestone in a cemetery sought of Elida.

AFTERTHOUGHTS

I told my story in the way I have because my own life is inseparable in my experience from certain other lives. Whether that is true of some or even all other human beings I need not argue here. For it seems to me that the peculiar license and limitation of autobiography is its unabashed rendering of the writer's experience as the writer construes it. Of course, the thing can be done badly or dishonestly, and it is bound to be a self-indulgence; self-indulgence might even serve as reasonably strict definition of autobiography. Moreover, I cannot claim that I necessarily have privileged access to my own experience, except for the specific purpose of telling that story that is doubly my own, as both the narrated and the narrator. It is simply the way I have come to understand this little commotion in the world to which with equal license I refer reflexively as myself. This intermittent commotion has always been set off in tandem with others, creating a more general uproar within which it would be difficult to establish strict lines of demarcation.

So after a good deal of deliberation I decided to tell my story by narrating certain relationships with others. The next thing was to decide which others. Various scruples dictated that I not focus on anyone still living: for instance, I did not wish to risk embarrassment of the living or to interfere with our continuing interaction by prematurely closing stories that require to be left in their vital openness and irresolution. I would use the occasion, then, to revisit the dead.

I have narrated my relationships with these three other members of the immediate family in which I grew up, the people with whom I was already having intimate dealings when I first awakened to self-awareness. As a consequence, the story told in these pages dwells primarily on my earlier years, with only occasional projections into adult life. I might have employed the same method to focus instead on relationships that developed later in life. But in that case, it would have been tempting to narrate my life as three stories rather than one: First and foremost there would be the story of my family life in the 30 years I lived in marriage with Gertrud Bremer Crites, of our rearing four daughters together, our mutual love of whom has kept our story open even after the marriage ended unhappily in divorce. The second story would concern my professional development and my career as a philosopher of religion, working primarily in the highly collegial atmosphere of Wesleyan University in Connecticut. The third story would relate my avocational demi-career as a singer. Each of these three stories would involve a different cast of characters and would violate my scruples against discussing the living.

But one of the things I have come to see in telling my story from its original locus in my childhood home is that it is indeed one story, not three. I have, to be sure, lived my adult life in diverse institutional settings, but whatever is distinctive in what I have brought to them all, including the flaws, derives from my formative experience with Ruth, Beryl, and Bill. Originality, the peculiar style of all my doings and blunderings, is rooted in origins. The husband and father, the academic philosopher, the singer are three branches growing from the same tangled roots that continue to nourish them. That has become evident to me, at least, in this effort to expose these roots.

In the process, I have also become aware of how much my dead continue to affect me, and in what ways: how powerfully they continue to speak, and to sing, in my voice. Of course I do not pretend to have represented them objectively. I have not tried to write family history, but a personal memoir, representing my dead as they live in my memory, recalled from my point of view at the time, in their relationships with me, even as I only know myself in intimate relation with them and with others whose lives I share.

NOTES

1. "The Old Refrain," Viennese popular song. Words by Alice Mattullath and arranged by Fritz Kreisler (New York: Carl Fischer, Inc., 1915).

2. Eiselen, Frederick Carl, Lewis, Edwin, and Downey, David G. (Eds.). *The Abingdon Bible Commentary* (New York & Nashville: Abingdon-Cokesbury Press, 1920).

11

Elementals: An Autobiography

Robert Detweiler

As God unlocked all elemental things,
Fire climbed celestial vaults, air followed it
To float in heavens below; and earth which carried
All heavier things with it dropped under air;
Water fell farthest, embracing shores and islands.

Ovid, *Metamorphoses*[1]

EARTH

In early fall of 1991 my older—and only—brother died. The burial service was held, with only family members present, on a Thursday morning in the cemetery of the Souderton Mennonite Church north of Philadelphia. It was a brilliantly clear day, already so cool that we shivered in the shadow cast by the canopy over the grave site. After various readings, songs, and prayers, the coffin was let down into its deep vault and the heavy lid, transported by a mechanical winch, placed on top of it. Then eight full-sized shovels were produced (perhaps they were there all the time), and as we sang the old hymns and familiar gospel songs in the rich four-part harmony of the Mennonites that I remembered from my adolescence, we shoveled in the grave from the pile of earth next to it. These were not ceremonial heaps dropped in with miniature spades. We shoveled in the grave. My brother's son, tall and strong and an earthmover by profession, rolled up his sleeves and went to work. He was joined by sisters, uncles, cousins, nephews; young wives, sons-in-law, and old men all took turns. Little girls in their frocks and white stockings grasped the shovel handles with their fathers—some both weeping and singing—and struggled to carry the earth from the diminishing mound to the steadily filling hole.

We shoveled until the pile was gone and the soft ground high and rounded over the grave. Then we turned our shovels over, and with the smooth backs of the blades we shaped the earth into its final oblong and after that we sang the Doxology: "Praise God from Whom All Blessings Flow."

My roots are in that earth. Three hundred yards from what is now my brother's grave, across Walnut Avenue and an asphalt parking lot where once stood the elementary school I attended for six years, is the patch—or *was* the patch. I didn't think to look, when I was there for the funeral, to see if it was still there.

The patch was a truck patch, a vegetable garden, part of a larger plot of land sloping down behind an assortment of garages, tool sheds, and chicken coops that belonged to the row of houses farther up the hill on West Chestnut Street. My maternal grandparents and an aunt and uncle shared a duplex in that row, and the patch that my father and I tended was my grandparents' property. I don't know if we rented it (I doubt it), or if we—more likely— simply had the use of it.

I just wrote "my father and I," but surely my brother and sister worked in the patch earlier with my father—we had it for many years. But I remember only being there alone with my father, beginning when I was eight or nine. In spring he gave me a hatchet and let me sharpen the long rough poles for pole beans into new points. In summer we picked beans, peas, tomatoes, and above all corn—"above all" because I loved fresh corn, almost as much as my father did. He taught me how to judge which ears were ready for plucking, just as he showed me the caterpillars curled up tightly in the silky tips of so many of the ears, and how to jar them loose with a sharp finger snap.

When the stalks were at their tallest, the rows of corn were a thick green jungle. My two cousins and I played hide and seek in there, rushing up and down the rows and now and then getting cut across the cheek or arm by a sharp blade. I would remember those stinging cuts, oozing blood, later in Germany when I saw the scars of men gained (gained?) ceremonially in the duels of the fraternities at the universities.

My father grew up on a farm ten miles distant from Souderton but moved there and became a town dweller when he married my mother. He had the farmer's knowledge and instincts, but I did not. I never learned to milk a cow or drive a tractor: something the children—even the girls—of my father's brothers could do. They stayed on farms; those were the family choices: you stayed on the farm or moved to town. But I did learn a fascination for growing things. In my suburban living, I find a need for a few cucumber plants, some tomato vines, parsley, and mint tea in my tiny backyard plot or patio planter.

Shovels and earth. In the fall of 1984, my daughter's dog died: Pamela, age 17—many doggy years. She died in my daughter's arms in the back seat of my station wagon as I drove them, knowing it was hopeless, to the vet, the one open at night for emergencies. I stopped the car by the side of the road as we wept and considered what to do next. One is never ready for death, even when it has announced itself long before its arrival.

We agreed to place Pammy in the backyard of the family house. We drove over, got the spade and a large black trashbag. My daughter held the flashlight while I dug the grave next to the fence, slicing through the tangle of roots from the loblollies and tulip poplars around us. We buried her deep, for a dog, three feet down, snugly wrapped in that flimsy plastic bag. Biodegradable. As we walked back to the carport, my daughter, lighting the way, said, "Let's give her two years, then dig her up for the bones." My daughter is a physical anthropologist, a pragmatist, and shares the family's mordant humor. Recently, over the Christmas holidays, we reminded each other that the task of digging up Pamela is long overdue.

Beginning in late August 1951, when I had just turned 19, I shoveled *Bimssteine* for six months in the German Rhineland. This was six years after the end of World War II, and I was in an American workcamp near the riverside town of Neuwied in French-occupied Germany, making blocks of cement and volcanic stone that would be hauled north, via autobahn, to a postwar Mennonite settlement in Westphalia, where they would be used to build homes for refugees from the east—German Mennonites and others who had fled west ahead of the advancing Soviet armies. I volunteered for a year of workcamp and ended up staying in Germany over six. During that time, the battered nation regained its sovereignty, and the "economic miracle" was in its early stages when I returned to the United States at last in late 1957.

We worked outside through the winter at the Neuwied block manufacturing site: some ten American young men, our American house parents, our German boss (a sawed-off volatile Rhinelander named August, pronounced "Ow-goost," whom we suspected of being an unregenerate Nazi), and assorted German locals and refugees who came and went. The block pressing machine, electric powered, was simple but effective: shovel the *Bimssteine* into a kind of trough, add cement and water, press the button and stand back while the machine churns, strains, and delivers two fresh wet blocks on a board. One of us on each end of the board, we carried the blocks away and stacked them six to eight rows high to dry (not too high or the weight of the blocks higher up would crush those underneath and the whole wall would collapse into a useless mess). Then the same process over and over again. We took turns working the machine, stacking the blocks, and digging the stones from our little so-called quarries. Much later, when

I first read Kafka's story "In the Penal Colony," which features an execution machine that etches the victim's sentence into his flesh and thus kills him, I thought of the Neuwied block-making machine. Sometimes we scratched our names into the half-dried blocks. My name today, stuccoed over, is part of a dozen or so houses in Westphalia.

I liked working in the quarries best. The area where we worked and lived was on the fringes of the Eiffel Mountains, close to the French border, a range of long-dead volcanoes that had produced the stones we used. *Bimsstein* is light, brittle, and porous and can be found in thick layers of pebble-sized fragments not far beneath the earth's surface all over this valley. Mixed with cement, it makes sturdy and inexpensive building blocks. Later on, during the following year, I worked on a site outside Lübeck on the Baltic, where we also constructed houses for refugees. There we used larger, much heavier reddish blocks made from the crushed rubble of bombed buildings; there were enough of these around throughout the country to provide material for years. Germany recycled its ruins in the forties and fifties, and out of them rebuilt itself.

In my early teens, growing up in Souderton, I became a trapper. The fields behind our barn and elsewhere on the fringes of town were criss-crossed by creeks (pronounced "cricks," of course), and in their banks the muskrats dug the tunnels, partly submerged, that led to their burrows. In late fall, my friends and I caught muskrats with the simple leg traps that we ordered via the Sears and Roebuck catalogue. Some of us had partners. Mine was the neighbor boy "Sonny." These were the months of colds, chapped hands, and wet feet. We tramped through the fields and claimed our spots— generally just by finding the holes first and setting our traps there.

It was an unwritten law that you did not set a trap near a hole that was already staked—and I mean staked literally, since we attached our traps to chains that were, in turn, wired to short wooden stakes that we pounded into the earth. Usually we honored each others' territory. Sometimes we'd even kill a trapped animal in someone else's trap, tell him about it that day in school, and let him come to pick it up. Poaching—stealing muskrats from another's trap—was bad form, but it happened often enough. If we suspected it (usually by someone ratting, as it were, on someone else), we'd punish the perpetrator: steal his traps, remove the name plates (generally pieces of tin with initials or symbols scratched on them), and hide them at home. It was not a good idea to use those traps that season; some of us etched tiny identifying marks on our traps, so that we could recognize them as our property. Accusations, confrontations, and fistfights out in the wintry fields were not uncommon.

Sonny and I set about 30 traps and checked them in the evening, after junior high basketball practice, and then again at four to five in the morning. Earlier was better, in order to get to the trapped animals before a marauding fellow trapper would. My alarm would wake me, and I'd force myself out of the warm bed, along with my pint-sized shorthaired terrier mongrel, who would be shivering with cold (he slept under the blankets with me, fleas and all) and excitement. I'd dress warmly, take my flashlight and hammer, and we'd walk the few hundred yards, often through snow, to Sonny's house. There I'd find the clothesline hanging from the second story window, opened just a slit, and tied around Sonny's ankle. Since he had no alarm, I'd rouse him by yanking on the line until I felt the answering tug and watched the line pulled up inside the window.

Soon my friend would appear, bundled up as much as I, and we'd walk the route, not saying much, checking the burrow entrances—we knew all the locations by heart—with our lights. The giveaway of a trapped muskrat was the chain stretched taut from its anchoring stake and vanishing inside the tunnel. We would loosen the stake, often difficult in the frozen ground, then drag the helpless animal out by the chain and kill it with a hammer blow to the skull.

In a good week, we'd catch four to six muskrats. We kept the little carcasses in my father's barn, where they were preserved or even frozen stiff in the cold weather. Wednesday evenings my father would drive us to a gas station north of town, out toward Franconia, where a fur dealer, unshaven and chainsmoking, waited with his pickup. The going rate for a muskrat was $1.50 to $2.00, depending on size and the quality of the pelt. We never had to skin them, for which I was thankful. Now and then someone would bring the dealer a skunk. He'd swear and refuse it or swear and pay 50 cents; I never figured out what made the difference. Every once and awhile some poor fool would try to sell him a possum. He would take it silently by the tail and pitch it across the highway into the gutter, while the others of us shook our heads in quiet contempt.

Now I think back on those few years of muskrat trapping, regret the cruelty I practiced, and am surprised that I was so callous. But perhaps—probably—that was what served as my initiation, my late-pubescent rite of passage giving me my earliest real feel of violence and death. I can still see the smashed yellow teeth, the bloody mouths, and the twisted rictus grins of the creatures I killed. I can feel their final death shudders. A decade later in Germany, when I first saw, nauseated, the photos of naked death camp corpses piled atop each other on open truck beds, I recalled the back of the trader's pickup and, by the garish light of the Sunoco sign, the mass of furry bodies that filled it.

The memory of one night almost redeems the brutality of trapping. One early morning at four I walked the trap lines alone, with my terrier—Sonny must have been sick. It had snowed, melted during the day, and frozen again, and the whole expanse of field behind our barn was a single sheet of ice shining brilliantly in the moonlight. It was utterly silent, except for the crunch of my boots as I broke through the crust every few steps. I caught no muskrats; the traps were buried beneath the ice. But I made my rounds anyhow: slid, skated, and stumbled across the slick and brittle white glaze in a kind of trance, and when I think of it now, it is as if I moved then to the strains of strange music.

I like to visit graveyards. Now and then, my brother and I, when I went north to see him and his family, explored cemeteries in (and outside of) small towns of eastern Pennsylvania. We read the names and dates on the tombstones, looking for our paternal and maternal family names, trying to resolve something of our vague heritage. Years ago I visited the Jewish cemetery in Prague, a graveyard so old and crowded that the weather-scarred, discolored tombstones jostled each other for space. Many of the inscriptions I could not read, for they were in Hebrew. It was an overcast gray day, and in the ancient trees that grew there, the roots of some further unsettling the troubled earth, big black rooks cawed and flapped from branch to branch. Was it macabre? That word is said to derive from the old *danse macabre* (Old French), the dance of death, which in turn may derive from the Danse Macabé, the Maccabean dance from the medieval morality plays recalling the massacre of the Maccabees.

I visit regularly the old cemetery behind Christ's Church on my island (more on this later) off the Georgia coast. There one can linger in the shade of the great live oaks, their impossibly long and twisted limbs bearded with Spanish moss, and learn a good deal of the island's history—its white history, that is. It is a tranquil place, far away from the beaches, the golf courses, the little shops, and there one finds the names of the generations that have inhabited the island for two centuries and more.

What am I looking for there, or in any cemetery? What sort of news? Nothing profound, I think. Reading tombstones is not unlike reading fiction. I create stories from these plots, spin interwoven lives from the names and times of family groups. Death stirs the imagination.

My parents are buried side by side in a field beside a narrow country road in rural Pennsylvania, near Souderton. It is a Mennonite cemetery that my father helped to tend in his spare time, mowing the lawn. Their graves, like all those there, are marked not by upright stones but by heavy bronze plaques set flat in the earth.

I can never quite remember the location of their graves. Two winters ago, when I was visiting relatives in that area, I asked my brother to take us to that cemetery. It had snowed the night before, and when we arrived we saw that the field was covered with a layer of white. My brother (how like him) had taken a broom along, and while I felt for the hard flat plaques with my shoes and scraped the snow off those I discovered, my brother did a better job, sweeping the plaques clean. We found, scraped, and swept two dozen of them, but still no sign of our parents. I had given up and was already heading, with cold feet, for the warmth of the car, when my brother shouted. "Here they are!" He swept vigorously, and by the time I reached him, they were bare, the letters standing out in relief. It is a favorite image that I have of my brother: in his dark overcoat and rubbers, briskly sweeping the snow from our parents' graves on a cold late-December afternoon.

AIR

In early 1955, I began study at the University of Hamburg. I was formally enrolled in the school of theology, but I also studied philosophy and "Germanistik," German language and literature. The buildings where my lectures and seminars were held were, in actuality, dingy and shabby, but when I recollect those years I see an exalted image. I see myself entering a vast high hall suffused in light that streams in from something like clerestory windows just beneath the ceiling.

That image stayed with me, to a degree, during the five semesters I spent at the university there. I felt as though, after just one year at a church college (Eastern Mennonite) in the United States in 1950–1951, I had miraculously been granted access to the great tradition of European learning. This was about a decade before the German Federal Republic's *Universitätsreform* that liberalized the curriculum; led to the founding of new universities that would compete with those begun in the late Middle Ages, the Renaissance, and Enlightenment; and offered the chance of a university education to a far larger group of German youth.

In the process, and inevitably, what had been a relatively elitist system sacrificed a degree of quality in the name of egalitarianism. Thomas Jefferson would have approved. I experienced this, since I studied under the old regimen and have taught on four occasions as visiting professor under the new. The reform was necessary; if anything, it has not been radical enough. German university education still takes place in a patriarchal, largely homogeneous, extremely tradition-bound environment, and it functions—or tries to—under conditions of scandalous overcrowding that hinder the best sort of learning.

At the time, in the fifties, I had no sense of the shortcomings of the old system. I had been exposed to the exhilarations of the life of the mind, to the heady atmosphere of the grand heritage of the *Geisteswissenschaften* (what we translate weakly as the human sciences), and I have never recovered from it. Those five semesters were a marvellous indulgence of languages studied (Greek, Latin, Middle High German), of reading Kant, Hegel, Goethe, Marx, Nietzsche, Freud, Kafka, Barth, Tillich in their native tongue (but notice the absence of women on that list), of absorbing phenomenology, neo-orthodoxy, existentialism, a still-vibrant historicism, and the beginnings of the New Hermeneutic. I wish every student the sense of excitement that I felt—however flawed its basis was—and that grew and deepened as I gradually recognized the infinitely rich potential of the intellectual enterprise itself. Keats's poem "On First Looking into Chapman's Homer" conveys it with a metaphorical power better than any sober analysis:

> Then felt I like some watcher of the skies
> When a new planet swims into his ken;
> Or like stout Cortez* when with eagle eyes
> He stared at the Pacific—and all his men
> Looked at each other with a wild surmise—
> Silent, upon a peak in Darien.

The "exalted image" I mentioned of the vast hall suffused with light also has a specific locale or, better said, many specific locales. Living in Europe for more than a decade, all told, I became a passionate, if quite amateur, connoisseur of cathedrals. A cathedral, strictly speaking, is the main church of a bishop's jurisdiction. I use the term in the popular sense to refer to the grand churches built first in the Middle Ages. I am interested in all styles and periods but am drawn most to the Gothic on the Continent and the equivalent Perpendicular in Great Britain. I do not know why a boy nurtured in the severely plain Mennonite churches of eastern Pennsylvania should have grown into an adult fascinated by cathedrals, although the answer may be right there: I may have sought (still seek) the compensation of adornment, of the intricate and complex structure of the grand design. I am in certain ways easily bored, yet a single cathedral, were I to devote myself to it, could occupy me for the rest of my life.

I have visited scores of them: in Prague, Vienna, Salzburg, Innsbruck, Munich, Passau, Regensburg, Speyer, Cologne, Münster, Schleswig, Bourges, Paris, Canterbury, Rochester, London, Winchester, Chichester, Salisbury, Exeter, Gloucester, Norwich, Ely, Lincoln, York, Ripon, and Edinburgh; still others in Florence, Venice, Zurich, Basel, Antwerp, and Amsterdam; also the two major ones in the United States: St. John's in Manhattan and St. Peter's in Washington. For a month during the summer of 1986, I lived at Hatfield College in Durham in northern England and almost literally in the shadow of the massive Norman edifice that dominates that city from its position on the highest hill in town. Lying on my narrow cot next to the window, I could see from my pillow the added-on (in the thirteenth century, actually quite late) Gothic facade and towers of the west end, and I absorbed the regular ringing of the bells. I visited that huge long sanctuary regularly, often two or three times a day, and learned to feel its rhythms. I took part in evensong, sat up with the choir and joined in the music and readings that animate the church.

It is, among other things, the play of light, stone, and glass in the cathedrals that intrigues and delights me. Even the dark (some would say gloomy) and

*Even if Keats did mean Balboa.

heavy atmosphere of the Durham structure strives for illumination. One needs to understand that light, as much as glass and stone, is a building material of the cathedrals, and then one senses much better the genius of their design and the extravagance of their beauty.

I have a slide of an annunciation painting by Jan van Eyck that shows Mary and the angel facing each other at the altar of a Gothic cathedral. From a great height a narrow shaft of light shines in through a clerestory window and angles down through the shadowed sanctuary to pierce the virgin's womb. It is one of the loveliest paintings I know, and it conveys the focused mystery of light that provides those great churches with at least some of their aura of the sacred.

Once, in the winter of 1956, when I was a theology student at the University of Hamburg, I preached to the tiny Mennonite refugee congregation that met on occasional Saturday afternoons in the cathedral of Lübeck. I was a substitute for the lay pastor who usually spoke there. The group met in a large chapel of the cathedral because they had no building of their own. I took a train from Hamburg to Lübeck on the Baltic Sea (right on the closed border to East Germany), walked through the old Hanseatic town to the church and arrived 30 minutes early. No one was there to greet me, and so I sat in the great nave—not in the chapel where I would preach—and listened to the organist practicing for the Lutheran service on Sunday morning, the following day.

He (or she—I never saw the person up in the loft) played Bach. The church was cold, unheated, and the frigid air seemed to charge the music with a clarity and intensity that penetrated me. It was a dull day outside and already darkening by mid-afternoon, as it does in north Germany in winter, but enough light still entered the high windows (only recently installed to replace those shattered in the wartime bombings by my countrymen) to create a spectral play of form with columns and arches.

I have no memory of what I preached on in the side chapel that day— probably something far too academic, in my theology student mode, for the two dozen aging refugees who came hoping for a nostalgic trip back to the prewar services in Danzig and East Prussia. But I know that before I joined them I had been transfixed by the convergence of the cold, the winter light in the great damaged church, the triumph of Bach on the organ filling the hushed space in and around me.

Some six years later I preached again. This time I filled in for a month at the University Lutheran Church in Gainesville, Florida, while that congregation was seeking to replace a pastor (named Kaiser, an unwitting reminder of my German sojourn) who had moved on. Since I had studied Lutheran theology in Hamburg and had attended the Gainesville church for some three years, the task was not totally unfamiliar, although wearing the robes and performing the liturgy (in my little black book I had marked my choreography: "turn now," "kneel here") had its ironies for this Anabaptist.

I never intended to become a pastor, however. I could have become a professor of religious studies, perhaps, but at the time when I was making those decisions, teaching religion seemed to mean purveying doctrines and ideologies that suggested more certainty about the substance of such matters than I felt, and so I turned instead to the other possibility, the other serious fiction: professing literature.

It was the right choice, although some of my friends and former students might claim that I have used the teaching of literature and the writing about it mainly as occasion to profess religious convictions after all. I don't mind that charge. I become less and less confident that distinct boundaries exist between disciplines that depend as crucially on metaphoric language and on personal narrative as literature and religion do. Indeed, I have tended more and more, in my academic career, to blur those boundaries and to explore the terrain of the overlap.

My reference to Bach a few paragraphs back makes me want to enlarge on the value of music in my life, and that will lead to a reflection on the importance of the German language for me.

Karl Barth once remarked something to the effect that he looked forward to seeing Mozart in heaven. To my sensibilities, Mozart—and Bach—have already provided far more than their share of heavenliness here and now. I find their sounds—of the short-lived Austrian Catholic (I lived in Salzburg, his town, for a glorious year) and the full-lived German Lutheran—to be not merely the most sensually and aesthetically satisfying that I know, but also to echo the most enduring mystery of genius that I can imagine. I do not comprehend how they poured forth the sheer complex beauty of their music so consistently (almost relentlessly) and richly. Mozart's *Requiem* (which I have sung in a local Atlanta choir) and *The Magic Flute*; Bach's organ works, his *Well-Tempered Clavier*, and his motets and cantatas: these overwhelm and delight me again and again.

If I had to compose a theology, it would begin with these—and might end with them as well (with a footnote from Brahms' *German Requiem*). These matter to me as much as the land, sea, and sky scapes I have written about (in a later section), as much as the light and stone that play together in the shape of cathedrals, almost as much as the people I love and about whom I cannot write here, not in these few pages.

The German language. The much praised, maligned, overvalued, underestimated, mythicized, and rationalized German language. Mark Twain in *A Tramp Abroad* called it "the awful German language" and had great fun spoofing it: "I'd rather decline two beers than one German noun," he wrote, or something close to that. I am, of course, a native English speaker, although my older relatives in eastern Pennsylvania spoke Pennsylvania German (Dutch or Deitch, they called it) while I was growing up. I never learned it, but I suppose my exposure to it gave me an ear for German later on. I learned German among the Germans as a young man and could eventually pass as one of them. Now sometimes my relationship to that language surprises me, like that with an old lover. I speak it, think or muse in it, and am just enough *other*, just enough distant from it to remark its strange familiarity. Anyone who has become comfortable in a second (or third, or fourth) language recognizes what I mean. How is it,one asks, that the images and the syntax *flow* in this language almost as they do in one's "own"?

Sometimes I dream in German, and that then reminds me of how one's involvement in another language is also participation in another life. My friends tell me that I am a different person in German. That is true. At least I am a different perso*n* then; I feel and perform another self.

To say all this still says nothing about the richness of German, about its literature. The verse of the Minnesänger, Goethe's and Rilke's poetry, the prose fiction of Thomas Mann, Robert Musil, and Ingeborg Bachmann include some of the greatest writing I have encountered. One of my enduring frustrations as a teacher happens when I attempt to show how Goethe rivals Shakespeare as a craftsman of language to students who read only English. If I had to select a single brief example to convey the genius of German literature at its best, it would be Goethe's deceptively simple, resonant "Wandrers Nachtlied":

> Über allen Gipfeln ist Ruh.
> In allen Wipfeln spürest du
> Kaum einen Hauch.
> The Vögelein schweigen im Walde;
> Warte nur, balde
> Ruhest du auch.

My translation, done with liberties, goes like this:

> Peace above the peaks on high.
> In all the treetops you'll feel
> Scarcely a sigh.
> The little birds in the woods are still.
> Just wait:
> Soon you'll rest too.

The things that have motivated the German imagination are here: the romantic sentiment, the celebration of the natural world, the drive for serenity, the persistent awareness of death that gives the final line its double meaning. Some of my friends, less generous about the Germans, would say that such poetry disguises a will to power that has resulted in the annihilation of millions, and I'd reply that this is also true. At the same time, it's a kind of verse that tries to tame the will to power—a will that, as the late twentieth century has demonstrated, far exceeds German appropriations of it.

In any case, I did not become a teacher of German literature as such but of that literature in comparison with its American and British counterparts, and it is surely an irony of sorts that the person who led me to this was not a prominent international scholar but an American college teacher. I have had many fine teachers in my lifetime (and some of the best have been my own doctoral students), but never one as influential as the young woman (scarcely five years older than me, I'd guess) who guided me through three semesters at Goshen College where I earned my B.A. degree after returning from Germany.

She ran a casual class with no obvious system. She lectured a good deal and involved us in some discussion, but she wasn't innovative. Sometimes she'd drift into the afternoon classroom, a wisp or two of blonde hair astray, look at us absently for a moment through her glasses, then murmur, "Oh dear, I seem to have forgot my books," and leave again to retrieve them. But when she talked to us about texts and authors and traditions, she was magnificent. I learned how to read modern fiction by watching her plot her way through Virginia Woolf's difficult *Mrs. Dalloway,* and that brilliant neurotic novel has remained central to my interpretive strategies. I learned as much usable philosophy from her glosses of Kafka and Faulkner as I did from all my courses in Hamburg. I learned from her that one can organize one's mind via the great literary texts. She taught me to think by literature.

She talked *to* us (and not just at us) in class, thinking out loud, taking us seriously enough for that, but I had little contact with her otherwise. A few times we crossed paths on the plain little campus, and once, I recall, she paused red-nosed and sniffling in January to tell me that she was allergic to the cold. I could sympathize: My hayfever struck regularly a few months later in the spring. Another time we talked after class, and I, still recovering from years of speaking German, pronounced "chaos" as "cah-ohs." "Cay-ahs," she said, interrupting me gently. I think of her like that, gracefully interceding, almost apologetically, to reinterpret disorder.

A few years ago, my partner and I found ourselves on a summer evening in a southeastern French town named Bourg-en-Bresse, a Saturday-night stopover on our way to visit friends in the French Alps. We wandered through the quiet streets and entered a little church. It was empty, cool, and silent. As usual, we went our separate ways as we explored the nondescript building, but then I called a few words to her and was startled at the transport of my voice.

She was standing near the altar. "Sing something," I said, and she sang the first stanza of "Amazing Grace" in her lovely soprano. The sound was crystalline, vibrant, and pure, and it brought tears to my eyes. The provincial church had acoustics that the designers of concert halls—and performers in them—dream of and pray for, and I heard, as if for the first time, the simple depth of that song and the fullness of that voice.

Not all of my airy experiences have been ethereal. I should probably write here about flying and how important commercial flying has been to me, the jets getting me back and forth on frequent trips, especially to Europe and home again, and making this modern mobile life possible. But flying actually doesn't interest me very much—unlike my son, a film maker who flies much more than I and, fortunately, still likes it.

I'll describe instead an evening in the spring of 1989, when I was teaching at a Bavarian university. I had driven to Amsterdam to visit friends, was on my way from there to Hamburg to see other friends before returning to southern Germany, and stayed for the night in the German town of Norden, not far from the Dutch border. My hotel was right behind the huge grassy dike built to keep out the ferocious flood tides, and I climbed it to make my way down the other side to the North Sea, now tranquil—as was the whole coastal area in the pre-tourist season. Atop the dike, I turned to look inland, the direction I had come from, and saw a half-mile distant six great pylons with three-bladed propellers attached—giant wind machines designed to generate electricity for this area. I had seen photos and films of these in California but never the real thing.

After walking along the water, I made my way inland in twilight along a narrow dirt road through pastures and drainage ditches to the wind machines. As I drew close, I saw that the propellers (each gleaming chromed blade must have been at least eight feet long) were fixed to cones that rotated easily on their axes (ball-bearing mounted, no doubt) to meet the breezes. They spun slowly but methodically, humming and throbbing high above me. I stood beneath them as the sky darkened, feeling their power as if I were in the gathered center of a vast natural force field. I imagined what it would be like when those long blades whirled fiercely in the windlashed rain, the cones swivelling silently to meet the gusts.

FIRE

Not long after I arrived in Germany for the first time, in 1951, I took a bus into town to cash traveller's cheques, as one did then, at the Neuwied post office. I stepped up to the counter and signed the cheques as the postal clerk, a thin and taciturn man seated on a chair, watched me. He studied my passport for a long time. Then, as he turned in his chair and shoved the bills and the passport to me, he gave me an unpleasant thin-lipped smile and spoke in German: "*Das, was Sie mit Dresden gemacht haben, war nicht nötig*" ("What you did to Dresden was not necessary").

What he meant, of course, was the bombing of Dresden by the British and Americans in February 1945, a devastating raid ordered by Churchill, it was said, both in retaliation for the German air attacks on British cities and to break the will of the German citizenry. It was a raid in which many thousands were killed in a few hours in the standard ways of aerial bombardment: concussion, collapsing buildings, suffocation, fire. That attack is in good part the substance of Kurt Vonnegut's searing novel *Slaughterhouse Five*.

I had no reply to that postal clerk (a man who practiced my father's vocation). In fact, at the time my German was so weak that I was not sure of what he had said, and I comprehended it only later. But I did, at that moment, recognize a hatred so strong that it overcame his fear of accusing me, a conqueror and occupier of his country.

In January 1953, I moved from the workcamp in Lübeck 50 miles west to Hamburg, and for three years I lived in the Hamburg Mennonite Church complex and served as youth worker in the North German Mennonite congregations—these a combination of old churches dating back as far as the early 1700s and recently formed fellowships of Mennonite refugees in areas where few or no Mennonites had lived before.

I organized summer camps along the Elbe River, in the Harz Mountains and in the lowlands of Schleswig-Holstein; bicycle tours to Mennonite families and churches in the Netherlands and South Germany; weekend retreats in Cologne, Frankfurt, Hannover, and dozens of other cities; and I held a virtually constant open house for teenagers and young adults in my snug parsonage quarters. Part of the time I lived and worked with a succession of two German volunteers and one American; some of the time I worked alone, traveling by train to the various areas or in a cranky old British panel truck that the American relief agency and the German church bought for us.

Atlanta, my home, since 1970, for over two decades, symbolizes itself by the phoenix, the mythical bird that rises reborn from the ashes. In Confederate history, of course, Atlanta was put to the torch by General Sherman on his notorious march to the sea. Hamburg, a former home to which I return periodically and gladly, is much more a phoenix city, for it was devastated by fire and rose again many times since its founding as the Hammaburg, a Saxon fortress, in the 800s. When I moved there in the early fifties, I found myself amidst the ruins of the latest catastrophe, the incredible firebombing of World War II that turned the city, in that fateful, abnormally hot July of 1943, into an inferno that took thousands of lives and razed vast sections of the town.

Less than ten years later when I arrived, parts of it still lay wasted, and I got used to the incongruities of rubble fields next to new highrises; of the massive concrete anti-aircraft bunker in the Holy Ghost Field hulking grotesquely over the hugely festive Dom, the twice-yearly fair held at Christmas and in mid-summer.

Hamburg and London (where I would live six months of the year if this were an ideal life) are in certain ways sister cities: cool (in every sense), cosmopolitan, understated merchants', bankers', and sailors' cities, wedded to great rivers, the Elbe and the Thames, that run to the sea. The psyches of both are severely scarred by fire—London also burned many times and suffered the bombardment conflagrations of the war. I am attracted to these cities tried by fire, where the nightly high-tech illuminations still reflect, for those with memories, the blazing skies of the *Blitz* and the *Feuersturm*.

Fire scorches the German collective memory. Remember the *Götterdäm-merung* of German myth, the twilight of the gods that is an apocalyptic cataclysm. Remember Brünhilde asleep inside the flaming circle in *The Song of the Nibelungs*. Remember the furnaces of Auschwitz and the ovens of Dachau. I visited Dachau, as well as Bergen-Belsen and Neuengamme, and I was sickened. I am just as sickened by American memories: Blacks in my part of the country hanged from branches of trees and slow-roasted over fires beneath them; the Ku Klux Klan burning crosses in a national park ten minutes from my house.

In summer of 1943 (about the time that Hamburg was being firebombed) the Apocalypse announced itself in Souderton. These were the Second World War years, and people were edgy in any case. My father, a rational man, had dreams of being chased by Hitler (the Antichrist?) and thrashed in his bed at night. The End seemed imminent first on one of those overwrought hot nights when the whole nation was tossing and turning, fretting over German tenaciousness in Europe and Africa ("There's no good news on the Western front tonight," Gabriel Heatter's mournful voice would intone on the five o'clock radio news in everybody's kitchen) and Japanese victories in the Pacific ("Every time you buy a bond, you slap a Jap across the pond," was one of the government propaganda slogans we learned in school, but the Japanese seemed to be doing most of the slapping): Someone saw a cross on the nearly full moon. Or better said, when one studied the moon, it seemed to elongate into a cross. The news spread across town the next day with the speed of doom, and that night many folks looked for the cross on the moon, the moon as cross. Some saw it; many didn't. For those who did, it was a sign and a portent, a natural omen warning of the Judgment. People examined Ezekiel and Revelation in their Scofield Bibles for evidence that the latter days would be signalled by crosses on/in/of the moon.

Then on the third night, some demystifier discovered the simple fact: look at the moon outside or through a window, and you see your standard non-apocalyptic lunar sphere. Look at it through a screen, and you see it pulled, stretched into a cross shape by the tiny wire squares.

That was it. One might say, the crux of it. No Second Coming advertised after all, just a quirk of optics and wire mesh technology. I, about ten at the time, remember feeling disappointment. I had little sense of what the Apocalypse was (we didn't call it by that big word, of course), although I connected it vaguely to the July nights agitated by heat lightning flickering across the skies, and by the recollection of my father's answer to a question. "What would happen," I asked him once, "if a flash of lightning wouldn't stop?" I was uneasy about lightning, the real kind and not just the heat displays. My father admired Ben Franklin (he'd take me to the Franklin Institute in Philadelphia now and then), but he was no student of electricity. "Why," he replied, "then the whole world would burn up." That struck me as so scary that it was delicious, so that I thought of the Apocalypse as stuck lightning that incinerated everything.

Two years later we dropped the bomb on Hiroshima and Nagasaki, and I imagined that the Beast was on the loose—just in time for my late adolescence and the fire in the loins.

Our workcamp in Lübeck on the Baltic was actually on the outskirts of town, and during one holiday, I went in alone to explore the old city. I was an innocent 20 at the time. Lübeck has many charming narrow alleyways off larger streets (like the mews of London), a vestige of its medieval past, and I was strolling through one of these, studying the glazed brick and half-timbered buildings crowded together, when I heard a tapping on a window above me. Startled, I looked up and saw the pretty young woman smiling down at me behind the glass. Her face was heavily made up, and her breasts were mostly naked. With her forefinger she beckoned me. I realized in a flash where I was—in the midst of the street set aside for the prostitutes—and I fled, blushing with shame.

Not long ago in Amsterdam: *déjà vu*. I was walking near the Nieuwe Kirk, looking for the entrance, when I heard a little call: "Hey!" I searched for the source of the voice and found her: way up at the garret window of an ornate old building. She gave me a flash of smile, a flash of thigh, and waved. I smiled, waved back, and found my way into the severe Dutch Calvinist church. Starving poets used to live in garrets, I thought; now it's young whores—although many of them in Amsterdam, as in Hamburg, display themselves at ground floor level behind large glass windows. She seemed merry, the one who waved to me, but I doubt that she was.

I have lived nearly half my life in Florida and Georgia, in the heat. When I told the dean of my Indiana college, back in the late fifties, that I planned to move to the South to begin graduate study, he tried to dissuade me. "You'll lose your soul down there," he told me, and he was serious.

Who knows? Maybe I did, in a way. I have, in any case, made my home here, and I do not intend to return to the North except to visit. My children and my grandchildren, others precious to me, are at home here. They are Southerners. I come close.

Heat marks the South. My family and I left my parents' home in Pennsylvania in late May of 1959 (I having finished college and seminary in Indiana) on our way to Florida and graduate school. We drove an old Dodge and pulled a trailer with all of our goods. On the first night, we stopped at a motel in southern Virginia, and I remember the heat there. It was sultry. It enveloped my body gently but insistently. It was the first time I had felt the pervasive presence of southern heat.

We lived in Florida for six years without air-conditioning, and thus I am a veteran of the force of southern summers. During my first summer quarter as an M.A. student in Gainesville, I had classes in un-air-conditioned buildings. I remember writing examinations that June and July in a linguistics course when it was so hot that the sweat ran down my arms as I wrote, and I held a handkerchief around my right wrist with my other hand, so that the perspiration would not drip onto the paper and blur the ink.

Later, when I taught at a college in St. Petersburg for four years, it was just as hot and still more humid, there on the Gulf Coast, but we had air-conditioning at last, and life became, finally, more comfortable and more productive. Nevertheless, we played tennis for hours in the full sun in the hottest months, just as we walked the dazzling beaches in swimming trunks and bikinis, courting skin cancer. Our son fished, caught snakes, and turned a deep tan. Both children swam incessantly in the college pool. I nurture an image of my daughter from those days, breaking through the surface in that pool one bright hot afternoon, shooting up and out like a dolphin, streaming sparkling water from her lithe brown body.

Atlanta has the pleasures, dangers, irritations of all big cities, but life is much enhanced by the climate. For six to eight months of the year, one can virtually live outdoors, when it is neither too hot nor too cold. In March or early April, the dogwoods and azaleas bloom, and one is astonished anew each spring by the extravagant beauty of it all. Warm weather teases us already in February, and abruptly the grassy quadrangle of my university campus is full of bare legs, bare feet, frisbees flying, somebody's dog chasing squirrels. Summer brings violent and spectacular electrical storms, cloudbursts that are called gullywashers here. Sometimes it brings weeks and months of drought that turns things brown, withers the corn, and exposes the rotting stumps as the lakes recede. It brings nights when the temperature will not drop below 90, when it is totally windstill and one hears, sweating lightly in bed in the cooled houses, the hum of air-conditioners working overtime throughout the neighborhood.

Then there are nights when it cools off and one sleeps with open windows. Often I will wake at two, or three, or four (I am a light sleeper) and hear the melancholy hu-u-u-u-u of the screech owl in the little woods behind the house. (Every neighborhood should have at least one screech owl; I am for making this a requirement.) Down on my island, when the wind is right, I can hear from my bed the sound of the surf on the beach or against the rocks at high tide. This is my world, heatstruck.

In 1951, for a few seconds, I glimpsed the most compelling fire of passion I have ever seen. I was in Germany then, and for reasons I cannot recall I was in the train station of Koblenz, a town on the Rhine River close to Neuwied where I lived and worked. It was in the evening around seven or eight, and the station was packed and agitated. I saw and felt the excitement, then watched as a small group pushed through the crowd from an arrived train to a waiting car.

"It's Kurt Schumacher!" someone said, and I (remarkably) knew what that meant. Schumacher was Germany's most prominent socialist, a hero; a man imprisoned during the Nazi era and tormented by those thugs. After the war, he had emerged as a charismatic leader, a fighter for the socialist alternative, even though he and his party could not prevail against the U.S.-backed Christian Democrats. But here he was, one arm amputated, gaunt, already harshly marked by the lung cancer that would kill him a few months later. He and his small entourage passed close by me. His daughter held his arm (his only arm) and guided him. I looked into his face and saw that the cliché "blazing eyes" could be a true description. Schumacher's eyes blazed. Perhaps it was from the fever of his illness, perhaps exhaustion. Perhaps it was those things but also the fire of his vision. He seemed to take in nothing around him. His eyes were focused on something far away, and they were very bright. I have never again seen anything like it.

WATER

In one of my earliest memories, I am under water. I am perhaps three years old, with my parents and other relatives (aunts? uncles? cousins?) during the summer at a lake near the Pennsylvania-New Jersey border. My adult conjecture tells me it must have been a state park near Washington's Crossing. People are jumping off the dock into the water. In my excitement I jump too. I cannot swim. As I descend, eyes open, I see vague shapes around me, swirling, emitting bubbles. The light above me seems radiant as I sink. I take a breath and choke. I thrash. Within seconds my father is there. Treading water, he catches me up and swims with me to the grassy bank, where I stand coughing and trembling. There I am chided for my foolishness. I am both elated and ashamed.

Three decades later, I went back under water and stayed, off and on, for three years. In 1962, about the time I was finishing my Ph.D. at the University of Florida in Gainesville, I began skin diving. For the first year, I limited myself to free diving: I employed mask, snorkel, and flippers and held my breath as I dove. I dove with family and friends in the sinkholes, underwater caves, and clear springs and rivers that penetrate and flow through the porous limestone substructure of northern and central Florida.

I dove without scuba diving equipment for the first year because I couldn't afford it. It was excellent training. Eventually I could hold my breath under water for two minutes and longer—plenty of time to explore cave formations at depths of 30 feet or to dive quickly to the bottom of a 90-foot sinkhole and reach the surface again before passing out.

Finally, I bought my compressed air tanks and regulator and learned scuba diving with friends from the Gainesville diving club. Never a very good surface swimmer, I became a passionate diver, and the lucid, cold deep waters of the Florida springs were the locus of my desire. We dove year round, summer and winter. The springs are a constant 68 degrees; in summer this feels shockingly cold: There is nothing more exquisitely agonizing than the water creeping up your back, under the wetsuit, during those first minutes after you've plunged into the spring. In winter, in contrast to the outside temperatures, the water seems warm.

We dove during the day and the night, and indeed our night dives were the most exhilarating. Three or four of us would arrive at Ginny Springs off the Santa Fe River in total darkness. Using our car headlamps for light, we would "tie off" a line to a tree or cypress root at water's edge. Once in the water, and with our diving gear on, we would pay out the line, one of us taking the lead and the others following him—or her—down into the cave. We'd descend to depths of 100, 120 feet and explore the labyrinth of tunnels, wielding our homemade diving lamps for illumination. The fish we encountered in the cave on the night dives seemed transfixed by the beam of our lights. They would drift, virtually motionless, close by, and sometimes they would follow us as if drawn along, dream-swimming, by our brightness.

On such a night, ascending from a dive, I experienced one of the loveliest epiphanies of my life. I emerged last from the mouth of the cave, still 30 feet down, turned over on my back and looked above as I floated slowly upward through the crystalline water. I could see the wavering treetops of pines, cypress, and live oaks form a circle that expanded and contracted, and beyond that I glimpsed the stars, shimmering points stretched into iridescent dashes, then back to dots: a cosmic morse code light years above me signaling the ineffable infinite clarity of things.

Once at the surface and standing waist deep in the little spring run above the cave, it was different. A hundred yards down the run, where it met the Santa Fe, we saw reflected in our flashlight beam the 'gators' red eyes and heard their sound, something combined of a honk and a bellow: waronkk!

A Saturday night in the summer of 1965 changed everything about cave diving for me. It was already nearly dark when I got the telephone call to come to Ginny Springs and look for the body of a fellow club member, 19-year-old Bob, who had gone diving into the cave alone (a cardinal sin among divers) that afternoon and had vanished in there. I was by then in the local water rescue unit (as Bob himself was, ironically enough) that worked with the Alachua County Sheriff's Department and was on that evening the only diver in town who could be located.

I threw my gear in the Volkswagen and sped to the site. Arriving at the end of the dirt road in the woods next to the run, I saw the flashing red light of the sheriff's vehicle and a small group gathered at the bank like some mysterious band of worshippers. Among them were the distraught grand-parents of my reckless friend, with whom he lived.

Two divers from Tampa who had happened to be exploring springs in the area that day were on the scene, but they were fearful of descending into that unfamiliar place at night. One of them volunteered to dive with me and search for Bob's body. We used his line, tied it off, and swam down on a long slant into the depths of the cave. At its base, it is over 100 feet deep. One comes first into a large, low vestibule studded with stalagmites and stalactites and beyond the vestibule is a labyrinth of tunnels, many of which my friends and I had ventured into on previous dives. We tied a line to a sturdy stalagmite and began to check out the tunnels, following them one by one until they ended in sheer limestone walls or until our line gave out. After 20 minutes my partner, who had been diving that afternoon, ran low on air and signaled that he had to quit. I ascended with him as far as the cave's entrance and waited there until his friend joined me in the continuing search.

It was treacherous business, for we kicked up bottom silt with our flippers as we swam, and whenever we turned to exit a tunnel we had to feel our way along the taut lifeline (that one of us reeled in as we swam) through a murk that our lights could scarcely penetrate. We searched until our air ran low, then gave it up. My partner left the cave for the surface, but I remained suspended inside the mouth of the cave, decompressing. Since I had been at those lower depths for over an hour, I needed to let my body adjust to normal atmospheric pressure and avoid the possibility of an aeroembolism, or the so-called bends. There, floating on my stomach in the darkness, my twin tanks clanking against the vault of the cave, I had time to think.

Except for the end of the unbearable tension it would have meant for Bob's relatives—who were still hoping hopelessly that we might find him alive—I was not sorry that we hadn't discovered his body. I had seen before what drowned divers look like, and I was not eager to come upon Bob in that condition. I thought about how foolish my friend had been—a far better diver than I—to dive alone and without a line, seduced by the false familiarity of the cave he thought he knew so well. I thought of what a waste it was, to be dead of carelessness at 19, and of how fortunate I had been to survive similar foolhardiness. I recognized my own selfishness in indulging this risky sport in spite of the fears of people who loved me, and I decided that I would give it up.

Other divers from our club found Bob's body the next day, a Sunday morning, at the dead end of a tunnel that we had missed the night before. I made a few harmless dives after that and then quit. Late that summer, we moved to New York, and I sold my gear. Every now and then, a quarter-century later, I wake up at night and remember myself deep in the cave of Ginny Springs, groping through narrow stone passageways for a body I wish not to find. Sometimes I have the uncanny feeling that I myself did not survive that night, and that my life since then has been an illusion. Dreamt by whom?

But water continues to attract me, as it always has. When I was a boy in Souderton I'd hear the whistles of the trains passing through town and imagine that they were the horns of ships. On our infrequent trips (one per summer, or less) to the New Jersey beaches—the "shore"—I would grow giddy with anticipation as my father drove us, in the sturdy black Buick, those last few miles over bridges and past marinas, taking us to the ocean at last.

In the early seventies, I taught for two terms at the University of Salzburg, and we lived in that stunning town, surrounded by the Austrian Alps, for a year. The area was beautiful, heady, bracing, and awesome; it had spectacular waterfalls and gorges carved by rushing Alpine streams—but it was not the sea. It was not half as interesting as the time, four years later, when I taught two semesters at the University of Hamburg and we lived for nine months on the hillside of Blankenese, a suburb overlooking the mighty Elbe River.

Hamburg is a good 60 miles from the North Sea, but the Elbe is navigable into the city's huge harbor even for the supertankers and the giant container ships. I spent many hours (often neglecting my research—and I've never been sorry) down at the Blankenese floating dock, watching the dense river traffic, above all the tugboats, sometimes ten or twelve at a time, swarming around the monstrous cargo vessels and maneuvering them toward a berth or, conversely, back out to sea. The tugs were fretful, busy, nagging little craft, pulling and shoving the huge recalcitrant bulks in the proper directions. Sooner or later another tug would appear and attach itself to the big ship. A rope ladder would be dropped down, and a figure would climb up slowly from the tug to the deck of the ship: the harbor pilot, the expert whose task it was to take the ship the final distance. I decided then that in one of my future lives I would like to take a break from academe and train to become a harbor pilot on the Elbe River, guiding the great ships those few crucial miles to and from their destinations. It is a profession with clean lines, where one gets immediate results. Pilot or perish.

Now, finally, I have found my place on the water. We own a house on an island off the southern coast of Georgia, an island of marshes and forests once inhabited by Indians, then by Spanish and British settlers, eventually the site of plantations and a home to slaves. Now it is quietly residential, at least semisuccessfully resisting "development" (a pernicious term, since development generally means environmental destruction) as a tourist center, a haven for persons who want a slower life. Our house, in the midst of massive live oaks that rise to form a canopy over us, is a five-minute walk from the beach and the Atlantic.

We drive there as often as we can, which is never often enough, and it is always worth the five-hour trip. The journey itself on the crowded freeways is a transition from the busy pace of the metropolis to the relative peace of the island. Once there and settled in, I work as intensely as at my Atlanta home, but more productively. On my island, I can interrupt my writing (*this* very writing, for example), my class preparations, with long ruminating walks on the beach. It is seldom crowded. For company there are the gulls, the plovers, the pelicans in single-file fishing formation just above the waves, an occasional exuberant dog splashing in the surf. Here one can sort things out, think uncluttered thoughts.

The light makes a difference. So do the cloud formations, the patterns in the sand, the shells and flotsam that the surf churns up especially after storms, the rhythms of the tides and winds. The seaside (this one still clean) lives in constant change, although much of it is subtle, nuanced, and is apprehended only gradually. Sometimes one has to be lucky. One night in a late summer, the full moon coincided with—perhaps helped to cause—an extremely low tide. The sky was clear, and in the brilliant moonlight, we walked barefoot far out on the damp ocean bed. We walked out so far that we could barely see the lights of the Coast Guard station a few hundred yards inland, and the sweeping beam of the lighthouse, down near the pier, seemed to come from some distant alien realm. There were no sounds; even the surf was hushed, and the radiance around us was like a vast veil that held out noise and rumor. We walked separately, in different regions of whiteness, and when we called out to each other, it was in chastened tones.

One late December day on a Sunday noon we walked the beach down to the pier. Above us and over the island, the sky was an emphatic blue, and a bright winter sun shone warmly. At water's edge, a thick wall of fog rose high, abruptly, like a barrier to another world. Gulls vanished into it and flew back out into our midst, crying some news about strange things there, bird versions of the twilight zone.

These are rare events, but every day, off the coast of our island—unless the fog is too thick or the sea too rough—one can see the shrimp boats harvesting, the long arms that hold the nets stretched out, raised up as if in blessing or in supplication, either way a sign of the abundance that still flourishes here.

(Why go on so about islands, the light, the sea? Because these are the phenomena that truly matter to me. They are more important than ideas. They are the stuff from which ideas spring. "The symbol gives rise to thought," says Paul Ricoeur's famous formula. Yes indeed, but the natural events birth the symbols that give rise to thought.)

I'm not yet quite finished with islands. I have always, at least in my adulthood, been drawn to islands. I suffer from what James Michener in his recent autobiography calls "nesomania" ("neso" is the Greek word for "island"), a near-obsession with islands, I have not humored this affliction very much; I have never been to Hawaii, the South Seas, or Greece, and to the Caribbean (Jamaica) just once for an instructive and disturbing week in the near Third World. But I have visited many islands off the Gulf Coast of Florida, Nova Scotia (for all practical purposes an island), Iceland, Helgoland and other North Sea islands closer to the German coast, the spectacular and overcrowded Mont Saint-Michel in Normandy. Manhattan (where I lived and taught for a year) appeals to me in good part because it is an island, and Venice, one of my favorite cities anywhere, attracts me not least because it survives precariously on many islands. In Great Britain I have been to Mersea Island south of Colchester, to the Holy Isle of Lindesfarne in Northumberland, to Mount St. Michael in Cornwall, and (my favorites of anywhere) the Orkneys off the north coast of Scotland.

In spring and summer of 1989, while I taught at the University of Regensburg in northern Bavaria, I lived for four months in a small village close to the Danube River. I could walk along a narrow forest road amidst tall evergreens and hardwoods a mile or so to the water. Now and then I would startle deer along the way, and they would bound off into the deeper woods. This was as idyllic as I have ever lived. My teaching schedule was light, and when I had done my professorial duties I would drive the ten miles from the busy old city (founded by the Romans) out to the rural solitude of Saxberg, my town of 30 houses. Often I would head down to the river—this venerable waterway that flows 1,750 miles, all told, through Germany, Austria, Yugoslavia, Hungary, between Bulgaria and Romania, and into the Black Sea at last—and I would sit on its bank at sundown, watching the clouds of tiny insects rising and falling above the current. Fish would leap clear of the water, lunging at the dancing clouds, slap down again and vanish, leaving spreading rings.

Sometimes I'd drive down to the river, cross the bridge at the spa town of Bad Abbach, park and walk along the bank on the other side. Here sedate little settlements front the Danube, strung-out neighborhoods reaching to the road that parallels the river and stretching back a few hundred yards to the low wooded hills. Here and there one sees a church, a beer garden shaded by large trees, a small grocery store. No doubt many inhabitants of these towns work in Regensburg; probably some of them even brave the Autobahn close by—taking courage and steering wheel firmly in hand for the daily 60-mile drive each way to jobs in Nuremberg. But life is still distinctly slower out there, still aligned in some measure to the rhythms of the river. In another life (perhaps after my career as an Elbe River pilot) I would like to live there: write my books, walk on the narrow path along the water and meditate, drink my evening glass of local wine at a table under the trees, slow my pace to that of the Danube.

Not long ago, early in 1992, I had a dream about my brother. We were together in a car, parked near a cliff high above the water. It could have been the Pacific or somewhere along the British coast—Cornwall, for example. In that multiperspective that we accept in our dreams, I sat in the car aside of my brother, who occupied the driver's seat, but I could also see straight down the face of the steep cliff, as if I were standing at the very edge. It was rocky down below. Slick black boulders surfaced and vanished as the water surged in and out. There was no beach at the base of the cliff, and the surf crashed directly into the sheer stone, sending up white spume and foam. The water was a deep blue, but I do not remember that the sun was shining. My brother was whole, healthy, and we talked quietly about unimportant things. Outside gulls wheeled and screamed, their soaring and diving bodies a brilliant white against a noncommittal heaven.

I awoke from the intensity of the dream, and my grief for him was sharp. Yet somehow, since then, I have missed him less.

CODA

I don't recall just when or how the idea occurred to me of organizing my autobiography according to the four elements of ancient and medieval cosmologies, but when it did, I knew immediately that it would be a productive grid to use. First, it led me to order the narrative of my life in a nonchronological way whereby I could emphasize significant moments and motifs. Second, I have been greatly influenced by landscapes, topographies, the physicality of places and structures, and this approach enabled me to stress such influence. Third, I decided (I am a relatively private person) that I would not write my story primarily in terms of my relationships to family and other loved ones: This seemed far too formidable an undertaking for an essay of such brevity. Thus, my "elemental" strategy permitted me to write about important *matters* that tell the context and plot of my narrative without dwelling on its characters. This tactic leaves out a great deal, obviously, but it tells what I want to have overtly told. Fourth, in my profession I teach a great deal of fiction, including experimental writing, and the idea of composing my story in this innovative way appealed to me as a student of literary narrative.

What have I learned from writing this autobiography? Partway into the composition of it, I remembered that my four elements are prominent Jungian archetypes. This realization bothered rather than pleased me, since I am no particular friend of Jungian thought. Yet as my story took shape, I found that this structuring prompted memories and revelations that probably would not have occurred to me otherwise. A case in point is the time years ago (described in the "air" section) when I preached in the cathedral in Lübeck. This was, on balance, a very minor moment, but the recollection of it, inspired by my "elemental" approach, made me realize how much my life has been marked, ordered, and made valuable by such little epiphanies.

My brother died around the time when I was starting to think seriously about writing this life narrative, and his death and the grief process permeated my story more than he himself would have if he were alive. His strong presence in my narrative confirmed what I already knew—his considerable influence on my life—but I also learned at first hand how "writing out" an emotionally fraught situation helps one to come to terms with it.

Finally, I rediscovered through the writing what a rich, stimulating, and blessed life I have led and lead, and how most of its grace has come from the persons, all unnamed, who inhabit my tale. Everyone has seen the drawings in newspapers and magazines that challenge one to find the figures disguised among the trees, the fields, the clouds. My story is something like that. Many precious persons are hidden in its detail. I hope that some of them, at least, will have the pleasure of discovering themselves there.

NOTE

1. From *The Metamorphoses* by Publius Ovidius Naso, translated by Horace Gregory, Translation copyright (c) 1958 by The Viking Press, Inc., renewed 1986 by Patrick Bolton Gregory. Used by permission of Viking Penguin, a division of Penguin Books USA Inc.

12

The Stories We Live By: Confessions by a Member of the Species *Homo Fabulans* (Man, the Storyteller)

George S. Howard

Miller Mair (1988) made a profound observation when he claimed that,

> Stories are habitations. We live in and through stories. They conjure worlds.
> We do not know the world other than as story world. Stories inform life. They
> hold us together and keep us apart. We inhabit the great stories of our culture.
> We live through stories. We are *lived* by the stories of our race and place. It
> is this enveloping and constituting function of stories that is especially impor-
> tant to sense more fully. We are, each of us, locations where the stories of our
> place and time become partially tellable. (p. 127)

We live in and through stories—the great stories of our race and place. We
are lured into playing roles in the compelling dramatic scripts that we have
the good fortune to read, see, hear, or imagine. People are neither reinforcement maximization machines; nor computer-like information proces-
sors; nor highly evolved biological organisms; nor the battlefield wherein
libidinal instincts struggle against societal repression; nor creatures composed of body and soul and made in the image and likeness of God; nor the
conduit whereby selfish genes make their way into the next generation's
gene pool; nor. . . .

According to Mair, *we are locations* where the stories of our place and
time become partially tellable. Thus, I must amend my earlier claim slightly.
B. F. Skinner was a reinforcement maximization machine—but George
Howard is not! That's probably why Skinner was wealthier and more famous
than I. And while a sociobiologist might see himself or herself as the pawn
of selfish genes—I surely don't see myself in that light! I'm thrilled to have

two sons—no more, no less. And, finally, my mother and my uncle Tom Mahon (you'll meet both of those people later in this story) were both convinced that the Baltimore Catechism's answer to the question "What is man?" was perfectly correct. Once upon a time, God—that great playwright/ director in the sky—chose to miraculously bring matter and spirit together. And John and Margaret Howard saw fit to name this child after his paternal grandfather, George. And, because my God is all-humorous, He chose to set the stage for this particular life story in Bayonne, New Jersey, at the threshold of the latter half of the twentieth century. And the rest, as they say, is psychohistory. (This chapter [like all Gaul] is divided into three parts. The first part is autobiography, it deals with my past—and the great stories that formed me as a person.)

THE PAST: A STORY OF GEORGE

My memories of Bayonne are almost all good. I even savor the few bad memories, as they make the entire package more realistic. "That which does not kill me, makes me stronger!" Nietzsche was right, although horribly overstated for my tastes. But it would be a mistake to tell tales of meaningful lessons and blindingly acute insights—for that isn't the way it was. It was all rather ordinary—really. My memories are of good pals, exciting games of stickball and basketball, caring and hardworking parents, days of school that took forever, wonderful summers that raced past like the blink of an eye, and of Sunday afternoons that were so depressing that I was regularly reduced to tears.

As my British friends would say, I grew up in a working-class family. Everyone in my family worked, and our announcements of someone between the stages of high school and retirement who did not work were always greeted with mild surprise. By the way, school didn't count as work—it was a natural thing people of a certain age just did. I mean, you don't take credit for breathing, do you? Work was what you did after you took care of the expected activities. Besides, an idle mind (or body, or anything) was the devil's workshop. So we worked hard, played hard, and generally tried to better ourselves. But to say that we were an achieving family would not be exactly correct.

My older sister Marion and my younger brother Billy always were much better in school than me. (In fact, I am dyslexic. But nobody in Bayonne even heard of the word *dyslexia* until 1990—and to this day, nobody there can spell it correctly.) But back then—in the 1950s—it was widely agreed (OK, universally accepted!) that, while I was a nice guy and a hard worker, I was a bit of a dunce. While it goes without saying that I was saddened by this analysis of my intellect, I had to admit that all the evidence suggested that it was correct. But I was very lucky—being a dunce had minimal impact on my spirits. After all, almost everyone in the neighborhood liked me; I had lots of good pals; I could run like the wind; jump like a kangaroo; throw a baseball like Sandy Koufax; and when we were choosing up sides for any game, I was always the first or second kid chosen. Hell, I was on a fast track to the National Basketball Association. You really didn't need to be a genius to be a star.

But I sure was a good boy—even in school. While I couldn't get too thrilled about getting terrible grades, I definitely wasn't going to get myself in trouble by making like I wasn't trying, or—worse yet—acting like a wise-acre. You see, I was born after the invention of the telephone. Those nuns wouldn't hesitate for an instant in calling up my mother and then I could kiss away play for the forseeable future (like a week).

If pressed to describe my grade school years, I would probably char-acterize them as being happy, safe (because I was in a very supportive environment), active, and simple. A word more needs to be said about why it was simple and uncomplicated. You see we are talking about the mid—and late—1950s—the Eisenhower years! Did anything of importance happen during the Eisenhower years? When people reminisce about a simpler, less complicated time, I know exactly what they are talking about. The weightiest issues with which I wrestled were momentous problems like having to do extra chores because I was late for supper; not knowing why everyone learned their multiplication tables faster than I; finding enough soda bottles to be able to replace the ball that had rolled down a sewer; and the like.

I lived in a ghetto—but really, it was more like a warm cocoon. We were all working class, Catholic, and of Western European ancestry (mostly second or third generation). In fact, my parents still live in the house where my mother was born. Families kind of grow together when they've been neigh-bors for 60 or 70 years. Besides, I had about a dozen close relatives (grand-parents, aunts, uncles, and cousins) who lived within 150 yards of our home. As I look back on it now, I was never alone—I never had to face anything alone. Come what may, there were always relatives and friends close at hand to walk (or talk) me through any difficulty. It was many years, and many tears, before I realized exactly how influential that constant, early support was for me. I did work as a psychotherapist for four years during and im-mediately after graduate school. The most difficult clients for me to listen to (let alone to be of some help to) were the ones who had encountered severely traumatic experiences during childhood. I become paralyzed with an overwhelming guilt (because unlike them I was blessed with a wonderful childhood) that rendered me somewhat (OK, totally!) ineffective as a helper for them. Thus, the career choice to be an academic psychologist was easy—and I never seriously looked back. To give you an idea how idyllic my childhood now appears to me (in retrospect), consider my lone "brush with the law" as a youth.

I was driving home from a bowling outing with friends late one Saturday afternoon. I clearly had the right of way, but she pulled out of her parking space and her left front fender ripped the entire right side of my car. The only voice I could hear was my father's. A few months earlier (when I was awarded my learner's permit) he had stated quite emphatically, "and if you ever get into an accident call the police immediately." As I phoned for police assistance, I was very shaken (from the accident) but enormously relieved that I knew "the right thing to do." The potential problems associated with my being a 17-year-old who had gotten into an accident with the wife of a prominent physician in town, and whose learning permit happened to be in the pocket of another pair of slacks, were still a million miles from my awareness.

I began to suspect that I was in trouble by the look in Officer Jones's eyes when I discovered that I didn't have my learner's permit with me. I knew I was in trouble when the physician's wife suggested she and the policeman have a private chat. And I was overcome with nausea when Officer Jones announced that I would sign a statement saying the accident was my fault— and my insurance company would pay to fix our cars—or he would throw me in jail. All I was able to choke out was the accident was not my fault, and that I wouldn't sign anything. Fortunately, the ride to the police station was sufficiently long to enable me to gather my senses and form a plan. As soon as I was led in tow to the desk sergeant, I shouted for everyone in the squad room to hear, "I wanna see my Uncle Bub! NOW!"

Officer Jones had no way of knowing it, but he had stumbled into the jaws of our family's only bona fide success story. By dint of hard work and fidelity to duty for over 30 years, Bub Mahon had risen from being an ordinary cop, pounding a beat, to the chief of police. The desk sergeant tried to pacify me by suggesting that "It wasn't necessary to disturb the chief with this small. . . . " "Get him now, or you're in trouble too," I cried. The sergeant, who knew an explosive situation when he saw one, wisely punted, "Chief, your nephew is here to see you." You see, Bub wasn't really my uncle (but yelling something such as "I wanna see my seventh cousin, twice removed!" would probably lack force). And, in fact, I never called him anything but Uncle Bub. (That's not completely true—if I caught him talking to someone "important"—like a mayor, or a Monsignor—I'd breeze by and nonchalantly chirp, "Hi ya Bubbles!" And, in fact, he never called me anything but "Nephew George" (unless, of course, I had just called him "Bubbles"). I was proud to think of him as my uncle—and so I adopted him.

But getting back to the story, no sooner did Bub appear, than Officer Jones and I began to blurt out parallel—but very different—versions of "the story." Eventually, I became so upset that I began to cry. I summarized with a sobbing, "Uncle Bub, you know I'd never tell you a lie." And in that moment of silence, one could almost hear the great court judge in the sky announce, "Advantage, young mister Howard." I silently thanked my lucky stars for all those times I had been compulsively honest with Bub. By the look in Bub's eyes—even if Officer Jones had been a cat (with nine lives)—

he still would have been dead as a doornail. "Murphy!" Bub snarled, "Get a squad car and take my nephew home. Jones! My office!"

About the fifteenth time I thanked Bub for "getting me out of trouble," and apologized for "causing him all that trouble," he said that it was probably for the best that it happened. People can be very cruel sometimes, and he was just happy that this time I was around friends when I needed help. As always, Bub was right—as I'd later find out. But more importantly, Officer Jones was young and would have to determine right from wrong as the representative of the law for many years to come. Bub was convinced that the experience was one Officer Jones would not soon forget—and that he would be a far better cop for it. I hope Bub was right.

If all this sounds like so much "truth, wisdom and beauty," or piles and piles of "happy horseshit," then I'm sorry. But that's the way I remember it. I had more than my share of fights as a child. I also broke more than my share of bones while playing sports. But life seemed so good, so fair, so understandable, and so predictable—in the good sense. If you take chances, you can sometimes come up with the short end of the stick. But, in general, life wasn't cruel, or threatening, or unfair, or uninteresting. I charged into adolescence and young adulthood with enthusiasm, confidence, and more than a little naïveté.

I've pretty much avoided what was an important part of my life at that time—my religion. Being a Catholic, for me, was a lot like being a male. I didn't know how I had become a Catholic. There was never any question about it—I would no more have thought, "Maybe I'll become a Protestant," than I would have imagined, "Maybe I'll become a female." And I certainly did nothing to earn the faith I had. (The catechism answer, "Faith is a gift from God," fit my experience perfectly.) But in Bayonne in the 1950s, being a Catholic was like being a human—everybody was one! I completely accepted the world-view of Catholicism and, thus, benefited from the warm, safe certainty that it offered. I knew right from wrong; I understood what was expected of me in life; and, through religion, I began to work out "my view of the world." I began to tell myself an increasingly more coherent story regarding why things were the way they were in my life, my community, and the world. As provincial, unrealistic, and idealistic as it was, it was at least a start, and that was important.

But with 20–20 hindsight, I can now see that the seeds of change were sown even than. It would just take a few years for those seeds to germinate. The religion I learned was liberally sprinkled with sin and damnation, stories of the fires of hell, and a deep suspicion of sinful human nature. I had more than my share of childhood nightmares of the devil and hell-fires. Finally, mysteries of faith were always my Achilles heel. Perhaps it was the first stirrings of the scientist in me, but even back then, mysteries were puzzles, challenges, and mind-teasers which were to be dissected, analyzed, and solved. "Just accept it on faith" was the standard advice I received. And even if it was good advice, I was constitutionally incapable of heeding it. I simply had to think everything through—even though the thinking was painfully slow and frequently faulty.

I need to talk a bit about my parents before we leave the topic of religion. My father is a Protestant, although even to this day, I don't know exactly to which denomination he belongs. He certainly never actively practiced. When he and my mother married, he was forced to sign an agreement that the children would be raised as Catholics. While there were times that he chafed under the terms of that agreement, to his credit he never seriously subverted it (to deliver an occasional joke or snide remark is only human—and, in fact, highly desirable if the jokes are funny). But I know that I learned at least two important lessons from his example in the religion domain: (1) a deal's a deal (you agree on something and you don't renege on it); and (2) you don't need to be religious to be a good person and lead a good life.

But I'm afraid that I've lapsed into pure autobiography, and I didn't want to do that. What I wanted to demonstrate is that all of us are formed by the great cultural stories that (as children) we are told are true. You know, stories such as Roman catholicism, the Protestant ethic, liberal democracy, the importance of family, the march of Western civilization, science, and the value of liberal education. Given that each of us must find some set of foundational mythologies with which we will make some sense out of our lives, I can't kick about the set that I was given—while I might have done a little better, I certainly could have done far worse. But, I need to make this last point, none of us can take credit (or blame) for our foundational myths, because these world-views are *given* to us as children. Like original sin, they are part of the human nature that we are given to work with. One might properly feel pride or shame in what one *does* with the hand they've been dealt, but not proud that one was born with (so to speak) an intellectual silver spoon in one's mouth.

THE PRESENT: I REMEMBER VINCE

Since I had never even attended a New Fellows talk at an APA Convention, I asked the chairwoman of the session, "What should I talk about?" She said, "Just tell us exactly what you will do for the rest of your career. Make a prophecy!" So here's what I said:

The title of this talk is *Quo Vadis?*—or Where are you going? Well, I'm not at all comfortable in the role of the prophet, and here's the reason why: If 20 years ago someone had asked me to predict in what career I would follow, the term *psychology* would definitely not even have been mentioned. If ten years ago I'd attempted to foresee my work of the next decade, the term *research* probably would have appeared only in the following context: "Since I've *finally* finished my dissertation *research*, I can get on to what I really want to do." And last, if a short five years ago I'd played the role of the futurist, the word *freedom* might have slipped into my account only in passing: something like, "Once I get tenure I'll finally have the *freedom* to conduct research on really important issues." *Psychology—Research—Freedom.*

So now I'm going to tell you that for the remaining years of my career I intend to—you guessed it—conduct *Research* on the *Psychology* of Personal *Freedom!*

Now let me be clear about what I'm asserting in seriousness: I do intend to conduct research on the psychology of free will (or self-determination, or personal causation, or volition, or agency) or whatever you want to call that human capacity. What I am not taking too seriously is my ability (or anyone else's) to accurately predict the future.

But if I don't believe in people's ability accurately to predict the future, how can I believe in their capacity to be self-determining, willful, or volitional? Let me approach an answer by analogy: I sometimes think of myself as if I were a fish! (I'd like to picture myself as a 25-inch rainbow trout—but an eight-inch sucker might be closer to the truth.) So here I am in this stream of life, and I think, "I could burrow into the mud today" or "Maybe I'll lie under that log for awhile" or "Perhaps I'll swim upstream and see what's happening." Well, one might say I'm self-determining—right? But we know that events, such as whether or not a worm gets washed downstream or a fly lands on the surface of the stream, are really important considerations in what a fish will eventually do. Whether or not those potential dinners are imbedded with hooks could be of more than minor import upon my life course. And we fish don't even like to think about the possibility of apocalyptic events such as droughts, acid rain, floods, hydroelectric plants, chemical spills, and the like. So you can see why it is problematic—even for a self-determining fish—to predict his or her life course.

While analogies are very important for science, it is crucial to know where analogies fail. For example, call me a speciesist, but I doubt that any fish in history ever thought the following: "I wonder by what methodology one could rationally partition the variance in a particular behavior attributable to self-determination from the variance caused by biological factors, psychic determination, environmental influences, social pressures, and the like?" However, I can guarantee that at least one human being (me!) has seriously considered that thorny problem. So humans are different from fish in some important ways. But fishy models of human behavior are not over-running psychology. (Pardon me, I meant to say: But *fish* models of human behavior are not over-running psychology.) We employ other kinds of models: hydraulic analogies, reinforcement maximization models, and, perhaps most commonly, computer analogies.

By the way, have you heard Gregory Bateson's (1979) comment upon the computer analogy of human behavior? Well, here it is,

A man [*sic*] wanted to know about mind, not in nature, but in his private large computer. He asked it (no doubt in his best Fortran), "Do you compute that you will ever think like a human being?" The machine then set to work to analyze its own computational habits. Finally, the machine printed its answer on a piece of paper, as such machines do. The man ran to get the answer and found, neatly typed, the words: THAT REMINDS ME OF A STORY.

Like all of you, I've been telling myself a story about my professional life—the most recent line of which you've already heard: "*I intend to conduct research on the psychology of personal freedom.*" Let me pull together these rambling thoughts by telling you a few things about *my story*.

Some readers will remember Vince Harren. Vince was the director of the counseling psychology program at Southern Illinois University when I was a graduate student there. Vince was a humanistic psychologist, a wonderful human being, and a good friend. I, on the other hand, was a semiserious graduate student who was hellbent on getting out of what I perceived to be silly course requirements. On one occasion I went to Vince's office and had the following conversation: "Vince, I can't stand another semester of psychological assessment. Would you please waive that requirement of a second semester?" To my utter amazement Vince winked at me and said, "Sure George, a course in assessment really isn't important *for the person who is going to make research in humanistic psychology respectable!*"

My mind was racing with thoughts such as "You've got to be out of your mind. . . . There isn't a snowball's chance in hell that I'd. . . . You're the humanistic psychologist, Vince, not me. . . . I don't think humanistic research can *ever* be made respectable."

But fortunately, whenever the potential for a serious, career-threatening event arises, a million years of genetically preprogrammed survival instincts automatically kick in; all semblance of free will evaporates completely; and I was mechanistically impelled to give the only answer a conniving, corner-cutting counselor could. I looked at Vince with a startled gaze and said "Vince—you sly dog—how did *you* know that's exactly what I want to do with my career???"

We now leap forward several years in my story. In spite of my deficiencies in the area of assessment, I landed a job at the University of Houston. There I was—a mere fingerling—swimming in a pool with some *really big suckers*. And they wanted me to summarize my first three years there and tell the story of the rest of my career. Well, what could I say? "In the first year I swam after two worms; one got published, the other one got me sick. Remember, in the second year, our stream got polluted, so nobody got any work done. And my third year was a complete wipe-out because I had that run-in with a red-eyed wiggler" (by the way, for those who may not know, that's a fishing lure).

No! I couldn't say that to a departmental review committee, so I told a story about "improving methodology by conducting research on research methods." I honestly don't remember if I noticed the slight similarity to the path Vince had urged. Shortly thereafter, Paul Secord taught me the *first principle of ethogeny,* which is, "For scientific purposes treat subjects as if they were human beings." And suddenly I was swimming with the current. By tenure review, my story spoke of person-centered methodologies—designs capable of appreciating those uniquely human characteristics such as volition, free will, meaningfulness, self-determination, and so forth.

So now I intend to research the psychology of personal freedom. Well, Vince is looking positively prophetic right now. I only wish he could be here to share the moment. (Vince died suddenly a few years ago.)

Many of you realize that I'm going after thorny issues that have plagued students of human nature for several millennia. Do I *really* think I am going to offer something important to that conversation? Frankly, no! For those of you inclined toward a friendly wager, I am currently offering 20 to 1 odds *against* my making a breakthrough. *But isn't that one bet I would love to lose!*

The chairwoman asked me where I'm going. And like Bateson I answered, "You know, that reminds me of a story. . . . About a dozen years ago, a good friend dangled a fat juicy worm in front of a frisky, young sucker and urged him to swim with it as far as he could. Vince asked me to be a part of a story—and a tradition. And, frankly, it's still the nicest story in which anyone has ever invited me to take part."

Well, that's the speech I gave, and that's my best guess as to where my professional story came from—and, more important, where it seems to be going. Giving talks at conventions are adventures that I generally do not enjoy, but my *Quo Vadis* talk was a delight! A number of people in the audience came up to me afterward to tell me their stories of Vince—"I was a grad student at Texas when Vince was director of the counseling center there. I don't believe that he actually let me gather data on . . . "; "You know, Vince waived those stupid summer practicum requirements for me the year before you arrived at SIU. Since I was married and had a family, I had to get a real job. But I felt I could never tell anyone about it because the other students would raise hell, and Vince would get into trouble. It wasn't until you mentioned his waiving the assessment course for you that I realized— I can't get Vince in trouble"; "Remember those poker games Vince used to hold? One night he was a big winner—and I was the last one out the door— and he just handed me his winnings. I don't know if he knew it, but I was broke. . . . " (Honesty demands that I question the veracity of that last report—Vince was *the worse* poker player I ever encountered. While his generosity goes without question, I simply can't imagine him winning!)

Now Vince was only human. So I would imagine that there were some people in the audience who could have told some true stories where Vince was the villain. But they didn't come forward to ensure that a "fair" or "balanced" or "objective" or "completely accurate" story of Vince emerged. And I'm glad that they didn't! At a funeral, you don't tell the family of the deceased what a jerk the person was. Getting an accurate picture of the life of the deceased is *not* the point of a funeral. Funerals are for the living to help them in their grief process and to urge them to remember the best in the deceased. After my talk, we were just trying to remember the best in what Vince gave to us in the hope that in the process, we might become better persons ourselves.

THE FUTURE: THE STORIES WE LIVE BY

If any part of this chapter could be labeled "conventional," it would have been the first part where I made some autobiographical reflections upon my childhood experiences in Bayonne. Biographies, autobiographies, clinical case histories, life stories, psychobiographies, and other related genres are standard fare in the humanities and also in psychology. In all such cases, one "looks back" over a life with an eye toward uncovering earlier roots that explain why the person has become the sort of person that he or she currently is.

The middle part of this presentation was a bit different in that it looked forward toward possible futures (for me and for psychology) as much as it looked backward (in my life, through the history of psychology) to understand how we arrived at the present moment (for me and for psychology). Figure 1 helps the reader to visualize this process as a large, diverse past being funneled into my present with diverse possible futures being open to me for the remainder of my life, and also for the enterprises of psychology and science. Of course, each person might imagine a similar figure for himself or herself. What might be common to readers is that we share the story of psychology. However, our life experiences to this point might have been quite dissimilar. Finally, while I see the story of science as key to the twists and turns my life has taken, others here might see quite different stories as foundational in their own life story. For example, there might be some cultural tale, a religious narrative, a family saga, or a political movement that you accord salience in your life, similar to the way the history of science plays a central role in the evolution of my life story. What I'm suggesting is that each of us could profit from a close examination of our own life stories dealing simultaneously with our pasts, presents, and possible futures.

So now I'll launch into my life's future by telling you a teleography. Teleographies are just like autobiographies but they face our futures, rather than our past (Howard, 1992). In this teleography, I will try to paint for you a picture of the invented reality of my life. For if our lives can be thought of as each of us painting our own life, then this teleography is a picture of me—painting myself. But I'm afraid that I wrote this paper at the end of a long, hard school year. Thus, I hope you will be patient with what I am struggling to say. My teleography is entitled:

Figure 1
The funneling of diverse past influences into a present that serves as a
springboard into one of many possible futures.

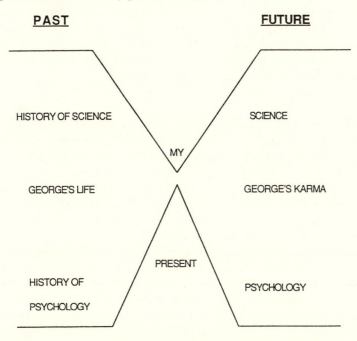

Two Steps Forward, One Step Backward: The Psychology of Patience

I believe that the practice of the virtue of patience will pay dividends—
patience well placed will work to the benefit of any person. Thus, I come
to praise patience—not to bury her. My optimistic title (*Two steps forward,
one step backward*) also reveals something about me. I still believe in the
idea of progress; I've never yet seen a half-empty glass; and I believe all's
well that ends! A virtue that I possess in abundance is optimism. Patience,
on the other hand, is but a dream for me.

Did you know that patience is a member of the gang of traditional virtues?
Its gang brothers and sisters being justice, temperance, wisdom, charity,
agreeableness, constancy, fidelity, fortitude, tactfulness, hope, mirth, and
many others. With that many siblings, patience would never want for back-
ups if she found herself sucked into a brawl. By the way, that list of virtues
was gleaned from a bevy of writers as diverse as Homer, Aristotle, the New
Testament, Jane Austin, Benjamin Franklin, and Alisdair MacIntyre. I left
off virtues such as faith, piety, and fear of the Lord so as *not* to overemphasize
one important cultural strain in my background, and similarly, I omitted
thrift, industry, acquisitiveness and cleanliness in order to downplay yet
another important developmental influence upon me. But, alas, somewhere

along the line I missed out on patience. For all the good work done on my behalf by John and Sis Howard, by Our Lady Star of the Sea Roman Catholic Church, by the Boy Scouts of America, by the Bayonne, New Jersey, Police Athletic League, by the Marist Brothers of the Schools, by the sons and daughters of Hibernia, by the counseling psychology program at Southern Illinois University, and by the usual Saturday night crowd at the Dewdrop Inn—in spite of their herculean efforts in the formation of my character—I never got patience. "So what?" you might ask.

So what, indeed. You see I am telling myself an important story about what's going on in my life—a story about what *the meaning* of my life is. And the virtue of patience is a crucial, but missing, part of that story.

Suppose I asked you, "What's your best guess as to how you will die?" Tell me what is the most likely candidate to be your killer—please *force* yourself to give a specific answer. Although no one knows for sure, I think I'll die of a heart attack or a stroke. As you may have already noted, I have more than my share of Type A characteristics—and a lack of patience is one of those characteristics.

When I try to think objectively about my life, I think of the important people in my life. First, I think of my sons. I know that they're doing fine, so I can't be screwing up too badly as a parent. But with a little more patience on my part, my sons would be a little bit better off. I'm a good-enough husband, but I push myself to be a little better nonetheless. My wife Nancy and I have an equal marriage, but it is an exhausting task to see to it that I always do my fair share in *every* domain. My track record as a researcher and writer is nothing to be embarrassed about. But I press myself daily to do more writing and better research. I'm surely an adequate teacher and advisor, but I press myself not to rest on my laurels. Finally, I am a good friend. I urge friends to call on me whenever I can be of assistance, and they feel comfortable enough to do so—often. Talk about multiple-role strain, you don't have to be a woman to experience that—as any *true* Type A knows all too well.

So, now I ask you, what kind of a life story am I creating here? What tale will be told of George Howard once he's dead and buried? Well, that depends, in part, on whether I die of a massive heart attack five minutes after I finish this chapter (even God wouldn't dare take an academic in the middle of a paper) or if I have a busy, productive life and slip away peacefully at the ripe old age of 100. Scholars in the humanities have been telling us for years that *endings* are by far the most important parts of stories. And this perspective is very different from what has been believed to be true by mainstream psychology. People such as Freud told us that the *past* was the most important part of our lives; people such as Skinner focus upon the ways in which the *present* controls us. But thanks to the constructivist revolution, we now realize that our lives can be understood as if we were being drawn forward by the *future*—the future as each of us now imagines it. This shift in temporal emphasis does not demand that we denigrate the importance of the past and the present in the formation of human action. Rather, it simply offers the possibility of influencing human actions by altering a person's imagined futures. We can now rewrite life stories by focusing the storytellers on different imagined possible futures.

So what does the future hold for me? If I am called to my final reward immediately after this chapter is completed, then the recounting of my life story might go something like this: "At age 43, he left Nancy and the young boys to fend for themselves. In spite of his degrees in psychology, his articles and books, he showed about the same amount of insight into self-destructive life styles as did Janis Joplin. What a waste!"

But if in the year 2006, I watch my youngest son graduate from Notre Dame, and if 12 years later I retire after a 40-year career of productive scholarship, then my epitaph will read quite differently. It might say something like this: "He retired with a TIAA-CREF total accumulation value of $1,742,388—which at that time, coincidentally, was the exact price of a Chevy Nova."

So, now you can see that the meaning of my vice of impatience looks quite different depending upon how my life story ends. But no one knows how their life is going to end! So, our lives represent acts of faith made in the hope that something like our desired, imagined futures might actually occur.

But I'm digressing a bit, and I did promise you some stories of the future, so let me get on to some future-creating stories. My first story is really just an anecdote: It comes from people in our admissions office who ask students, who've been accepted at Notre Dame, why they chose to either accept or reject Notre Dame's offer. One student, who decided to accept, wrote the following: "Because I'm a Catholic, I thought it would be more meaningful to attend a religiously-*afflicted* school!" Out of the mouths of babes and freshmen!

But what I found most interesting about that story was that this future freshman claimed it would be *more meaningful* to further afflict his life with religion. It caught my attention because I'd just completed a series of experiments that demonstrated beyond reasonable scientific doubt that human beings can self-determine a portion of their actions in various domains with all other possible nonagentic explanations methodologically controlled (Howard, 1993; Howard & Conway, 1986). That is, we now can assess the proportion of variance in human action attributable to freedom of the will. Did you notice how I melded two different language systems in that sentence: "proportion of variance" attributable to "freedom of the will"? I'll be doing lots more of that shortly. But intellectual honesty demands that I level with you first. You see, I believe that experiments themselves are nothing but *another form of stories*. I'll be telling you more stories from the "scientific culture" in a minute. In addition, I'll continue telling you stories from my "common sense culture." And I will argue that both types of stories are cut from the same cloth. But, again, honesty demands that I note that I have borrowed this insight from Ken Gergen.

In a letter to me, Ken wrote the following, "It is my view at this point that the separation between fact and fiction is only one of style, and that the scientific style is the inferior in many ways because of the enormous number of limitations by which it is encumbered. (How many experiments do you know, *about which anybody cares*?)" Notice how Ken also blurred genres? Is "caring" one of the criteria of good experimentation? But talk of blurred genres reminds me of a story.

Two years ago, I was asked to participate in a debate on the following question, "Can a university be great in both academics and athletics?" The debate took place a few days before Notre Dame's football game with Miami, so the crowd of alumni, subway alumni, and students was enormous. I was debating the "pro" position. A triple domer from the class '53 named O'Malley was debating the "con" position. O'Malley was wearing one of those blue ties with gold Notre Dame shamrocks all over it; garish green slacks; the loudest gold sport coat you've ever seen, and a hat shaped like the Golden Dome. I figured I could beat him on style points alone—until I looked out at the audience and noticed they were all dressed exactly like O'Malley.

O'Malley spoke first, and gave a ten-minute, rambling diatribe peppered with statements such as "The Rock never wouldda stood for this," and "The Gipper wouldda done that," and on, and on, and on. If it weren't for the frequent blasts of spontaneous applause, I would have thought I'd been transported backward in time to a Ronald Reagan press conference.

Then I got my ten-minute chance to debate the "pro" position. Here's what I said, "Can a university be great in both academics and athletics? Why of course it can. Not only is it possible, it's already been done—several times. I cite as evidence for my claim, Stanford University and Duke University." What an argument—clear, crisp, and to the point. I began to unfasten the microphone as I waited for the avalanche of applause—but all I got was stunned silence—so I figured I better hold on to the mike. O'Malley was the first to comment. He leaned forward and asked, "Excuse me professor, let me be certain I understand what you're suggesting. You want us to become more like a school whose football team hasn't *even* won the ACC championship in over 20 years?" Before I could even say "I guess so," the senior who was dressed as a leprechaun yelled from the third row, "We can already beat Stanford in basketball—this joker wants us to get *worse* in hoops!" The leprechaun then threw his shillelagh at me. Things were turning ugly, so I looked around for campus security. But the only cop I could see was angrily shaking his billy club at me. Somebody yelled, "Hey look! The professor's got a sunburn. He's probably a Miami spy!" As the angry crowd pressed forward, I remembered an important saying, "When the going gets tough . . . don't give up the mike." I knew my only hope was to seize the moral high-ground, so I started singing:

♬ "Cheer, cheer for old Notre Dame; wake up the echoes cheering her name." ♪

Every member of the subway alumni in the audience reflexively began singing.

♪ "Send a volley cheer on high, shake down the thunder from the sky." ♬

The sophomores instinctively linked arms and swayed to the rhythm of the "Fight Song." There wasn't a dry eye in the crowd.

♪ "What though the odds be great or small. Old Notre Dame will win over all." ♬

"STOP!" I yelled into the mike. The crowd stared at me in astonishment, and I returned it with my harshest, most God-like, professional glare.

"For shame," I scoffed, "Some of you people don't even know the words to the Notre Dame Fight Song."

You could have heard a pin drop. I had them in the palm of my hand.

"Old Notre Dame will win over all."

"Some of you think over all is two words. If that were true we'd have to go undefeated every year in order for us to feel successful. That kind of absolutism and perfectionism will inevitably lead to failure. *Moderation in all things* is the virtue we should strive to develop. Fanaticism, even in the service of a good cause, is to be deplored by reasonable people." I was winding up for my grand finale when the debate moderator yelled, "Time! Mr. O'Malley, you now have the opportunity to rebut that nonsense."

I never got the chance to say that while most of us generally agree that Catholicism represents a reasonable religious story to be telling ourselves, that even religious fanaticism can lead to problems. After all, we *are* the religion that gave the world the Crusades, the Thirty Years War, and the Inquisition—and we really shouldn't be proud of that part of our history— should we?

O'Malley swaggered to the podium, adjusted his clip-on shamrock tie and began, "Let me be certain I've got your argument straight, professor. If over all is one word in the Fight Song then we should be happy if we only win more games then we lose? You mean we should be satisfied with a 6 and 5 season? Is that right?"

Before I could even mumble, "Well, I guess so," O'Malley turned to the horror-struck audience and shouted, "If 6 and 5 was good enough, we'd still be led into battle against Miami by Gerry Faust!" Chaos! Pandemonium broke out! O'Malley was declared the debate winner by acclamation, and everyone adjourned to The Huddle for a round of drinks and a discussion of the finer points of moderation. *End of story*!

I imagine you're wondering where these stories are leading, so I need to start tying down some loose ends. First, I guess I should come clean about these stories I've been telling to you. The experimental stories are all true. By that I mean that I conducted and faithfully reported the experiments I mentioned. All of the other nonexperimental stories I've told are also true—except for that story about a debate with O'Malley. I mean, I did participate in a debate prior to the Miami game about whether a university can be great both academically and in sports, and we did debate the prevalent belief that single-minded fanaticism is required in order to achieve excellence in any field—that much is true! The debate revealed intense differences of opinion regarding the place of sports in an academic institution that is striving to be a great center of learning. Any institution of higher education would be honored to have sponsored the debate that actually occurred. But there was no O'Malley—or a near riot—that part was all caricature and burlesque.

While there are O'Malley types in the Notre Dame community, they have little power or role in steering the course of the university. But members of the faculty and administration frequently joke about them. Why do we joke about them? To scare ourselves into taking them very seriously. You see, that's the problem with fanatics: They are so single-minded that they can come to exert an inordinate and inappropriate amount of influence on the course of an institution. Because of their myopia; because of their single-minded fanaticism; because they are *so* convinced that they know what's best for Notre Dame, the O'Malleys of the world are *extremely dangerous*. Left to have its own way, *fanaticism can ruin your life*—I mean, your university.

And now the clinicians reading this chapter all move forward in their seats and think, "We're not talking about O'Malley, the fanatic, are we, George? We're talking about George, the fanatic! Aren't we?"

"Well, yes, I guess we are," is my honest answer. There is a part of me that really would like to be the world's greatest father, the world's greatest teacher, and so forth. I know I'm good enough in both domains, but there is a part of me that would really like to go undefeated and be the national champion husband and psychologist. But I'm frightened that I would have to become a fanatic about any of these four dreams in order to make it come true. Suppose (following O'Malley's lead) I told myself the story that I *had* to be the very best psychologist in the world—I would quickly become a workaholic. Then what kind of a husband and father would I be?

You see it is potentially very dangerous to be telling oneself a story about the meaning of one's life. In time, it can become true that not only do we live out this life story, in time our lives can become dominated by the story. Shakespeare said, "Beware of what you desire, for you will surely have it." A gloss on that would be: Beware of the stories we choose to tell ourselves, for we will surely be lived by them.

I should also say something about the role of humor in my life and stories.

Miller Mair set up my explanation by noting that our lives are told (in part) by the great stories of our race and culture. As I said earlier, I grew up in a ghetto of a peculiar sort. It was really a warm, Irish-Catholic cocoon. All of my grandparents and relatives (who were also our neighbors) grew up in Ireland and immigrated to Bayonne as young adults. Any group that referred to Bayonne, New Jersey, as "The Promised Land," and "The Land of Milk and Honey" or "God's Country" either experienced ghastly childhoods, or they had extraordinary senses of humor. I can assure you that it was the latter. In our crowd, one of the ways you prepared yourself to face any terror—whether unemployment, or surgery, or failure in school, or even death—was by cultivating friendships. The most important tools in building friendships are *virtues* like honesty, warmth, fidelity, and compassion. Our crowd also emphasized the importance of songs, story-telling, a shared drink, and a shared joke in friendship-creating. While I haven't yet offered to buy you a drink, please don't give up hope, for the chapter is not yet ended. As you probably already know, humor is under attack these days, and I think that's *sad*. We interviewed a young woman for a job a few years ago, and she began her colloquium with the following joke:

"Did you hear about the tremendous breakthrough by a dyslexic theologian? He proved there was no dog!"

She did not get a job offer from us, in part, because of that joke. People argued vociferously that it showed her insensitivity toward the handicapped. It mattered not a whit that Janice Normoyle and I—the only two dyslexics in our department—thought it was a great joke and not at all offensive. The chair of psychology at Vanderbilt, Howard Sandler, is a good friend of mine, who constantly jokes with friends. But Howard advises me to not joke in professional papers. Howard chooses *not* to joke in professional settings because he says jokes are always at someone's expense. I've told a number of jokes here, and if anyone has been offended by them, I am truly sorry. I consider all readers to be friends, and I have no desire to hurt any of you in any way. As I said earlier, I joke about precisely those people and things that I care *most* about: my family, my friends, my profession, my heritage, my academic institution, my religion, and myself. Jimmy Buffett had it about right when he claimed: "With all of our running, and all of our cunning; If we didn't keep laughing, we'd all go insane."

Let's think of joking from a virtue perspective, as was discussed in the beginning of this teleography. Howard Sandler's advice—to not joke in formal settings—honors the ethical principle *to do no harm*. But there is another equally important ethical obligation, namely, *to do good*. My task in this chapter is to *do some good* for you. And when I think back on the most significant learnings in my life, humor has often been an important part of those insights. For example, one day in 1964, five of my 16-year-old male buddies and I were hanging around our kitchen one summer day. My mother was trying, unsuccessfully, to get some work done, and my great-uncle, Tom

Mahon—our designated family philosopher—was just trying to be where the action was. You see, that was the job description for pensioners in Bayonne. Like most 16-year-old boys, we were "in heat," and all we talked about was girls, girls, girls. Finally, my mother could take it no longer, and she blew up at us. She was not pleased with the attitudes toward women that were exhibited in our conversation. In the stunned silence, my Uncle Tom cleared his throat. Everyone knew that meant, "Shut-up! Uncle Tom's got some philosophizing to do." He slowly puffed on his pipe, and said, "Do you know what's the most overrated act in the whole world? The Sex Act." And then he cleared his throat again, and we all knew what not to do. Finally, he continued, "And do you know what's the most underrated act in the whole world? It's a good shit."

Now if Tom had simply said, "Sex is overrated, boys," who would have ever remembered it? Adults are always talking at teens like that. But because Tom wrapped it in a joke—none of us could ever forget it. Although honesty demands that I report that Tom went to his grave, swearing on a stack of Bibles, that *he wasn't joking.* I could go on and on with stories from my past of significant learnings where humor was an important element, but since space is limited, I must go on. For, as an old Chinese proverb says so well, "One who spends too much time living in the past has no future."

Life stories aren't authored at one point in time, at a desk, by an independent author, as is fiction. At most, each of us is only a co-author of our own life story. Miller Mair sees race and culture as significant co-authors; my earlier points about the importance of religion, academic psychology, and Notre Dame in my life story hint that these institutions deserve co-authorship in my life story. And who can doubt that our parents, grandparents, and other forebears from generations back live on in us and our life stories. I am one acorn who would have considered it an absolute tragedy, if I had fallen far from my family tree. That's why I spend so much time reliving and re-appreciating my roots. You see, what I've been doing up to now is constructing and reconstructing my life for you. Philosophically, I am a constructivist as well as an objectivist. Briefly, objectivism believes in a free-standing reality, the truth about which can eventually be discovered. The constructivist assumes that all mental images are creations of people, and thus speak of an invented reality. Objectivists focus on the *accuracy* of their theories, whereas constructivists think of the *utility* of their models. Watzlawick (1984) claimed that the shift from objectivism to constructivism involves a growing awareness that any so-called reality is—in the most immediate and concrete sense—the construction of those who believe they have discovered and investigated it. Objectivists are *inventors* who think they are discoverers—they do not recognize their own inventions when they come across them. Good constructivists, on the other hand, acknowledge the active role they play in creating a view of the world and interpreting observations in terms of it (Efran, Lukens, & Lukens, 1988). I'd love to go

on talking about constructivist metatheory and related epistemological issues, but I can imagine my readers' eyes glassing over, so I'll have to leave
the topic with just these spartan comments.

But before we leave constructivism, imagine with me a Pantheon of Patron
Saints of Constructivism. Who would get on our all-star team of constructivist
super-heros? Giambattista Vico and Immanuel Kant would be pioneer constructivist super-heros. Jean Piaget and George Kelly are more recent stars
who we psychologists know more closely. To this august list, I would like
to volunteer a dark-horse candidate, another psychologist, the late, great
Don Bannister. I never met him—he died far too soon. But he lives on in
me, through his writing. I only have time to mention one of his many, many
great quotes. Don was worrying about the problematic relationship between
experimenters and their human subjects in psychological research, when he
made the following point:

> I am reminded of a recurrent theme in certain types of science fiction stories.
> The master chemist has finally produced a bubbling green slime in his test
> tubes, the potential of which is great *but the properties of which are mysterious.*
> He sits alone in his laboratory, test tube in hand, brooding about what to do
> with the bubbling green slime. Then it slowly dawns on him that the bubbling
> green slime is sitting alone in the test tube brooding about what to do with
> him. This *special nightmare* of the chemist is the permanent work-a-day world
> of the psychologist—the bubbling green slime is always wondering what to do
> about you. (Bannister, 1966, p. 22)

When I thought of writing a teleography for this volume, I despaired.
What could I possibly say to you folks that hadn't already been said—and
said far better than I am able? And then the voice of my friend Don Bannister
spoke to me, and he said, "Wake up, stupid! You're not just a chemist—
you're also a slime!" You see, Don was a lifelong patron saint of the oppressed,
the downtrodden, and the little guy. He asked me, "Who'll be the voice for
the slimes?" And as I began to write this chapter, it came out as a semiproper
slime-to-chemist paper. At every turn in the writing, whenever I lapsed into
scholarese, Don whispered: " 'Cop-out'; 'whitewash'; 'academic bullshit.'
Don't talk slime-to-chemist to them; talk to them slime-to-slime! They can
take it!"

"I know they can take it," I shouted back at Don. "I don't know if I can
take it. There are going to be some pretty impressive people reading this
book. I might look like nothing more than a sentimental, slobbering wimp.
I'm frightened, Don."

Don's voice grew soft and caring.

"George, what you're experiencing is the special nightmare of the academic psychologist, but that's the work-a-day world of every clinician. Day
in, day out, clinicians are up to their asses in the primordial ooze of the
human condition, as they struggle to help their client-slimes. They're con-

stantly forced to wrestle with fear, sickness, depression, anger, confusion, pain, death, and despair. Georgie-boy you got lucky. You're not just speaking to academics—you're also talking with a bunch of clinicians! Don't reason with their academic-slime heads; whisper to their clinician-slime hearts."

I figured Don might be right, so like a good little academician I just kept writing. "Don," I said, "while I've still got you on the line, can you tell me why I can't just let myself end this chapter?"

"Endings are always tough," Don replied.

"Don," I whispered, "tell me about death."

"Sorry, I can't," Don replied. "I'm a psychologist—a life expert. I'm not allowed to practice outside of my area of competence. Death belongs to the philosophers and theologians, not psychologists. But, you won't believe how lucky you got, kiddo. Guess who is the Dean of Theology and Philosophy up here? It's your great-uncle, Tom Mahon! George, Tom hasn't changed a bit. He's still joking, cursing, and smoking that smelly old pipe. He's your friend, George, he'll tell you all you need to know about death. Just call on him."

"Thanks, Don," I said. Then I whispered, "Tom? Uncle Tom, can you hear me?"

"Ara Georgeen (which is Gaelic for little George)," Tom replied, "why would you be callin' on me now, after havin' missed my last 24 birthdays?"

"The birthday cards are in the mail, Tom," I replied.

"Ah, you still have a sharp tongue, Georgie-boy. Where'd you learn that?"

"At your knee, Tom," I replied.

"So you did. So you did. What can I do for you?"

"Tom, you gotta tell me about death. It's driving me nuts."

"'Tis a damn short drive," he teased. But when I didn't laugh, he knew I was serious, but he still wouldn't budge. I decided to try flattery.

"Tom," I said, "I hear you're the Dean of Philosophy and Theology up there. That's quite a feather in your cap—and you, who never set foot in high school."

"Oh, things are much different up here, laddie," Tom replied. "Degrees don't mean a thing. Advancement is based solely upon *competence* and *hard work*."

I was impressed! "Tom, now that you're the head man, I'll bet you're giving a real hard time to dogmatists, liturgists, logicists, and all analytic philosophers."

"Oh, none of *them* ever make it to heaven," he joked.

"Tom, I can't believe you'd leave them alone. You would never get off their case here on earth."

"Sure, inasmuch as I'd like to, I give them no trouble at all," he replied. After a long, uncomfortable pause, Tom noted feebly, "Georgeen, did Don Bannister tell you that up here, a deanship is an elected position?"

"*You* won an election? *You?* A lousy politician? Tom, are you *sure* you weren't condemned to hell?"

"Be not too hard, Georgie-boy," Tom replied, "heaven's a lot like earth in that we all do what we must do in order to get by."

Now *that* was the Tom I knew and loved.

"Tom?" I asked, "Are you going to be able to help me on this death thing?"

"Well, *yes* and *no,*" he replied, "*No* because death and heaven are different for everyone. But *yes* because there are some things you can do to get ready for death."

"What can I do to get ready, Tom?"

"Well, you can lead a good life," he shot back.

"How do I do that, Tom?"

Tom thought for a moment, and then slowly replied, "You know that Bannister fellow is smart as a whip—for an Englishman—and he's always talking about those 'special nightmares' of his. Georgie, you might learn something about life and death by running yourself through a 'special nightmare' about death."

"Tom, if you think it might help, then I'll try it," I replied. "So, how do I do it, Tom?"

"Close your eyes, George. Imagine that you just died. Now open your eyes to being dead, and tell me what you see."

I opened my eyes and said, "Nothing! I see nothing when I'm dead. I no longer exist, so I can't even feel the biting cold, or see the black nothingness."

"And how does that make you feel?" Tom asked, sounding for all the world like a psychologist.

"Awful!" I replied. "Absolutely terrible. I'm depressed and terrified at the thought of death being the end of everything for me. If that's the way it is, I see no good in life, and no point in going on."

"Right!" Tom shouted. "And right now, that depressive outcome seems to you like the most probable scenario after your death. But you now sound like a depressed, suicidal adolescent who can only see his or her life getting worse—becoming a tragedy. Life looks black—you have no hope. Now aren't you just-after-tellin' us that the future looks terrible until one begins to imagine a better, more hopeful possible future? That's not the right end for you, Georgie. Despair doesn't fit with the rest of your life. *Don't settle for less from God and death* than you've expected from yourself in life. Come on, kiddo, give us an ending fitting of your life—a proper ending for your life story. Georgeen, let me take the role of a therapist for a moment, and help you to imagine a different ending to your death. When therapists rewrite clients' life stories, they don't completely change good stories, they make small but important alterations—changes that make all the difference in a life. Go ahead, Georgeen, I'll do the speaking for God."

"Okay, Tom," I replied. "I'm game!"

"Close your eyes," Tom whispered. "You die. Then you open your eyes, and you are staring face to face with God. Talk to Him, Georgeen. Work it out with Him. I'll answer for God. There He is George—talk to Him—He doesn't bite. What would you say?"

"Well, God, what do you know, you *do* exist!"

"Yep," God replied. "Does that make you feel uncomfortable?"

"It does," I stammered, "because you could be pissed that for a long time I couldn't imagine you—I didn't believe in you."

"If I'd wanted you to believe in me down there, I'd have given you more faith. I'd have made myself more real to you. I'm not in danger of being forgotten down there—why a recent Harris poll shows that 94 percent of all Americans believe in God. But I had different plans for you."

"You did?" I asked excitedly. "How'd I do? Did your plan for me work out? Did I live a good life?"

"Slow down," God said. "That's not the way things work up here. You tell your life story, and we decide from that story whether or not you honored the two commandments."

"Two commandments?" I queried.

"Yep!" God replied. "Do good! And do no evil! Now, George, where do you want to tell your life story?"

"You wouldn't happen to have a pub up here, where they sing songs, tell jokes, and spin tall tales—would you?"

"I know just the place," God replied. "Come walk with me. It's just two clouds over." God looked at me sadly, and said, "I always have such mixed emotions about Irish pubs. They're both a source of great joy and camaraderie, and the soil of the great Irish tragedy—the weakness—alcoholism."

"Yes—the weakness," I replied. "I remember my grandmother consoling a young widow at an alcoholic's funeral. His drinking buddies were standing around saying things like 'Poor Martin, he had the weakness,' 'Sure the poor devil had the weakness.' My grandmother thought they were trying to exonerate the deceased and themselves of their role in producing this tragedy. She gave them a withering glare and snarled, 'Tis a damn strong weakness ye all have.' "

God nodded his assent and asked, "George, who should we assemble to speak on your behalf at your final judgment?"

"I get to bring along friends?" I asked excitedly. "Okay! Let me see: my parents; my brother and sister, my wife Nancy; and our boys. They'll say that I *did good*. And my Uncle Tom Mahon—I want him there also."

"George, Tom Mahon would try even an all-patient God," the Almighty replied. "Are you sure you want him? Besides, he keeps grousing about how many of his birthdays you've missed."

"It's okay, God," I replied. "You see, I wrote him this great part in a chapter I'm writing—it's the best role he's ever played. Don't worry, he'll forget the birthday cards. Besides, Lord, I'm assuming that we don't have to be perfect in this examination—we don't need to get a letter grade of 'A.' This is gonna be 'Pass-Fail' isn't it? I mean, my family is gonna bring up this patience problem of mine, so a grade of 'A' is absolutely out of the question."

"Sure! Sure, George! Relax! You don't have to be perfect. To err is human—to constantly err becomes a problem. That reminds me of a story, George, the guy who got the lowest passing grade ever on the final judgement is named Billy Bob Widebody. Do you know what we call him up here?"

"Saint Billy Bob," I replied, to God's dismay. And it made me feel better to know that even God—who is perfect—can't make every joke work.

"God," I asked cautiously, "are there many people in heaven?"

"Relax, George," God replied. "The greatest wisdom of all decreed that human lives would be graded 'Pass-Fail'—one doesn't have to be perfect. Just try your best to 'do good' and 'do no evil,' and that will be good enough. Heaven is mobbed! All my friends are here—and all their friends also. But, of course, there's always room for a few more."

"God, can you round up a bunch of my former students and faculty colleagues and my childhood friends and relatives to be there?"

"I know just the ones," God replied.

"I'd like Knute Rockne at my final judgment also," I volunteered.

That one surprised God a bit.

"The Rock? You never even met the Rock."

"It's this Notre Dame connection. Rockne loved Notre Dame, and I think I've represented Notre Dame well, so I thought. . . . "

"Okay," God replied. "But I think you're reaching a bit."

"Well, how about Saint Patrick?" I queried.

Now the all-just God was clearly angry, "George, for someone who has never even set foot on 'The Old Sod,' you've soaked this Irish thing for all it's worth."

"I guess so, Lord," I mumbled. "But now I'm worrying about the 'do no evil' commandment, and I'm thinking about this fictitious character named O'Malley, and I guess I really made him look like a jerk, and if he shows up. . . . "

"Two points you need to know," God explained. "First, we have a hard enough time dealing with the facts of things that actually occurred. What you imagined in your life is of no concern to us. That's called the 'Twain principle.' You see, Mark Twain's final judgment had to be held in a stadium—over 100,000 people attended. And Twain went on and on—'Oh, the tragedies I've seen in my life—Oh, the tragedies.' He had the entire house in the palm of his hand. At times you could scarcely hear what he said, for all the weeping and wailing. And then, at the end, he says, 'Fortunately, most of these tragedies never occurred!' So now we have the 'Twain Principle': Whatever goes on in your imagination is your own business! It's a good principle because people need some free space to plan out, test out and weight the value of different possible life stories. We only hold folks responsible for the story they actually chose to live."

"My second point," God continued, "is that *you* get to invite those who will speak on your behalf—those who will speak against you choose to attend of their own free will. When you die you have no means to influence what will be said by those who choose to testify against you. So you might want to do what you can about those matters, while you still have the chance. Oh, by the way, George, did I tell you that because of the number of people who'll be at your final judgement, we've had to reschedule it for the stadium?"

I clutched my chest and staggered backward in horror.

God, seeing my reaction, became extremely upset and blurted out, "Joke! Joke, George! It was meant to be a joke. Gee, I'm sorry! It was just a joke—I guess it was in bad taste. I didn't mean any harm by it. Everybody makes mistakes."

"Don't you know that jokes are always at someone's expense?" I fired back. "There's a time and a place for everything, and a joke like that is. . . ."

"You're right, George!" God countered, "it was stupid of me—but not malicious. Everyone is entitled to their moments of stupidity—it goes along with being human. All I can do is say I'm truly sorry and assure you it was done without malice. If I could turn back the hands of time, and undo that stupid joke, I'd do so immediately. But what's past is past—even for God—we can only strive to do better in the future."

We arrived at the pub and could hear the singing, joking, and story-telling going on within. But I was still frightened.

"Jude!" I blurted out. "I want St. Jude in there for me. Things might turn ugly, and St. Jude has lots of experience with hopeless cases."

"George," God replied, "you had no special devotion to St. Jude in life. You have to *earn* the testimony of people who'll speak on your behalf. Besides, you won't need Jude. Come on, George. Where's that old optimism? This is no time to turn cowardly on us. Do you think I've been stringing you along your whole life just to pull the rug out from under you at the last moment? What kind of a God do you think I am? Now, you shouldn't keep your guests waiting. Let's go in."

"Would you mind if you went in first, Lord, and I took a moment to collect my thoughts?" I asked. God smiled, squeezed my arm reassuringly, and went in. I felt alone and friendless as I summoned the courage to tell my life's story. Then I heard someone singing an Elton John song in an Irish brogue, as he hurried through the clouds. It was a familiar song to me. The one that calls us to make friends of everyone and that if our friends are there, then everything will be all right.

It was my Uncle Tom Mahon.

"Tom! You sing Irish rebel tunes—Clancy Brothers songs. You couldn't stand rock and roll. What are you doing singing Elton John?"

"Oh, that's the wonderful thing about heaven, Georgie-boy," Tom bellowed. "You're finally able to see beyond the petty biases of time and culture. Turns out, I love rock and roll."

Heaven was sounding more remarkable by the minute, and so I tried to press credulity. "Tom, tell me, do you now also like 'The Talking Heads' and 'The Sex Pistols'?"

Tom slowly removed the pipe from his mouth, cleared his throat, and whispered, "Georgeen, a lack of bias does *not* imply a lack of taste!"

Then, as he moved past me to the pub door, Tom said, "I'm glad I'm not late—I wouldn't have missed your final judgment for the world." Tom, seeing the worry on my face, asked, "Ara Georgeen, you're not still worried about those 24 birthdays of mine that you missed, now are ye? Sure, I've put them behind me long ago. And I sold my stock in Hallmark Cards back in the fifties. Have no doubt, sonny, I'm in your corner all the way. In fact, I need to thank ye for the part you gave me in that chapter on autobiography. Now you need to be followin' up on that character—write some more stories for me. Have me helpin' St. Patty drive the snakes out of Ireland; I could be whisperin' in young Jack Kennedy's ear during the Cuban missile crisis. I tell you, laddie, those stories have got great potential for a series on television."

"Tom," I interrupted. "I can't do that. I'm a psychologist."

"Ah, Georgeen," Tom said softly as he patted my shoulder, "this is no time to be runnin' yourself down like that."

Tom reached for the door, stopped, and turned to me one last time.

"About that problem you've been having in ending that chapter," he began, "I think I've finally figured it out. Your teleography isn't about patience, or humor, or virtues, or culture, or friendship, or heaven, or any of those things. It's about human nature. End the paper by thanking *them* kindly for their patience, and then tell them the nature of human nature."

"And just how might I be tellin' them the nature of human nature?" I asked, while also mocking his brogue.

Tom let the dig pass and simply said, "Ye might try using that wonderful Gregory Bateson quote. You know, the one about stories."

"Oh, you mean the one that goes,

A man wanted to know about mind, not in nature but in his private large computer. He asked it (no doubt in his best Fortran), "Do you compute that you will ever think like a human being?" The machine then set to work to analyze its own computational habits. Finally, the machine printed its answer on a piece of paper, as such machines do. The man ran to get the answer and found, neatly typed, the words: THAT REMINDS ME OF A STORY.

"No! No! No!" Tom said, "That's the story he used to tell back when he was a scientist on earth. I mean the one he's using now as a philosopher/theologian up here in heaven."

Tom stuffed a piece of paper into my hand, grabbed the doorknob to the pub, and said, "And now you'll be excusin' me, as I have to be buying a pint of stout now. You see, they close the bar the moment a judgment begins."

Before entering the pub myself, I read Tom's gloss of Bateson's quote:

> A man wanted to know about human nature, not through the eyes of a science, but through the eyes of human beings themselves. So he asked himself: Where did we humans come from? What is it like to have a human nature? and What is the meaning of life? And suddenly God appeared to the man to give an answer. And, God (looking for all the world like Charlton Heston) pointed to a rock, and a lightning bolt traveled from His hand to the rock. And one could see that some words were neatly emblazoned upon the rock. The man ran to the rock to find the answer to his questions. And the message was: GOD MADE HUMANS BECAUSE HE LOVES GOOD STORIES.
>
> —Last line adapted from Robert Murphy

Uncle Tom opened the door to the pub and hissed at me, "Laddie, have ye gone daft? The grim reaper waits for no man. Now get in here—for the mood of the jury for your final judgment is turning ugly."

"Tom," I sobbed, "how can I—how can anyone—justify their life? Help me, Tom."

"Georgeen, don't you know that everyone in that pub is exactly alike? Who among us is more than only human? Just remind them of themselves, and they'll be your friends. And if your friends are there, then everything's all right. Why don't you start out by singing them that sad, lonely song by Neil Diamond? You know, the one that reminds us that we've all worked and wondered, and then wept when life ends because it was done too soon."

Tom took my hand and slowly led me into the pub. He turned to me, winked, and said, "And when you're done tellin' your story, laddie, be sure to thank *them* for *their* patience."

Well, that's my teleography—at least for now. You can see that I'm wrestling with the meaning of life and the meaning of death. That makes me quite similar to a great many other people in their early forties. I guess I'll go to my grave reflecting upon my Irish-Catholic background. Like other psychologists, I'll wonder about the nature of human nature until I can wonder no more. And, when I reach the far side of death, I hope to encounter a loving and understanding God—and lots of good friends who made safe the way before me. Until then, I'll teach, and think, and write about science and about human nature. I'll also befriend and love a lot of people and institutions and generally try to leave this world a better place than I found it. And in those respects, I'm not very different from any of you—or from our clients or our research subjects, for that matter. Is that because my self-analysis was good? Or because we all share the same human nature? Or both? And, finally, I'll continue leading the life story that I've chosen because, frankly, I can't think of anything better to do between now and death. And so I'll close by saying,

Thank you for your patience.

Afterword

D. John Lee

It is not uncommon for autobiographers to learn something about themselves through the process of writing their story. For example, Theodore Sarbin had "an awakening" to an oppositional pattern of his work that led him to speak to the academy's anti-Semitism, which placed him on the margins. And, although Joseph Rychlak was aware of his marginality when he began his essay, his blue-collar theme emerged as an unexpected insight. Donald Spence was surprised by his discovery of why he had been fascinated by the Orpheus myth. He also learned afresh how plastic memory can be or how easily recollections "can be fitted into a particular narrative frame." The frame of "a younger brother's cry for power and justice" was used to present a picture of Brian Sutton-Smith's life. Rachel Hare-Mustin was keenly aware of the particularity or selectivity of the "narrative frame" as was Leon Rappoport and Robert Detweiler, who emphasized that what was unsaid and who was unnamed was just as important as what was said and who was named.

Another common effect of autobiography is an experience of connectedness. Theodore Sarbin asserted that "self-narratives are not solipsistic enterprises but the resultant of social interaction"; and Karl Scheibe confirmed this proposition by expressing his relatedness to both his father and mentor. Mary and Ken Gergen's "duography" embodied an "ever shifting relational matrix" where they reaffirmed that it is not *my* life or *your* life but *our* lives. Also, it became obvious as Stephen Crites remembered himself with his parents and brother that our connection stretches to our dead as well. And besides organizing his memoir, Detweiler's use of the four elements of earth, air, fire, and water revealed the sensory quality of memory and our connection to nature.

The act of autobiography reveals the dynamic tension between the past and future simultaneously existing in the present. One cannot focus on one without also considering the others. This condition is supported by Rappoport's comment that "while busy excavating the past, you can't help keeping an eye on the present and future." Thus, another effect of autobiography is to move one into the future. Spence affirmed this teleological propulsion (and therapeutic value) of autobiography when he wondered "what other discoveries lie ahead?" A review of the past in the present propels one into the future, but as George Howard's teleography revealed, considering one's possibilities in the present cannot avoid remembering the past.

While all of the contributors would agree that time cannot be severed, there would be disagreement over the form in which their time or narrative was moving. Some would argue that their narratives are moving in a progressive linear fashion which could be considered the modernist ideal. Others might argue that their narrative is proceeding as a tragedy (regress), or a comedy (a tragedy with a happy ending), or a romance (ups and downs with no progress or regress). Finally, a circular narrative (which simultaneously contains tragedy, comedy, and romance), would represent the hermeneutical arguments of the postmodernists (and several "ancient" traditions as well!). Autobiography can both construct and disconstruct narratives. There might also be disagreement among the contributors over what moves their narratives. Are humans passive respondents/machines or are they active participants/storytellers? Jesse Hiraoka suggests a resolution to this debate within the title of his essay, "Conditions *and* Will."

Jerome Bruner (1987) suggested that listening to how people tell their stories can reveal how they structure their experience, and possibly, how they will live their lives. His initial inquiries found that there were consistent differences between the way in which men and women autobiographize. I have not systematically analyzed the language of this collection but it may prove useful to someone to do so. Also, it would be fascinating to hear how the contributors would tell their stories ten years from now.

It seems appropriate to end this book with the metaphor with which it began. This collection contains the stories of some of my favorite magicians. And recently, I have been spinning some magic of my own. I hope my magic reaches beyond illusion to reveal islands, princes, and princesses, and maybe even God.

Bibliography

Adorno, T. W., Frenkel-Brunswik, E., Levinson, D. J., & Sanford, R. N. (1950). *The authoritarian personality*. New York: Harper and Row.

Allen, V. L., & Scheibe, K. E. (Eds.). (1982). *The social context of conduct: Psychological writings of Theodore R. Sarbin*. New York: Praeger.

Ashby, W. Ross (1956). *An introduction to cybernetics*. London: Chapman & Hall.

Avedon, E. M., & Sutton-Smith, B. (1971). *The study of games*. New York: Wiley.

Bannister, D. (1966). Psychology as an exercise in paradox. *Bulletin of the British Psychological Society, 19*, 21–26.

Barnes, Julian. (1985). *Flaubert's parrot*. New York: Alfred A. Knopf.

Bateson, G. (1979). *Mind and nature: A necessary unity*. New York: Dutton.

Berger, B. (1990). *Authors of their own lives: Eighteen intellectual autobiographies of American sociologists*. Berkeley, CA: University of California Press.

Bruner, J. (1987). Life as narrative. *Social Research, 54*, 11–32.

Bruner, J. (1986). *Actual minds, possible worlds*. Cambridge, MA: Harvard University Press.

Cameron, N. (1943). The development of paranoic thinking. *Psychological Review, 50*, 219–233.

Chick, G. (1991). Editorial note: Studies in honor of Brian Sutton-Smith. *Play and Culture, 4*, 85–86.

Christie, J. F. (1991). A quantitative survey of Sutton-Smith's impact on the social science literature. *Play and Culture, 4*, 139–143.

Chun, K., & Sarbin, T. R. (1970). An empirical study of metaphor to myth transformation. *Philosophical Psychologist, 4*, 16–20.

Efran, J. S., Lukens, R. J., & Lukens, M. D. (1988). Constructivism: What's in it for you? *The Family Therapy Networker, 12*, 27–35.

Fisher, S., & Fisher, R. L. (1981). *Pretend the world is funny and forever*. Hillsdale, NJ: Erlbaum.

Foucault, Michel. (1988). The political technology of individuals. In Luther Martin,

Huck Guttman, & Patrick Hutton (Eds.), *Technologies of the self: A seminar with Michel Foucault*. Amherst, MA: University of Massachusetts Press.

Foucault, Michel. (1980). *Power/knowledge*. New York: Pantheon.

Frankl, Viktor. (1960). Paradoxical intention: A logotherapeutic technique. *American Journal of Psychotherapy, 14*, 520–535.

Freeman, Joann. (1973). The tyranny of structurelessness. *Ms. Magazine*, July, 76–78, 86–89.

Freud, S. (1920). *A general introduction to psychoanalysis*. New York: Permabook.

Friedlander, J. W., & Sarbin, T. R. (1938). The depth of hypnosis. *Journal of Abnormal and Social Psychology, 33*, 453–475.

Frye, N. (1971). *Anatomy of criticism*. Princeton, NJ: Princeton University Press.

Gadamer, Hans-Georg. (1976). *Philosophical hermeneutics*. Berkeley, CA: University of California Press.

Garvey, C. (1977). *Play*. Cambridge, MA: Harvard University Press.

Gergen, K. J. (1973). Social psychology as history. *Journal of Personality and Social Psychology, 26*, 309–320.

Gergen, K., & Gergen, M. (1988). Narrative and the self as relationship. In L. Berkowitz (Ed.), *Advances in experimental social psychology*. New York: Academic Press.

Hare-Mustin, Rachel. (1992). Cries and whispers: The psychotherapy of Anne Sexton. *Psychotherapy, 29*, 406–409.

Hare-Mustin, Rachel. (1991). Sex, lies, and headaches: The problem is power. In T. J. Goodrich (Ed.), *Women and power: Perspectives for therapy* (pp. 63–85). New York: Norton.

Hare-Mustin, Rachel. (1987). The problem of gender in family therapy theory. *Family Process, 26*, 15–27.

Hare-Mustin, Rachel. (1983). An appraisal of the relationship between women and psychotherapy: 80 years after the case of Dora. *American Psychologist, 38*, 593–601.

Hare-Mustin, Rachel. (1978). A feminist approach to family therapy. *Family Process, 17*, 181–194.

Hare-Mustin, Rachel. (1974). Ethical considerations in the use of sexual contact in psychotherapy. *Psychotherapy, 11*, 308–310.

Hare-Mustin, Rachel, & Marecek, Jeanne. (1990). *Making a difference: Psychology and the construction of gender*. New Haven, CT: Yale University Press.

Hare-Mustin, Rachel, & Marecek, Jeanne. (1988). The meaning of difference: Gender theory, postmodernism, and psychology. *American Psychologist, 43*, 455–464.

Hare-Mustin, Rachel, & Marecek, Jeanne. (1986). Autonomy and gender: Some questions for therapists. *Psychotherapy, 23*, 205–212.

Heidbreder, E. (1933). *Seven psychologies*. New York: Appleton-Century.

Heider, F. (1958). *The psychology of interpersonal relations*. New York: Wiley.

Heider, F., & Simmel, E. (1944). A study of apparent behavior. *American Journal of Psychology, 57*, 243–257.

Hermans, Hubert, Kempen, Harry, & van Loon, Rens. (1992). The dialogical self: Beyond individualism and rationalism. *American Psychologist, 47*, 23–33.

Hollway, Wendy. (1989). *Subjectivity and method in psychology: Gender, meaning, and science*. London: Sage.

Howard, G. S. (1992). Behold our creation: What counseling psychology has become—and might yet become. *Journal of Counseling Psychology* 39, 419–442.

Howard, G. S. (1993). Steps toward a science of free will. *Counseling and Values, 37,* 116–128.

Howard, G. S. (1991). Culture tales: A narrative approach to thinking, cross-cultural psychology, and psychotherapy. *American Psychologist, 46,* 187–197.

Howard, G. S., & Conway, C. G. (1986). Can there be an empirical science of volitional action? *American Psychologist, 41,* 1241–1251.

James, W. (1902). *The varieties of religious experience.* New York: Longmans, Green & Co.

James, W. (1890). *Principles of psychology.* New York: Holt.

Jarrett, R. F., & Scheibe, K. E. (1962). Association chains and paired-associate learning. *Journal of Verbal Learning and Verbal Behavior, 1,* 264–268.

Koch, S. (1959). Epilogue. In S. Koch (Ed.), *Psychology: A study of a science* (Vol. 3). New York: McGraw-Hill.

Korzybski, Alfred. (1958). *Science and sanity.* Lakeville, CT: International Non-Aristotelian Library Publishing Co.

Kren, G., & Rappoport, L. (1980). *The Holocaust and the crisis of human behavior.* New York: Holmes and Meier.

Lee, D. J. (1993). *Storying ourselves.* Grand Rapids, MI: Baker Books.

Lee, D. J. (1988a). Book review of "Narrative Psychology," edited by T. R. Sarbin, 1986. *Christian Scholar's Review, 18*(1), 97–99.

Lee, D. J. (1988b). Book review of "Autobiographical Memory," edited by D. Rubin, 1986. *Christian Scholar's Review, 18*(2), 203–205.

Levin, H. (1970). The Quixotic principle. In M. W. Bloomfield (Ed.), *The interpretation of narrative: Theory and practice* (Harvard English Studies I). Cambridge, MA: Harvard University Press.

Lewis, J. H., & Sarbin, T. R. (1943). Studies in psychosomatics. The influence of hypnotic stimulation on gastric hunger contractions. *Psychosomatic Medicine, 5,* 125–131.

MacIntyre, A. (1981). *After virtue.* Notre Dame, IN: University of Notre Dame Press.

Mair, M. (1988). Psychology as storytelling. *International Journal of Personal Construct Psychology, 1,* 125–138.

Mancuso, J. C., & Sarbin, T. R. (1983). The self-narrative in the enactment of roles. In T. R. Sarbin & K. E. Schiebe (Eds.), *Studies in social identity.* New York: Praeger.

McAdams, D. P. (1985). *Power, intimacy, and the life story.* Chicago: Dorsey Press.

Mead, G. H. (1934). *Mind, self, and society.* Chicago: University of Chicago Press.

Michotte, A. E. (1946). *The perception of causality* (T. R. Miles & E. Miles, Trans.). London: Methuen.

Mischel, W. (1968). *Personality and assessment.* New York: Wiley.

Mishler, E. G. (1986). *Research interviewing: Context and narrative.* Cambridge, MA: Harvard University Press.

Newcomb, T. M., & Hartley, E. L. (1947). *Readings in social psychology.* New York: Henry Holt & Co.

Olney, J. (1988). *Studies in autobiography.* New York: Oxford University Press.

Orne, M. T. (1962). On the social psychology of the psychological experiment: With particular reference to demand characteristics and their implications. *American Psychologist, 17*, 776–783.

Orne, M. T., & Scheibe, K. E. (1964). The contribution of nondeprivation factors in the production of sensory deprivation effects: The psychology of the "panic button." *Journal of Abnormal and Social Psychology, 68*, 3–12.

Parsons, Talcott, & Bales, Robert. (1955). *Family, socialization, and interaction process*. Glencoe, IL: Free Press.

Pepper, S. (1942). *World hypotheses*. Berkeley, CA: University of California Press.

Pitcher, E., & Prelinger, E. (1963). *Children tell stories: An analysis of fantasy*. New York: New York University Press.

Platt, John (1976). Hierarchical growth. *Bulletin of Atomic Scientists, 2-4*, 46–48.

Polkinghorn, D. (1988). *Narrative knowing and the human sciences*. Albany, NY: State University of New York Press.

Polti, G. (1916). *The thirty-six dramatic situations* (trans. by L. Ray). Boston: Writer, Inc.

Rappoport, L. (1984). Dialectical analysis and psychosocial epistemology. In K. Gergen & M. Gergen (Eds.), *Historical social psychology*. New York: L. Erlbaum Associates.

Rappoport, L. (1965). Interpersonal conflict in cooperative and uncertain situations. *Journal of Experimental Social Psychology, 1*, 323–333.

Reynolds, P. C. (1986). Play, language, and human evolution. In J. S. Bruner et al. (Eds.), *Play*. New York: Basic Books.

Rorty, R. (1989). *Contingency, irony, and solidarity*. New York: Cambridge University Press.

Rosenberg, B. G., & Sutton-Smith, B. (1971). *Sex and identity*. New York: Holt, Rinehart, & Winston.

Rotenberg, M. (1987). *Re-biographing and deviance*. New York: Praeger.

Rubin, D. C. (Ed.). (1986). *Autobiographical memory*. Cambridge, UK: Cambridge University Press.

Runyan, W. M. (1982). *Life history and psychobiography*. New York: Oxford University Press.

Rychlak, J. F. (1991). *Artificial intelligence and human reason: A teleological critique*. New York: Columbia University Press.

Rychlak, J. F. (1982). *Personality and life style of young male managers: A logical learning theory analysis*. New York: Academic Press.

Rychlak, J. F. (1979). *Discovering free will and personal responsibility*. New York: Oxford University Press.

Rychlak, J. F. (1977). *The psychology of rigorous humanism*. New York: Wiley-Interscience. (Second edition, 1988, New York: New York University Press.)

Rychlak, J. F. (1973). *Introduction to personality and psychotherapy: A theory-construction approach*. Boston: Houghton Mifflin. (Second edition, 1981.)

Rychlak, J. F. (1968). *A philosophy of science for personality theory*. Boston: Houghton Mifflin. (Second edition, 1981, Malabar, FL: Robert E. Krieger.)

Sarbin, T. R. (1993). The narrative as a root metaphor for contextualism. In S. Hayes, L. Hayes, H. Reese, & T. R. Sarbin (Eds.), *Varieties of scientific contextualism*. Reno, NV: Context Press.

Sarbin, T. R. (1991). The social construction of schizophrenia. In W. Flack, M.

Wiener, & D. Miller (Eds.), *What is schizophrenia?* New York: Springer Verlag.

Sarbin, T. R. (1990). The narrative quality of action. *Theoretical and Philosophical Psychology, 10,* 49–65.

Sarbin, T. R. (1989). Emotions as narrative emplotments. In M. J. Packer & R. M. Addison (Eds.), *Entering the circle: Hermeneutic investigations in psychology.* Albany, NY: State University of New York Press.

Sarbin, T. R. (1988). The moral climate of trust and betrayal. *Proceedings of the Personnel Security Research Symposium.* Monterey, CA: Naval Postgraduate School.

Sarbin, T. R. (1986a). *Narrative psychology: The storied nature of human conduct.* New York: Praeger.

Sarbin, T. R. (1986b). The narrative as a root metaphor for psychology. In T. R. Sarbin (Ed.), *Narrative psychology.* New York: Praeger.

Sarbin, T. R. (1986c). Two models of care: Contract and covenant. In E. E. Rutherford (Ed.), Ethics and practice of care in public and private settings. *Proceedings of the American Association for the Advancement of Science,* Pacific Division.

Sarbin, T. R. (1984). Role transitions as social drama. In V. L. Allen & E. van Vliert, (Eds.), *Role transitions: Explorations and explanations.* New York: Plenum.

Sarbin, T. R. (1982a). The quixotic principle: A belletristic approach to the psychology of imagining. In V. L. Allen & K. E. Scheibe (Eds.), *The social context of conduct: Psychological writings of Theodore R. Sarbin.* New York: Praeger.

Sarbin, T. R. (1982b). The root metaphor of metaphor: Application to psychological problems. In V. L. Allen & K. E. Scheibe (Eds.), *The social context of conduct.* New York: Praeger.

Sarbin, T. R. (1982c). A preface to a psychological theory of metaphor. In V. L. Allen & K. E. Scheibe (Eds.), *The social context of conduct.* New York: Praeger.

Sarbin, T. R. (1982d). A prolegomenon to a theory of counter-deception. In D. Daniels & K. Herbig (Eds.), *Strategic military deception.* Elmsford, NY: Pergamon Press.

Sarbin, T. R. (1977). Contextualism: A world view for modern psychology. In A. W. Landfield (Ed.), *1976 Nebraska Symposium on Motivation.* Lincoln, NE: University of Nebraska Press.

Sarbin, T. R. (1968a). Ontology recapitulates philology: The mythic nature of anxiety. *American Psychologist, 23,* 411–428.

Sarbin, T. R. (1968b). The transformation of social identity: A new metaphor for the helping professions. In L. Roberts, N. Greenfield, & M. Miller (Eds), *Comprehensive mental health programs: The challenge of evaluation.* Madison: University of Wisconsin Press.

Sarbin, T. R. (1964). Anxiety: The reification of a metaphor. *Archives of General Psychiatry, 10,* 630–638.

Sarbin, T. R. (1954). Role theory. In G. Lindzey (Ed.), *Handbook of Social Psychology* (Vol. 1). Reading, MA: Addison-Wesley.

Sarbin, T. R. (1943). The concept of role-taking. *Sociometry, 6,* 273–284.

Sarbin, T. R. (1939). Rorschach patterns under hypnosis. *American Journal of Orthopsychiatry, 9,* 315–318.

Sarbin, T. R., & Adler, N. (1971). Self-reconstitutive processes: A preliminary report. *Psychoanalytic Review, 57,* 599–616.

Sarbin, T. R., & Allen, V. L. (1968). Role theory. In G. Lindzey & E. Aronson (Eds.), *Handbook of Social Psychology* (2d ed.). Reading, MA: Addison-Wesley.

Sarbin, T. R., & Coe, W. C. (1972). *Hypnotism: The social psychology of influence communication.* New York: Holt, Rinehart, & Winston.

Sarbin, T. R., & Coe, W. C. (1979). Hypnosis and psychopathology: On replacing old myths with fresh metaphors. *Journal of Abnormal Psychology, 88,* 506–526.

Sarbin, T. R., & Juhasz, J. R. (1970). Toward a theory of imagination. *Journal of Personality, 38,* 52–76.

Sarbin, T. R., & Kitsuse, J. I. (Eds.) (1993). *Constructing the social.* London: Sage Publishers.

Sarbin, T. R., & Mancuso, J. C. (1980). *Schizophrenia: Medical diagnosis or moral verdict?* New York: Praeger.

Sarbin, T. R., & McKechnie, G. E. (1986). Prospects for a contextualist theory of personality. In R. Rosnow & M. Georgoudi (Eds.), *Contextualism and understanding in behavioral science.* New York: Praeger.

Sarbin, T. R., & Scheibe, K. E. (Eds.). (1983). *Studies in social identity.* New York: Praeger.

Sarbin, T. R., & Scheibe, K. E. (1980). The transvaluation of social identity. In C. J. Bellone (Ed.), *The normative dimension in public administration.* New York: Marcel Dekker.

Sarbin, T. R., Taft, R., & Bailey, D. (1960). *Clinical inference and cognitive theory.* New York: Holt, Rinehart, & Winston.

Sass, Louis (1988). The self and its vicissitudes: An "archaeological" study of the psychoanalytic avant-garde. *Social Research, 55,* 551–607.

Scheibe, K. E. (in press). *Self studies.* Westport, CT: Praeger.

Scheibe, K. E. (1993). Cocaine careers: Historical and individual constructions. In T. R. Sarbin & J. Kitsuse (Eds.), *Constructing of the social.* Westport, CT: Praeger.

Scheibe, K. E. (1983). The psychology of national identity. In T. R. Sarbin & K. E. Scheibe (Eds.), *Studies in social identity.* New York: Praeger.

Scheibe, K. E. (1979). *Mirrors, masks, lies, and secrets.* New York: Praeger.

Scheibe, K. E. (1970). *Beliefs and values.* New York: Holt, Rinehart, & Winston.

Scheibe, K. E. (1964). The effect of value on statements of expectancy under four experimental conditions. *Psychological Record, 14,* 137–144.

Scheibe, K. E., & Sarbin, T. R. (1965). Towards a theoretical conceptualization of superstition. *British Journal for the Philosophy of Science, 62,* 143–158.

Scheibe, K. E., Kulik, J. A., Hersch, P. D., & La Macchia, S. (1969). *College students on chronic wards.* New York: Behavioral Publications.

Schwartsman, H. (1978). *Transformations: The anthropology of children's play.* New York: Plenum.

Sennett, Richard. (1980). *Authority.* New York: Alfred A. Knopf.

Shaver, P. R., & Scheibe, K. E. (1967). Transformation of social identity: A study of chronic mental patients and college volunteers in a summer camp setting. *The Journal of Psychology, 66,* 19–37.

Smedslund, J. (1955). *Multiple probability learning*. Oslo: Akademsk Forlog.

Spariosu, M. I. (1989). *Dionysus reborn*. Ithaca, NY: Cornell University Press.

Spence, D. P. (1982). *Narrative truth and historical truth*. New York: W. W. Norton.

Spender, Dale. (1984). Defining reality: A powerful tool. In Cheris Kramarae, Muriel Schulz, & William O'Barr (Eds.), *Language and power*. Beverly Hills: Sage.

Squire, C. (1990). Crisis? What crisis? Discourses and narratives of the "social" in social psychology. In Ian Parker & John Shotter (Eds.), *Deconstructing social psychology*. London: Routledge.

Steele, R. S. (1982). *Freud and Jung: Conflicts in interpretation*. London: Routledge.

Sutton-Smith, B. (in press). *In search of play*. Cambridge, MA: Harvard University Press.

Sutton-Smith, B. (1993). Dilemmas in adult play with children. In K. McDonald (Ed.), *Parents and playing*. Albany: State University of New York Press.

Sutton-Smith, B. (1989). Games as models of power. In R. Bolton (Ed.), *The content of culture: Constants and variants* (Studies in honor of John M. Roberts). New Haven, CT: HRAF Press.

Sutton-Smith, B. (1986). *Toys as culture*. New York: Gardner Press.

Sutton-Smith, B. (1983). Piaget on play, revisted. In W. F. Overton (Ed.), *The relationship between social and cognitive development*. Hillsdale, NJ: Erlbaum.

Sutton-Smith, B. (1981). *The folk stories of children*. Philadelphia: University of Pennsylvania Press.

Sutton-Smith, B. (1979). The play of girls. In C. B. Kopp & M. Kirkpatrick (Eds.), *Becoming females*. New York: Plenum.

Sutton-Smith, B. (1978). *Die Dialecktik des Spiels*. Schorndorf, Germany: Verlag Karl Hoffman.

Sutton-Smith, B. (1976). *The cobbers*. Wellington, New Zealand: Price Milburn.

Sutton-Smith, B. (1970). The psychology of childlore. *Western Folklore, 29*, 1–8.

Sutton-Smith, B. (1961). *Smitty does a bunk*. Wellington, New Zealand: Price Milburn.

Sutton-Smith, B. (1950). *Our street*. Wellington, New Zealand: Reed.

Sutton-Smith, B., & Rosenberg, B. G. (1970). *The sibling*. New York: Holt, Rinehart, & Winston.

Sutton-Smith, B., & Savasta, M. (1972). Sex difference in play and power. In B. Sutton-Smith, *Die Dialektikdes Spiels* (pp. 143–150). Schorndorf, Germany: Verlag Karl Hoffman.

Swain, Sally. (1988). *Great housewives of art*. New York: Penguin.

Tavris, Carol. (1992). *The mismeasure of woman*. New York: Simon & Schuster.

Thom, R. (1975). *Structural stability and morphogenesis*. Reading, MA: W. A. Benjamin.

Todd, F. J., & Rappoport, L. (1964). A cognitive structure approach to person perception: A comparison of two models. *Journal of Abnormal and Social Psychology, 68*, 469–478.

von Glasersfeld, E. (1984). An introduction to radical constructivism. In P. Watzlawick (Ed.), *The invented reality* (pp. 17–40). New York: W. W. Norton.

Wakefield, Neville. (1990). *Postmodernism: The twilight of the real*. London: Pluto Press.

Watzlawick, P. (Ed.). (1984). *The invented reality*. New York: W. W. Norton.

Watzlawick, Paul, Weakland, John, & Fisch, Richard. (1974). *Change: Principles of problem formation and problem resolution*. New York: W. W. Norton.

Werner, H. (1961). *Comparative psychology of mental development*. New York: Science Editions, Inc.

Yeatman, Anna. (1990). A feminist theory of social differentiation. In Linda Nicholson (Ed.), *Feminism/postmodernism*. New York: Routledge.

Zeigarnik, Bliuma. (1927). On the retention of completed and uncompleted tasks. *Psychologische Forschung, 9*, 1–85.

Index

About the Contributors

STEPHEN CRITES is professor of philosophy at Wesleyan University where he has taught both religion and philosophy since 1961. He has published work on nineteenth-century philosophical and religious thought, particularly on the writings of Hegel and Kierkegaard. He has also published a number of articles on the role of narrative and other aesthetic media in the construction of personal and cultural identity. He is currently working on a book entitled *The Aesthetic Formation of Experience.*

ROBERT DETWEILER is professor of comparative literature in the Graduate Institute of the Liberal Arts at Emory University. He has published books and articles on literary criticism, recent fiction, and the relationship between literature and religion. He has been active in the American Academy of Religion and has taught as visiting professor at the Universities of Copenhagen, Hamburg, Regensburg, and Stuttgart.

KENNETH GERGEN is professor of psychology and director, Interpretation Theory Program, Swarthmore College, Swarthmore, Pennsylvania. He is the author of *Toward Transformation in Social Knowledge, The Saturated Self,* and the forthcoming *Realities and Relationships, Soundings in Social Construction.*

MARY GERGEN is associate professor of psychology and women's studies at Penn State University, Delaware County Campus, in Media, Pennsylvania. She is the editor of *Feminist Thought and the Structure of Knowledge* and is authoring *Social Construction and the Practice of Feminist Psychology.*

RACHEL T. HARE-MUSTIN is a feminist theorist and clinical psychologist who has taught at Harvard, Columbia, and the University of Pennsylvania. As a researcher, clinician, and theorist she has published numerous articles on feminist theory, psychotherapy, family therapy, and professional issues.

Her book on postmodern theory with Jeanne Marecek, *Making a difference: Psychology and the construction of gender,* was published in 1990.

JESSE HIRAOKA grew up in the then rural San Joaquin Valley in California. After removal to Gila River, Arizona, in 1942, he spent the next ten years in a number of places for purposes of education, military service and travel. He recently retired from university life after long service as professor/administrator and as editor of *The Journal of Ethnic Studies.*

GEORGE S. HOWARD is professor of psychology at the University of Notre Dame. His research has focused upon theoretical, methodological, and philosophical problems in several applied areas of psychology. Among his books are *Dare we develop a human science?*, *A tale of two stories: Excursions into a narrative approach to psychology, Adaptive counseling and therapy: A systematic approach to selecting effective treatments,* and he has published over 120 articles and chapters.

D. JOHN LEE is associate professor of psychology at Calvin College in Grand Rapids, Michigan. He has published several articles and chapters on a variety of topics and recently edited *Storying ourselves: A narrative perspective on Christians in psychology.* He plans to continue exploring the usefulness of a narrative root metaphor for doing and teaching psychology.

LEON RAPPOPORT is professor of psychology at Kansas State University. Major publications include a textbook on personality development, anthologies on human judgment and psychohistory, and (with George Kren) *The Holocaust and the crisis of human behavior.*

JOSEPH F. RYCHLAK is the Maude C. Clarke Professor of Humanistic Psychology at Loyola University of Chicago. He has for many years been formulating and empirically testing his Logical Learning Theory, which is an explanation of human behavior that subsumes agency, free will, and self-determination. His books have covered such topics as the philosophy of science, history of ideas, and a critique of artificial intelligence.

THEODORE R. SARBIN joined the faculty of the University of California in 1949. He served the Berkeley campus for 20 years before being called to the Santa Cruz campus. He was granted the emeritus title in 1976. He has contributed over 200 titles on topics of role theory, hypnosis, schizophrenia, imagination, metaphor, emotion, criminology, and narrative psychology.

KARL E. SCHEIBE is professor of psychology at Wesleyan University since 1973—with several interruptions for visiting professorships in Brazil and California. He is currently working on two books entitled *Self studies* and *The drama of everyday life.*

DONALD P. SPENCE is professor of psychiatry at the Robert Wood Johnson Medical School. He is author of *Narrative truth and historical truth,*

The Freudian metaphor, and is currently completing *The rhetorical voice of psychoanalysis* to be published in 1994.

BRIAN SUTTON-SMITH is a professor emeritus of the University of Pennsylvania. He is author, coauthor, or editor of 25 books and 300 articles. He was the director of the Program of Interdisciplinary Studies in Human Development from 1977–1990; and director of the Program in Developmental Psychology at Teachers College, Columbia University, New York, from 1967–1977.